CW01072655

(*continued on back*)

Delusional Beliefs

Edited by
Thomas F. Oltmanns
Brendan A. Maher

WILEY

A WILEY-INTERSCIENCE PUBLICATION

JOHN WILEY & SONS

New York • Chichester • Brisbane • Toronto • Singapore

Copyright © 1988 by John Wiley & Sons, Inc.

All rights reserved. Published simultaneously in Canada.

Reproduction or translation of any part of this work
beyond that permitted by Section 107 or 108 of the
1976 United States Copyright Act without the permission
of the copyright owner is unlawful. Requests for
permission or further information should be addressed to
the Permissions Department, John Wiley & Sons, Inc.

This publication is designed to provide accurate and
authoritative information in regard to the subject
matter covered. It is sold with the understanding that
the publisher is not engaged in rendering legal, accounting,
or other professional service. If legal advice or other
expert assistance is required, the services of a competent
professional person should be sought. *From a Declaration
of Principles jointly adopted by a Committee of the
American Bar Association and a Committee of Publishers.*

Library of Congress Cataloging-in-Publication Data:
Delusional beliefs.

    (Wiley series on personality processes)
    "A Wiley-Interscience publication."
    Bibliography: p.
    Includes index.
    1. Delusions. I. Oltmanns, Thomas F. II. Maher,
Brendan A. III. Series.

RC553.D35D45 1988   166.89   87-25328
ISBN 0-471-83635-4

Printed in the United States of America

10 9 8 7 6 5 4 3 2 1

Contributors

Jean P. Chapman, Ph.D.
Professor of Psychology
University of Wisconsin
Madison, Wisconsin

Loren J. Chapman, Ph.D.
Professor of Psychology
University of Wisconsin
Madison, Wisconsin

Stephen R. Dunlop, M.D.
Assistant Professor of Psychiatry
Indiana University School of
    Medicine
Indianapolis, Indiana

Nizar El-Khalili, M.D.
Clinical Assistant Professor
    of Psychiatry
Indiana University School of
    Medicine
Indianapolis, Indiana

Atwood D. Gaines, Ph.D., M.P.H.
Associate Professor of
    Anthropology and Psychiatry
Case Western Reserve University
Cleveland, Ohio

Martin Harrow, Ph.D.
Professor of Psychiatry and of
    Behavioral Sciences
University of Chicago;
Director of Psychology
Michael Reese Hospital and
    Medical Center
Chicago, Illinois

Douglas W. Heinrichs, M.D.
Assistant Professor of Psychiatry
University of Maryland School of
    Medicine; and
Maryland Psychiatric Research
    Center
Catonsville, Maryland

David R. Heise, Ph.D.
Professor of Sociology
Indiana University
Bloomington, Indiana

Kenneth Heller, Ph.D.
Professor of Psychology
Indiana University
Bloomington, Indiana

Hugh C. Hendrie, M.B.Ch.B.
Albert E. Sterne Professor of
   Psychiatry
Indiana University School of
   Medicine
Indianapolis, Indiana

E. Tory Higgins, Ph.D.
Professor of Psychology
New York University
New York, New York

Irene P. Hoyt, M.A.
Graduate Student in Psychology
University of Wisconsin
Madison, Wisconsin

Marcia K. Johnson, Ph.D.
Professor of Psychology
Princeton University
Princeton, New Jersey

John F. Kihlstrom, Ph.D.
Professor of Psychology
University of Arizona
Tucson, Arizona

Brendan A. Maher, Ph.D.
Henderson Professor of the
   Psychology of Personality
Harvard University
Cambridge, Massachusetts

Marlene M. Moretti, Ph.D.
Assistant Professor of Psychology
University of Waterloo
Waterloo, Ontario
CANADA

John M. Neale, Ph.D.
Professor of Psychology
State University of New York
Stony Brook, New York

Thomas F. Oltmanns, Ph.D.
Professor of Psychology
University of Virginia
Charlottesville, Virginia

Francine Rattenbury, Ph.D.
Postdoctoral Fellow in Psychiatry
Michael Reese Hospital and
   Medical Center
Chicago, Illinois

Frank Stoll, Ph.D.
Research Associate in Psychiatry
Michael Reese Hospital and
   Medical Center
Chicago, Illinois

John S. Strauss, M.D.
Professsor of Psychiatry
Yale University School of
   Medicine
New Haven, Connecticut

Milton E. Strauss, Ph.D.
Professor of Psychology
Johns Hopkins University
Baltimore, Maryland

Joseph Westermeyer, M.D.
Professor of Psychiatry
University of Minnesota
   Hospitals
Minneapolis, Minnesota

Series Preface

This series of books is addressed to behavioral scientists interested in the nature of human personality. Its scope should prove pertinent to personality theorists and researchers as well as to clinicians concerned with applying an understanding of personality processes to the amelioration of emotional difficulties in living. To this end, the series provides a scholarly integration of theoretical formulations, empirical data, and practical recommendations.

Six major aspects of studying and learning about human personality can be designated: personality theory, personality structure and dynamics, personality development, personality assessment, personality change, and personality adjustment. In exploring these aspects of personality, the books in the series discuss a number of distinct but related subject areas: the nature and implications of various theories of personality; personality characteristics that account for consistencies and variations in human behavior; the emergence of personality processes in children and adolescents; the use of interviewing and testing procedures to evaluate individual differences in personality; efforts to modify personality styles through psychotherapy, counseling, behavior therapy, and other methods of influence; and patterns of abnormal personality functioning that impair individual competence.

IRVING B. WEINER

Fairleigh Dickinson University
Rutherford, New Jersey

Preface

Delusional beliefs are among the most common and intriguing phenomena in the field of psychopathology. Their clinical and social significance cannot be overstated. The expression of delusional beliefs—and taking action based upon them—is frequently the crucial consideration leading to the conclusion that a person is mentally ill. This is especially true in forensic applications of psychopathology, as in the Hinckley case.

Delusions may also be among the most poorly understood phenomena in psychopathology. Although most experienced clinicians can describe delusional beliefs and can distinguish between ideas that are delusional and those that are not, it is very difficult to obtain consensus on a specific definition of delusions. The etiology of delusions is similarly unclear. In comparison to other specific features of psychosis, such as formal thought disorder and hallucinations, relatively little effort has been spent in attempts to describe and explain the development and maintenance of delusional beliefs. Clinicians are frequently frustrated by the intractable nature of many delusional beliefs, in spite of more general improvements in the patient's affect or social interactions. Few treatment studies have examined specific changes in delusional beliefs as an outcome measure, focusing instead on global adjustment ratings.

Several factors may account for the tendency of theoreticians and investigators to ignore delusional beliefs. One consideration may be that delusions are associated with so many forms of psychopathology. They are frequently expressed by patients with schizophrenic and affective disorders, substance abuse disorders, organic psychoses, and numerous other conditions. For that reason, many prominent clinicians have argued that they are not of primary importance from a diagnostic point of view. Delusions are taken to be accessory phenomena that develop as a function of more fundamental problems. According to this line of reasoning, the examination of delusional beliefs might be about as useful as the classification and study of fevers. One might conclude that the time of clinicians and investigators is better spent by focusing on clusters of symptoms, or syndromes, that might be etiologically distinct, or by studying basic processes, the disturbance of which is fundamentally related to the development of the syndrome.

The fact that delusions appear in many disorders in addition to schizophrenia does not, however, necessarily put them in the same category as fevers in infections, because many—and perhaps most—of the patients who suffer from psychiatric disorders do not have delusions, while almost all patients with infections do have fevers. Psychopathologists should be interested in determining why some patients with a given disorder develop delusions while others with the same disorder do not. The analogy between delusional beliefs and fever is therefore basically invalid.

Even if delusions were common to all psychiatric patients, it would be necessary to study their development and maintenance. To dismiss the study of delusions as trivial because they are not unique to a given disorder is as indefensible as dismissing the study of the immune response on the grounds that it operates in a wide range of biological disorders. Understanding mechanisms involved in the etiology of delusions is important in just the same way as is the study of stress and adaptation.

Delusions have received some attention in the traditional psychiatric literature. Unfortunately, their description has not always been accompanied by systematic attempts at explanation. Some clinicians have incorporated certain forms of delusional belief into their diagnostic systems, but have discouraged attempts to understand their development and maintenance. Jaspers (1963), Schneider (1959), and other members of the Heidelberg school of psychiatry, for example, emphasized the distinction between primary and secondary delusions. Primary delusions, which were considered to be of importance diagnostically, were also presumed to be completely inexplicable (e.g. Schneider, 1959, pp. 106–107). Their development was presumably unrelated to psychosocial variables. The acceptance of this argument has impeded the systematic investigation of delusional beliefs.

There have, of course, been other clinicians who have favored the consideration of specific symptoms. For example, Freud was one of the few major, early figures in psychiatry to argue that the function of specific symptoms such as delusional beliefs could be understood in terms of psychological processes. Many attempts to understand delusional beliefs have developed within a psychodynamic perspective. We share some of these general interests, but would argue that it is possible to understand delusional beliefs without appealing to unconscious motivations or the symbolic content of symptoms.

While there is good reason for caution in studying the overt symptoms of psychopathology, there is also a lot to be gained by this type of endeavor. Cognitive theories of schizophrenia and depression, for example, might benefit from a consideration of the ways in which specific deficits in information processing might manifest themselves at the level of specific symptoms, such as delusions. Classification efforts may also be improved by a more careful delineation of the criteria by which some beliefs are determined to be delusional. Finally, the efforts of clinicians may be aided by further information regarding the mechanisms that maintain and perpetuate delusional beliefs once they have developed.

The purpose of this book is to review existing knowledge and generate new ideas, with an eye toward the encouragement of further theoretical speculation and empirical study. The description of clinical phenomena, as well as their relationship to other symptoms of psychopathology, is obviously an important starting point for this type of inquiry. It is also necessary to know something about the processes by which nondelusional beliefs are generated and tested in nonpsychopathological populations.

The following list of questions was presented to all of the authors in order to stimulate discussion and enhance continuity across chapters:

1. By what criteria should delusions be identified, described, and classified? How do we know that a particular person is delusional?
2. What personal, interpersonal, and/or situational variables might predispose certain individuals to the development of delusional beliefs?
3. Through what processes are these beliefs perpetuated or reinforced?
4. Given a particular view of the development of such beliefs, how might one go about trying to change a particular delusional belief (or minimize its impact on the person's behavior)?

In an effort to provide a variety of perspectives on each of these issues, we invited the participation of clinicians and research scientists whose training and experience cross a variety of professional boundaries, including psychology, psychiatry, anthropology, and sociology. We have included perspectives from investigators who study the development of beliefs and attitudes in people without psychological problems as well as from those who are concerned primarily with the study of psychopathology.

Following a set of introductory remarks, the book is organized in four general sections. The first includes a variety of theoretical perspectives regarding the development and maintenance of delusions. Several authors in this section point out ways in which knowledge gained by the study of nonpathological beliefs can be applied to the analysis of delusions. The second general section includes chapters that present empirical evidence regarding the description of delusions from the perspectives of clinical research and cross-cultural psychiatry. The evidence includes studies of groups of delusional patients as well as descriptions of individual cases. The third section includes three chapters that discuss approaches to the treatment of delusional patients. The fourth and final section includes general summaries by John Strauss and Brendan Maher, whose comments integrate and expand upon several issues raised in previous chapters.

Preliminary drafts of several of these chapters were presented and discussed at the Indiana University Conference for Research on Clinical Problems in April, 1985. The conference was supported in part by funds from a Clinical Research Training Grant awarded by the National Institute of Mental Health to the Department of Psychology at Indiana University. We would like to express our sincere gratitude to Richard M. McFall, who was then Director of Clinical Training in Psychology at Indiana University. This project would not have been possible without his leadership and encouragement. Additional thanks are due to several other Indiana University faculty members who also participated in that conference, including Alex Buchwald, Laura Carstensen, Russ Fazio, Jim Sherman, and George Bohrnstedt. Their thoughts and comments stimulated considerable discussion and undoubtedly influenced several of the chapters in this book. We also acknowledge the support of the Indiana University President's Committee for the Social Sciences and the Office of Research and Graduate Development.

Finally, special appreciation is due to Joshua Oltmanns who was born on April 17, 1985, one day after the completion of his father's remarks for the conference and six hours before the arrival in Bloomington of other conference participants. His company has been a source of great pleasure during the completion of this volume.

THOMAS F. OLTMANNS
BRENDAN A. MAHER

Charlottesville, VA
Cambridge, MA

REFERENCES

Jaspers, K. (1963). *General psychopathology* (H.S. Hoenig, Trans.). Chicago: University of Chicago Press.

Schneider, K. (1959). *Clinical psychopathology*. New York: Grune & Stratton.

Contents

Introductory Remarks

CHAPTER 1

Approaches to the Definition and Study of Delusions

THOMAS F. OLTMANNS

University of Virginia

Any discussion of factors leading to the development of delusional beliefs must necessarily begin with a consideration of their defining features. What is a delusional belief and how can delusions be distinguished from other kinds of beliefs and attitudes? Most of the chapters in this volume deal with this question in one way or another. One purpose of the following comments is to summarize various suggestions and issues that have been raised with regard to the definition and description of delusions, and to discuss a general solution to problems that have characterized previous definitions. Subsequent sections of these introductory remarks will summarize approaches to the etiology and treatment of delusional beliefs.

BY WHAT CRITERIA SHOULD DELUSIONS BE IDENTIFIED?

Many definitions of delusional beliefs have focused on the notion of *false* ideas (e.g., American Psychiatric Association [APA], 1987; Moor & Tucker, 1979). This approach encounters problems associated with the identification of truth, which is generally a difficult enterprise (Heise, this volume). In an effort to avoid this dilemma, some clinicians have proposed that the term *delusional* should be applied only to those beliefs that are truly incredible or completely impossible (e.g., Jaspers, 1963). Unfortunately, this definition also has serious limitations, including the low reliability of judgments regarding the bizarreness of beliefs (Kendler, Glazer, & Morgenstern, 1983; Winters & Neale, 1983). These considerations suggest that, for any given idea or belief, it is not always possible to determine whether it is false or truly incredible.

This difficulty is frequently compounded by ambiguity surrounding the presence or absence of cultural support for the person's belief. Delusions are

3

typically considered to be idiosyncratic beliefs, utterly lacking in social validation. The clinician must be quite knowledgeable regarding the social context in which the belief is expressed before it is possible to determine whether any of the person's peers might share the same view (see Gaines, this volume; Westermeyer, this volume). Again, this standard is sometimes difficult to apply in actual practice.

Most definitions of delusional beliefs also address the degree of conviction with which the patient holds the belief. Jaspers (1963), for example, maintained that delusions are held with extraordinary conviction. The definition presented in the Diagnostic and Statistical Manual of Mental Disorders (DSM-III-R) (APA, 1987) suggests that delusions are "firmly sustained in spite of what almost everyone else believes." This criterion presents further problems for those who seek to distinguish delusional from nondelusional beliefs (Garety, 1985). Most patients fluctuate in their conviction, moving from periods of absolute certainty to intervals in which they recognize the implausibility of their ideas. Sacks, Carpenter, and Strauss (1974) have suggested that the process of recovery from delusions involves three phases: the delusional phase, the double-awareness phase, and the nondelusional phase. During the double-awareness phase, patients are able to question the validity of their delusional beliefs although they have not abandoned them entirely. Definitions that require absolute conviction as a criterion for the identification of delusional beliefs are therefore in the awkward position of maintaining that a specific idea is delusional at one moment and not delusional at some later point in time, simply as a function of diminished conviction and in spite of the fact that its content has not changed.

The problems listed above suggest that it may not be useful to continue to search for, or insist upon, a specific definition that draws a neat boundary between ideas that are delusional and those that are not. Several authors have proposed an alternative approach to the description of delusions, beginning with the observation that the distinction between delusional and nondelusional phenomena is frequently less than obvious. John Strauss (1969) suggested that delusions should be seen as points on a continuous distribution from the normal to the pathological. He argued, "Although it is possible conceptually to dichotomize almost any variable, it is not valuable to do so if such a categorization ignores significant qualities of the variables being classified" (p. 584). Strauss identified four criteria that could be used to describe delusional beliefs: conviction, absence of cultural determinants, preoccupation, and implausibility. His list was expanded by Kendler, Glazer, and Morgenstern (1983), who suggested that additional consideration be given to variables such as extension (the degree to which the delusional belief involves various areas of the patient's life). Similar dimensions have been studied by Harrow, Rattenbury, and Stoll (this volume).

Strauss, Kendler, Harrow, and their colleagues have proposed these dimensions for descriptive purposes, but they might also be adapted for the purpose of definition. Any given belief may possess one or more of these features. Beliefs that clearly exhibit all of these features will undoubtedly be considered delusional. As some of the defining features are omitted or become less obvious, there will be less agreement about the classification of the belief. The following list includes several features that have been used to describe delusions. They might also be seen as defining characteristics, with none being considered to be either necessary or sufficient conditions.

a. The balance of evidence for and against the belief is such that other people consider it completely incredible.
b. The belief is not shared by others.
c. The belief is held with firm conviction. The person's statements or behaviors are unresponsive to the presentation of evidence contrary to the belief.
d. The person is preoccupied with (emotionally committed to) the belief and finds it difficult to avoid thinking or talking about it.
e. The belief involves personal reference, rather than unconventional religious, scientific, or political conviction.
f. The belief is a source of subjective distress or interferes with the person's occupational or social functioning.
g. The person does not report subjective efforts to resist the belief (in contrast to patients with obsessional ideas).

These defining characteristics draw attention to the fact that specific beliefs may be considered more or less delusional, depending largely upon the number of specific features that are present. It is not reasonable to assume, however, that all of these features are equally important. Future research may indicate that one or more features, singly or in combination, is particularly important with regard to predicting response to specific treatment methods or with regard to particular etiological mechanisms.

It should be noted that some of these characteristics may not be unique to delusional beliefs. Most notable may be the criterion involving firm conviction. As Maher (this volume; see also Nisbett & Ross, 1980) has pointed out, people who are not delusional may also refuse to abandon certain ideas in the face of contradictory evidence. Scientists' resistance to theories that compete with their own views serves as an example. The point of including this criterion in the definition of delusions is not to argue that anyone firmly convinced of the correctness of his or her ideas is delusional. On the other hand, it would be a mistake to omit conviction and resistance to contradictory evidence from consideration in a definition of delusional beliefs. Firm conviction is a salient characteristic of some though not all beliefs, and when it is present along with other relevant features it increases one's confidence in the judgment that a specific belief is delusional.

This approach to definition underlines the complexity of the problem of delusions. The elements noted above should be explained by any theory of delusional development and maintenance. Investigators should be concerned with the identification of factors that influence a patient's conviction in, or preoccupation with, a belief and the way in which these features of the belief can fluctuate over time. Investigators should be interested in the ways that delusional patients collect and interpret information from their social environment and the manner in which that evidence is used to support or disconfirm their beliefs. Finally, any explanation of the development of delusional beliefs must account for the wide variety of clinical conditions, including numerous psychopathological and neurological disorders, in which delusions are found (e.g., Cummings, 1985; Maher & Ross, 1984). A truly useful theory will account for as many of these variables as possible.

HOW ARE DELUSIONS DEVELOPED AND MAINTAINED?

Numerous theories have been proposed in an attempt to answer the question of how delusions are developed and maintained, and the present volume includes several contemporary perspectives on this problem. Personality theorists have pointed to several traits that might predispose an individual to the development of delusions, ranging from unconscious homosexual desires (Freud, 1911/1958) to fear of loss of control (Melges & Freeman, 1975) and sensitivity to humiliation (Colby, 1975, 1977). Despite the clinical popularity and intuitive appeal of psychodynamic notions, they have not been tested empirically (see Arthur, 1964, for a review of the early evidence). In the present volume, chapters by Higgins and Moretti and by Neale outline contemporary motivational accounts of delusion formation that depend on the use of personality constructs. These formulations offer considerable promise for further research because the concepts these authors employ lend themselves to specific measurement procedures.

Another view holds that delusional beliefs are determined, at least in part, by faulty thinking or information processing. Winters and Neale (1983) have reviewed several hypotheses linking delusions to underlying cognitive defects, such as failures in logical reasoning. More recently, Hemsley and Garety (1986) have discussed the possible relationship between delusional beliefs and failures in specific stages of belief formation, such as formulating hypotheses, assessing component probabilities, and examining the probabilities of competing hypotheses. In the present volume, chapters by Johnson and by Kihlstrom and Hoyt present hypotheses regarding the etiology of delusions that capitalize on recent progress in the study of memory, consciousness, decision making, and social cognition.

Maher (this volume) has offered a view of the problem that does not depend upon personality traits or cognitive defects. He argues instead that delusional beliefs are founded in an attempt to explain anomalous experiences (see also Maher, 1974; Maher & Ross, 1984). Delusional beliefs are not, according to this model, produced by faulty logic. Chapman and Chapman (this volume) discuss this idea in light of evidence collected from individuals who are considered to be at risk for the development of psychotic disorders. The evidence they present provides mixed support for Maher's proposal. Chapman and Chapman suggest another explanation based on their hypothesis regarding excessive yielding to normal response biases, which is more closely related to the cognitive orientations mentioned above.

One additional point of view deserves mention, in part because it is not well represented in the other chapters of this volume. Cameron (1959a, 1959b) emphasized the importance of interpersonal variables in the development of paranoid beliefs. He argued that predelusional patients are anxious, fearful, socially withdrawn, and reluctant to confide in other people. In addition to these personality characteristics, Cameron recognized the importance of social skills (most notably the ability to understand the motivations of other people) and the ongoing process of interaction between the person and his or her social environment. According to this model, interpersonal incompetence and the ensuing social isolation may foster the formation of bizarre ideas because the person does not receive the benefit of social validation for beliefs and attributions. Having formed a delusional belief, the patient is likely to behave in a manner that will elicit from other people further confirmation of the original misconception. Thus, Cameron's formulation allows for a complex interaction of personality traits, social skills, and environmental events. Unfortunately, the theory is based exclusively on clinical experience. We do not know whether delusional patients are, indeed, more anxious than other people, whether they are deficient in specific social skills, or whether the response of other people has an important effect on the maintenance and further crystallization of delusional beliefs. A more detailed description of Cameron's suggestions has been presented by Winters and Neale (1983). Arguments similar to those made by Cameron have been presented more recently by Bandura (1986).

HOW SHOULD DELUSIONAL BELIEFS BE TREATED?

Practicing clinicians express frustration and occasional pessimism regarding their attempts to help patients who have developed systematic delusional beliefs. Therapists may report, for example, that patients still harbor vestiges of their delusions, even though they are less preoccupied by them. Many clinicians simply advise their patients to avoid talking about the ideas, but this may not always be the most effective strategy. Rudden, Gilmore, and Frances (1982) have suggested that there may be certain types of patients (or certain points during a patient's disorder) for whom therapeutic efforts aimed at confrontation with reality will meet with positive results.

In comparison to the attention directed at various syndromes of psychopathology, the treatment of delusions has received relatively little attention in the literature. The most common form of treatment for delusional patients may be the use of antipsychotic medication, because many delusional patients also exhibit other symptoms of schizophrenia in the absence of affective or neurological disorder. The efficacy of medication is somewhat difficult to evaluate because most investigators have measured improvement in terms of global adjustment rather than changes in specific symptoms. Some studies have reported that paranoid and grandiose delusions do not respond as well to neuroleptics as other schizophrenic symptoms (e.g., hallucinations and formal thought disorder) (Cole & Davis, 1969).

Some behavior therapists have claimed modest success in the treatment of delusions. For example, Liberman, Teigen, Patterson, and Baker (1973) used operant learning procedures to train delusional patients simply not to talk about their strange ideas. Unfortunately, the restriction in their verbal behavior did not generalize to situations other than those in which the specific contingencies were enforced. Furthermore, the elimination of verbal expression does not necessarily signal the disappearance of the delusion. Unwarranted suspicions, grandiose ideas, and other bizarre beliefs may continue to have a serious influence on the manner in which the patient behaves, regardless of whether or not he or she discusses these ideas in the presence of particular people. Indeed, the deliberate elimination of social feedback pertaining to the patient's belief system may ensure that it becomes further entrenched and even more idiosyncratic.

Three chapters in the present volume are specifically concerned with treatment issues. Hendrie and his colleagues have reviewed the literature concerning treatment of delusions in patients with paranoid and affective disorders, and Heinrichs has done the same for patients with schizophrenic disorders. The organization of these chapters is somewhat orthogonal to the approach taken in most of the other chapters in the present volume, which is to focus on delusions per se rather than as manifestations of more general syndromes.

The authors of the first two treatment chapters adopted this strategy as a way of maximizing coverage of the relevant data while minimizing overlap between the two chapters. Heller's chapter is concerned with the treatment implications of several theoretical perspectives outlined elsewhere in the book. His suggestions should stimulate efforts to evaluate various specific intervention and prevention procedures.

HOW CAN DELUSIONS BE STUDIED?

The purpose of this volume is to draw attention to the study of delusional beliefs—their etiology, maintenance, and treatment. Various theoretical perspectives are presented and discussed in the following pages. Their utility, as well as the value of different approaches to the definition of delusional beliefs, must be evaluated in future empirical studies. Numerous disciplines, including psychology, sociology, anthropology, and psychiatry, can offer relevant expertise in the search for further information. Converging evidence should be sought using research designs that focus not only on the study of patients who are already delusional, but also on the study of the formation of aberrant beliefs in otherwise healthy individuals. The methods described by Chapman and Chapman in the present volume are particularly promising as they provide the opportunity to study delusions as they unfold over time.

In the context of an effort to encourage empirical investigations of delusional beliefs, it may also be useful to discuss a few methodological problems that will be encountered in such endeavors. One serious difficulty involves the fundamentally private nature of delusions. They are beliefs whose presence is inferred primarily on the basis of verbal behavior. Investigators must therefore rely heavily upon self-report measures. It is important to remember that the person's statements about the belief are manifestations of the delusion and should not be taken as being synonymous with the delusion. A belief must be expressed verbally before a delusion is said to be present. On the other hand, once a patient has expressed a delusional belief, its absence cannot be inferred from a simple refusal to discuss the belief with others.

Another important methodological consideration is the need to describe the patient's mental status in careful detail. For example, some investigators might choose to compare the performance of a group of delusional patients with a group of patients who do not express delusions. This design might be useful for some kinds of questions, but it should be taken into account that the delusional patients are likely to be heterogeneous in several ways. They might vary with regard to any of the criteria listed previously in this chapter, as well as with regard to the content of their beliefs (paranoid vs. grandiose), the length of time since the onset of their delusions, and the presence of various associated psychopathological symptoms. Investigators should make every effort to describe their patients and the patients' beliefs and to reduce the heterogeneity of the delusional beliefs that are being examined.

Experimental designs have considerable appeal for the study of belief formation because they provide an opportunity to draw strong inferences regarding potential causal mechanisms. Hypotheses generated through the observation of clinical patients may be tested, in part, by attempting to manipulate the attitudes or behaviors of nonpathological groups (e.g., Zim-. bardo, Andersen, & Kabat, 1981). As Milton Strauss (this volume) has argued, experimental studies of this sort must be interpreted with caution, particularly regarding the extent of the similarity between the analogue condition and the form of psychopathology that is presumably being modeled. It may be interesting to demonstrate that certain conditions cause people to become suspicious, hostile, and critical of other people, but that evidence should not be taken to mean that the subjects have developed paranoid beliefs. The characteristics of delusions listed previously in this chapter might be useful in evaluating the similarity between beliefs and attitudes that are manipulated in the laboratory and delusions that appear in clinical populations. Investigators should consider, for example, whether delusionlike beliefs are incredible, held with firm conviction, and unresponsive to contrary evidence. Analogue studies that are able to induce or manipulate several of these characteristics will provide particularly compelling evidence regarding the etiology of delusions.

REFERENCES

American Psychiatric Association. (1987). *Diagnostic and statistical manual of mental disorders* (3rd ed.-revised) (DSM-III-R). Washington, DC: Author.

Arthur, A.Z. (1964). Theories and explanations of delusions: A review. *American Journal of Psychiatry, 121,* 105–115.

Bandura, A. (1986). *Social foundations of thought and action: A social cognitive theory.* Englewood Cliffs, NJ: Prentice-Hall.

Cameron, N. (1959a). The paranoid pseudo-community revisited. *American Journal of Sociology, 65,* 52–58.

Cameron, N. (1959b). Paranoid conditions and paranoia. In S. Arieti (Ed.), *American handbook of psychiatry* (1st ed.). New York: Basic Books.

Colby, K.M. (1975). *Artificial paranoia: A computer simulation of paranoid processes.* New York: Pergamon Press.

Colby, K.M. (1977). Appraisal of four psychological theories of paranoid phenomena. *Journal of Abnormal Psychology, 86,* 54–59.

Cole, J.O., & Davis, J.M. (1969). Antipsychotic drugs. In L. Bellak & L. Loeb (Eds.), *The schizophrenic syndrome.* New York: Grune & Stratton.

Cummings, J.L. (1985). Organic delusions: Phenomenology, anatomical correlations, and review. *British Journal of Psychiatry, 146,* 184–197.

Freud, S. (1958). Psychoanalytic notes on an autobiographical account of a case of paranoia (dementia paranoides). In *Standard edition of the complete works of Sigmund Freud* (Vol. 12, pp. 9–82). London: Hogarth. (Original work published 1911.)

Garety, P. (1985). Delusions: Problems in definition and measurement. *British Journal of Medical Psychology, 58,* 25–34.

Hemsley, D.R., & Garety, P.A. (1986). The formation and maintenance of delusions: A Bayesian analysis. *British Journal of Psychiatry, 149,* 51–56.

Jaspers, K. (1963). *General psychopathology* (H.J. Hoenig & M.W. Hamilton, Trans.). Chicago: University of Chicago Press.

Kendler, K.S., Glazer, W.M., & Morgenstern, H. (1983). Dimensions of delusional experience. *American Journal of Psychiatry, 140,* 466–469.

Liberman, R.P., Teigen, J., Patterson, R., & Baker, V. (1973). Reducing delusional speech in chronic paranoid schizophrenics. *Journal of Applied Behavior Analysis, 6,* 57–64.

Maher, B.A. (1974). Delusional thinking and cognitive disorder. In H. London & R.E. Nisbett (Eds.), *Thought and feeling: Cognitive alteration of feeling states.* Chicago: Aldine.

Maher, B.A., & Ross, J.S. (1984). Delusions. In H.E. Adams & P.B. Sutker (Eds.), *Comprehensive handbook of psychopathology.* New York: Plenum Press.

Melges, F.T., & Freeman, A.M. (1975). Persecutory delusions: A cybernetic model. *American Journal of Psychiatry, 132,* 1038–1044.

Moor, J.H., & Tucker, G.J. (1979). Delusions: Analysis and criteria. *Comprehensive Psychiatry, 20,* 388–393.

Nisbett, R., & Ross, L. (1980). *Human inference: Strategies and shortcomings of social judgment.* Englewood Cliffs, NJ: Pretice-Hall.

Rudden, M., Gilmore, M., & Frances, A. (1982). Delusions: When to confront the facts of life. *American Journal of Psychiatry, 139,* 929–932.

Sacks, M.H., Carpenter, W.T., & Strauss, J.S. (1974). Recovery from delusions: Three phases documented by patient's interpretation of research procedures. *Archives of General Psychiatry, 30,* 117–120.

Strauss, J.S. (1969). Hallucinations and delusions as points on continua function. *Archives of General Psychiatry, 21,* 581–586.

Winters, K.C., & Neale, J.M. (1983). Delusions and delusional thinking in psychotics: A review of the literature. *Clinical Psychology Review, 3,* 227–253.

Zimbardo, P.G., Andersen, S.M., & Kabat, L.G. (1981). Induced hearing deficit generates experimental paranoia. *Science, 212,* 1529–1531.

PART 1

Theoretical Perspectives

CHAPTER 2

Anomalous Experience and Delusional Thinking: The Logic of Explanations

BRENDAN A. MAHER

Harvard University

Each contributor to this volume has been asked to provide answers to certain basic questions about delusions, both in general and, presumably, from the individual perspective that each brings to the topic. The present chapter will approach these questions in the context of a particular model of delusions. The classification, genesis, and nature of delusions will be considered within that framework. This process will be used to elaborate and modify the explanatory model that the author has offered elsewhere (Maher, 1970, 1974; Maher & Ross, 1984).

DEFINITION AND CLASSIFICATION

By what criteria might delusions be identified, described, and classified? How do we decide that a particular person is delusional? Any answer to these questions can well begin with current formal diagnostic definitions. Turning to the Glossary of Technical Terms in the *Diagnostic and Statistical Manual of Mental Disorders* (DSM-III) (American Psychiatric Association [APA], 1980) we find the following: "A false personal belief based upon incorrect inference about external reality and firmly sustained in spite of what almost everyone else believes and in spite of what constitutes incontrovertible and obvious proof or evidence to the contrary" (p. 356). DSM-III then goes on to provide a classification of delusions under the following headings: Control; Bizarre; Persecutory; Grandiose; Poverty; Jealousy; Reference; Nihilistic; and Somatic. The Present State Examination (PSE) (Wing, Cooper, & Sartorius, 1974) identifies 13 different kinds of delusion, while the Schedule for Affective Disorders and Schizophrenia (SADS) (Spitzer & Endicott,

I am greatly indebted in the formulation of the content of this chapter to extensive discussions with my wife and colleague, Dr. Winifred B. Maher.

1978) gives 11 types. All of these systems base their classifications on analyses of the content of the delusion, not on the logical features of the explanation that the delusion seeks to provide. Thus, for example, the SADS distinguishes between "Thought broadcasting" and "Thought insertion" but does so without considering whether this distinction reflects a valid distinction in pathology, or in the cognitive processes that lead to one kind of content rather than the other. The PSE classifies on such content bases as, "Special Mission," "Religious," "Fantastic," and the like.

Classification by content has a long history. Look, for example, at the classification proposed by Dr. Thomas Arnold in 1806:

> "*Notional Insanity:* I have placed under this division that species of insanity which has a peculiar title to the appellation of Delusive, because . . . with the sound and unimpaired use, in every other respect, of the rational faculties, which in some cases have even been observed to be remarkably acute, the Patient, in relation to some particular subject, or subjects, is under the influence of the most Palpable, and extraordinary Delusion. Under this variety may be enumerated the cases of such as have imagined themselves to be dead,—to be deprived of their proper nature as human beings.
>
> *Scheming Insanity:* . . . the patient thinks himself . . . by his superior knowledge or cunning capable of doing great things, which few, or none, but himself, are able to accomplish.
>
> *Vain or Self-Important Insanity:* . . . with which they who are possessed, have a very exalted opinion of their own imaginary dignity, opulence . . . learning, or some other valuable quality.
>
> *Whimsical Insanity:* in which the patient is possessed with absurd, and whimsical fancies, aversions, fears, scruples and suspicions.
>
> *Hypochondriacal Insanity:* in which the patient is for ever in distress about his own state of health"
>
> *(cited in Hunter & Macalpine, 1963, pp. 470–471).*

This kind of classification can be found certainly as far back as Burton's "Anatomy of Melancholy"—and probably before that were we to take the trouble to examine the matter more closely.

In most discussions of the definition of delusions there is added the cautionary note that where a belief that might otherwise be regarded as delusional is shared by members of a culture as part of a religious ideology, it is incorrect to classify it as delusional, a comment that echoes the observation made long ago by Bucknill on a patient who believed in Osiris:

> "had there been a few hundreds or even a few scores of persons entertaining the same belief, his [the patient's] ideas on this subject would have been of infinitely less value as a symptom of insanity"
>
> *(Bucknill, 1854, cited in Skultans, 1975, p. 83).*

The fact that this caution is necessary at all tells us either that social consensus defines the irrationality of an idea, or that psychopathologists have concluded that it is politic not to get into controversy over matters of ideology. In either event it gives rise to the uncomfortable reflection that if consensus is to be the overriding criterion for judging the delusional character of a belief system, then perhaps we have undermined the basis upon which we criticize certain psychiatric practices in the Soviet Union. There, we are told, dissidents are hospitalized with the diagnosis that they are suffering from "reformist delusions" (Medvydev & Medvydev, 1971).

The most important implication of all this is that we cannot always, or perhaps often, decide that a belief is delusional on the face of it. The matter was put succinctly by Southard in 1916, when he pointed out that "the majority of false beliefs are not prima facie fantastic or incredible. They on the contrary require the test of experience. They represent pragmatic situations" (Southard, 1916b, p. 453). Every psychopathologist is familiar with those cases in which the patient who seemed to be deluded was in fact correct; the embassy in Moscow was indeed being affected by microwaves; and the bag lady on the beach in Florida who claimed that her cousin had been the British Ambassador to the United States turned out to be telling the truth. What might perhaps be called the Martha Mitchell Effect* does turn up with some frequency. Such cases also tell us that determining whether a statement is delusional is often exceptionally difficult. It is far from clear that the DSM-III criterion that there is frequently "incontrovertible proof or evidence to the contrary" in cases of delusions is often actually met.

The purpose of this chapter will be to suggest that the classification of delusions on the basis of their content has been relatively unfruitful, and that the analysis of delusions may profit from another approach. Classifications are, of course, fruitful only to the extent that the groups discriminated by them turn out to have other differences between them, such as etiology, prognosis, response to treatment, and the like. Interrater reliabilities in the form of high kappa values are, of course, an essential requirement of any classification system, but they do not, of themselves, testify to the scientific usefulness of the system. Nor is there much value in demonstrations that the classification system predicts diagnosis unless the criteria for the diagnosis have strictly and completely excluded the class of delusion. Unless this is the case, the discovery that (for example) high percentages of patients suffering

---

*Many readers will recall that Martha Mitchell, wife of the then attorney general of the United States, alleged that illegal activity was taking place in the White House, and that it involved her husband. This was regarded as evidence that Mrs. Mitchell was suffering from some kind of psychopathology until the revelations of the Watergate affair cast a new light on it all. The writer has found the term "Martha Mitchell Effect" an apt label to describe those people who correctly report what seem to be improbable events, and are judged to be deluded for doing so.

from delusions of control are diagnosed as either schizophrenic or paranoid (World Health Organization, 1973) leaves us still unsure whether a previously unknown correlation has been discovered, or whether we are witnessing the reliability with which certain clinical phenomena influence the diagnostic decision. As yet, the literature on delusions contains little evidence that classification by content conveys incremental knowledge about some other aspect of the disorder, other than the probability that the diagnostic classification will be associated with it.

What other kinds of definition and classification might be possible? Oddly enough, when we turn to the study of the processes by which models of explanation (i.e. belief systems) are created by nonpsychiatric subjects—such as scientists—we find little emphasis placed on the content of the theories. Much more emphasis is placed on the explanatory structures that are employed. Beginning with our own field—psychology—we note the long history of concern with the differences between idiographic and nomothetic approaches to knowledge formulation. More recently, students of epistemology have emphasized the differences between empirical-falsifiable theories, and hermeneutic or interpretive theories, the contrast between the positions of Karl Popper on the one hand and Freud and Marx, for example, on the other.

The possibility that delusions might be classified in terms of their logical structure was raised nearly three quarters of a century ago by Southard (1916a, 1916b). He proposed that delusional beliefs might be classified in accordance with the moods of grammar that their form reflected. Grammarians of his day distinguished between four moods in which a sentence might be formed in English: the subjunctive, the indicative, the imperative, and the optative. The first of these, the subjunctive, expresses a proposition conditionally, that is, with the implication of a probability of truth, but not a certainty of it—in brief, in a form or mood typical of empirical science. The indicative mood asserts a finished and established truth. The imperative mood reflects an attempt to control others, while the optative mood expresses a wish or desire. That these moods were present in the grammar of language, and owed nothing of their existence to psychologists' perceptions was, Southard felt, a good thing, suggesting as it did that the distinction was inherent in the forms of the language of propositions and not simply laid onto language to suit some psychological theory about the nature of thought.

Using these mood categories, Southard suggested that delusions fall into two categories. One set of delusions is in the subjunctive mood. These delusions take the form of miniature scientific theories about the patient's experiences, are formed on the basis of empirical observation, are amended from time to time when further observations demand it, and, like all scientific theories, are never entirely satisfactory. In a series of pioneering studies of the bodily pathologies found in autopsies of deceased delusional patients, Southard was able to demonstrate a close correspondence between the explanatory function of the delusion and the sensory experiences associated with the specific diseases from which the patients suffered. The following example (Southard, 1912) will serve to illustrate his approach:

> Case III was a case in which the somatic delusion was again a belief not far transformed from the truth. In fact Case III might almost be regarded as a "symptomatic psychosis". He was thought to be full of hypochondriacal ideas, as, "*My stomach is full, and I can't eat anything.*" Patient, who was an Irish currier of uncertain but advanced middle age, was a quiet, feeble, amnestic, sad man who had apparently been irritable and perhaps subject to delusions of persecution for some months before admission. Signs of *intestinal obstruction* shortly appeared, and other signs warranting a tentative diagnosis of abdominal cancer. Autopsy, by Dr. H.A. Christian, about six weeks after admission, showed a carcinomatous obstruction of splenic flexure of the colon .... (p. 330)

Another case involved a woman who was admitted to the hospital with the delusion that her skull was filled with bees; she kept her fingers in her ears in an attempt to block out these distressing sounds. Autopsy examination of this patient revealed that she suffered from a softening of the bones of the skull, with consequent pressure on the brain and probable mechanical stimulation of receptor areas. Delusions such as the ones that these two patients expressed, could be seen, Southard argued, as having the form of crude scientific theories about the somatic experiences that plagued the patients (e.g., Southard & Stearns, 1913; Southard & Tepper, 1913; Southard, 1912, 1915, 1916a, 1916b).

The other kinds of delusions, Southard proposed, arose from the imperative mood (delusions of grandeur) or the optative mood (delusions of a bizarre or fantastic nature that are the expression of wishes). As such they do not rest upon the interpretation of experience, but lay upon external reality a set of interpretations determined largely by personal motives. Southard was, of course, writing at a time when Freud's ideas had become influential in Western psychiatry, and he readily identified the optative form of the delusion with the wish-fulfillment model proposed by Freud.

There is no need to enter into the details of Southard's proposal; it is important here mainly to note that the idea of the profitability of examining the logical status of a delusional system is not at all new. It will be obvious from the foregoing that Southard long ago proposed the notion that the cognitive operations of the patient with a somatic delusion are best understood as an attempt to explain experiences for which the patient has not been able to find a "correct" (i.e., medical) explanation. In this important regard his proposal anticipates the model that this author has sought to develop to cover delusions of a wider spectrum of content.

It seems useful to proceed further with the notion that a delusion is the same as a normal theory, extending the latter term to include theories of a nonfalsifiable sort. As a prolegomenon to this, it may be helpful to summarize the main components of this conception. A full and more recent account is given in Maher and Ross (1984). Some psychopathologists have described it as an attributional model and others as a perceptual model.

DELUSIONS AS NORMAL THEORIES

The formal propositions of this model are as follows:

1. Delusional thinking is not, in itself, aberrant. This means that the cognitive processes whereby delusions are formed differ in no important respect from those by which nondelusional beliefs are formed.

2. Delusions are best thought of as theories—much like scientific theories—that serve the purpose of providing order and meaning for empirical data obtained by observation. The following propositions about delusions thus apply equally well to the development of scientific theories.

3. The necessity for a theory arises whenever nature presents us with a puzzle. Puzzles arise when a familiar and hence predictable sequence of observation fails to occur in the expected fashion, but occurs instead in a new and unpredicted fashion. Puzzles are surprises. The events that are surprising are seen as significant. Another way of stating this is that when there is a discrepancy between what we expect to observe and what we do observe, we experience the discrepancy as significant. We notice it; we are brought into a state of alertness and tension; it puts us into what might colloquially be termed a "search mode."

4. Puzzles demand explanation; the search for an explanation begins and continues until one has been devised.

5. When an explanation for such a puzzle has been developed, it is accompanied by marked feelings of relief and tension reduction, or even exhilaration. This occurs whenever the explanation appears to account satisfactorily for a substantial range of the discrepant observations, and for their departure from the predicted pattern.

6. Data obtained subsequently that contradict the explanation create cognitive dissonance and are unwelcome. Data that are consistent with

the explanation reduce dissonance and are given particular status in the explanation.

7. Theories will be judged delusional by others if (1) the data upon which they are based are not available to those who are judging—the Martha Mitchell Effect is an instance of a belief system being dismissed as pathological because those who judged it to be delusional did not have personal access to the data upon which it is based; and (2) the data are available but most observers do not experience puzzlement or sense the significance that the patient does. This happens when events do occur as expected. The deluded patient nevertheless experiences puzzlement in the manner suggested in paragraph 8 below.

The foregoing propositions may be summarized schematically as a sequence from observation to delusion, as follows:

E. Expected sequence of experiences.

O. Observed sequence of experiences.

E matches O.

No discrepancy and nothing to be explained.

E differs from O.

Discrepancy is noticed—Experience of puzzlement or perception of significance arises—A search procedure is activated, involving further observation—Development of hypotheses follows and these will be tested against new observations—Rejection of hypothesis when new observation fails to confirm it—Renewal of search, and so forth, until a satisfactory fit of observation to hypothesis is obtained—Feeling of relief—Reduction of dissonance—Raised resistance to new contradictory data together with low threshold for recognition of confirmatory data.

8. The experiences of "significance" and "relief" are assumed to have a real locus in the central nervous system, probably mediated by the matching of, or failure to match, one neurally defined template (the expected sequence of observations) with another neurally defined template (the experienced sequence of observations). If the neural locus hypothesis is correct, it is reasonable to suppose that the feeling of significance, with its accompanying tension and activation of the search mode, may well be produced endogenously by various neuropathologies that affect the relevant neural tissue, and that this may occur in the absence of any actual discrepancy in the environmental sequences or between the neural templates themselves. Thus the observation of an expected, trivial, or irrelevant event may be accompanied

fortuitously by a feeling of significance and puzzlement even though the experienced event may not be discrepant from its expected form. The concept of "delusional mood" fits this formulation (i.e., the experience that familiar objects or situations seem to have acquired an unexplained significance). When this happens, the task of the patient is to discover why this seemingly trivial event or object is now significant.

9. Delusional theories based upon data unavailable to the public should develop whenever there is (1) a real impairment in sensory functioning, including the sensation of pain, kinesthetic and visceral sensations, and the like, that has not been identified and diagnosed as such to the patient; (2) a defect in the processes that select incoming information for processing (i.e., an attentional deficit); or (3) the experience of disturbance in personal expressive behavior, such as language disturbances or motor impairment, that have not been given an independent diagnosis.

10. A delusional theory, like other theories, is not readily abandoned until it can be replaced by a theory that better explains the experiences that the patient is having. Hence the folk-clinical observation that delusional patients do not readily abandon their theory in the face of critical contradictory evidence does not indicate a pathology of reasoning. It merely tells us that deluded patients are like normal people—including scientists—who seem extremely resistant to giving up their preferred theories even in the face of damningly negative evidence.

The clear implication of this model is that delusional beliefs are developed in much the same way that normal beliefs are, and that they serve essentially the same purposes. Some important criticisms have been directed at the model. They will be addressed later in this chapter and in a set of concluding comments at the end of the volume. There are also various kinds of evidence that are consistent with the model, including the following:

First, delusions have been reported in association with a very large number of disorders of all kinds. These have been described in some detail in an earlier paper (Maher & Ross, 1984). Various sources list well over 70 conditions with which delusions have been associated as part of the clinical picture (e.g., Giannini, Black, & Goettsche, 1978; Manschreck, 1979). They range all the way from paranoid schizophrenia to 20 neurological syndromes, 16 metabolic and endocrine disorders, and a very large number of syndromes associated with alcohol and other substance abuse. Delusions are much more likely to be secondary, reactive responses to some personal situation arising in connection with bodily disability, with sensory or motor features, or both, as opposed to primary disturbances of cognitive functioning arising from a predominantly motivational-conflictual basis. It is very difficult to imagine what all of the conditions in which delusions occur might have in common other than that they all involve some degree of disturbed bodily function.

Second, there is no independent evidence of actual impairment of reasoning ability in delusional patients, apart from the inference that is made from the presence of the delusions themselves. To verify the existence of such impairment requires proof that these patients typically perform less well than other groups on tasks involving logical inference, induction, and deduction, and so forth. Von Domarus proposed that delusional patients were suffering from a specific inability to reason syllogistically. As he put it (Von Domarus, 1944), and as elaborated later by others (Arieti, 1955; Nims, 1959), this inability rests upon a failure to distinguish between the identity of *subjects* and the identity of *predicates* in logical propositions.

According to the Von Domarus principle, a patient might reason thus:

Napoleon was exiled and incarcerated
I am incarcerated
Therefore I am Napoleon.

From this logical error other errors flow. If I am Napoleon my wife must be Josephine, the hospital staff must be British jailers, and they are never going to let me go home.

All of the data relevant to this proposition, the so-called von Domarus principle, came from the interpretation of clinical cases. Two investigators, Nims (1959) and Williams (1964), performed appropriate tests by presenting delusional patients with experimental tasks in which it was necessary to solve various kinds of syllogism. From the results of both of these studies it was clear that (1) nondeluded subjects made errors of logical reasoning, some types of errors being more common than others; and (2) deluded patients made the same kinds of error and showed the same pattern of error-type frequency as that found in nondeluded subjects; they did make more total errors than the controls. However, as these patients showed performance deficit in a wide range of tasks, it is not possible to conclude that they suffered from any unique deficit in reasoning. These studies seem to have put an end to the viability of this hypothesis, as no further significant work on the problem has appeared recently.

Finally, the study of normal subjects under anomalous environmental conditions suggests strongly that irrational beliefs can be readily provoked. Studies on delusions in subjects with hypnotically induced sensory impairment (Zimbardo, Andersen, & Kabat, 1981), sensory deprivation (Jones, 1966), and undiagnosed hearing loss (Cooper & Curry, 1976; Cooper, Kay, Curry, Garside, & Roth, 1974) confirm that delusional beliefs are of some frequency under these anomalous conditions.

Further data on this point are provided by the outcome of an investigation conducted some years ago at the Psychological Laboratory at the University of Copenhagen. The central purpose of the study, which was designed and conducted by Nielsen (1963), was to establish the threshold for the magnitude of a discrepancy between a planned motor movement and the actual execution of it—that is, the threshold at which the subject would cease to regard the discrepancy as an error on his or her own part, and would search for some other explanation. Each subject engaged in a simple motor tracking task with a joystick and received visual information about the achieved time on target. After several legitimate trials a rather complex device presented a false hand, visually located at the point at which the subject's hand should be. This artificial hand proceeded to produce a motor performance timed to coincide with the movement of the real hand, but with varying degrees of off-target error. A full description of the procedure may be found in Nielsen (1963).

Each subject was later interviewed, and, before debriefing, was asked to explain the unexpectedly poor performance on the key trials. All subjects were normal Danish adults and residents of Copenhagen. Here are some of their explanations:

It seems that my hand was moved by magnetism or electricity.

It was done by magic.

My hand took over and my mind was not able to control it.

I tried hard to make my hand go to the left, but my hand tried harder and was able to overcome me and went off to the right.

My hand developed automatic motion.

The apparatus has some magnetism in it.

I looked to see if there were electrodes on my hand, but I could not see any; they were there, but I was deceived about them.

I was hypnotized.

I don't know, but I began to wonder if it was happening because I am homosexual.

My hand was controlled by an outside physical force—I don't know what it was, but I could feel it.

Many subjects commented that they could feel their hand being moved in the wrong direction, even though the entire discrepancy was, in fact, created purely through visual cues. Several subjects suggested explanations verging on the correct one, that the effect was some sort of optical illusion, or—in only 2 cases out of 28—that there was an artificial hand involved in the technique. It should be noted here that the actual duration of the experience was very brief, not more than half an hour, and that we might assume that there is some a priori reason for subjects to expect technical deceptions in a psychology laboratory! Nonetheless, these subjects quite easily turned to notions of external influence to account for their experience. The main point of this brief summary of evidence is to suggest strongly that we may too readily assume that normal people develop their beliefs about experience with a solid foundation of probabilities or common sense against which they test their beliefs, and most often reject those that seem implausible.

CRITICISMS OF THE MODEL

Before proceeding to a modification and elaboration of this model, some of the thoughtful criticisms that have been directed at the model should be addressed. Some of the most incisive have been offered by Neale, whose contributions have been of great value. Some of the questions raised have to do with the specific data on the correlation between one specific sensory defect—hearing loss—and delusions. Winters and Neale (1983) point out the classic problem of causative inference from correlations and urge the necessity of establishing the nature of the predelusional experience if we are to make etiological inferences. In this, they are, of course, quite correct. In a hypnotic analogue setting Zimbardo et al. (1981) did succeed in showing a chronological cause and effect relationship between functional hearing loss and delusional ideation, but analogues are never as wholly convincing as the real thing. In brief, the criticism is apt. Their second criticism, often made by colleagues more informally, is to ask why the delusional patient rejects the more natural explanation. This criticism arises from the assumption that people free from psychopathology naturally reject implausible explanations in favor of reasonable, empirically testable ones, and/or are ready to change their beliefs when counterdata are presented. If this assumption is generally true then any substantial failure to conform to this standard is, presumably, pathological.

The central response to this criticism comes in several parts.

1. Normal people, including scientists, do not readily change their beliefs once the ideas have taken coherent form. It is this imperviousness of human beings to changing their beliefs that leads Popper to assert that the conduct of science is ultimately social—it is the development of competing theories by other scientists that leads to change. Change rarely comes about through an actual change of mind by an individual scientist giving up the theory with which he or she is identified merely because data have refuted it! (Popper,

1945). For experimental demonstrations of this we may turn to the studies of Ross and his colleagues (e.g., Ross & Lepper, 1981; Ross & Anderson, 1981; Anderson, Lepper, & Ross, 1980). The strongly supported theme of the findings emerging from these investigations is as follows:

> People often cling to their beliefs to a considerably greater extent than is logically or normatively warranted ... initial beliefs may persevere in the face of a subsequent invalidation of the evidence on which they are based, even when the initial evidence is as weak and inconclusive as a single pair of dubiously representative cases ... causal explanations or scenarios that continue to imply the correctness of one's initial beliefs even in the later absence of any directly relevant evidence.
>
> *(Anderson et al., 1980, p. 1045)*

2. The model that is under scrutiny here asserts that deluded patients may not be ready to abandon their delusion for a naturalistic explanation, for the good reason that their actual experiences are better explained by the delusional theory than by the naturalistic one. This is so because the delusion explains data—the patients' experiences—that the naturalistic theory fails to explain. To ask patients to abandon the delusion is, from this point of view, tantamount to asking them to trust the evidence of other people's senses in preference to their own—something that is not impossible to do, but something that is not readily done by most people.

3. Any casual survey of the media suggests that a substantial proportion of the normal population is prone to believe in the Bermuda Triangle, flying saucers, spoon-bending by mental power, the Abominable Snowman, and return to life after the out-of-body experience of death. This list does not even mention such marginalia of normal science as prebirth hypnotic age regression, multiple personalities (including a recent case presented by a psychologist in a federal agency in which the alleged number of personalities exceeded a score), and so forth. Nor should we overlook the recent expenditure by a military agency of substantial sums of money to see if extrasensory perception could tell us what is happening behind the Iron Curtain. The common preference for magic and mystery rather than science has been described in some detail by Roszak (1981). Let us consider some of his observations:

> A prominent psychotherapist remarks to me over lunch that people sleep and die only because they have been mistakenly programmed to believe that they have to ... and goes on to suggest how this erroneous programming might be therapeutically undone ... A psychologist shows me photos of himself being operated on by Philippine psychic surgeons whom he has seen penetrate his body with their bare hands to remove cartilage and tissue ... I come upon a

physicist writing in *Physics Today* about "imaginary energy" and the supposedly proven possibilities of telepathic communication and precognition . . . A historian tells me of his belief that we can, by altering consciousness, plug into the power points of earth's etheric field and by doing so move matter and control evolution . . . An engineer I meet at a party explains how we might influence the earth's geomantic centers and telluric currents by mental manipulations, which he believes to be the technology that built Stonehenge and the Pyramids.

(p. 56)

Roszak goes on to propose that there is a widespread need for the mystic and marvelous, and that this need is at odds with the cold, empirical, rationalism of the scientific method; he adds, further, that devotees of the latter are far outnumbered by the former. In brief, it may well be argued that it is the rational, data-oriented, skeptical, "subjunctive" scientist who is statistically aberrant—not the deluded patient with his beliefs about the FBI, or waves from outer space. We have already seen that normal people readily offer implausible explanations for anomalous experience, and while it may be argued that they prefer magic and mystery because it is entertaining, the most parsimonious position—given all of the data—is that this preference typifies human explanations more generally than that.

A major problem for the model proposed here, however, is that although a substantial proportion of deluded patients do present evidence that they are having anomalous experiences, many other patients do not. Partly in an attempt to tackle this problem, and partly because any consideration of normal epistemology suggests that the empirical-falsifiable explanatory mode is far from universal, or even common, in the genesis of human beliefs, it may be profitable to turn to the role of coincidence in delusional thinking.

THE LOGIC OF EXPLANATIONS: COINCIDENCE AS A PROBLEM

The experience of surprise and puzzlement does not arise only from the failure of events to match expectations. It also seems to arise when patterns of different realms of events turn out to match each other when this was not expected. By way of illustration, let us look at the fascination that mathematicians, esthetic philosophers, and lately some psychologists, have found in the contemplation of the Golden Section and the Fibonacci series of numbers.

The mathematician Pythagoras gave us the solution to the problem of the Golden Ratio (or Golden Section, Golden Rectangle, etc.). The problem is to determine the ratio that should exist between two lines of uneven length such that the ratio of the total length of both to the length of the longer of the two is the same as the ratio of the length of the longer to that of the shorter. If we label the two lines *a* and *b*, then the problem may be simply stated as that of calculating the lengths necessary for

$$(a + b)/a \text{ to equal } a/b$$

To cut the mathematics of it short, the answer is that where *b* equals 1.00, *a* should equal 1.61803. If we draw a rectangle with sides of these dimensions, and then impose a square on the shorter side (*b*), the sides of the rectangle remaining outside the square will continue to have the same Golden Ratio— and of course repeating the process will produce a series of rectangles of decreasing size, but with a constant ratio of the same value. The diagram in Figure 2.1 shows the process.

The Fibonacci series is a series of numbers, beginning with any two, such that the third in the series is the sum of the first two, the fourth is the sum of the second and third, the fifth is the sum of the third and fourth, and so on. When we calculate the ratio of each pair of successive numbers in that series, we soon reach a value of 0.61803 (when we divide any one number by the number that immediately succeeds it in the series), or 1.61803, if we reverse the order of division. In brief, the Golden Ratio appears in another way.

At this point we might well wonder what this has to do with anybody other than mathematicians. However, many people have been intrigued with this ratio. The façade of the Parthenon has been calculated to conform to it; one British art historian has computed that the ratio is observed in the

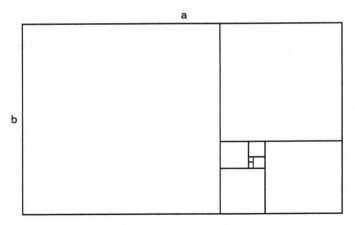

Figure 2.1

proportions of Botticelli's Venus. The ratio has been observed in the serial development of the chambers of the Chambered Nautilus, and so forth.

Finally it has been reported recently that the Golden Ratio is to be found when we establish the ratio of favorable to unfavorable adjectives that people are likely to ascribe to persons they know. Indeed, in this latter connection, the investigators concluded that the appearance of this ratio in the adjective assignment habits of schizophrenic subjects warrants the conclusion that the deep structure of their thinking processes is essentially unimpaired (Kahgee, Pomeroy, & Miller, 1982).

What seems to be important here is the explanatory strategy, which proceeds from a numerical coincidence to search for evidence that this coincidence reflects a pattern in nature that underlies the operation of many different systems. Note that no explanation of the relevant mechanism is really offered—the strategy is that of the various forms of structuralism, namely to describe a pattern that is then hypothesized to exist at some profound level of the human psyche—or, better still—in the basic wiring of the central nervous system. The obvious problem with this kind of explanatory model is that there is no satisfactory way to falsify it. While the Parthenon may have the proportions of the Golden Rectangle, the Empire State Building doesn't; the Chambered Nautilus reveals the ratio, but the giraffe doesn't; the ratio was detected in Botticelli's Venus by Theodore Cook, but only when he was free to determine the points on the body that should be regarded as the bases of the units of length. Like all structural strategies, the ultimate goal appears to be the discovery of universals. Originally sought in the spirit of Plato's Ideals, the search now points toward the nervous system, or perhaps the genetic code. Whatever the goal, it is, by definition, impossible to falsify.

Turning to clinical examples of this kind of explanation, we might note the following capsule cases known to the writer.

1. A patient who, finding himself in front of a house numbered 11 on Armistice Day, November 11th, is struck by the coincidence and concludes that he was responsible for World War I.

2. A patient who, noticing from his reading that the conflict between the assertions of science and those of religion places pressures on the individual, and that the same is true of the forces exerted on a football by the two opposing teams, concludes that the major figures in the history of religion and science can only be comprehended by discovering their analogues on football teams—quarterback, guard, and so forth.

3. A patient who, noticing that the buses of a British city travel along streets that meet in a triangle, the angles of which correspond somewhat approximately to those of the Great Pyramid, concludes that the angles contain the secret to the beginnings of man.

4. A patient who, noticing that the letters of his name, when rearranged as an anagram, produce the name of a famous American Indian chief, concludes that he is the reincarnation of that man.

Delusions of this kind take the logical form of argument by analogy, or coincidence. We have already seen that coincidences may stir the curiosity of scientists and other nonpsychiatric subjects, and indeed may provide the first important clue to a new scientific discovery. The problem, however, is that coincidence-based delusions seem unreasonable because they apparently rest upon the detection of trivial or manufactured coincidences. For example, the patient in the fourth case above notices the coincidence of his name with that of a Native American chief only when he rearranges the letters of his name.

Here it is suspected that the normal person may, in fact, be surrounded by much the same kind of detectable coincidences in the environment but simply does not notice them. Why might the potentially delusional patient notice this kind of pattern in the environment? Several possibilities arise.

1. The patient is hypervigilant, that is, has a characteristic pattern of close scanning of the environment; this pattern may constitute a personality variable predisposing the person to delusions.

2. The search for coincidences occurs at a later stage in delusional development; it does not begin until the patient has already needed to develop an hypothesis to account for some experiential anomalies.

3. Coincidence sensitivity represents a natural outcome of a basic delusional mood condition; this, in turn, arising from some neuropathological activation of brain centers responsible for mediating the experience of significance. The coincidence is detected in the course of a very close scrutiny of the environment, which, in turn, was provoked by the need to discover the basis of felt significance.

QUESTIONS TO BE ANSWERED

In this chapter, the writer has attempted to elaborate a model of delusional beliefs presented earlier. The model proposes that classification might be dealt with in terms of logical structures of belief rather than semantic content:

1. The mechanisms that produce delusions do not differ in terms of the cognitive psychology of the believer from those that determine the beliefs of people generally.

2. A predisposition to delusional thinking might be related, in some cases of coincidence delusions, to characteristic scanning patterns, but a common basis is the existence of experiential anomalies unrelated to prior personality attributes.

3. Delusional beliefs are perpetuated in part by the self-fulfilling prophecy mechanism; the delusion of persecution becomes valid as a result of the antisocial behavior of the patient.

4. The question of how delusional beliefs are perpetuated and reinforced carries with it an implication that under normal circumstances human beliefs are constantly modified by their experiential validation or refutation, and that we therefore need to postulate some special and powerful factors to account for the failure of deluded patients to modify their delusions in the face of poor validation. But a major part of the answer to this question may be simply that nobody changes beliefs easily—no matter what the counterevidence, and that the belief itself has a major selective effect upon determining what is, and what is not, perceived as evidence. In brief, the delusion is perpetuated and reinforced by exactly the same processes as those that maintain normal beliefs in spite of poor empirical support.

How might we change a delusional belief? The logic of the model presented here is such that the main prospect lies in prevention rather than change. Early detection of developing delusions, and the presentation of counterevidence, before the "solution-relief" experience has been reached, would seem to be more likely to succeed than later interventions.

In closing, it is important to note that we are ourselves ignorant about many features of delusional pathology, and that we need to gather good data bearing on the following questions.

1. Is it true that delusional patients cannot be systematically argued out of their beliefs by the organized provision of counterevidence? I can find no systematic study of this problem.

2. What are the stages of development in delusions; that is, what is the natural course (or courses) of delusional belief systems?

3. What personality attributes are associated empirically with delusions of particular logical structures?

4. To what extent is the presence of the delusional belief a source of social difficulty? Or is it the case that the preoccupation with the belief, the effort spent to communicate it to others, and the conduct of behavior in accordance with it, are what bring the patient into the hands of the clinician? If this should prove to be the case, then in focusing on the

delusion we overlook the possibility that it is the activities that the delusion produces that are pathological. The literature of fiction, as well as of psychopathology, reminds us that the individual who tries to act wholeheartedly upon a set of religious beliefs is in some danger of being diagnosed as delusional, while those who adhere to religious beliefs but practice them only moderately are not.

REFERENCES

American Psychiatric Association. (1980). *Diagnostic and statistical manual of mental disorders* (3rd ed.). (DSM-III). Washington, DC: Author.

Anderson, C.A, Lepper, M.A., & Ross, L. (1980). Perseverance of social theories: The role of explanation in the persistence of discredited information. *Journal of Personality and Social Psychology, 39*, 1037–1049.

Arieti, S. (1955). *Interpretation of schizophrenia.* New York: Robert Brunner.

Cooper, A.F., & Curry, A.R. (1976). Pathology of deafness in the paranoid and affective psychoses of later life. *Journal of Psychosomatic Reasearch, 20*, 97–105.

Cooper, A.F., Kay, D.W.K., Curry, A.R., Garside, R.F., & Roth. M. (1974). Hearing loss in paranoid and affective disorders of the elderly. *Lancet, 2*, 851–854.

Giannini, A.J., Black, H.B., & Goettsche, R. (1978). *Psychiatric, psychogenic and somatopsychic disorders handbook.* New York: Medical Examination Publishing.

Hunter, R., & Macalpine, I. (1963). *Three hundred years of psychiatry.* London: Oxford University Press.

Jones, A. (1966). Information deprivation in humans. In B.A. Maher (Ed.), *Progress in experimental personality research, Vol. III.* New York: Academic Press.

Kahgee, S.L., Pomeroy, E., & Miller, H.R. (1982). Interpersonal judgments of schizophrenics: A golden section study. *British Journal of Medical Psychology, 55*, 319–325.

Maher, B.A. (1970). *The psychology of delusions.* Paper presented at the meeting of the American Psychological Association, Miami Beach, FL.

Maher, B.A. (1974). Delusional thinking and perceptual disorder. *Journal of Individual Psychology, 30*, 98–113.

Maher, B.A., & Ross, J.S. (1984). Delusions. In H.E. Adams & P.B. Sutker (Eds.), *Comprehensive handbook of psychopathology.* New York: Plenum Press.

Manschreck, T.C. (1979). The assessment of paranoid features. *Comparative Psychiatry, 20*, 370–377.

Medvydev, Z., & Medvydev, R. (1971). *A question of madness.* London: Macmillan.

Nielsen, T.I. (1963). Volition: A new experimental approach. *Scandinavian Journal of Psychology, 4*, 225–230.

Nims, J.P. (1959). *Logical reasoning in schizophrenia: The Von Domarus principle.* Unpublished doctoral dissertation, University of Southern California.

Popper, K. (1945). *The open society and its enemies*. London: Routledge, Kegan Paul.

Roszak, T. (1981, January). In search of the miraculous. *Harper's Weekly*, pp. 54–62.

Ross, L., & Anderson, C. (1981). Shortcomings in the attribution process: On the origins and maintenance of erroneous social assessments. In D. Kahneman, P. Slovic, & A. Tversky (Eds.), *Judgment under uncertainty: Heuristics and biases*. New York: Cambridge University Press.

Ross, L., & Lepper, M.R. (1981). The perseverance of beliefs. Empirical and normative considerations. In R.A. Shweder & D. Fiske (Eds.), *New directions for methodology of behavioral sciences; Fallible judgment in behavioral research*. San Francisco: Jossey-Bass.

Skultans, V. (1975). *Madness and morals*. London: Routledge, Kegan Paul.

Southard, E.E. (1912). On the somatic sources of somatic delusions. *Journal of Abnormal Psychology, 7*, 326–339.

Southard, E.E. (1915). Data concerning delusions of personality with a note on the association of Bright's disease and unpleasant delusions. *Journal of Abnormal Psychology, 10*, 241–262.

Southard, E.E. (1916a). On descriptive analysis of manifest delusions from the subject's point of view. *Journal of Abnormal Psychology, 11*, 189–202.

Southard, E.E. (1916b). On the application of grammatical categories to the analysis of delusions. *The Philosophical Review, 25*, 424–455.

Southard, E.E., & Stearns, A.W. (1913). How far is the environment responsible for delusions. *Journal of Abnormal Psychology, 8*, 117–130.

Southard, E.E., & Tepper, A.S. (1913). The possible correlation between delusions and cortex lesions in general paresis. *Journal of Abnormal Psychology, 8*, 259–275.

Spitzer, R.L., & Endicott, J. (1978). *Schedule for affective disorders and schizophrenia* (3rd ed.). New York: Biometrics Research.

Von Domarus, E. (1944). The specific laws of logic in schizophrenia. In J. Kasanin (Ed.), *Language and thought in schizophrenia*. Berkeley, University of California Press.

Williams, E.B. (1964). Deductive reasoning in schizophrenia. *Journal of Abnormal and Social Psychology, 69*, 47–61.

Wing, J.K., Cooper, J.E., & Sartorius, N. (1974). *The measurement and classification of psychiatric symptoms*. London: Cambridge University Press.

Winters, K.C., & Neale, J.M. (1983), Delusions and delusional thinking in psychotics: A review of the literature. *Clinical Psychology Review, 3*, 227–253.

World Health Organization. (1973). *The international pilot study of schizophrenia*. Geneva: Author.

Zimbardo, P.G., Andersen, S.M., & Kabat, L.G. (1981). Induced hearing deficit generates experimental paranoia. *Science, 212*, 1529–1531.

CHAPTER 3

Discriminating the Origin of Information

MARCIA K. JOHNSON

Princeton University

INTRODUCTION

There is an issue lurking in perception, in the recollection of specific, auto-biographical episodes, and in the expression of knowledge and beliefs. How do we know that an apparent perceptual object is actually "out there"? How do we know that the events that we think make up our life actually happened? How do we know that knowledge or beliefs accurately reflect the infomation we have obtained through experience rather than guesses, our deepest fears, wishful thinking, or prejudice? We constantly attribute information to *sources*, both internal (e.g., dreams, imagination), and external (e.g., TV, a friend) in a kind of ongoing monitoring or judgment process. Most of the time we are not particularly conscious of this judgment process and not too concerned about errors in it. Sometimes, however, we are made quite aware of the process, for example, when we think we see a burglar lurking in the corner and it turns out to be the laundry bag, or when we awake suddenly from a nightmare, or when a colleague challenges us about the origin of an idea. Benign failures in these monitoring processes are called misperceptions, errors in memory, and unfounded or self-deceptive beliefs. Less benign failures lead to hallucinations and delusions.

Nowhere is the importance of the distinction between the real and the imagined clearer than in the topic of delusions. Most of us have erroneous memories and beliefs. We even cultivate a few self-serving self-deceptions, but we continue to function reasonably well all the same. What differentiates ordinary failures in source monitoring from those experienced by psychotic

Preparation of this article was supported by grants from the National Institute of Mental Health (MH 37222) and the National Science Foundation (BNS 8510633) and a fellowship from the John Simon Guggenheim Memorial Foundation. I would like to thank Carol Raye, Ron Finke, and Mary Peterson for their helpful comments on earlier drafts of this chapter.

individuals? We may be able to make progress toward answering this question by considering how such judgments are normally made.

Delusional patients are sometimes described as unable to differentiate perceptions from ideas, but this characterization of the problem is too global. It may mean any or all of the following: (1) difficulty discriminating ongoing perception from ongoing imagination, (2) difficulty discriminating internally generated from externally derived memories for particular events, and (3) difficulty discriminating the self-generated basis (thought, inference, etc.) from the perceptually derived basis of knowledge and beliefs. I think it is useful to reserve the term *reality testing* for the first case, which deals with present events, and *reality monitoring* for the other two cases, which deal with past events. It may help us analyze both normal and abnormal failures in discriminating the origin of information if we adopt this classification scheme. I will briefly consider false perceptions, false event memories, and false beliefs separately, and then turn to some general issues. The major theme of the chapter is that, in all these cases, discriminating the origin of information is a judgment process, and like all judgments, it is limited by both the quality of the evidence and by characteristics of the judgment process.

FALSE PERCEPTIONS

As Helmhotz (1878, cited in Kahl, 1971) noted some time ago, it isn't obvious why the objects in the space around us appear to be red or green, cold or warm, to have an odor or a taste. These qualities of sensations belong only to our nervous system and do not extend at all into the space around us. Thus a classic perceptual problem is why objects are perceived "out there" when the processing that is our immediate experience is "in here" (see also Gregory, 1970). However, there is another equally puzzling class of experiences—some objects and events are clearly experienced as "in here." That is, an equally central problem for cognitive psychologists is why we experience ourselves as the source of activities such as imagination, dreams, or thoughts. If *some* mental experiences are projected into the outside world, why are not *all* mental experiences projected into the outside world? This is especially curious considering the apparent similarity between perception and imagination.

The Similarity Between Perception and Imagination

Perky's (1910) studies were perhaps the first experimental exploration of the relation between ongoing imagination and ongoing perception. The observer looked at a screen while imagining a colored object (e.g., a banana) and describing it. At the same time, a faint color stimulus (e.g., a yellow banana shape) was raised from a subliminal value to just above threshold (based on pretesting of Perky and Titchner). Almost all Perky's Cornell student subjects mistook the perceptual stimulus for an imagination and incorporated aspects of the perception in their report (e.g., the orientation of the banana). They were quite indignant or surprised later when asked if they had really imagined the objects.

Half a century later, Segal and her colleagues replicated and extended Perky's results. Segal (1970) suggested that several factors probably combined to increase the probability that Perky's subjects would attribute their experience to imagination rather than perception: Introspections about imagery were common in 1910; the instructions focused subjects' attention on their imagery; nothing suggested the possibility of externally presented stimuli. Segal and Nathan (1964), "with the hard-headed, suspicious students of 1959 and 1960" (Segal, 1970, p. 105), found that only about 25 percent of the subjects failed to detect the perceptual stimuli after six images. However, Segal then changed the procedure and got better results. Subjects looked in a large translucent plastic cylinder that limited their field of vision. They were told that the experiment was concerned with the kinds of imagery experienced by normal people under conditions of reduced visual stimulation, simulating the environment of astronauts, pilots, deep-sea divers, or polar explorers. An object was named and about the time that most subjects began describing their images a slide was back-projected onto the screen of the cylinder. With this procedure and "cover story," some of the students were just as surprised and indignant as Perky's observers when they were later told that real pictures might have been projected onto the plastic hood. Even after the apparatus was explained, the majority of the students concluded that, for them, no stimuli had been projected.

Segal and her colleagues also found that subjects who felt relaxed from a pill (actually a placebo) reported vivid images, but few perceptions of the stimulus (Segal & Nathan, 1964); subjects reported more images and fewer detections of the stimulus when lying down than when standing (Segal & Glicksman, 1967), and reported more detections when they were expecting stimuli to be projected than when they weren't. A prior series of discrimination trials on the projected pictures improved detection of them during the image trials. In general, stimuli that were more intense, of longer duration, more angular, or enclosed in a square frame were more likely to be classified as external; stimuli that were less clear, or that were shown for a more brief interval or on an opaque background so only the figure was projected, were attributed to imagination more often (Segal, 1970).

Although this was potentially the beginning of an interesting line of research on conditions that affect the attribution of origin to experiences, it was not pursued. Rather, another aspect of Segal's work subsequently had greater impact and is more characteristic of current work on imagery—the demonstration that imagining interferes with perceiving. Segal and Fusella (1970) required subjects to generate either visual or auditory images while detecting either visual or auditory signals. Imagined sounds interfered more with detection of auditory signals and imagined pictures interfered more with detection of visual signals. These results suggested that imagery generates some local effects in the same pathways used by perception itself. This led Segal to conclude that "in the final analysis, an image and a percept are indistinguishable" (Segal, 1970, p. 111).

Other work in the Perky-Segal tradition emphasized the mutually interfering aspect of imagination and perception (e.g., Brooks, 1968; Bower, 1972) or investigated in more detail their common properties (e.g., Cooper, 1975; Finke, 1985; Finke & Shepard, 1986; Kosslyn, 1980; Shepard, 1984). In considering the relation between perception and imagination, psychologists have been preoccupied with their similarities, and for good reason.*

Much less attention has been given to the problem of how, given the similarites between imagination and perception, they are ordinarily distinguished, and the conditions that favor better or worse discrimination. The fact that origin is a judgment call, subject to contextual influences and the biases of judgment processes, is important. Though Segal (1970) emphasized the similarity between imagination and perception, she did hint at the importance of judgment processes as well:

Thus we all perceive, we all image, we all hallucinate; there is no difference in the cognitive experiences of the schizophrenic, the hallucinating drug addict, and the college student in this regard. What varies are the patterns of past experience, individual differences, contextual probabilities, expectancies and biases that each one brings to the task, a process that passes as judgment. Presumably, the judgment of the schizophrenic is different, a broader range of experiences may appear ambiguous to him, and his actions in the face of this ambiguity are probably idiosyncratic. However, the visual hallucinations of an alcoholic or drug addict are phenomenally in the same class as images, dreams, and perceptions; and as we have found the same effects for audition as for the visual mode . . . it is probably also true that the "voices" of the schizophrenic and a melody imagined by a composer are similar events, and may be further equated to the normal sensory processing of physical sounds.

(p. 111)

---

*As Casey (1976) points out, philosophers, as well as psychologists, may have neglected the unique characteristics of imagination.

Are Hallucinations Real Perceptions?

Added to the problem of the apparent similarity between perception and imagination is the possibility that what might at first seem like a hallucination may be a response to an actual perceptual experience (Maher, 1974; Maher & Ross, 1984). For example, Saravay and Pardes (1967; 1970) suggested that the elementary auditory hallucinations of alcohol withdrawal can be divided into two major categories, prolonged or sustained sounds, and short, phasic sounds. Gross (cited in Saravay & Pardes, 1970) studied the first group (buzzing, humming, and whistling sounds) and concluded that these phenomena are not hallucinations but examples of intrinsic tinnitus—real noises produced by the muscles of the middle ear. Saravay and Pardes (1970) drew similar conclusions about the second, phasic, type (shots, knocking, crackling, snapping, etc.), which were sometimes described by patients in alcoholic withdrawal as shots, firecrackers, a door slamming, something slammed against a wall, spiked heels walking, or water dripping.

Like auditory hallucinations, visual hallucinations have also been linked to sensory experiences. Hughlings Jackson (cited in Horowitz, 1978, p. 225) described how floaters (*muscae volitantes*) in the eye might develop into visions of rats. When Horowitz (1978) had hallucinating patients draw what they imagined, he found that "vicious snakes" were drawn as wavy lines, "two armies struggling over my soul" were drawn as moving sets of dots. One patient saw bugs on one occasion and the faces of the Holy Trinity on another, but the drawings produced were nearly identical simple drawings of dots. During an ophthalmologic examination, the subject reported the bugs again. Another chronic schizophrenic patient reported he saw his "eyeball burning." As he improved he reported that he no longer thought of his eyeball burning and that he saw "just flames" or "just wavy lines" (again, the drawings produced were quite schematic).

Horowitz obtained drawings and descriptions of visual experiences from psychiatric staff members who were asked about visual impressions they had while falling asleep, while looking at a bright light or space such as the sky, or from being struck on the head. They were also asked to close their eyes and press on their eyeballs and to draw and describe their visual impression, and were asked about any unusual visual experiences. The reports resembled those of patients who reported visual hallucinations—both groups reported or drew, for example, stars, pinwheels, wheels, marbles, dots, specks, circles, snakes, spiders, worms, bugs, spots, swirls, wavy lines, and filigrees.

Horowitz argues that hallucinations and other image experiences may be elaborated from elementary sensations that might arise either in the retinal ganglionic and postretinal neural network and/or from anatomic bodies within the eyeball. As evidence, he cites a study suggesting that mild electric or mechanical stimulation of the optic system yields drawings and descriptions similar to those obtained in his study. Horowitz also discussed a particularly vivid example of the likely perceptual base of a visual hallucination: the case of a woman who told her minister she was seeing "the blood of Christ." The phenomenal experience seemed to be a shower of sparks followed by darkness. It turned out she had a partially detached retina.

Although delusions will be discussed below, it should be noted here that actual perceptual experience may form the basis of delusions as well as of hallucinations. Maher (1974; Maher & Ross, 1984) particularly has emphasized the role of impaired or anomalous sensory experience in the formation of delusions. The patient, faced with an unusual and perhaps intense experience, arrives at an explanation of it that constitutes the delusion. To the extent that hallucinations and resulting delusions have a perceptual basis, the nature and relative frequency of anomalous perceptual experience in normal and pathological groups is a central issue.

I would like to emphasize a different aspect of these observations. Although patients often may really "hear" or "see" something, we should remember that this is not hearing or seeing in the usual sense—that is, hearing or seeing that has all the characteristics of perceiving real external events. The woman in Horowitz's example didn't actually see the blood of Christ. Rather, she had an ambiguous visual experience that she interpreted as the blood of Christ. Many similar cases of detached retina do not result in such interpretations. Similarly, it takes a great deal of interpretation to turn lines into snakes, or spots into the Holy Trinity. These interpretive processes may be analogous to normal ones in some ways, but they clearly differ in important respects, not the least of which is the proportion of interpretation to visual experience. Rather than having a vivid *visual* experience, some of these patients seem to be having a particularly compelling *interpretive* experience.* In fact, Horowitz makes the intriguing observation that patients could sometimes distinguish a form that they "saw with their eyes" from the more elaborate images described as their hallucinations. Furthermore, he mentions that the same recurring hallucination might become simpler as the patient's clinical state improves. This suggests that it would be interesting to collect systematic data on changes in hallucinations in order to investigate the relative contribution of visual information and interpretation. Also, having patients be explicit about differentiating the visual characteristics of an experience from other characteristics (e.g., emotional qualities), and having patients examine nonhallucinatory perceptions as well as hallucinatory ones, may have therapeutic consequences.

---

*A parallel observation might be made about dreams. Although we usually think of dreams as vivid visual experiences, they may, like hallucinations, instead be vivid interpretive experiences.

Another point of interest is that auditory hallucinations seem more frequent in clinical populations than visual hallucinations (Leach, 1985; see Jaynes, 1977, for some thought-provoking ideas about the origin of auditory hallucinations). This is perhaps because visual stimuli typically are relatively continuous and hence easy to submit to reality testing (moving your head, attempting to touch the object, asking someone else if they see it too). It is harder to disconfirm intermittent auditory impressions through normal reality testing procedures and, hence, easier to maintain belief in their reality.

FALSE MEMORIES

Not only do we have the possibility of confusing ongoing imagination with ongoing perception, but we also face the even more likely prospect of confusion in *remembering*. The products of previous imaginal activity may be confused with the products of previous perceptual activity, producing a failure in reality monitoring (Johnson & Raye, 1981). Even when the source of an event was clear initially (e.g., purposeful fantasy or imagination), there is some possibility that later, in remembering, we will be mistaken about its origin. The attributed origin of memories is not only important to the individual, but it also greatly influences the nature of theories about the origin of psychological problems (e.g., Freud, 1914/1957; Masson, 1984).

A paradox is that imagination both helps and hurts memory. Imagining the relation between incoming information and what is already known or believed can greatly increase accurate recall (e.g., Bransford & Johnson, 1973; Chase & Simon, 1973). On the other hand, interpretive and imaginative processes are also a frequent source of errors in remembering. For example, Johnson, Bransford, and Solomon (1973) read several brief stories to high school students (e.g., "It was late at night when the phone rang and a voice gave a frantic cry. The spy threw the secret document into the fireplace just in time, since thirty seconds longer would have been too late.") On a subsequent memory test, subjects were likely to claim they heard that *the spy burned the secret document.* In order to "remember" that the spy burned the document, subjects had to infer a great deal of not necessarily true information: that the spy intended to destroy rather than to hide the document; that the document was made out of paper or some other combustible material; that the fireplace was full of wood and burning rather than, say, ready but not yet burning so that the spy could hide the document behind the wood; and so forth. These sorts of errors illustrate interpretive processes that draw on a range of prior knowledge and also suggest that people sometimes have a difficult time discriminating what they perceived from what they generated themselves (see also Sulin & Dooling, 1974; Bower, Black, & Turner, 1979).

Reality Monitoring

Johnson and Raye (1981) emphasized that many errors of memory may not reflect inaccurate or malleable storage mechanisms, but rather, fallible decision processes. We proposed that the memory system preserves both the results of perceptual processing and the results of more self-generated processing such as thought, imagination, and certain types of inferential thinking. Because the system is veridical (it preserves whatever it has processed), we sometimes see evidence of accurate memory for very specific detail, for example, memory for typeface (Hintzman & Summers, 1973) or particular wording (Bates, Masling, & Kintsch, 1978; Christiaansen, 1980). However, people will sometimes confuse the origin of information, misattributing to perception something that was only imagined, or confusing information from one source (e.g., visual input) with information from another source (e.g., verbal input).

Johnson and Raye (1981) proposed a framework for understanding the processes by which perceived and self-generated events are discriminated and confused in memory (the processes of reality monitoring). Briefly, with respect to class characteristics, memories originating in perception should have more perceptual information (e.g., color, sound), time and place information, and more meaningful detail, while memories originating in thought should have more information about the cognitive operations (such as reasoning, search, decision, and organizational processes) that took place when the memory was established. Differences between externally and internally derived memories in average value along these dimensions or attributes form the basis for deciding the origin of a memory. For example, a memory with a great deal of cognitive operations information and not very much sensory information could be judged to have been internally generated. More extended reasoning processes include retrieving additional information from memory and considering whether the target memory could have been perceived (or self-generated) given these other specific memories or general knowledge. For example, a memory of a conversation with another person might correctly be attributed to a fantasy on the basis of the knowledge that you are not acquainted with the person. In addition, judgments will be affected by people's opinions or by "metamemory" assumptions about how memory works. Thus there are at least two ways for reality monitoring to break down—a target memory may be uncharacteristic of its class (e.g., an especially vivid imagination) or the subject may fail to engage in reasoning (or engage in faulty reasoning) based on prior knowledge.

The results of a number of experiments provide support for the reality monitoring model. For example, (1) the class characteristics of memories from external and internal sources seem to differ, and discriminations within a class are more difficult than discriminations between classes (Foley, Johnson, & Raye, 1983; Foley & Johnson, 1985; Johnson & Foley, 1984; Raye & Johnson, 1980); (2) confusion is increased by sensory similarity between memories from the two sources (Johnson, Foley, & Leach, in press; Johnson, Raye, Wang, & Taylor, 1979); (3) confusion is reduced with increases in the information about cognitive operations associated with internally generated memories (Johnson, Kahan, & Raye, 1984; Johnson, Raye, Foley, & Foley, 1981); (4) memories based in perception have better spatial, temporal, and sensory information, and people's tacit assumptions about these characteristic differences are reflected in metamemory assumptions that influence reality monitoring judgments (Johnson, 1985; Johnson, Raye, Foley, & Kim, 1982); and (5) reality monitoring and recognition may draw on different characteristics of memories (Johnson, 1985; Johnson & Raye, 1981; Kahan & Johnson, 1984). This last point is important because it emphasizes the fact that information can be quite familiar (hence memory for it is good), yet people can be mistaken about its origin.

The reality monitoring model predicts that the more imaginations are like perceptions in sensory detail, the more subjects should confuse imaginations with perceptions. Consistent with this, Johnson, Raye, Wang, and Taylor (1979) found that the more often subjects thought about a picture, the more often they thought they had seen it. Furthermore, compared to poor imagers, good imagers were more affected by the number of times they had imagined a picture. In another experiment (Johnson et al., in press), subjects imagined themselves saying some words and heard a confederate saying other words. Later, subjects were quite good at discriminating the words that they had thought from the words the confederate had actually said. In another condition, the procedure was the same except that subjects were asked to think in the confederate's voice; in this case subjects later had much more difficulty discriminating what they had heard from what they had thought. (It is probably not accidental that auditory hallucinations are usually in someone else's voice.) Like the good/poor imager study, this study is consistent with the idea that the more sensory overlap there is between memories derived from perception and memories generated via imagination, the greater will be the confusion between them.

To explore the role of cognitive operations in reality monitoring, Johnson, Kahan, and Raye (1984) investigated people's ability to distinguish their own dreams from those told to them by someone else because dreams are a class of internally generated events with relatively little information about operations. Briefly, pairs of people who lived together read instructions each night assigning them to one of three conditions: They either read a dream or made up a dream and reported it to their partners the next morning, or they reported an actual dream from the night before. The taped morning reports were transcribed and identification of origin tests constructed by sampling sentences from the reports. Distractor (new) items for one pair of people were drawn from the test items of another pair of people. Subsequently, each subject received a surprise memory test on which they were pressed to respond quickly. On both read items and made up items subjects were better able to identify sentences from their own reports than from their partners'. In contrast, subjects could *not* better identify their own dreams compared to their partners'. This pattern is consistent with the idea that dreams are deficient in the kinds of information about cognitive operations that help identify waking self-generations (such as the items that were read and made up). In their involuntary quality, dreams are like perceptions.

In a second experiment, in which subjects were provided with better cues and more time, the deficit for identifying the origin of real dreams was eliminated. Thus, if subjects have sufficent cues and the opportunity to think about the dreams in light of other memories, their reality monitoring improves. We also had subjects explain the basis of their origin attribution. One interesting observation was that subjects would occasionally make misattributions of origin on the basis of general beliefs (e.g., "That couldn't have been mine because it is just not the sort of thing I dream.").

In another series of studies, we are investigating reality monitoring for various kinds of naturally occurring, autobiographical events. In one study, we asked subjects to remember an event from their own experience (a trip to the library, a social occasion, or a trip to the dentist, a dream, a fantasy, or an unfulfilled intention), and then we asked them how they knew that the event actually had (or hadn't) happened. Three types of explanations were clearly used differentially for actual and imagined events: (1) For actual events, subjects were very likely to refer to characteristics of the target memory trace itself such as temporal information (e.g., time of the school year), location information ("I know exactly where it happened."), or sensory detail ("I remember the exact color of his shirt."). (2) For actual perceptions subjects were very likely to refer to supporting memories. Actual events are embedded in anticipations before the fact (such as buying something to wear) and consequences after the fact (such as later conversations about the event or later regrets). People frequently refer to these supporting memories to justify their belief that an event really happened. (3) For imaginations, people referred to characteristics of the target memories or to supporting memories much less often. Rather, the overwhelmingly most frequent response for imaginations involved reasoning, such as pointing out inconsistencies with their general knowledge of the world (e.g., "In this fantasy I was a doctor but really I was too young to be a doctor, so it must be only a fantasy." Or, "The event breaks physical laws about time and space.").

In addition to judgments about whether events derive from the external world or from the self, we also constantly must discriminate among various types of memories within each class. As Figure 3.1 shows, within the domain of memories for perceptually derived events, we attribute events to *particular* sources (e.g., Raye & Johnson, 1980; Foley, Johnson, & Raye, 1983); abnormal failures in external source monitoring are sometimes called "source amnesia" (e.g., Schacter, Harbluk, & McLachlan, 1984). Within the domain of self-generated events, one of the most interesting discrimination problems is that between ideas and ideas realized in action (e.g., "Did I say something or only think it? Did I turn off the stove or only intend to?" Foley et al., 1983; Foley & Johnson, 1985; Johnson & Foley, 1984; Anderson, 1984). All orderly thought and skilled action depends on this latter type of self-monitoring process. There is some evidence that children, while not generally disrupted in ability to monitor the origin of external versus internal events or between external events from two sources, are less able than adults to discriminate between their ideas and the ideas that they have realized in action

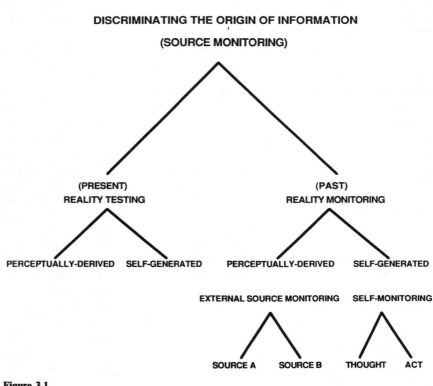

Figure 3.1

(Johnson & Foley, 1984; see also Harvey, 1985, for a similar result with thought-disordered schizophrenics).

The reality monitoring model offers an alternative to a number of other current approaches to the problems of distortion, errors, and intrusions in memory. In some memory models, imagined information and perceived information are assumed to have essentially the same underlying representation (e.g., Loftus, 1979); in other models, they are distinguished simply by tags specifying the external or internal origin of the information (e.g., Anderson, 1983). In the former accounts, there would be no basis in memory for separating externally derived and internally generated information. In the latter accounts, confusion is thought to result from lost tags and memory for origin to result from retrieval of the correct tag. In contrast, our model assumes that the representation of information in memory reflects its processing history (e.g., Kolers, 1975; Johnson, 1983) and emphasizes the role of decision processes in both confusing and discriminating memories from these two sources. Johnson and Raye (1981) emphasized that memory for origin is actually the outcome of a judgment process that evaluates the characteristics of revived or activated information. This judgment process is sensitive to many factors (e.g., the amount of sensory detail expressed in a memory, whether it gives rise to supporting memories, how it fits with prior knowledge); the notion of an all-or-none retrieval of a tag does not do justice to the importance of these many factors. In addition, the present approach provides a general framework for investigating similarities and differences in reality testing, reality monitoring, external source monitoring, and self-monitoring processes (see also Lindsay & Johnson, 1987).

Can Reality Monitoring Be Improved?

There are some indications that reality monitoring can be improved. For example, Raye, Johnson, and Taylor (1980) examined confusion between perceived and imagined words as reflected in subjects' frequency judgments about how often a particular word occurred. Half of the subjects were given an upper limit for their judgments and half were not given any limit. The effect of the limit was to selectively reduce the impact of inappropriate events—that is, it reduced the effect of generating a word on estimates of the number of times it was perceived. This suggests that a more stringent criterion can help edit out inappropriate memories (see also, Gauld & Stephenson, 1967; Hasher & Griffin, 1978).

Schooler, Gerhard, and Loftus (1986) used a misleading question paradigm to suggest to some subjects that a sequence of slides depicting a traffic accident had contained a yield sign when, in fact, no sign was present. Other subjects were actually shown a yield sign. Subsequently, subjects were asked whether they had seen a yield sign and were asked to describe their memories. The verbal descriptions of subjects who had actually seen the sign and those of subjects who had not seen the sign, but who reported they had, were compared. Descriptions that resulted from suggestion were longer and contained more hedges, more reference to cognitive operations, and fewer sensory details. These results are what would be expected based on Johnson and Raye's (1981) reality monitoring model and are consistent with subjects' justifications about the origin of autobiographical memories (Johnson, 1985). Schooler et al. (1986) reported two subsequent experiments investigating the ability of new subjects to accurately classify the descriptions given by other subjects as real or suggested memories. Classification was better than chance and improved with instruction about the ways in which real and suggested memories differ. If people can become better at classifying the origin of others' memories, presumably they can become better at classifying the origin of their own memories.

In addition, there is evidence that subjects are more confident about (1) correct origin decisions than incorrect origin decisions (Johnson et al., 1981), (2) presented than generated information (Gauld & Stephenson, 1967), and (3) seen than suggested information (Schooler et al., 1986). Thus a number of findings suggest that subjects could improve the accuracy of their decisions about origin by applying a stricter criterion during remembering.

FALSE BELIEFS

Perceptions and imaginations yield events or episodes, and episodes yield knowledge, beliefs, and attitudes. Knowledge (or beliefs, or attitudes) is distinguished from memory for episodes in that beliefs represent summary conclusions about "states of affairs."* The information is decontextualized. I "know" Columbus discovered America in 1492, and believe that one person's vote counts, and neither of these cognitive experiences (knowing or believing) seems the result of a particular event that I can remember. Under many circumstances, this inability to get back to the source of information is not a problem and, in fact, is an advantage. It allows us to use words and concepts facilely without reference to how we learned them.

---

*The distinction here is similar to Tulving's (1983) episodic-semantic memory classification, but without the implication of separate memory systems underlying memory for events and more generic memories (Johnson, 1983). The difference between knowledge and beliefs is a matter of judgment. Beliefs seem more removed from perception than does knowledge. Knowledge is associated with greater certainty perhaps. However, the line is fuzzy because for different people with similar experiences, the same idea (e.g., "There is a God.") may be a matter of knowledge or belief.

There is some controversy over how we should characterize the representation in memory of general information such as knowledge and beliefs—how to behave in restaurants; what birds, or blacks, or women, or the self are like (e.g., Markus, 1977; Schank & Abelson, 1977). One possibility is that individual, related events are combined into an abstract, conceptual representation (e.g., a schema or prototype) that is used in perception, learning, judgment, and so forth (Nisbett & Ross, 1980; Posner & Keele, 1968; Rosch, 1975; Schank & Abelson, 1977). Alternatively, knowledge may not be represented in any abstract format, but rather may be computed when needed from memory representations of individual episodes (Hintzman, 1986; Jacoby & Brooks, 1984; Kahneman & Miller, 1986).

Regardless of how knowledge and beliefs are represented, the veridicality of a belief, attitude, or knowledge depends on the origin of the information. If imagined events have contributed to the construction of a schema, the schema itself may be inaccurate; in addition, details generated by a schema during recall of a particular event may be normatively true but factually inaccurate for a particular episode. Reality monitoring processes may fail to distinguish schema generated (i.e., imagined) from perceptually derived information. On the other hand, if knowledge is computed when needed from individual memories for events, specific imaginal episodes may be miscounted as perceptual episodes by the knowledge computation process. Thus, reality monitoring is critical, however, knowledge and beliefs are represented. The factors emphasized by the Johnson–Raye (1981) reality monitoring model should be important in reality monitoring of knowledge and beliefs as well as in reality monitoring of specific events.

In addition, failures in reality monitoring may contribute to a number of other factors that produce errors in memory or knowledge. For example, the ease with which people can recall instances will often influence judgments of frequency, probability, or causality (Tversky & Kahneman, 1974; Nisbett & Ross, 1980). Insofar as self-generated instances are highly available and become confused with actual instances, or rehearsals of perceptual events become confused with actual perceptual events (Johnson, Taylor, & Raye, 1977), self-generated information may have an inappropriate effect on beliefs and judgments about states of affairs. There are other common biases in the interpretation of events; for example, people attribute other people's actions to traits and their own actions to situational demands (Jones & Nisbett, 1972). Similarly, people often blame others for the negative things that happen to them and take credit for the positive things (Greenwald, 1981). These sometimes may be instances of failures to discriminate the origin of information if the person making the attribution mistakes an interpretation (self-generated) for perceptually derived evidence.

The possible relations among false perceptions, false autobiographical memories, and false beliefs remain to be specified. Hallucinations are not invariably turned into false memories; people sometimes remember a hallucination but feel certain the experience was self-generated and not perceived. On the other hand, imaginations that we knew full well at the time were imaginations, later—in remembering—can be confused with previous perceptions (e.g., Johnson, Raye, Wang, & Taylor, 1979; Johnson et al., in press). Episodes that are misattributed to perception (either initially or during remembering) are likely to be viewed as evidence for a belief, but beliefs do not depend on conscious recollection of any particular episode (whether based on accurate source identification or not). For example, amnesics can believe that one man is nicer than another without remembering the information that produced that belief (Johnson, Kim, & Risse, 1985).

Delusions are usually defined as false or implausible personal beliefs that are firmly held in spite of evidence to the contrary (see chapters by Maher and by Oltmanns, this volume). They are usually classified in terms of content (e.g., paranoia, grandiosity, etc). Another potentially interesting way to classify delusions is in terms of whether they (1) seem to involve (false) perceptions or memories of specific episodes or whether they (2) have more the character of (false) beliefs or knowledge that is independent of memory for particular episodes. It is likely that delusions of the first type are a precursor of delusions of the second type and thus may signal the eventual development of a full-fledged delusional system. Furthermore, there may be differences in prognosis or effective treatment depending on whether the delusion centers around the interpretation of particular events or represents a belief that has become independent of the "evidence" that originally gave rise to it.

One particularly interesting aspect of delusional beliefs is that people's conviction in them does fluctuate. Sacks, Carpenter, and Strauss (1974) suggested that there is a "double awareness" phase in many patients' recovery from delusional thought (see also Hilgard, 1977). For example, one patient said, "Forty-nine percent of me knows that what I am thinking is too weird to be real," and another asked a member of the staff to take him around the hospital grounds to see whether it really was a political prison.

It is possible that this monitoring activity could be encouraged by having patients report in detail about the qualitative characteristics of their mental experiences of both a delusional and nondelusional sort (similar to the suggestion above that hallucinations could be compared with actual perceptual experiences). Perhaps a modified version of our Memory Characteristics Questionnaire (MCQ) (Johnson, 1985; Johnson et al., 1984; Suengas & Johnson, 1985) could be developed, asking subjects to rate various specific memories and beliefs for sensory content, contextual information, meaningfulness, affect, and so forth. It would be quite useful to have more specific information about the qualitative characteristics of delusions, how these change, and whether changes in conviction about a delusion follow or are independent from other qualitative characteristics of the memory or belief.

DELUSIONS AND REALITY MONITORING

This section highlights a number of factors that may contribute to the development of delusions and that are particularly interesting from the reality monitoring perspective.

Perceptual Characteristics of Imagination

Insofar as there is a real perceptual basis for delusions (e.g., Maher, 1974), or insofar as imagination is similar to perception (e.g., Finke, 1985; Johnson et al., 1979b; Perky, 1910; Segal, 1970), the feeling that the delusion is based in fact should be compelling because perceptual information typically is weighted very heavily in reality monitoring judgments (Johnson, 1985).

Rehearsal

Delusions sometimes develop in cases of social isolation, lack of social skills, and deafness (Maher & Ross, 1984; Winters & Neale, 1983). One obvious consequence of these states is that the person does not have the benefit of testing ideas against social consensus. Another strong possibility is that these are conditions in which the number of internally generated episodes increases relative to the number of externally derived episodes. If you are cut off from perceptual (especially social) stimulation, more time is spent in self-generated processes. What are the consequences of thinking about events, especially thinking about events repeatedly?

One consequence is that the frequency of occurrence of certain perceptual events may be inaccurately inflated (Johnson et al., 1977; Johnson, Raye, Wang, & Taylor, 1979; Johnson, Raye, Hasher, & Chromiak, 1979; Raye et al., 1980). Thus, if you think repeatedly about the various times people have seemed to ignore you or slight you in some fashion, your subjective estimate of the number of times such events happen will be inflated. In addition, thinking about an event increases its availability for recall, and highly available events may exert a special influence over various judgments. For example, if your neighbor appears unfriendly today, and you can remember an earlier, similar episode, it will affect whether you attribute your neighbor's behavior today to his mood (a transient factor unrelated to you) or to his attitude toward you. Another potential consequence of thinking about events is that they may seem more true the more often they are thought about. For example, Hasher, Goldstein, and Toppino (1977) showed that when people were asked to judge the truth of obscure facts, repeated judgments about the same facts increased subjects' ratings of the truth of the statements.

We have recently begun to explore the consequences of thinking about complex events (Suengas & Johnson, 1985). We developed a paradigm in which autobiographical events are simulated in the lab. Students perceived some situations and imagined other situations (e.g., meeting a Korean woman, making a pot of clay, visiting a computer lab, having coffee and cookies, writing a letter of complaint to the university administration). Situations were counterbalanced so that a given situation was perceived and imagined by an equal number of subjects. On perception trials, subjects actually experienced the event and on imagination trials, imagination was guided by a script read by the experimenter (e.g., "Imagine that I am offering you a cup of coffee . . . Please try to imagine the steaming cup of coffee in front of you as clearly and as vividly as possible . . . I also offer you some milk and sugar . . .). Several seconds between sentences in the script allowed subjects time to imagine what was suggested. The next day, subjects filled out the MCQ, which involves rating each memory on several dimensions (e.g., sensory detail, personal relevance, etc.).

Subjects' responses on the MCQ indicated that, relative to imagined memories, perceived memories were sharper, had more color, more visual detail, more sounds, more touch, seemed more comprehensible, had clearer spatial arrangement of objects and people, and produced more of a feeling of being a participant. For perceived memories, subjects could also better remember how they felt, thought the memory was more revealing about them, and had fewer doubts about the accuracy of their memory. Imagined memories seemed longer (when, in fact, the imagined events were, on the average, shorter). Imagined and perceived memories did not differ on a number of other dimensions—in amount of smell, taste, or temperature information; in complexity, bizarreness, tone, intensity of feelings they evoked; or in how unique the events seemed. These findings are generally consistent with those we have found for naturally occurring autobiographical memories.

In this study we also manipulated the number of times events were thought about after the initial ratings were obtained. Subjects were instructed to think about each situation either 0, 8, or 16 times (distributed equally across second and third sessions that were one day apart). On each rehearsal trial, subjects were cued with an event label (e.g., "Think about making the pot of clay.") and were allowed 15 seconds. As with assignment to perceived and imagined conditions, particular events were assigned equally often across subjects to number of rehearsals. Final ratings of the memories were obtained at the end of the third day.

Rehearsal affected some aspects of the memories but not others. For a number of rating dimensions, instructions to think about the events had parallel effects on perceived and imagined memories, maintaining initial differences between them: If situations were not rehearsed, the availability of visual infomation diminished (e.g., clarity, color, detail). If situations were rehearsed, initial levels of visual information were maintained, but not exceeded. Other questions followed a similar pattern—that is, if not rehearsed, perceived and imagined memories became more sketchy and confusing, and rehearsal decreased the confusing and doubtful quality of perceived and imagined memories equally. On the other hand, some characteristics of memories appeared to become less available over time and instructions to rehearse had no effect. For example, rehearsal did not affect memory for the sound, touch, temperature, what people thought at the time of the event, and how much the situation revealed about themselves.

These results seem promising for a number of reasons. The initial ratings (before rehearsal) replicated the general pattern we have found for natural autobiographical memories, suggesting that differences between perceived and imagined memories are consequences of the processes of perception and imagination, and not a function of differences in the usual "topical" content of what is perceived and what is imagined (which, of course, is uncontrolled in the autobiographical studies). Thus, these findings are consistent with those indicating that when subjects are asked about their reasons for believing that something happened or that they just imagined it, they often refer to perceptual and contextual attributes of the situation as evidence for its occurrence and sometimes to the lack of those attributes as evidence for mere imagination (Johnson, 1985). In addition, the results suggest that rehearsal has a selective effect on complex memories. For the types of events we studied, thinking about an event very much seems to involve the activation of visual features, and much less so other types of information.

The finding that thinking about an event maintains certain types of information to the same degree for perceived and imagined memories suggests that thinking about events alone might not be a sufficient condition for producing later confusion between fact and fantasy. However, the *differential* rehearsal of events (thinking more about imagined than perceived events) could, in principle, produce a situation in which memories for previous imaginations are actually more vivid than memories for previous perceptual events from the same time frame. This provides one potential mechanism for the development of delusions. Those conditions (e.g., isolation, deafness) that would be expected to increase thinking about self-generated events relative to thinking about perceptually derived events would tend to reduce the difference in qualitative characteristics of the two types of memories and hence, make the self-generated memories seem more real.

An interesting question that follows from this is whether only those aspects of an event included in a rehearsal are affected (maintained or potentially distorted), or whether all aspects are affected. For example, in thinking about events we sometimes focus on the physical characteristics of the event, and sometimes on our feelings, thoughts, or reactions. Especially if an event evokes strong feelings or reactions, we are likely in subsequently thinking about the event to focus on our feelings. One consequence of this may be that the perceptual features of the event become less available than they would have been with an equal number of "unemotional" rehearsals. This suggests one mechanism by which emotional involvement might reduce our ability to later give an accurate physical description of events, even if emotion did not disrupt initial encoding of physical features of the event. Furthermore, events that initially had high emotional content often later have an "unreal" quality—people know the events happened because they remember reacting, but they can't revive the events themselves (dreams are a particularly striking example of this phenomenon, but waking events can suffer the same fate). Again, this loss of a sense of reality surrounding an event may be a consequence of earlier rehearsals focused primarily on the emotional qualities of the event. Emotion may produce "repression" not because an event is "expelled" from consciousness, but because (relative to an unemotional event) certain critical (e.g., perceptual) features of the event do not receive the attention they would otherwise have received. This also would tend to increase the similarity of perceived and imagined memories and make reality monitoring more difficult.

Another important consequence of rehearsal is that it may embed an event in a network of other events or beliefs. When people think about something, they may look for other events that fit with or confirm the target event. For example, if subjects are told that a test indicated that they were particularly socially sensitive, they may remain convinced that they are even after they are told the test was not genuine (Ross, Lepper, & Hubbard, 1975). Presumably, this is because the initial information causes them to remember events that are consistent with the idea that they are socially sensitive. Similarly, if subjects initially liked their lab partner, thinking about the partner was likely to increase this feeling, but if they initially disliked the partner, thinking about the partner tended to increase the dislike (Sadler & Tesser, 1973; Tesser & Conlee, 1975). Presumably, thinking about a person includes thinking about reasons why you feel the way you do. The bias is to think of evidence consistent with the feeling; hence, the feeling becomes exaggerated. Through thought, particular events become embedded in a network of other, related events. We know from our studies of autobiographical memories that people often take the existence of supporting memories as evidence for the reality of an event. Thus, the quality of embeddedness implies the reality of a perception, the perceptual origin of a memory, or the reasonableness or truth of a belief.

Control over Self-Generation

There are several reasons that dreams, hypnotic events, hypnogogic images, hallucinations, and delusions might seem real. When we are asleep or hallucinating, perceptual memories that are normally suppressed by reflective functions might become activated and recruit attention (Johnson, 1983). That is, remembered reflections may ordinarily recruit attention more easily than remembered perceptions, but if reflective activity is somehow "turned off" or attenuated, then perceptual activity can dominate phenomenal experience. Another possibility is that the reduction of reflection does not result in a more vividly perceptual phenomenal experience, but rather in the reduction of the criteria used to decide what an object is. That is, ordinarily the features of a stimulus may suggest several possibilities for its identity and the correct one is selected through a hypothesis-test cycle (Hochberg, 1968; Neisser, 1967). If this normal cycle is suspended, a stimulus may be assigned an incorrect identity selected at random or because of its association with other ongoing events or ideas.

Finally, a critical factor (and one that I think may be particularly interesting) is that the self-generation is not under conscious control. Most of the time, we have a sense of control over our imagination. One way, for example, of differentiating a present perception from a present imagination is to attempt to change the appearance of the object. Perceptions are more stable, whereas imaginations can be changed at will (e.g., Casey, 1976). Loss of control makes a self-generated event seem like a perceptual event. For example, take the case of dreams. One obvious possibility is that dreams seem real because they are particularly vivid experiences; that is, they have the perceptual detail characteristic of perception. However, the vividness of dreams may be overestimated. Often, upon waking, we realize that although a dream seemed as real as life, we are not sure of the identity of people in the dream. Also, although we may have a strong sense that the action took place in a certain location, the specifics of the location are not clear. In fact, when Johnson, Kahan, and Raye (1984) had subjects rate the characteristics of real dreams and dreams subjects had either read or made up, memories for the real dreams were not rated as having significantly more detail on perceptual dimensions. Perhaps more critical than the visual aspect of dreams is the fact that they are not under reflective control—and this is the characteristic they share with perception that makes them seem so real. Similarly, the ideas that occur under hypnosis, or posthypnotic suggestion, may not be more vivid or realistic than the ideas that can normally be conjured up during consciously controlled imagination. However, the very fact that they do not come and go with conscious intention is perhaps what makes them seem real. Experiences that are the basis of hallucinations (e.g., visual experiences of stars and jagged lines, or auditory experiences of clicks and buzzes) also do not appear to have great perceptual detail. Rather, it is their unbidden quality (Horowitz, 1978), augmented by interpretation (especially embedding), that perhaps creates the sense of something happening "out there."

Another consequence of loss of control is disruption of temporal ordering of events. Events do not come with "time tags." Rather, they are ordinarily ordered with reference to other events (Friedman & Wilkins, 1985; Loftus & Marburger, 1983). Events should be particularly easy to order when they are a part of a goal directed sequence (Johnson, 1983). Melges and Freeman (1975) emphasize the importance of temporal disorganization in the development of persecutory delusions, and point out that it has consequences for reality monitoring:

> Memories, perceptions, and expectations, which are ordinarily separated by geophysical time, seem to be interconnected in psychological time. Such temporal confusion might blur the distinction between inside events (memories and expectations) and outside events (perceptions). In short, that which is lost in time may also be lost in space, and internally generated threats and predictions may seem to be coming from the outside. . . . The blurring of temporal boundaries would also enhance the interaction between threats and predictions . . . since predictions would be endowed with a sense of reality similar to the present-time or past occurrences. That is, rather than thinking, "They might attempt to control me," the temporarily confused individual would be more likely to think, "They are (or have been) controlling me."
>
> *(p. 1043)*

Inappropriate Criteria

Most of the time, we adjust our criteria for deciding the origin of information according to the situation. For example, we are more likely to adopt a lax criterion for detecting peaches in a tree than for detecting enemy planes in the sky, or for telling an autobiographical anecdote on a social occasion (Johnson, 1985) than for testifying as a witness, or for expressing beliefs about politics than for beliefs about psychology (a political scientist would perhaps show the reverse effect). We also adjust our criteria as a function of the same sorts of biases that lead us to look for confirming evidence of hypotheses we favor and disconfirming evidence of hypotheses we do not favor (Smedslund, 1963; Ward & Jenkins, 1965; Wason & Johnson-Laird, 1972). That is, a memory (or belief) that we find pleasant or comforting might not be examined for accuracy, whereas one that we find disturbing might well be. Ordinarily, we are governed by our notions of plausibility—if a perception, memory, or belief does not seem plausible, it should be scrutinized more carefully than if it does seem plausible. Delusions may not represent the operation of unusually lax criteria, but rather of inappropriately lax criteria.

Individual Differences

There may be habitual differences in attitude with which experience is approached. Generally, if you are unaware of how much imagination may fill in for perception, you may not consider the possibility in a particular case. Some people are more willing to trust their first impression than others; some are more willing to jump to conclusions on the basis of little evidence. It is less likely to occur to some people than to others to doubt their memory. For example, after talks that I have given on reality monitoring, people have told me that they were reminded of something they had always assumed had happened but now they were not so sure. Also, we have found a normal bias that adults show in reality monitoring experiments: If they feel that something is familiar but are not sure of the source, they are more likely to attribute it to perception than to generation (e.g., Johnson et al., 1981). Perhaps people differ in the extent to which this bias operates. Reserving judgment and living with the ambiguity of not attributing an experience to a source is an option that some people may find more difficult than others, or that individuals may find more difficult under some conditions (e.g., stress) than others. Although we know that delusional patients do not differ from normals on logic problems (Nims, 1959; Williams, 1964; both cited in Maher & Ross, 1984), it would be nice to have more information about their general style of thought, especially to have more information about their habitual mode of dealing with the ambiguity of the origin of information of nondelusional as well as delusional content.

Reality Monitoring as a Skill

Reality monitoring may be a skill that develops with experience. For example, although young children behave like adults in some reality monitoring tasks, they are sometimes worse at discriminating the source of information (Johnson & Foley, 1984). As Austin (1962) suggests, because all of us cannot tell subtle differences in vintages of wines, we do not assume they are indistinguishable, or because a child may at first confuse a bent stick with a refracted stick, we do not assume that the child cannot learn something about the differences in the stimulus array that signal refractedness rather than crookedness. Similarly, a person prone to hallucinations might perhaps be taught to examine the "stimulus" for characteristics that reveal that it is a hallucination.

With respect to beliefs, a good deal of the best part of higher education is helping people adopt a critical attitude toward what they think and teaching them to differentiate between beliefs that are supported by evidence and beliefs that are not. If this were easy, many college courses would be unnecessary. As Tversky and Kahneman (1974) have so clearly pointed out, we all, even quite sophisticated scientists, make errors. Because delusions often involve false beliefs about other people, one of the most important issues is whether delusional people have, during the time preceding the development of their delusions, adequate opportunity for the social interactions that provide the opportunity to come to some accurate reading of the social environment (e.g., Swann, 1984). As Swann points out, accuracy in social perception is achieved through a process of interaction.

Delusions may be a response to intense and otherwise unexplained sensory experiences, or a response to traumatic experiences or other stressful events (Maher & Ross, 1984). Delusions are ways of coping, and may be produced by cognitive processes that produce other sorts of memories and beliefs (e.g., interpretation, selective rehearsal, selective confirming of hypotheses, etc.). However, delusions are the result of a dysfunctional, rather than a functional, coping strategy. What do people do who successfully cope with anomalous sensory experiences, traumatic events, social isolation, deafness, and so forth? Perhaps some research patterned after the novice versus expertise literature in cognition (e.g., Chase & Simon, 1973) would be useful. As well as studying the dysfunctional coping strategies of people who fail (and become delusional), perhaps we should study people whose coping succeeds, and pattern preventative treatments and educational programs after successful individuals. If we assume that reality monitoring is a complex skill (as is mental health), there are many points for it to go awry. Perhaps people could at least be partially protected against the future development of delusions by learning to anticipate the types of mental processes and activities (and the types of social contexts) that help and hurt their ability to discriminate the origin of information. Prevention is particularly important because once a complex delusional system develops, the probability of being able to change a person's habits of thought and life situation (e.g., social isolation) may be very low.

Availability of Alternatives

Another important variable in reality testing and reality monitoring is the availability of alternative explanations. People need not only the disposition to consider alternatives, but also some specific alternatives to consider. Again, environmental and social factors are critical. For example, suppose you are having mood swings that seem unconnected with events in your life. If you have read something suggesting that hormones (or blood sugar, or magnesium) affect mood, and you have social support for this idea, you may be less likely to conclude that some abstract force is controlling you. Similarly, if you are skeptical of miracles (or magic) to begin with, you should be less likely to conclude that a visual experience is the blood of Christ, and more inclined to look for other possibilities. Delusions should be affected by patients' cultural and social experience, particularly when the delusions are not sufficiently driven by perceptual experience to determine their character and are not constrained by alternative possibilities that are salient because of prior experience. Especially important may be the availability of alternative explanations for people's own *feelings*.

SUMMARY AND CONCLUSIONS

Reality is not given by experience, but by judgment processes. The characteristics of mental experience that provide it with the quality of reality are similar for perception, event memories, and beliefs: sensory detail; embeddedness in spatial and temporal context; embeddedness in supporting memories, knowledge, and beliefs; and the absence of consciousness of or memory for the cognitive operations producing the event or belief. Reality testing of ongoing perception and reality monitoring of memories and beliefs are complex judgment processes that are subject to error and more difficult in some situations than others.

For example, discriminating origin is limited by the quality of the information. In a situation such as Perky's (1910), in which imagination and perception are made quite similar, distinguishing between them may be difficult. Similarly, in some of our lab experiments, in which subjects perceived some words and generated others, the ability to later judge origin was quite poor (Johnson et al., 1981). But it would be a mistake to conclude from such work that perception and imagination are the same. These lab situations are only a subset of the possible judgment tasks, and not a random subset at that. Austin (1962) nicely makes the point that it is a mistake to assume that because perception and imagination are sometimes confused, they are the same:

> Could it be seriously suggested that having [a dream that I am presented to the Pope] is "qualitatively indistinguishable" from *actually being* presented to the Pope? Quite obviously not. After all, we have the phrase "dream-like quality"; some waking experiences are said to have this dream-like quality, and some artists and writers occasionally try to impart it, usually with scant success, to their works. But of course, if the fact here alleged *were* a fact, the phrase would be perfectly meaningless, because [it would be] applicable to everything. If dreams were not "qualitatively" different from waking experiences, then *every* waking experience would be like a dream; the dream-like quality would be, not difficult to capture, but impossible to avoid. It is true, to repeat, that dreams are *narrated* in the same terms as waking experiences: these terms, after all, are the best terms we have; but it would be wildly wrong to conclude from this that what is narrated in the two cases is *exactly alike*. When we are hit on the head we sometimes say that we "see stars"; but for all that, seeing stars when you are hit on the head is *not* "qualitatively" indistinguishable from seeing stars when you look at the sky.
>
> Again, it is simply not true to say that seeing a bright green after-image against a white wall is exactly like seeing a bright green patch actually on the wall; or that seeing a white wall through blue spectacles is exactly like seeing a blue wall; or that seeing pink rats in D.T.s is exactly like really seeing pink rats; or (once again) that seeing a stick refracted in water is exactly like seeing a bent stick. In all these cases we may *say* the same things ("It looks blue," "It looks bent," etc.) but this is no reason at all for denying the obvious fact that "experiences" are *different*.
>
> *(pp. 48–49)*

Assuming that perceived and imagined experiences are different, discriminating origin is also limited by the nature of the tests and judgment processes applied to information. What kind's of tests are possible? If an ongoing perception seems doubtful, you can move your head, try to touch something you see, ask someone else if they heard it too. In remembering, you can compare the qualitative characteristics of a memory you are uncertain about to one you are more certain is accurate. As with ongoing perception, social verification ("How do *you* remember it?") is an extremely important reality monitoring device for memories and beliefs.

Segal's (1970) suggestions that Perky's subjects made their judgments during a time when introspections about imagery was common and under conditions in which they had no reason to doubt that their experiences were imaginal illustrates the cultural and contextual factors operating in making origin decisions. Segal's work, as well, suggests that detecting the origin of experiences is influenced by a range of conditions that presumably affect a person's set or bias (e.g., whether they are relaxed) as well as by conditions that presumably affect the quality of the information (e.g., stimulus intensity).

Taking into account the nature of both the information and judgment processes, I have suggested several specific aspects of delusional thinking that seem particularly important from a reality monitoring viewpoint. Delusions are likely to involve imagined sensory information (e.g., another person's voice) that is difficult to distinguish from actual perceptual events (Johnson et al., in press). Delusional people experience a loss of control over their thoughts and may spend considerable time thinking about and embellishing the delusion. Such a loss of control, even without any increase in frequency or vividness of imagined experiences, would tend to make thoughts seem external. Furthermore, frequent rehearsals and embellishments of a delusion should make it seem even more real, both because sensory aspects are preserved that normally would become less available, and because of the process of embedding. (At the same time, rehearsal of actual events that focuses on their emotional as opposed to perceptual aspects may decrease the discriminability between actual and imagined events.) Social isolation may not only decrease opportunites for social verification, but may also produce increases in rehearsal and embedding. In addition, delusions may be sustained by lax reality monitoring criteria (which we all use on occasion) applied inappropriately. Together, loss of control, frequent rehearsals, embedding, and inappropriately applied lax criteria should contribute to producing compelling interpretive experiences that (like perceptually vivid imaginations) might seem real.

I also suggested there may be important individual differences in how ambiguous information is dealt with. Reality monitoring is a complex skill and some of us are better at it than others. There are hints in the literature that editing of false memories can be improved (e.g., Raye et al., 1980; Hasher & Griffin, 1978), or that people can be given instructions that help them differentiate descriptions of constructed versus perceived events (Schooler et al., 1986). In addition, certain aspects of reality monitoring appear to develop with age (Johnson & Foley, 1984). These facts suggest that reality monitoring is not fixed but is subject to change. Similarly, there are hints in the social cognition literature that people can be made more aware of the biases that operate in processing incoming information (Lord, Lepper, & Thompson, 1980, cited in Fiske & Taylor, 1984). Presumably, if people became aware of these biases as they occur, they will entertain the hypothesis that past biases have influenced the quality of remembered evidence as well. Horowitz's (1978) report that sometimes patients seemed capable of differentiating between visual and nonvisual qualities of a hallucination is quite interesting, as is the fact that people recovering from delusions go through a "double awareness" phase in which delusions are questioned (Sacks et al., 1974; see also Hilgard, 1977). These observations suggest the intriguing possibility that there is some potential for dissociation between the delusional experience and judgments about it. This is perhaps the heart of the answer to what differentiates delusional beliefs from ordinary fantasy.

There may be some fundamental discontinuity between normal and delusional thinking; that is, delusions may involve factors other than those involved in nondelusional memory and judgment processes. However, it seems clear that there is much room for the conditions and processes that are typically involved in discriminating the origin of information to contribute to the formation and maintenance of delusions. Conversely, considering the formation and maintenance of delusions should provide hypotheses about and insights into normal reality testing and reality monitoring processes.

REFERENCES

Anderson, J.R. (1983). A spreading activation theory of memory. *Journal of Verbal Learning and Verbal Behavior, 22,* 261–295.

Anderson, R.E. (1984). Did I do it or did I only imagine doing it? *Journal of Experimental Psychology: General, 113,* 594–613.

Austin, J.L. (1962). *Sense and sensibilia.* New York: Oxford University Press.

Bates, E., Masling, M., & Kintsch, W. (1978). Recognition memory for aspects of dialogue. *Journal of Experimental Psychology: Human Learning and Memory, 4,* 187–197.

Bower, G.H. (1972). Mental imagery and associative learning. In L.W. Gregg (Ed.), *Cognition in learning and memory.* New York: Wiley.

Bower, G.H., Black, J.B., & Turner, T.J. (1979). Scripts in memory for text. *Cognitive Psychology, 11,* 177–220.

Bransford, J.D., & Johnson, M.K. (1973). Considerations of some problems of comprehension. In W. Chase (Ed.), *Visual information processing.* New York: Academic Press.

Brooks, L.R. (1968). Spatial and verbal components of the act of recall. *Canadian Journal of Psychology, 22,* 349–368.

Casey, E.S. (1976). *Imagining: A phenomenological study.* Bloomington: Indiana University Press.

Chase, W.G., & Simon, H.A. (1973). Perception in chess. *Cognitive Psychology, 4,* 55–81.

Christiaansen, R.E. (1980). Prose memory: Forgetting rates for memory codes. *Journal of Experimental Psychology: Human Learning and Memory, 6,* 611–619.

Cooper, L.A. (1975). Mental rotation of random 2-dimensional shapes. *Cognitive Psychology, 7,* 20–43.

Finke, R.A. (1985). Theories relating mental imagery to perception. *Psychological Bulletin, 98,* 236–259.

Finke, R.A., & Shepard, R.N. (1986). Visual functions of mental imagery. In K.R. Boff, L. Kaufman & J.P. Thomas (Eds.), *Handbook of perception and human performance* (Vol. 2), New York: Wiley-Interscience.

Fiske, S.T., & Taylor, S.E. (1984). *Social cognition.* Reading, MA: Addison-Wesley.

Foley, M.A., & Johnson, M.K. (1985). Confusion between memories for performed and imagined actions: A developmental comparison. *Child Development, 56,* 1145–1155.

Foley, M.A., Johnson, M.K., & Raye, C.L. (1983). Age-related changes in confusion between memories for thoughts and memories for speech. *Child Development, 54,* 51–60.

Freud, S. (1957). On the history of the psycho-analytic movement. In J. Strachey (Ed.), *The standard edition of the complete psychological works of Sigmund Freud* (Vol. 14). London: Hogarth. (Original work published 1914.)

Friedman, W.J., & Wilkins, A.J. (1985). Scale effects in memory for the time of events. *Memory & Cognition, 13,* 168–175.

Gauld, A., & Stephenson, G.M. (1967). Some experiments relating to Bartlett's theory of remembering. *British Journal of Psychology, 58,* 39–49.

Greenwald, A.G. (1981). Self and memory. In G.H. Bower (Ed.), *The psychology of learning and motivation* (Vol. 15). New York: Academic Press.

Gregory, R.L. (1970). *The intelligent eye.* New York: McGraw-Hill.

Harvey, P.D. (1985). Reality monitoring in mania and schizophrenia. *The Journal of Nervous and Mental Disease, 173,* 67–73.

Hasher, L., Goldstein, D., & Toppino, T. (1977). Frequency and the conference of referential validity. *Journal of Verbal Learning and Verbal Behavior, 16,* 107–112.

Hasher, L., & Griffin, M. (1978). Reconstructive and reproductive processes in memory. *Journal of Experimental Psychology: Human Learning and Memory, 4,* 318–330.

Hilgard, E.R. (1977). *Divided consciousness: Multiple controls in human thought and action.* New York: Wiley.

Hintzman, D.L. (1986). "Schema abstraction" in a multiple-trace memory model. *Psychological Review, 93,* 411–428.

Hintzman, D.L., & Summers, J.J. (1973). Long-term visual traces of visually-presented words. *Bulletin of the Psychonomic Society, 1,* 325–327.

Hochberg, J. (1968). In the mind's eye. In R.N. Haber (Ed.), *Contemporary theory and research in visual perception.* New York: Holt, Rinehart & Winston.

Horowitz, J.M. (1978). *Image formation and cognition* (2nd Ed.). New York: Appleton-Century-Crofts.

Jacoby, L.L., & Brooks, L.R. (1984). Nonanalytic cognition: Memory, perception, and concept learning. In G.H. Bower (Ed.), *The psychology of learning and motivation: Advances in research and theory* (Vol. 18). New York: Academic Press.

Jaynes, J. (1977). *The origin of consciousness in the breakdown of the bicameral mind.* Boston: Houghton Mifflin.

Johnson, M.K. (1983). A multiple-entry, modular memory system. In G.H. Bower (Ed.), *The psychology of learning and motivation: Advances in research and theory* (Vol. 17). New York: Academic Press.

Johnson, M.K. (1985). The origin of memories. In P.C. Kendall (Ed.), *Advances in cognitive behavioral research and therapy* (Vol. 4). New York: Academic Press.

Johnson, M.K., Bransford, J.D., & Solomon, S.K. (1973). Memory for tacit implications of sentences. *Journal of Experimental Psychology, 98,* 203–205.

Johnson, M.K., & Foley, M.A. (1984). Differentiating fact from fantasy: The reliability of children's memory. *Journal of Social Issues, 40,* 33–50.

Johnson, M.K., Foley, M.A., & Leach, K. (in press). The consequences for memory of imagining another person's voice. *Memory and Cognition.*

Johnson, M.K., Kahan, T.L., & Raye, C.L. (1984). Dreams and reality monitoring. *Journal of Experimental Psychology: General, 113,* 329–343.

Johnson, M.K., Kim, J.K., & Risse, G. (1985). Do alcoholic Korsakoff patients acquire affective reactions? *Journal of Experimental Psychology: Learning, Memory & Cognition, 11,* 22–36.

Johnson, M.K., & Raye, C.L. (1981). Reality monitoring. *Psychological Review, 88,* 67–85.

Johnson, M.K., Raye, C.L., Foley, H.J., & Foley, M.A. (1981). Cognitive operations and decision bias in reality monitoring. *American Journal of Psychology, 94,* 37–64.

Johnson, M.K., Raye, C.L., Foley, M.A., & Kim, J. (1982). Pictures and images: Spatial and temporal information compared. *Bulletin of the Psychonomic Society, 19,* 23–26.

Johnson, M.K., Raye, C.L., Hasher, L., & Chromiak, W. (1979a). Are there developmental differences in reality-monitoring? *Journal of Experimental Child Psychology, 27,* 120–128.

Johnson, M.K., Raye, C.L., Wang, A.Y., & Taylor, T.H. (1979b). Fact and fantasy: The roles of accuracy and variability in confusing imaginations with perceptual experiences. *Journal of Experimental Psychology: Human Learning and Memory, 5,* 229–240.

Johnson, M.K., Taylor, T.H., & Raye, C.L. (1977). Fact and fantasy: The effects of internally generated events on the apparent frequency of externally generated events. *Memory & Cognition, 5,* 116–122.

Jones, E.E., & Nisbett, R.E. (1972). The actor and the observer: Divergent perceptions of the causes of behavior. In E.E. Jones, D.E. Kanouse, H.H. Kelley, R.E. Nisbett, S. Valins, & B. Weiner (Eds.), *Attribution: Perceiving the causes of behavior.* Morristown, NJ: General Learning Press.

Kahan, T.L., & Johnson, M.K. (1984, April). *Memory for seen and imagined rotations of alphanumeric characters*. Paper presented at the meeting of the Eastern Psychological Association.

Kahl, R. (Ed.). (1971). *Selected writings of Hermann von Helmholtz*. Middletown, CT: Wesleyan University Press.

Kahneman, D., & Miller, D.T. (1986). Norm theory: Comparing reality to its alternatives. *Psychological Review, 93*, 136–153.

Kolers, P.A. (1975). Specificity of operations in sentence recognition. *Cognitive Psychology, 7*, 289–306.

Kosslyn, S.M. (1980). *Image and mind*. Cambridge, MA: Harvard University Press.

Leach, K. (1985). *Cognitive factors differentiating hallucinating and nonhallucinating schizophrenics*. Unpublished doctoral dissertation, State University of New York, Stony Brook.

Lindsay, D.S., & Johnson, M.K. (1987). Reality monitoring and suggestibility: Children's ability to discriminate among memories from different sources. In S.J. Ceci, M.P. Toglia, & D.F. Ross (Eds.), *Children's eyewitness memory*. New York: Springer-Verlag.

Loftus, E.F. (1979). *Eyewitness testimony*. Cambridge, MA: Harvard University Press.

Loftus, E.F., & Marburger, W. (1983). Since the eruption of Mt. St. Helena, has anyone beaten you up? Improving the accuracy of retrospective reports with landmark events. *Memory & Cognition, 11*, 114–120.

Maher, B.A. (1974). Delusional thinking and perceptual disorder. *Journal of Individual Psychology, 30*, 98–113.

Maher, B., & Ross, J.S. (1984). Delusions. In H.E. Adams, & P.B. Sutker (Eds.), *Comprehensive handbook of psychopathology*. New York: Plenum Press.

Markus, H. (1977). Self-schemata and processing of information about the self. *Journal of Personality and Social Psychology, 35*, 63–78.

Masson, J.M. (1984). *The assault on truth: Freud's suppression of the seduction theory*. New York: Farrar, Straus & Giroux.

Melges, F.T., & Freeman, M.A. (1975). Persecutory delusions: A cybernetic model. *American Journal of Psychiatry, 132*, 1038–1044.

Neisser, U. (1967). *Cognitive psychology*. New York: Appleton-Century-Crofts.

Nims, J.P. (1959). *Logical reasoning in schizophrenia: The von Domarus principle*. Unpublished doctoral dissertation, University of Southern California.

Nisbett, R.E., & Ross, L. (1980). *Human inference: Strategies and shortcomings of social judgment*. Englewood Cliffs, NJ: Prentice-Hall.

Perky, C.W. (1910). An experimental study of imagination. *American Journal of Psychology, 21*, 422–452.

Posner, M.I., & Keele, S.W. (1968). On the genesis of abstract ideas. *Journal of Experimental Psychology, 77*, 353–363.

Raye, C.L., & Johnson, M.K. (1980). Reality monitoring vs. discriminating between external sources of memory. *Bulletin of the Psychonomic Society, 15*, 405–408.

Raye, C.L., Johnson, M.K., & Taylor, T.H. (1980). Is there something special about memory for internally-generated information? *Memory & Cognition, 8,* 141–148.

Rosch, E. (1975). Cognitive representations of semantic categories. *Journal of Experimental Psychology: General, 3,* 192–233.

Ross, L., Lepper, M.R., & Hubbard, M. (1975). Perseverance in self-perception and social perception: Biased attribution processes in the debriefing paradigm. *Journal of Personality and Social Psychology, 32,* 880–892.

Sacks, M.H., Carpenter, W.T., Jr., & Strauss, J.S. (1974). Recovery from delusions. *Archives of General Psychiatry, 30,* 117–120.

Sadler, O., & Tesser, A. (1973). Some effects of salience and time upon interpersonal hostility and attraction during social isolation. *Sociometry, 36,* 99–112.

Saravay, S.M., & Pardes, H. (1967). Auditory elementary hallucinations in alcohol withdrawal psychosis. *Archives of General Psychiatry, 16,* 652–658.

Saravay, S.M., & Pardes, H. (1970). Auditory "elementary hallucinations" in alcohol withdrawal psychoses. In W. Keup (Ed.), *Origin and mechanisms of hallucinations.* New York: Plenum Press.

Schacter, D.L., Harbluk, J.L., & McLachlan, D.R. (1984). Retrieval without recollection: An experimental analysis of source amnesia. *Journal of Verbal Learning and Verbal Behavior, 23,* 593–611.

Schank, R., & Abelson, R. (1977). *Scripts, plans, goals, and understanding: An inquiry into human knowledge structures.* Hillsdale, NJ: Erlbaum.

Schooler, J.W., Gerhard, D., & Loftus, E.F. (1986). Qualities of the unreal. *Journal of Experimental Psychology: Learning, Memory & Cognition, 12,* 171–181.

Segal, S.J. (1970). Imagery and reality: Can they be distinguished? In W. Keup (Ed.), *Origin and mechanisms of hallucinations.* New York: Plenum Press.

Segal, S.J., & Fusella, V. (1970). Influence of imaged pictures and sounds on detection of visual and auditory signals. *Journal of Experimental Psychology, 83,* 458–464.

Segal, S.J., & Glicksman, M. (1967). Relaxation and the Perky effect: The influence of body position on judgment of imagery. *American Journal of Psychology, 80,* 257–262.

Segal, S.J., & Nathan, S. (1964). The Perky effect: Incorporation of an external stimulus into an imagery experience under placebo and control conditions. *Perceptual and Motor Skills, 18,* 385–395.

Shepard, R.N. (1984). Ecological constraints on internal representation: Resonant kinematics of perceiving, imagining, thinking and dreaming. *Psychological Review, 91,* 417–443.

Smedslund, J. (1963). The concept of correlation in adults. *Scandinavian Journal of Psychology, 4,* 165–173.

Suengas, A.G., & Johnson, M.K. (1985, March). *Effects of rehearsal of perceived and imagined autobiographical memories.* Paper presented at the meeting of the Eastern Psychological Association, Boston.

Sulin, R.A., & Dooling, D.J. (1974). Intrusion of a thematic idea in retention of prose. *Journal of Experimental Psychology, 103,* 255–262.

Swann, W.B., Jr. (1984). Quest for accuracy in person perception: A matter of pragmatics. *Psychological Review, 91,* 457–477.

Tesser, A., & Conlee, M.C. (1975). Some effects of time and thought on attitude polarization. *Journal of Personality and Social Psychology, 31,* 262–270.

Tulving, E. (1983). *Elements of episodic memory.* New York: Oxford University Press.

Tversky, A., & Kahneman, D. (1974). Judgment under uncertainty: Heuristics and biases. *Science, 185,* 1124–1131.

Ward, W.C., & Jenkins, H.M. (1965). The display of information and the judgment of contingency. *Canadian Journal of Psychology, 19,* 231–241.

Wason, P.C., & Johnson-Laird, P.N. (1972). *Psychology of reasoning: Structure and content.* London: Batsford.

Williams, E.B. (1964). Deductive reasoning in schizophrenia. *Journal of Abnormal and Social Psychology, 69,* 47–61.

Winters, K.C., & Neale, J.M. (1983). Delusions and delusional thinking in psychotics: A review of the literature. *Clinical Psychology, 3,* 227–253.

CHAPTER 4

Hypnosis and the Psychology of Delusions

JOHN F. KIHLSTROM and IRENE P. HOYT

University of Arizona   University of Wisconsin

Hypnosis is a social interaction in which a person experiences anomalies of perception, memory, and action that have been suggested by the hypnotist. What unites the various phenomena of hypnosis is that all involve compelling subjective experiences that do not correspond to objective reality. For example, hypnotic subjects may hallucinate, perceiving objects that are not present in the stimulus field. Alternatively, they may fail to perceive stimuli that are actually present, as in the case of hypnotic analgesia. They may experience a regression to a previous period in their lives (or, for that matter, an ostensibly previous life altogether), and other changes in self-concept. After hypnosis has been terminated, they may forget the events and experiences that transpired therein. Even so, they may feel an urge to carry out some activity that was suggested to them while they were hypnotized—though if amnesia is in place they may not know why this is so.

Since the late nineteenth century there has been considerable controversy over the nature of hypnotic effects (Sheehan & Perry, 1976; Shor, 1979). Stated bluntly, and without regard for nuance, the principal question has been whether such effects are real or the products of deliberate deception. In part the controversy is due to the social matrix in which hypnosis takes place, and the fact that mere words seem to have so much power to control experience, thought, and action. In large part, however, the problem of hypnosis is the larger epistemological problem of the knowledge of other minds. The

The point of view represented in this paper is based on research supported in part by Grant MH-35856 from the National Institute of Mental Health. Preparation of this paper was also supported by an H.I. Romnes Faculty Fellowship from the University of Wisconsin. We thank Lyn Y. Abramson, Nancy Cantor, Jean P. Chapman, Loren J. Chapman, Russell H. Fazio, Paget Gross, Reid Hastie, Marcia K. Johnson, Rebecca Laird, Brendan A. Maher, Thomas F. Oltmanns, Patricia A. Register, and Steven J. Sherman for their many helpful comments. This paper is dedicated to Julius Wishner on the occasion of his retirement.

effects suggested in hypnosis are entirely subjective and private, and these changes in experience are mirrored only imperfectly in objective behavior. We have no way of knowing *for sure* whether what a hypnotic subject reports is faithful to his or her actual subjective experience.

The historical conflict in theories of hypnosis was summarized aptly by Sutcliffe (1960, 1961), who described two opposing points of view. According to the *credulous* view, the mental (chiefly perceptual) processes affected by suggestion are assumed to be the same as those instigated by actual stimulus conditions. By contrast, the *skeptical* viewpoint assumes that mental processes are unaffected by the hypnotic procedure, but the subject acts as if the world were as suggested by the hypnotist. Whereas the credulous view takes the subject's testimony at face value, Sutcliffe claimed, the skeptical view discounts this testimony and focuses on overt behavior (for critiques of Sutcliffe's dichotomy, see Evans, 1968; Hilgard, 1965; Sheehan & Perry, 1976; Weitzenhoffer, 1963, 1964). As an examplar of the credulous position, Sutcliffe nominated Milton Erickson—who generally seemed to hold that the sensory content of hypnotic experiences such as hallucinations was identical to that engendered by an actual, physical stimulus condition corresponding to the suggestion (e.g., Erickson & Erickson, 1938). Sutcliffe's representative of the skeptical view was White (1941), who argued that hypnotic behavior was the product of the motivated subject's striving to act like a hypnotized person, as defined by the hypnotist and understood by the subject.

The contrast between the two points of view may be illustrated with respect to hypnotic analgesia—the suggestion that the subject will feel no pain. From the credulous point of view, the effect of this suggestion would be analogous to a nerve block, preventing afferent impulses from being transmitted to the central nervous system. The skeptical point of view assumes that the subject will report feeling fine even though he or she feels intense pain—much as postoperative patients might reply to the queries of medical personnel that they are "feeling fine." The two points of view might be evaluated by a specimen experiment in which subjects are hypnotized and given an analgesia suggestion, and then their arms are plunged in circulating ice water. If highly hypnotizable the subjects will report little or no pain; nevertheless, psychophysiological responses to a pain stimulus (heart rate, GSR, etc.) will be unaffected (for reviews of this type of experiment see Hilgard & Hilgard, 1983).

At first glance, the available research findings would appear to favor the skeptical point of view—the subjects *report* no pain, but their covert behavior gives clear evidence that a painful stimulus is being processed. However, there is another possible perspective—Sutcliffe's own version of the skeptical view. Sutcliffe argued that subjective conviction distinguishes hypnosis from simulation. This kind of subjective conviction, in the case of analgesia, leads patients to return for treatment or to recommend hypnosis to others (Bowers, 1976). Thus, hypnosis involves an alteration in self-awareness, or, perhaps more precisely, in the subject's awareness of his or her relation to the external world. In the case of analgesia, for example, the hypnotic subject processes a veridical mental representation of the pain stimulus, but is not *aware* of doing so. Because the subject's verbal reports of pain reflect his or her subjective experience, he or she denies feeling pain. The psychophysiological responses do not contradict these self-reports, but rather indicate that the subject's assessment of the stimulus state of affairs is incorrect. Sutcliffe argued that because hypnotized individuals are unaware that objective reality has characteristics other than those suggested by the hypnotist, they are essentially deluded. Sutcliffe characterized his point of view as a variant on skepticism, because there was no implication that hypnotic experiences would be isomorphic with actual sensory experience.

Sutcliffe's idea, that hypnotized subjects are essentially deluded, is interesting for a number of reasons. First, it makes hypnosis relevant to an ancient problem in psychology: the nature and function of consciousness, and the relations between conscious and unconscious mental processes (Kihlstrom, 1984). Moreover, from a historical point of view hypnosis has been of interest largely because of the phenotypic similarities between the phenomena observed in hypnosis and the symptoms of clinical psychopathology (Kihlstrom, 1979). The parallels are especially profound between the classic phenomena induced by hypnotic suggestion and the symptoms of the dissociative neuroses of depersonalization, derealization, hysteria, fugue, and multiple personality (Hilgard, 1977; Kihlstrom, 1984). However, the parallels go further than this. In the classic case, hypnotic phenomena—both subjective experiences and their accompanying behaviors—are associated with a degree of involuntariness bordering on compulsion, and subjective conviction bordering on hallucination and delusion. These similarities between hypnosis and psychopathology—in experience, thought, and action—suggest that hypnosis may serve as a laboratory model for the study of a wide variety of psychopathological conditions, including delusional states (Kihlstrom, 1979).

CREDULITY AND SKEPTICISM IN HYPNOSIS

Sutcliffe characterized hypnotized subjects as deluded because their reports of perceived and remembered experience, made with apparent conviction, were counterfactual in two senses: (1) They contradicted objective evidence concerning what was registered and available in their perceptual-cognitive systems; and (2) the material they denied knowing actually affected their ongoing thought and action. For example, he found that hypnotized subjects reporting reduced pain following a suggestion for analgesia nevertheless gave normal GSR responses in electric shock. Similarly, subjects reporting that they could not hear their own voices following suggestions for deafness nevertheless showed performance impairments due to the administration of delayed auditory feedback (Sutcliffe, 1961). In later research, Sutcliffe (1972) found that subjects asked to imagine a color patch generally failed to show the appropriate negative after-image upon termination of the suggestion. These results were largely in accord with Sutcliffe's (1958) review of previous research. As he noted, "The occasional well-designed study tends to refute the credulous view; and so all told the evidence can be said to directly support or be consistent with the skeptical point of view" (p. 97).

Sutcliffe's review gave rise to a large number of experiments that pitted the subject's self-report of experience following suggestions against some objective (often nonverbal, sometimes physiological) index of response. These experiments were not always expressly designed to test the credulous versus skeptical views of hypnosis. In fact, some of the experiments were designed by those who were critical of Sutcliffe's classification and its implications. Nevertheless, this line of inquiry bears directly on the credulous-skeptical distinction, and on Sutcliffe's claim that hypnotized subjects are essentially deluded into believing that the world is as it is suggested by the hypnotist, rather than as it appears to an objective observer.

Accordingly, it seems appropriate to essay a brief and selective survey of this literature, covering a wide variety of hypnotic suggestions, to bring his review up to date. Sutcliffe's theoretical analysis was couched in terms of the subject's awareness of actual stimuli, and the equivalence in content between real and imagined sensory experiences. Therefore, it seems most appropriate to begin with the effects of hypnosis on sensation and perception: suggested analgesia, anesthesia, deafness, and blindness (see also Bowers, 1976; Hilgard, 1965, 1975, 1977; Kihlstrom, 1984, 1985a). Later, we turn to effects involving memory functioning and personality. In short, Sutcliffe seems to have been more right than wrong; the reader who is not interested in the details of hypnosis research can skip to the next section.

Hypnotic Analgesia

When administered appropriate suggestions, hypnotizable subjects can dramatically reduce the perceived intensity of a painful stimulus, an effect known as *hypnotic analgesia*. The pain relief produced through such suggestions can be enough to relieve pain in a wide variety of clinical syndromes (Hilgard & Hilgard, 1983; Hilgard & LeBaron, 1984). There are, in fact, numerous case reports of major surgery performed with hypnosis as the sole analgesic agent. In a recent laboratory study in which subjects were exposed to both cold pressor and ischemic muscle pain, hypnosis proved more effective than any of the other challenging agents tested, including morphine and diazepam, in reducing self-reported pain (Stern, Brown, Ulett, & Sletten, 1977).

Despite the subjectively compelling reduction in pain experienced by many subjects during hypnotic analgesia, the suggestions do not necessarily modify psychophysiological responses to the pain stimulus. For example, anecdotal reports from the clinic indicate that hypnotized subjects undergoing medical or surgical procedures with hypnotic analgesia frequently perspire and show other signs of tension. Formal experiments using measures such as GSR and heart rate confirm the earlier findings of Sutcliffe (1961) that these indices of stimulation do not follow the pattern of verbal reports (for a review, see Hilgard & Hilgard, 1983). These sorts of somatic responses indicate that the pain stimulus is not blocked at the periphery, but rather is registered more centrally in the cognitive system. In other words, the body is feeling pain that the person denies experiencing.

Hilgard's "hidden observer" technique provides additional evidence contradicting the credulous view. After analgesia has been established, it may be suggested to the subject that there is a hidden part of the person that may have registered, and can report, the true level of pain stimulation. Under these circumstances, some (but not all) hypnotic subjects give pain reports that are comparable to those collected under normal waking conditions. The hidden observer is a metaphor for this continuing cognitive (but subconscious) representation of pain, and the method by which it may be accessed (Hilgard, 1977, 1979). The hidden observer has been replicated in other laboratories. Although some controversy has arisen over its interpretation (Coe & Sarbin, 1977; Kihlstrom, 1984, 1985a; Laurence, Perry, & Kihlstrom, 1983; Sarbin & Coe, 1972, 1979; Spanos, 1986), hidden observer reports clearly show that some representation of pain is permanently registered in the cognitive system, despite the subject's denial of awareness of the stimulus.

Positive and Negative Hallucinations

In some sense, analgesia seems to involve a diminution in sensory acuity, resulting in a raising of the threshold for pain detection or pain tolerance. A somewhat different form of sensory-perceptual effect is the *negative hallucination*, in which the perceptual effect is selective rather than generalized, and focuses on only some portion of the stimulus. For example, research in the visual domain has studied hypnotic suggestions for selective blindness for location, form, or color. Such phenomena inherently involve a paradox, in that the targeted aspect of the stimulus must be registered, and processed at some level, before the person can construct the negative hallucination. In other words, one has to know what is there before one can block it out of awareness. Thus, these phenomena would seem especially likely to yield the paradoxical effects that are the hallmark of hypnotic delusion. And so they do. For example, despite a widely cited early report to the contrary (Erickson & Erickson, 1938), those who receive hypnotic suggestions for color blindness do not mimic the performance of the congenitally color-blind on rigorous formal tests of color sensitivity (Cunningham & Blum, 1982); nor do they eliminate interference on the Stroop color-word test (Harvey & Sipprelle, 1978).

Several experiments have examined the effect of hypnotic suggestions on some phenomenon to which the veridical perception is coupled. In theory, perceptual couplings are inviolate, in that one percept requires another. The argument is that if hypnotic suggestions truly affect sensory processing, there should be a palpable effect on other, coupled percepts. Perhaps the clearest evidence on this question is found in research by Blum, Leibowitz, and their colleagues on suggested tubular vision. In a case study, Blum (1975) found that such suggestions yielded an impairment in the detection of stimuli that was unresponsive to monetary incentives. However, the reported restrictions in the visual field remained constant over varying viewing distances, much in the manner of functional (but not organic) amblyopia. Moreover, when the stimuli were experimentally associated with strong positive or negative affect, their presentation elicited appropriate emotional responses in the subject—even though she was unable to detect the stimuli themselves. Leibowitz, Lundy, and Guez (1980) found that estimates of stimulus size varied with viewing distance—again, an effect that does not occur with true tubular vision. Finally, Leibowitz and his colleagues compared conventional perimetry procedures with a more subtle evaluation of peripheral acuity, roll vection, in which feelings of egomotion are induced by a stimulus rotating around the line of sight. Conventional perimetry confirmed the subject's verbal reports of tubular vision, but roll vection was unaffected by the negative hallucination (Leibowitz, Post, Rodemer, Wadlington, & Lundy, 1981).

In contrast to negative hallucinations, suggestions for *positive hallucinations* concern the hallucinated *presence* of some object or event. In a manner directly analogous to contemporary studies of mental imagery (Finke, 1980), the goal of many of these studies has been to determine whether the hallucination has the same perceptual consequences as an external stimulus. Again, however, the few studies performed in this area seem to reveal a contradiction between self-report and other indices of perception. For example, MacCracken, Gogel, and Blum (1980) employed a combination of positive and negative hallucinations in an attempt to alter the perceived distance between the subject and a point of light. Such suggestions altered estimated distance in the appropriate direction, but not the apparent motion of the target when the subject's head was moved from side to side.

Thus, the general thrust of the research on the sensory-perceptual effects of hypnotic suggestions is consistent with the conclusions drawn from research on pain. By the evidence of their self-reports, hypnotized subjects do appear to experience alterations in functioning in accord with the suggestions. Subjects given suggestions for deafness indicate that they cannot hear; subjects given suggestions for selective blindness indicate that they cannot see the critical properties or objects. Nevertheless, performance on other tasks (analogous to the psychophysiological indices used in the pain studies) shows that the stimuli in question have been fully registered within the perceptual system. Additional evidence is available from an experiment in which partially deaf subjects interrogated with the hidden observer technique show no reduction in auditory acuity (Crawford, Macdonald, & Hilgard, 1979). Thus, the bulk of the evidence tends to go against the credulous viewpoint, and shows that the features of suggested hypnotic experiences do not necessarily parallel those of the actual stimulus conditions to which they correspond.

Posthypnotic Amnesia

Similar conclusions may be drawn from the domain of memory. Just before hypnosis is terminated, it is common for subjects to receive a suggestion that they will find it difficult or impossible to remember the events and experiences that transpired while they were hypnotized—a phenomenon known as *posthypnotic amnesia* (Cooper, 1979; Kihlstrom, 1977, 1983a, 1985b; Kihlstrom & Evans, 1979). Nevertheless, it is easy to demonstrate that the material covered by the amnesia suggestion remains available in memory storage, even if it is not accessible on a particular attempt at retrieval. For example, both complete and partial amnesia can be reversed by administration of a cue, arranged during the suggestion, that will cancel the original suggestion. Thus, the amnesia does not represent the failure to encode the relevant memories, or their loss from storage. In other words, the memories covered by the amnesia suggestion remain available in memory, even if they are temporarily inaccessible (Tulving & Pearlstone, 1966).

Furthermore, it appears that the available but inaccessible memories are not merely latent, but continue to actively influence ongoing cognitive and behavioral performance during the time they are covered by the amnesia suggestion. In an experiment by Williamsen, Johnson, and Eriksen (1965), hypnotized subjects memorized a list of familiar words and then received a suggestion for posthypnotic amnesia. On a free recall test, the subjects of highest hypnotizability showed a dense amnesia for the word list. In a later phase of the experiment, however, the subjects were shown a set of words that had been degraded by eliminating portions of their constituent letters, and were asked to indicate what the words were. Some words were those that had been previously memorized; others had not been presented previously in the experiment. Although the two sets of stimuli had been carefully matched in terms of task difficulty, the subjects were much more successful in identifying the critical compared to the neutral items. The enhanced perceptual fluency reflects a priming effect familiar in the semantic memory literature, wherein prior presentation of an item facilitates later processing of identical or closely related material. Interestingly, the degree of fluency was uncorrelated with response to the suggestion: Amnesic subjects showed just as much facilitation as those who remembered the contents of the word list perfectly well. Thus, the memories covered by the amnesia suggestion actively influenced performance on a perceptual task.

A later experiment by Kihlstrom (1980) revealed an analogous effect on memory per se. Following Williamsen's procedure, the subjects memorized a list of familiar words and received a suggestion for amnesia. Those subjects of highest hypnotizability, as expected, responded with almost total amnesia, as measured by a test of free recall. In the next phase, the subjects were asked to give word associations to stimuli likely to elicit those items, as well as control stimuli targeting items that had not been previously memorized. Although the critical and neutral lists had been closely matched for stimulus-response probabilities, the subjects were more likely to produce the critical associates than those targeted by the neutral stimuli—another reflection of priming. A second experiment, in which subjects memorized a list of taxonomically related words and then were asked to give instances of critical and neutral categories, again yielded evidence of priming. In neither case was there any difference in the magnitude of priming displayed by amnesic and nonamnesic subjects.

In such experiments as these, we see the counterpart in memory of the effects observed in the perceptual domain. Hypnotic subjects deny memory of certain past experiences, yet evidence from other indices shows clearly that the critical memories were encoded, remained available in storage, and actively influenced ongoing task performance. If amnesia is construed as encoding failure or loss from storage, then the research on posthypnotic amnesia would tend to support the skeptical over the credulous view. The critical memories remain present, despite the amnesic subject's assertion to the contrary.

Hypnotically Induced Paramnesia

While posthypnotic amnesia effectively denies the subject conscious access to memory, the high responsiveness of hypnotized subjects to suggestions calling for perceptual-cognitive distortions means that memory can also be distorted through hypnosis. Sometimes, these distortions can arise quite innocently. For example, it has become rather common in forensic situations for witnesses and victims to be hypnotized and given suggestions for improved memory for the details of a crime in which they have been involved. With one exception (Geiselman, Fisher, MacKinnon, & Holland, 1985), laboratory studies indicate that such suggestions do little or nothing to influence the actual accessibility of the critical memories (for reviews, see Kihlstrom, 1985a; Orne, Soskis, Dinges, & Orne, 1984; Sanders & Simmons, 1983; Smith, 1983). For example, Register and Kihlstrom (1987) found that insertion of hypnotic suggestions for improved memory had no discernible effect on memory, over and above the hypermnesia often observed in the normal waking state (Erdelyi, 1984). Score another point against the credulous view: Hypnotic hypermnesia is not the same as remembering better.

Nevertheless, the subjects may well *believe* that their memory has been refreshed, and attach unwarranted confidence to new material produced after the suggestion has been given. For example, Dywan and Bowers (1983) found that both false and accurate recall increased following hypnotic suggestions, that the former outnumbered the latter by a large margin, and that subjects expressed equal confidence in both types of productions. Because the subjects seem to believe in their false recollections (as well as in their accurate ones), they may fairly be said to be deluded about what happened in the past. These delusions can be quite mischievous, as indicated by the substantial number of false prosecutions and convictions instigated by hypnotically "refreshed" memory (Orne, 1979; Orne et al., 1984).

In addition, memory may be actively distorted by explicit or subtle leading questions raised by the interrogator. The result can be a subjectively compelling *paramnesia*—a false but believed-in memory. Of course, distortions can be deliberately induced in the normal waking state by means of leading questions (e.g., Loftus, 1979). Being hypnotized does not render subjects immune from these effects (Sheehan, 1985), and may well make things worse. Just how powerful this effect can be was recently demonstrated by Laurence and Perry (1983), who asked hypnotized subjects to recount the events of an arbitrarily selected evening one week before. After recounting their memories, the subjects received a suggestion that they had heard a noise in the night that had awakened them. Although none of the subjects had reported such an event in the pretest, fully half of the subjects incorporated the false memory into their posttest recall. Moreover, for half of these subjects, one quarter of the entire sample, this pseudomemory remained unshakable even after the experimenter informed the subjects that it was the product of suggestion. We may call these subjects truly deluded.*

Of all the suggested changes in self-concept or self-image, perhaps the most dramatic is the phenomenon of age regression. In this case, it is suggested that the subject has returned to a previous period in his or her life—a childhood birthday party, for example, or a pleasant day in elementary school. In response, hypnotizable adults may take on a childlike demeanor and appear to relive an experience associated with that period in their past life. The experience can be quite compelling for subject and observer alike, entailing changes in voice quality and handwriting, mannerisms, and sophistication of speech (Hilgard, 1965). Still, the age-regressed adult does not behave exactly as a real child would (for a review, see Kihlstrom, 1982, 1985a). The "child" may well retain access to his or her adult fund of knowledge. Childhood memories ostensibly revived during age regression are not necessarily veridical. And ontogenetically prior modes of mental functioning are not actually reinstated—any more than the subject becomes smaller in the chair.

Contradiction, Metacognition, and Belief in Hypnosis

Given the terms in which Sutcliffe originally framed the issue, then, the available literature—past and present—seems to support the skeptical rather than the credulous view of hypnosis. Hypnotized subjects responding to suggestions report experiences that do not correspond to the actual stimulus state of affairs. In the case of analgesia and the negative hallucinations, there is the true absence of adequate stimulation; in amnesia, the absence of available memory. With the hypnotic paramnesias, especially those involving age regression, the phenomena of hypnosis take on an even more delusional quality, because specific counterfactual beliefs about the self—about one's past experiences, or present personality—are formed as the subject responds to suggestion.

---

*Hypnotically induced paramnesias have long been a staple of experimental psychopathology (see reviews by Blum, 1967, 1979; Levitt, 1967; Levitt & Chapman, 1979; Reyher, 1967; Silverman, 1976). Adapting a procedure invented by Luria (1932; see also Huston, Shakow, & Erickson, 1934), Reyher asks hypnotized subjects to imagine themselves the subject of a story designed to arouse socially disapproved sexual and aggressive ideas, wishes, and impulses. Similarly, Blum (1961, 1967, 1979) has suggested that some conflict-inducing event occurred during the subject's early childhood, and observed the effects of the paramnesia on projective test performance. These suggestions appear to have profound effects on measures of emotional state (for a dissent, see Sheehan, 1969). However, in both Reyher's and Blum's paradigm, the paramnesia is covered by a suggestion for amnesia. Because these subjects do not have a conscious memory to believe in, it is not clear that they should be classified as deluded.

However, these experiments do not permit us to distinguish between the two versions of the skeptical view described by Sutcliffe (1958). From one view, subjects are seen as strategically complying with demands placed on them by the hypnotist and the wider sociocultural situation in which hypnosis takes place. From the other view, subjects are seen as deluded about the nature of reality, and their self-reports are seen as reflecting subjective conviction and belief. The problem is set out well by recent theoretical accounts of hypnotic analgesia. For example, Coe and Sarbin (1977; Sarbin & Coe, 1979) have suggested that the hidden observer technique gives the subject permission to report pain that he or she has actually felt all along. From this point of view, analgesia represents less a matter of delusion than one of false reporting—calling for skepticism in Sutcliffe's first sense. Hilgard (1973, 1977, 1979), on the other hand, has suggested that the instructions somehow penetrate an amnesic barrier that prevents conscious awareness of stimuli that ordinarily would be perceptually salient. Such a lack of awareness would certainly qualify the individual as deluded in Sutcliffe's second sense.

It might in principle be possible to distinguish between these formulations, on the basis of subjective convictions and belief. However, such a program is complicated because some skeptical theorists resort to the concept of self-deception. According to Sarbin and Coe (1979), for example, hypnotic subjects engage in "rhetorical communication" (p. 517) in order to enhance the credibility of their self-reports. In the course of enacting a convincing performance, subjects may come to convince themselves that their reports are factual rather than counterfactual. Similarly, Spanos (1986) has claimed that contextual features of the hypnotic situation may lead subjects to interpret their behavior as involuntary, rather than as a product of strategic, goal directed action. Once self-deception enters the theoretical picture, we must abandon hope of differentiating between the first and second forms of skepticism about hypnosis.

Still, evidence supporting such a distinction is provided by other types of experiments. Consider, first, the contradictions between self-report and other indices that have been cited as undermining the credulous view of hypnosis. These anomalies have sometimes been taken as evidence impeaching the testimony of hypnotic subjects. However, it is important to note that similar anomalies are apparent in the behavior of normal subjects who have no reason to simulate, and in clinical patients complaining of perceptual-cognitive deficits secondary to unambiguous organic brain syndrome. The parallels are particularly striking in the case of posthypnotic amnesia, which shares many features in common with Korsakoff's syndrome, traumatic retrograde amnesia, and normal forgetting caused by poor initial encoding or long retention intervals (for reviews, see Jacoby, 1982; Jacoby & Dallas, 1981; Moscovitch, 1982; Rozin, 1976; Schacter & Tulving, 1982). It is often observed that the behavior of amnesic patients is influenced by recent events that they cannot remember. Yet it would be absurd to claim, on the basis of such observations, that the patients are playing the role of amnesiacs in accordance with the explicit and implicit demands contained in the clinical situation.

The point is not that hypnotic suggestion induces brain damage, or lengthens the retention interval, or is the psychological equivalent of a blow to the head. The point is merely that the kinds of anomalies observed in hypnosis are not confined to hypnosis. Therefore, observation of such anomalies, while certainly undermining the credulous point of view, does not necessarily call for Sutcliffe's first form of skepticism. In Sutcliffe's sense, amnesic patients are deluded about what they do, and do not, have available in memory. In an important sense, then, analgesia, amnesia, and other hyp-notic phenomena represent disorders of *metacognition*. Hypnotic subjects appear to be unaware of mental contents that influence their current cognitive and behavioral activities; and their current cognitive and behavioral activities seem to be influenced by beliefs about themselves and the world that are false but are nonetheless held with conviction.

AWARENESS, BELIEF, AND EXPLANATION

The literature on descriptive psychopathology contains several classic views of delusions, especially as these are encountered in schizophrenia. Pride of place, of course, goes to Bleuler's formulation in *Dementia Praecox, or The Group of Schizophrenias* (1911/1950). Later treatments of delusions were offered by Jaspers (1923/1963) in *General Psychopathology*, and by Reed (1974) in his beautiful but little-known *Psychology of Anomalous Experience*. From these sources, and from contemporary texts, we can piece together a picture of what delusions look like.

Pathological delusions are anomalies of judgment or belief commonly revolving around themes of persecution, grandeur, love and jealousy, and inferiority. They are false and even implausible beliefs that are assumed to be self-evident, and they are held with intense conviction by the believer, who shows a great deal of ego-involvement and preoccupation with them. Al-though incorrect, and even implausible, delusions are incorrigible in the face of persuasion, counterargument, and counterdemonstration. Although the stereotype of the delusional patient is the paranoid with a clearly worked-out system of beliefs, Bleuler (1911/1950) noted that delusions were not necessar-ily logically coherent. Then, if the patient is intelligent, his or her ideas may be highly systematized. But it is also possible for deluded patients to successively or simultaneously maintain sets of unconnected, even mutually contradictory ideas. In other instances, however, this feature is not so prominent. Rather, delusions can also be vague, fragmentary, and indefinite.

In the scientific literature and the popular press alike, most attention has been given to the systematized delusions of the classic paranoid schizophrenic. However, Jaspers (1923/1963) noted that these delusional beliefs are actually secondary to the primary delusional experience, which has a more perceptual quality. Thus, psychotic patients believe that objects and events have special significance—that they are somehow uncanny, mystifying, and ineffable, and that they have some kind of personal significance. A similar special significance accrues to the individual's ideas and memories (as distinct from his or her percepts). Jaspers held that this primary delusion was *contentless*. The patient's specific delusional beliefs, then, were secondary—reflecting the individual's attempt to structure the diffuse experience of the primary delusion by giving it some sort of content.

Delusions as Beliefs

Delusions are, first and foremost, false beliefs. In that limited sense, as Sutcliffe (1958) noted, hypnotic subjects are certainly deluded on matters that relate to their current experiences and memories of the past. The primary delusion of hypnotized subjects is that they, and the world around them, are as the hypnotist suggests. Despite the analgesic subject's lack of pain, a painful stimulus really is being applied to this or her skin, and his or her body is not really insensitive to it. Despite the amnesic subject's lack of memory, certain events did in fact transpire during hypnosis, and mental representations of them have been adequately encoded and remain available in storage. And despite the tunnel-blind subjects' assertion that they can see nothing in the periphery, parafoveal events are being processed by their visual systems, and are influencing both behavior and experience.

Even the most mundane hypnotic suggestions have this delusory quality. For example, it may be suggested that the subject's outstretched arm is heavy, as if his or her hand were holding a heavy book; or that his or her outstretched arms are being drawn together as if magnets were attached to the hands. As others have noted, hypnotic subjects frequently become so involved in imagining these experiences that they drop the "as if" qualifier, transforming a metaphor into mythological—we might say delusional—reality (Coe & Sarbin, 1977; Sarbin, 1950; Sarbin & Coe, 1972, 1979). For this reason, Sarbin and Coe refer to hypnosis as a condition of believed-in imaginings. Interestingly, Bleuler (1911/1950) recorded a similar aspect of schizophrenic delusions: The patients, he noted, "believe in their interpretations which they take for perceptions" (p. 383).

Bleuler also noted a kind of double awareness in deluded schizophrenics, in which they entertained the delusion and its opposite, or failed to act in accordance with their delusions but instead behaved in a manner consistent with the actual stimulus state of affairs. Similar phenomena occur in hypnosis. Orne (1959) used the term *trance logic* to denote the ability of hypnotized subjects to maintain in consciousness simultaneous representations of mutually contradictory states of affairs. For example, he noted that subjects who were given suggestions for a hallucination reported both the suggested object and other, real, objects that would have been obscured if the hallucinated object had actually been present in the perceptual field—a finding that has been repeatedly confirmed by others (e.g., Sheehan, Obstoj, & McConkey, 1976; Spanos, deGroot, Tiller, Weekes, & Bertrand, 1985; Stanley, Lynn, & Nash, 1986). Or, age-regressed subjects may experience duality—that is, perceive themselves both as children, participating in the suggested events, and as adults, watching themselves (Laurence & Perry, 1981; Nogrady, McConkey, Laurence, & Perry, 1983; Perry & Walsh, 1978). Orne (1951) and others observed that age-regressed subjects often behave incongruously, drawing on their adult repertoires of skills and world knowledge while presenting themselves as having returned to a childlike state (see also Perry & Walsh, 1978; Nogrady et al., 1983; McConkey, Sheehan, & Cross 1980; Spanos et al., 1985).

But while psychotic patients typically display a great deal of emotional investment in their delusions (see the chapter by Harrow, Rattenbury, & Stoll in this volume), the delusional beliefs of hypnotic subjects are rarely defended with conviction and vigor. The analgesic subject denies experiencing pain, but he or she is perfectly willing to acknowledge that his or her arm is immersed in circulating ice water that is objectively painful. Similarly, the amnesic subject is perfectly prepared to accept the experimenter's account of what happened during the session, even though it does not correspond with his or her personal recollections (McConkey & Sheehan, 1981; McConkey et al., 1980). On the matter of personal investment, then, the analogy between hypnotic subjects and psychotic patients begins to break down.

Absorption, Dissociation, Awareness, and Delusions

At one level of analysis, the hypnotic subject seems to hold a delusional belief about reality, and holds it with some degree of conviction, because of his or her involvement with the suggestions offered by the hypnotist. A number of investigations have indicated that hypnotizable subjects have a capacity for vivid mental imagery (e.g., Sheehan, 1979, 1982), and for deep absorption in both sensory experience and fantasy (e.g., Hilgard, 1970; Tellegen & Atkinson, 1974). If a subject constructs an extremely vivid mental image in response to the hypnotist's suggestion, and then focuses his or her attentional resources on that image to the virtual exclusion of all else, the imaginary experience may well become subjectively convincing, and the object of a delusional belief in its objective reality.

But absorption in imagination is only one aspect of hypnosis. Shor (1959, 1962, 1970, 1979) argued that the essence of hypnosis lies in the suspension of the subject's generalized reality orientation (GRO), which he defined as the mental framework (nowadays we might say schema or cognitive structure) that provides the individual with an informational context for interpreting experience and organizing action. Fading of the GRO results in an isolation of ongoing experience from external reality and critical self-appraisal. According to Shor, imaginative experiences can become subjectively real only with the fading of the GRO. Otherwise, the subject retains awareness that his or her experiences are only imaginary, and it would seem that imaginings could not become objects of delusional belief.

The fading of the GRO has two consequences. First, the subject experiences a diminished awareness of objective reality. In the present context, this means that he or she will not be aware of percepts and memories that would contradict the imaginings. Moreover, it is important to underscore that many hypnotic phenomena—age regression and the positive hallucinations are good examples—require constructive and reconstructive activity on the part of the subject in order to create a mental representation of the suggested state of affairs. Just as the subject is not aware of information that could contradict imagination, he or she is also not aware of his or her own active role in creating the experience. As a result, response to the hypnotic suggestion is perceived as involuntary and effortless.

Such an alteration of awareness is the topic of Hilgard's (1973, 1977, 1979) neodissociation theory of divided consciousness. Hilgard proposes that under certain circumstances the stream of consciousness can be divided, so that several mental activities proceed in parallel. Further, he argues, under certain circumstances an organized system of thought and action can proceed outside of phenomenal awareness. Hilgard refers to this state of affairs as one of dissociation. Recently, an attempt has been made to assimilate dissociation into the associative network models of memory, which form a central component in contemporary information processing theories of cognition (Kihlstrom, 1984, 1985b).

It is possible that dissociation is only a secondary product of absorption. That is, to the extent that attentional resources are focused on the suggested imagining, there may be little left over to focus on external reality, or on oneself as agent of the imagined experience. However, there are at least two reasons for thinking that separate mechanisms might be involved. First, many hypnotic phenomena do not involve acts of positive imagination.

Analgesia, amnesia, and the negative hallucinations can be brought about even though the subject does not actively imagine some corresponding state of affairs. Second, certain other phenomena seem to involve absorption in the suggested state of affairs without diminished awareness of objective reality. This is seen to greatest effect in the logical incongruities generically labeled as "trance logic." Because absorption and dissociation are at least somewhat independent, it seems more fruitful to think of them as separate cognitive processes.

Conceptually, dissociation involves two cognitive states of affairs. First, there must be a division of consciousness into multiple, simultaneous streams of mental activity influencing experience, thought, and action. In addition, one of these streams must influence mental life outside of phenomenal awareness and voluntary control. The first requirement is compatible with contemporary resource views of attention (e.g., Kahneman, 1973; Norman & Bobrow, 1975), which hold that attention can be allocated among several activities as long as the total requirements of the tasks do not exceed the total amount of available resources. In trying to integrate neodissociation theory with contemporary cognitive psychology, then, this aspect poses no special problems.

But what of the second aspect? Contemporary cognitive psychology is willing to discuss *pre*conscious mental processes in terms of preattentive semantic processing and the like (Dixon, 1971, 1981; Erdelyi, 1974; Klatzky, 1984; Marcel, 1980, 1983a, 1983b; Shevrin & Dickman, 1980; but see Holender, 1986). It also has a place for *un*conscious mental processes, in terms of overlearned, automatized, procedural knowledge (Anderson, 1983; Hasher & Zacks, 1979; Posner & Synder, 1974; Schneider & Shiffrin, 1977; Shiffrin & Schneider, 1977). But most contemporary theories do not propose a ready mechanism for the kinds of subconscious processing implicated by the phenomena of normal and pathological dissociation (Kihlstrom, 1984, 1985b). Nearly a century ago, in *Principles of Psychology*, James (1890) considered this problem and gave us the essential clue to its solution: "The universal conscious fact is not 'feelings exist' and 'thoughts exist' but 'I think' and 'I feel'" (p. 221). The key to conscious awareness of reality, then, is self-reference. Some link is forged between two classes of mental representations residing in working memory: On the one hand, some internal representation of current percepts, memories, thoughts, and actions; on the other, a representation of the self as agent or experiencer (Kihlstrom & Cantor, 1984, 1986).

Conscious perception requires the forging of this link, while conscious recollection requires its maintenance or recovery. Thus, in conscious perception the subject essentially reports access to two mental representations—one of the stimulus event, and the other of him or herself as the *experiencer* (or the *agent*) of that event. In recall, the subject follows the link from the self to the event; in recognition, the reverse direction is traced. Some recent research indicates that in posthypnotic amnesia these links are broken or weakened, although both representations remain activated (Kihlstrom, 1985b). Thus, recall and recognition fail while priming and transfer effects are spared. A similar kind of process may be involved in the hypnotic hallucinations, especially the negative hallucinations, and in the amnesia that is part and parcel of classic posthypnotic suggestion. Put briefly, it seems that mental representations of some experience, thought, or action become conscious only when a direct link is established and maintained in working memory between them and an activated mental representation of the self. This, literally, is the basis for the phenomenal experience of consciousness of which James wrote. When this situation does not obtain, there occurs a dissociative loss of phenomenal awareness and the experience of voluntary control (Kihlstrom, 1984).

Thus, dissociation creates two conditions essential for the formation of delusions in hypnosis. First, the hypnotized subject is able to believe in a false view of reality—the one suggested by the hypnotist—because he or she is simply not aware of objective evidence to the contrary. But the relevance of hypnosis goes somewhat further than this, because hypnotic subjects are not passive automatons, overcome by the power of the hypnotist's technique. Rather, they actively construct mental representations according to the hypnotist's suggestions, drawing on information supplied by the hypnotist as well as preexisting knowledge stored in memory. However, by virtue of dissociation they fail to recognize their own roles as agents of this constructive process. Delusions occur not just because subjects do not know any better, but also because they are unaware of the internal origins of their current experiences (Johnson & Raye, 1981; see also Johnson's chapter in this volume). Delusional beliefs reflect not only the subjects' lack of access to the contradictory information, but also their lack of awareness of their own role in constructing the experiences, and the fact that the constructive activity was instigated by the hypnotist's suggestion.

This dissociative account of hypnotic delusions may have some bearing on pathological delusions as well. Interestingly, Jaspers (1923/1963) noted that the core of pathological delusions was a "diminished awareness of Being and of one's own existence" (p. 95). Many of the aberrant experiences of the schizophrenic described by Schneider (1959) seem to have dissociative qualities. Auditory hallucinations, for example, may be nothing more than the patient's own thoughts, or vivid mental images constructed from memory (McGuigan, 1966)—except that the patients are not aware of their internal sources, or of their own active role in generating the images. Similarly, thought insertion, and "made" feelings, acts, and impulses have their involuntary qualities precisely because the patients are not aware of their actual source in their own mental activities. Jaspers' primary delusion (Schneider's delusional percept) may reflect the priming of some preexisting mental representation by an internal or external event of which the person was not aware.

Still, the analogy between hypnotic and pathological delusions should not be taken too far. Hypnotized subjects are not aware of current environmental stimuli, or of past events, or of the reasons for their current behavior. Moreover, subjects construct hallucinations and delusions in accordance with the hypnotist's suggestions. Even if a loss of awareness plays some part in the formation of pathological delusions, and some sort of dissociative process is responsible for the loss, the parallels end there. The reason is simple: Whereas hypnotic subjects act on suggestion and accept the hypnotist's view of reality as their own, no such instigator or guide is present in the case of psychotic patients. These individuals come up with their delusional beliefs entirely on their own. In order to understand how this happens, however, we should first take a closer look at the nature of pathological delusions themselves.

Delusions as Explanations

Reed (1974) has noted that delusions are highly valued false beliefs, but they are not *just* that. For example, delusional beliefs are similar to overvalued ideas in that people have a great deal of emotional investment in both, but the two phenomena differ in that the latter often possess some degree of consensual validation, and at any rate are psychologically comprehensible in terms of the individual's personality and life experience. Overvalued ideas typically deal with social, political, and religious issues, while delusions have a more personal, self-referential flavor. Delusions are, first and foremost, beliefs about *oneself*: "Their content is crucially related to the individual's personal fears, needs, or security" (Reed, 1974, p. 144).

Like Jaspers, Reed distinguishes between primary and secondary delusions. Primary delusions consist in the patient's illusory awareness of a change in significance of some object, event, idea, or memory. The deluded patient interprets these primary delusions (e.g., of depersonalization or derealization) in terms of a shift in the schemata, or cognitive structures, that are used to organize and interpret perception, memory, and thought. This event then precipitates an attempt to fit the new meanings into the person's body of world knowledge. By this account, delusional beliefs—secondary delusions—reflect the patient's attempts to describe, form attributions about, and explain primary delusional experiences. These explanations draw on the person's fund of world knowledge and repertoire of inferential processes. Secondary delusions are unusual largely because the experiences they explain are unusual. Returning to his earlier discussion of overvalued ideas, Reed (1974, p. 152) concludes that delusions are also psychologically comprehensible:

> Given the necessary information, the observer can empathize with the subject; if he himself were to have such an unusual experience he would express beliefs about it which would be just as unusual as those of the subject. . . . They can occur in anybody who experiences disturbing phenomena, whilst retaining the ability to think clearly enough to devise explanations of those phenomena.

A more thorough account of the attributional origins of delusional beliefs has been suggested by Maher (1974; Maher & Ross, see also Maher's chapter in this volume). He argues that delusions begin in the individual's unusual perceptual experience—one that is intense and pervasive, but not shared by others. These attributes lead the patient to conclude that the experience is personally significant. Like any strange experience, this unexplained perceptual anomaly arouses anxiety. It also demands explanation, which is arrived at by thought processes that are essentially normal, and the coherence of which is correlated with the intellectual ability of the patient. Of course, the particular explanation constructed by the patient will be shaped by aspects of his or her present and past experience. Moreover, the content of the delusion will be affected by both personal factors such as the person's history of guilty secrets and past triumphs, as well as cultural factors such as his or her society's focus on concealed agents and enemies. In any case, once an explanation is arrived at, the patient experiences relief from anxiety. This outcome diminishes the person's subsequent motivation to question his or her original conclusions, and increases resistance to contrary information.

Maher's essential point is that delusions do not reflect *thought disorder*, but rather that they reflect essentially normal thought processes engaged in by people trying to explain the occurrence of *perceptual disorder*. At a descriptive level, the pathological delusions commonly observed in patients seem consistent with the proposal. Goodwin and Guze (1984, p. 43) write:

> Common delusions in schizophrenia are those of persecution and control in which patients believe others are spying on them, spreading false rumors about them, planning to harm them, trying to control their thoughts or actions, or reading their minds. Patients may express the belief that they are the victims of conspiracies by Communists, Catholics, neighbors, the FBI, etc. Delusions of depersonalization are also common. These may be feelings that bizarre bodily changes are taking place, sometimes as a result of the deliberate but obscure actions of others. . . .

In addition, patients may show delusions of being possessed by demonic forces, or of being inanimate objects. On the surface, at least, these contents appear to reflect the sorts of explanations that people could give for anomalous perceptual experiences.

Other descriptive data are also consistent with Maher's proposals. For example, he argues that the age of onset of the perceptual anomaly determines the extent of the delusional explanation. That is, anomalies with an early onset may be less likely to demand explanation, simply because they have become ego-syntonic, and thus part of the individual's normal experience. In fact, it seems that delusions are most likely to be observed in cases of acute schizophrenia in which the patient has had a history of good premorbid adjustment. There is also the extensive literature indicating that paranoid patients, who characteristically show delusions, have higher levels of cognitive functioning than other schizophrenics.

Although these observations are consistent with Maher's proposal, formal empirical tests are difficult to come by. It is, of course, extremely difficult to catch acute schizophrenics at precisely the time of their initial breakdown—when presumably they first form their delusions. And, of course, we cannot induce schizophrenic episodes in normal subjects in order to watch their thought processes at work. Of course, it *is* possible to induce psychotomimetic phenomena in normals through psychedelic drugs and sensory deprivation. In fact, Maher notes that such procedures often elicit delusional thoughts in otherwise normal experimental subjects. However, there is a subtle problem with this kind of evidence. The attributional hypothesis asserts that delusions are secondary to the individual's *unexplained* anomalistic experiences. But experimental subjects are aware that they are participating in an experiment involving the administration of drugs or sensory deprivation. Because they have at hand a satisfactory explanation for any unusual experiences that might occur—they know that they have just been given a drug, or that they are suspended in a water tank—there should be no motive to come up with a delusional explanation. Thus, Maher's proposal is extremely plausible, but it has not yet been subjected to empirical test.

Delusions and Posthypnotic Suggestion

Hypnosis would seem to offer the possibility of such an empirical test. As noted earlier, anomalies of perception, memory, thought, and action are part and parcel of the experience of hypnosis and can be readily induced in hypnotizable subjects by means of suggestion. Moreover, by means of posthypnotic amnesia it is possible to restrict the subject's conscious awareness that the true source of these experiences resides in the hypnotist's suggestion. Under these circumstances, if the subject has an unexplained anomalous experience, we should expect to observe delusional explanations of the kind discussed by Maher.

In fact, clinical and experimental lore on hypnosis included many such observations. In the phenomenon of posthypnotic suggestion, for example, it is suggested that the person will perform some action in response to a prearranged cue; it is further suggested that the individual will not remember that a suggestion to this effect was given during hypnosis. On the Stanford Hypnotic Susceptibility Scale, Form A, for example, it is suggested that the subject will shift from one chair to another when the experimenter raps a pencil on the desk (Hilgard, 1965). A substantial proportion of subjects respond positively to this suggestion, with concomitant amnesia. When asked why they switched chairs so abruptly in the middle of the experiment, they will commonly confabulate a reason. This explanation is typically plausible and rational, so it does not have all the qualities of a full-fledged delusion. Yet it is an incorrect explanation, arrived at through the subject's attempt to understand (and explain) why he or she did something out of the ordinary. Thus it is the stuff of which genuine delusions are made.

Similar observations have been made in cases of automatic writing, or in cases of uncanceled hypnotic suggestions that persist after hypnosis has been terminated, outside the experimental context. Consider, for example, the results of an experiment on posthypnotic suggestion by Damaser (1964; see also Hoyt & Kihlstrom, 1986; Orne, 1970). In this study, a small group of highly hypnotizable subjects received a suggestion that they mail one postcard per day to the experimenter. When they were aroused from hypnosis, they opened their eyes to find a stack of 150 preaddressed, stamped postcards waiting for them. Although the experimenter never referred to the postcards in the normal waking state, all the subjects took the cards with them when they left the laboratory. A control group was hypnotized, but received the instruction about the postcards in the normal waking state. A third group received both the posthypnotic suggestion and the waking instruction.

As it happens, compliance was poorest among subjects who received only the posthypnotic suggestion, and the experiment was terminated after 69 days. But in the present context, more interest attaches to the subjects' reflections concerning their behavior. Many of the highly hypnotizable subjects, who were densely amnesic for the events of the hypnotic session, attributed their behavior to something that had occurred during hypnosis— regardless of whether, in fact, they had received a posthypnotic suggestion. Some of the control subjects inferred, incorrectly, that they had been given a posthypnotic suggestion that countermanded the waking request. One control subject, who was relatively insusceptible to hypnosis and thus had no posthypnotic amnesia, falsely concluded that he had been given a posthypnotic suggestion precisely because he did not remember that anything had been said about postcards during hypnosis.

An experiment by Zimbardo, Andersen, and Kabat (1981) also illustrates the way in which delusions might arise as a result of posthypnotic suggestion. The experiment involved a group of highly hypnotizable subjects, known to be capable of responding positively to suggestions for both partial deafness and posthypnotic amnesia. None of the subjects showed evidence of preexisting psychopathology, and in fact individual differences in hypnotizability were uncorrelated with indices of neurosis or psychosis. During an otherwise routine hypnosis session, some of these subjects were given a posthypnotic suggestion that they would experience partial deafness whenever a particular visual cue was presented; others were given a suggestion that they should scratch their left ears when the cue appeared. Half the deafness subjects, and all the scratching subjects, also received a suggestion of posthypnotic amnesia.

The posthypnotic cue was visually presented while the subjects were engaged in a problem-solving task with two experimental confederates, who were at the time talking with each other in a normal tone of voice at some distance from the subject. Independent raters, blind to the conditions of the experiment, then rated the subjects on a number of scales of emotional arousal and paranoid tendencies. In addition, the subjects completed a set of self-ratings of affect, and wrote stories to TAT cards depicting ambiguous relationships. Although the effects were somewhat weak, the trends were all in the predicted direction. Those subjects given suggestions for deafness plus amnesia experienced more dysphoria, and more signs of paranoia, than comparable groups who received suggestions for deafness alone, or for scratching plus amnesia.

The measures of paranoia employed by Zimbardo et al. included aspects other than delusions. Nevertheless, assuming that at least *some* delusional content was tapped by the paranoia measures, the findings are consistent with the attributional account. Of course, the deafness group without amnesia had a ready, and correct, explanation for their problem: They were able to remember that it had been suggested to them earlier. The amnesic group did not remember, and, hearing the confederates "whispering," the explanations they concocted on their own commonly took the form of delusions of conspiracy and secrecy. It is important to note that the same sorts of delusions did not form in the group given a posthypnotic suggestion, with accompanying amnesia, for scratching their ears. In this case, however, it is likely that the posthypnotic response was not experienced as anomalous—if indeed it was given any notice at all: We scratch our ears all the time, automatically and unconsciously. Thus, there was nothing to explain, and no opportunity for a delusion to arise.

The importance of conscious awareness of anomalies is underscored by a recent extension of Damaser's (1964) experiment (Hoyt & Kihlstrom, 1986).

In this study, subjects received a suggestion of amnesia for a list of words memorized during hypnosis. After an initial test of posthypnotic amnesia, they were asked to mail one postcard a day to the experimenter, reporting whatever they could remember of the list. In addition, the subjects were given a posthypnotic suggestion to underline the preprinted date on each postcard as they filled it out. The request to mail the postcards was made in the normal waking state; although the task itself was somewhat intrusive the subjects were aware of its rationale. The posthypnotic response of underlining the date, however, was quite unobtrusive. Although the subjects responded to the suggestion at a high rate, they did not develop any delusions concerning their behavior.

Thus, the attributional account of delusions receives some tentative support from the results of experiments on posthypnotic suggestion. In these studies, hypnosis was employed as a technique for inducing anomalous experiences and behaviors in subjects, and for preventing them from becoming aware of the origins of these anomalies. Apparently, the subjects' efforts to account for their experiences led them to develop delusional ideas and other features typically associated with clinical paranoia. Therefore, it seems appropriate to examine the attributional account of delusions in light of contemporary trends in the psychology of human thought.

ATTRIBUTIONS, INFERENCES, AND DELUSIONS

During the early years of the cognitive revolution investigators of thinking and problem solving focused on normative rationality: categorization in terms of proper sets, syllogistic reasoning, and the like. These trends reflected the common conceptualization of persons as naive scientists, attempting to classify, explain, and predict events in their worlds—trends reflected in the classic literature on thought disorder in schizophrenia, as reviewed by Chapman and Chapman (1973). Beginning in the early 1970s, however, there occurred a dramatic shift in the conceptualization of thought processes. Without abandoning the model of persons as scientists, this contemporary work questions, if it does not abandon, the assumption of normative rationality. Thus, Tversky and Kahneman (1974) began to argue that human judgment is based on heuristic principles rather than algorithms, and Nisbett and Ross (1980) pointed to a number of biases and shortcomings that affect judgments of every sort. The history of this empirical and theoretical effort forms an important backdrop for testing the attributional account of delusions—whether those tests occur with clinical patients suffering from psychosis or with experimental subjects serving in a laboratory analog.

Normative Inference Rules

Since the seminal work of Heider (1944, 1958), cognitive and social psychology has made important advances in understanding the process of causal explanation—an enterprise known as attribution theory (for reviews, see Kelley, 1972; Kelley & Michela, 1980; Ross & Fletcher, 1985). The earliest formal theory of causal attribution, elaborated by Kelley (1967), consisted of a set of logical or normative inference rules patterned after the analysis of variance. Essentially, Kelley proposed that individuals abstracted, over multiple observations, information concerning the consensus, consistency, and distinctiveness of events, and used this information to attribute these events to the actor, to the target of the action, to the context in which the action occurred, or to some interaction among these factors. For example, Kelley argued that high levels of consistency coupled with low levels of distinctiveness and consensus drive attributions toward the actor. In the first empirical test of the theory, McArthur (1972) showed that the "covariation calculus of causal attribution" (Brown, 1985) could predict with reasonable accuracy the attributions made by subjects given various combinations of consistency, distinctiveness, and consensus information. More recently, Brown (1985) has shown that the calculus can account for a wide variety of real-life attributional phenomena, from the thoughts of the characters in *A Long Day's Journey into Night* to the blame assigned for the deaths at the Cincinnati Who concert.

Kelley's calculus was subsequently adapted by Weiner and his colleagues (Weiner et al. 1972) in a model of attributions concerning performance outcome in achievement situations. The model is somewhat complex because the canonical elements of actor, target, and context, on the one hand, and consistency, distinctiveness, and consensus, on the other, do not map directly onto achievement situations. Weiner argued that the basic attributional possibilities in such situations were ability, effort, task difficulty, and luck; these can be classified as internal (ability and effort) versus external (difficulty and luck), and as stable (ability and difficulty) versus variable (effort and luck). In general, Weiner argued, high consistency drives attributions toward stable factors (such as ability and difficulty), while low consensus drives attributions toward internal factors (such as ability and luck). However, the nature of the outcome—success or failure—complicates the attributions: In general, we tend to attribute successes to internal factors and failures to external factors. Again, experiments by Frieze and Weiner (1971) showed that the adapted calculus accurately predicted people's attributions concerning success and failure. More recently, Abramson and her colleagues have extended the general model to take account of individual differences in prevailing mood state and in attributional style (e.g., Abramson, Seligman, & Teasdale, 1978).

The covariation calculus seems intuitively plausible, and it is supported by considerable empirical data. Nevertheless, its applicability to schizophrenic delusions is doubtful. Let us assume, for purposes of employing the covariation calculus, that the anomalistic experiences of schizophrenics are highly consistent, indiscriminate, and have low consensus: They occur repeatedly, in a wide variety of situations, and to few other people. In Kelley's model, then, the schizophrenic should conclude from the covariation calculus that the origins of these experiences lie within the actor—that is, within the schizophrenic him- or herself. A similar prediction is made by Weiner's model. The combination of high consistency and low consensus should lead to attributions involving stable, internal factors. The problem is that these attributions are precisely those that schizophrenics do *not* draw. The delusions of persecution and control that figure so commonly in the presenting complaints of paranoid schizophrenics invoke *others*—Martians, the CIA or KGB, someone's spell—as the source of the patient's anomalous experiences. Because schizophrenics make external rather than internal attributions, it appears that we cannot look to the convariation calculus for an explanation of how they arrive at their deluded explanations for their anomalistic experiences.

After Kelley's proposal appeared, there ensued a substantial debate over whether people in fact used these rules as assiduously as Kelley seemed to suggest they did, and the accretion of a butterfly collection of heuristics, biases, and other errors that affect the attributions that people make (Nisbett & Ross, 1980; Reeder & Brewer, 1979). This point of view has been systematized to some extent in a theoretical approach known as judgment heuristics theory. It should be noted that this theory, and the research on which it is based, remains somewhat controversial. It is by no means clear that the shortcomings in human judgment and inference are as pervasive as the strong form of judgment heuristics theory suggests (Hastie, 1983; Sherman & Corty, 1984). Nevertheless, from this literature we can identify a number of heuristics, errors, and biases that may serve to generate or maintain delusions or false beliefs about the nature of anomalistic experiences. The strong version of judgment heuristics theory is not necessary for this exercise. All that is required is acceptance of a weak form stating that human judgment and inference are not always logical and rational, and that certain types of errors creep into the process.

Expectation and Arousal, Explanation and Affect

A revised attributional account of delusions should begin at the same place as the original: with the assumption that schizophrenics generate causal explanations concerning their own perceptual-cognitive experiences—that is, things that happen to them. A man predisposed to schizophrenia, walking down the street minding his own business, suddenly and unexpectedly has an anomalous experience—he hears his name, perhaps; or he has an abrupt shift in the direction of his stream of thought, or the stream stops entirely. Or he momentarily loses his balance or motor coordination; perhaps a strange or unpleasant idea crosses his mind, or a vague feeling sweeps over him. These are some of Schneider's first-rank symptoms of schizophrenia. According to some contemporary theories, these symptoms reflect a perceptual-attentional disorder that is the fundamental psychological deficit in schizophrenia (Kihlstrom, 1983b).

But the schizophrenic himself does not know this. All he knows is that something unusual has happened to him. Assuming that this is the onset of an acute psychotic attack, nothing like it may ever have happened before; or, at least, similar occurrences will have been rare. The occurrence of such an unexpected event will have two consequences. First, the person will initiate a search for the cause of that event, or a least some predictors of it. People seem to have a general propensity toward causal explanation (Mischotte, 1963), but anomalous, unexpected, schema-incongruent events especially demand explanation (Hastie, 1985). In addition, the subject's orientation to the event will increase his or her level of autonomic arousal (Mandler, 1984). Although some theories have held that unexplained arousal is affectively neutral, there exists considerable evidence that carries a negative affective valence (Marshall & Zimbardo, 1979; Maslach, 1979; Maslach, Marshall, & Zimbardo, 1979)—just as unpredictable events seem to arouse anxiety (Mineka & Kihlstrom, 1978). Thus, the anomalous event is both unpleasant and demands explanation.

Self-Other Differences

In this context, it is important to recall the assertion by Jones and Nisbett (1972) that attributions made by actors to explain their own behavior differ considerably from those the same individuals would make to explain the behavior of other people. As they put it, "There is a pervasive tendency for actors to attribute their actions to situational requirements, whereas observers tend to attribute the same actions to stable personal dispositions [of the actor]" (1972, p. 80; see also Albright & Kihlstrom, 1986; Watson, 1982). If the Jones-Nisbett hypothesis is correct, then schizophrenics seeking explanations for their anomalous experiences will look to the environment outside them. This is especially the case with unpleasant events: Greenwald (1980; see also Greenwald & Pratkanis, 1984) has noted a beneffectance bias in causal attribution, such that people perceive themselves as responsible for positive outcomes and tend to deny responsibility for negative outcomes. If we can generalize from the outcomes of actions to the affective valence of experience, then it would seem especially likely that acute schizophrenics would look to the environment, rather than themselves, for explanations for their experiences. This, in fact, they seem to do.

Contiguity, Precedence, and Salience

Kelley and Michela (1980) have noted that causal attributions are also influenced by certain assumptions that people intuitively make about causal relations. For example, people seem to assume that causes and effects are spatially and temporally contiguous—that effects occur near to their causes in space and time. (In addition, people seem to assume that causes appear prior to effects.) Finally, there seems to be a salience bias, such that people tend to attribute causal significance to the most salient aspects of the perceptual field at the time that the event actually occurred (Taylor & Fiske, 1978). Returning to our acute schizophrenic, suppose that something else unusual has happened to him that day. He got a solicitation in the mail from a radical political group, or he heard a radio broadcast about the search for extraterrestrial life, or a spy was captured in Germany. Or, he refused the request of a street person for money, and was cursed violently by the solicitor. These things happen. The schizophrenic, unknowingly experiencing the early stages of an acute episode, is likely to perceive the event in the environment as somehow connected—causally connected—to his perceptual-cognitive anomalies.

The Fundamental Attribution Error

The environment, of course, includes other people. From a social-psychological perspective, people are the most salient aspects of the external world (Cantor, Mischel, & Schwartz, 1982). It would seem likely that schizophrenics, in making judgments about the causes of their anomalous experiences, would focus on the people around them. Thus, in the course of explaining his own experiences, the schizophrenic comes naturally to focus on the actions of others. Having made the judgment that other people are somehow involved in causing his anomalous experiences, the schizophrenic is led to ask the next question: *Why?*. At this point, somewhat paradoxically, the covariation calculus becomes relevant once again.

Although she confirmed the general outlines of the covariation calculus, McArthur (1972) also observed that consensus information—the actions and experiences of other people—had relatively little impact on causal attributions. This departure from normative inference was reflected in a general tendency for subjects to attribute an actor's behavior to the actor, regardless of the pattern of available information—a tendency anticipated by Heider and enshrined by Ross (1977) as the Fundamental Attribution Error (see also Jones, 1979; Nisbett & Ross, 1980). This bias is so fundamental, at least with English-speaking people (and perhaps universally), that it has been enshrined in language: There are far more action verbs the derived adjectives of which are attributive to actors than to targets (Brown & Fish, 1980).

Once an effect has been attributed to an actor, the next question is *why*— that is, what internal dispositions led the actor to behave as he or she did? The movement from acts to dispositions has been traced by Jones and Davis (1965) in their theory of *correspondent inference*. The theory holds that people assume that actions correspond to intentions, and that intentions correspond to dispositions. Therefore, dispositions can be inferred directly from actions. Jones and Davis hold that the assumption of correspondence is especially strong under conditions of *hedonic relevance*—that is, when the actor's behavior affects the perceiver's welfare. Such conditions obviously obtain in the case of the schizophrenic's unpleasant anomalous experiences. Further, these unpleasant effects should be assumed to correspond to hostile, aggressive, unfriendly dispositions on the part of the actor.

In this way, the apparent paradox of the covariation calculus—that schizophrenics make external attributions when they should make internal ones—may be resolved by tracing a two-step process. First, by virtue of the self-other difference in causal attribution, and the beneffectance bias in self-attribution, their unpleasant, anomalous experiences are attributed to factors residing in the external environment, and particularly to the behavior of others. Then, by virtue of salience and the fundamental attribution error, the behavior of others is attributed to their internal dispositions—their abilities, traits, attitudes, beliefs, and intentions. Finally, by virtue of correspondent inference, others are characterized as hostile in intent. At this point, we have attributions that somewhat more closely resemble the delusions of persecution and control by others that characterize the paranoid schizophrenic.

Judgment Heuristics

Self-other differences in causal attribution, the fundamental attribution error, biased hypothesis testing, and the like all illustrate some of the departures from normative inference that affect information processing in general, and causal attribution in particular. Beginning in 1972, an important series of papers by Kahneman and Tversky started to outline another set of such departures, collectively described as judgmental heuristics—in contrast to judgmental algorithms (e.g., Kahneman & Tversky, 1972, 1973, 1982; Kahneman, Slovic, & Tversky, 1982; Tversky & Kahneman, 1973, 1974, 1982).

Algorithms are judgmental procedures that adhere to the rules of logical inference, and that are guaranteed to yield the correct solution. Unfortunately, there are some circumstances in which algorithms cannot be applied. Under conditions of uncertainty, either no algorithm is suitable to the task at hand or the information needed by an algorithm is not available. Even when an appropriate algorithm is available, and the person has access to all the information necessary to its use, the procedure still may not be employed. The reason for this is that human judgment is constrained by capacity limitations on human information processing. Algorithms are often complex, and we may not be able to handle all the information that is needed to employ them, especially under conditions of time pressure, low motivation, or—somewhat paradoxically—high personal involvement.

Under such circumstances, people seem to shift to heuristics—shortcut approaches to judgment that violate one or more rules of normative inference, but that nonetheless have some likelihood of leading to the correct solution to some problem. Heuristics are useful precisely because they are shortcuts: They permit judgments to be made when algorithms or the information algorithms require are not available, or when the requirements of a judgmental task exceed available cognitive capacity. Unfortunately, the fact that heuristics depart from the rules of logical inference means that their use increases the risk of error—that the judgment made may be wrong. Errors are produced because judgmental heuristics ignore or misuse information in a way that algorithms do not. In fact, observations of systematic errors and biases in judgment provide the most compelling evidence that people do in fact use heuristics in judgment. Kahneman, Tversky, and their colleagues have identified four major heuristic principles guiding judgments of frequency, likelihood, co-occurrence, and causality (for reviews, see Kahneman, Slovic, & Tversky, 1982; Sherman & Corty, 1981).

In *representativeness*, judgments are based on the degree to which any sample event is similar to the presumed parent population of that event. In a causal context, this means that people tend to assume that the features of a causal agent ought to resemble the features of its outcome: Weird, unpleasant effects should have weird, unpleasant causes. Kelley and Michela (1980) suggested that a similarity principle may account for such phenomena as conspiracy theories of political assassination. Such theories are not necessarily paranoid (or even necessarily incorrect), but similarity may underlie the kinds of conspiracy theories to which paranoid patients are prone. Additionally, people's causal judgments seem to be greatly influenced by their a priori theories about causation: If someone has the idea that many unpleasant events in the outside world reflect the activities of an international terrorist conspiracy, those same terrorists may be held responsible for unpleasant internal events as well. Thus, in seeking an explanation for his or her distressing anomalous experiences, the person experiencing them may be especially likely to focus on members of out-groups, individuals and classes of people who are generally feared in his or her culture, and the like.

In *availability*, judgments are affected by the ease with which specific instances can be brought to mind. Availability is observed whenever judgments are inordinately influenced by concrete, vivid, extreme cases. In a causal context, availability may be illustrated by perceptual salience, which affects judgments of causality by drawing attention to certain events in the internal or external world. In one respect, this only makes sense: Causal attributions are made when people search for explanations or predictors of surprising or unexpected events. In this process, their attention naturally focuses on other events that are also surprising or unexpected. After all, a routine event—something that happens all the time—cannot be a very good predictor of a rare event, because the probability of the rare event, given the occurrence of the routine event, must be relatively low. Accordingly, the search for predictors of unexpected happenings must focus on relatively infrequent causal agents. Given that all vertebrate organisms possess a capacity for classical conditioning—that is, an ability to determine the contingent relations between CSs and USs—it may be that the salience bias in judgments of covariation is part of our phylogenetic endowment.

The *simulation* heuristic is conceptually similar to availability, in that the basis for judgment is the ease with which a plausible scenario can be constructed mentally. For example, judgments of causality may be affected by the ease with which the person can imagine a path from a presumed cause to a known effect. Prediction in advance, given knowledge only of potential causes, is of course difficult and uncertain. However, given sure knowledge of outcomes, it is often an easy matter to trace causal links to prior events— even if the purported causes are totally unrelated to their ostensible effects. These errors are frequently made by psychoanalysts, biographers, and others who try to explain the actions of individuals in terms of prior events drawn from a rich body of historical knowledge. By virtue of simulation, events appear to be inevitable consequences of their antecedents.

Again, consider an acute schizophrenic searching the environment for a likely cause of his or her anomalous experiences. Salient objects and events— a honk or a wave from a passing driver, perhaps, or a member of a minority group standing on a street corner—will inevitably draw attention, and be given special weight as likely causes of the troublesome internal events. If there is nothing salient in the perceptual field, salient events retrieved from memory—a curse uttered in anger by a coworker, perhaps, or a sin unconfessed to a priest—may seem to be involved. If no event is generated by the availability heuristic, through either perception or memory, the simulation heuristic may come into play. The person may imagine possible causes, and grasp the first one that comes to mind as the most likely explanation. Perhaps someone slipped something into his morning coffee; perhaps there is a conspiracy afoot to prevent him from becoming aware of the true reasons for his experiences.

While representativeness, availability, and simulation seem to be involved in the initial generation of irrational causal explanations, another heuristic, *anchoring and adjustment*, may be important in the maintenance of such explanations. Many judgments begin as hypotheses, tentative conclusions that can be revised on the basis of newly arriving evidence. However, it has long been appreciated that final judgments are inordinately influenced by first impressions: The initial judgment serves as an anchor on the final one, in that there is relatively little subsequent adjustment. The heuristic of anchoring and adjustment reflects a general tendency to rely on initial or partial judgments, giving too little weight to newly obtained information. Although this heuristic plays a role in judgments of magnitude and frequency, it can also influence judgments of causality. By virtue of its use, judgments of causality tend not to accommodate to new information that should instigate revision. Instead, knowledge gained subsequent to the initial judgment may be distorted so as to fit the original causal theory.

Anomalies in Hypotheses Testing

Delusional explanations and other erroneous judgments are also maintained by other processes. While initial judgments may be regarded as hypotheses, we are not always given the opportunity to actively test them by collecting additional data. If we had such an opportunity, of course, the rules of normative inference would make us behave the way professional scientists are supposed to behave in the course of formal experimentation. That is, we would search for information that is inconsistent with our hypothesis—or, better, for information that is diagnostic with respect to our hypothesis, consistent with the hypothesis but inconsistent with some plausible alternative. Instead, people seem to adopt nonoptimal hypothesis-testing strategies. Thus, Snyder and Swann (1978) claimed that subjects tended to adopt verificationist strategies, seeking and paying special attention to information that is consistent with their hypothesis. Alternatively, Fischoff and Beyth-Marom (1983) argued that people tend to adopt inefficient strategies of hypothesis testing, wasting effort on nondiagnostic data (see also Trope & Bassok, 1982). The outcome is the same in both cases: People tend to hold onto incorrect hypotheses long after they should have been abandoned.

Another inferential shortcoming contributing to the maintenance of incorrect hypotheses is the *feature-positive effect*—the tendency to focus on the positive/positive cell in the contingency matrix. Having initially observed an (adventitious) association between some external event and some anomalous experience, repetitions of the event experience would ordinarily give the person repeated opportunities to observe the actual correlation between the two events—that is, to assess the conditional probability of the experience, given that the event has occurred. However, judgments of contingency and covariation often seem to be based only on the number of co-occurrences, and people tend to ignore the information provided by nonoccurrences. Thus, even though the actual association may be random, the feature-positive effect will lead individuals to focus attention, and memory, on instances when both the effect and its presumed cause were present. Furthermore, formal hypothesis testing is known to be inefficient, and some claim that it is subject to a confirmatory bias. Thus, again, if individuals seek to test their attributional hypotheses, they will retain incorrect ones longer than would be the case if they sought out diagnostic information.

In either case, it seems unlikely that people will subject their initial causal judgments, however derived, to rigorous testing. Left to their own devices, the normal and the schizophrenic alike will fail to turn up much information that definitively contradicts their hypotheses. And when confronted with representative data, people selectively encode and retrieve events that are consistent with it. The most clever, faced with incongruent information, will find a way to discount or rationalize it, and perhaps incorporate the rationalization into the explanatory system itself. For these reasons, delusions and other irrational explanations would not seem to be self-correcting as long as the anomalous experiences that they are designed to explain persist, and in the absence of any better explanation. In this context, we note with interest a report that delusions remit as schizophrenics recover from the acute phase of illness (Sacks, Carpenter, & Strauss, 1974), and a case study in which a nonpsychotic patient's delusional belief was corrected by means of attributional therapy (Johnson, Ross, & Mastria, 1977).

Why Are Schizophrenics so Vulnerable to Delusions?

The judgments and inferences made by ordinary people are often governed by heuristics, and so are subject to certain shortcomings and biases, at least to some degree. However, ordinary people are not usually thought of as delusional. So what makes schizophrenics special in this respect? One answer, of course, is that schizophrenics have more anomalistic experiences to explain, and the fact that these schizophrenic anomalies are relatively rare in the population means that there aren't readily available the sorts of normative explanations that the rest of us use—when, for example, we get a headache or toothache. Schizophrenics have more to explain, and more that is mysterious, which means that they have more need to reduce anxiety by finding a causal explanation. Normals, whose anomalies (if indeed they have them at all) are quite minor, may be more likely to pass the episodes off as "just one of those things."

Just as important, we have the evidence from Chapman and Chapman (1973; see also their chapter in this volume) that schizophrenics manifest excessive yielding to normal response biases. Heuristics are employed, when they are employed, in order to save cognitive effort. They reduce complex judgmental tasks to manageable proportions, and diminish task demands on information processing. In this context, we note in passing the important role historically ascribed to attentional deficits in schizophrenia. If schizophrenics have less attentional capacity than normals, or less ability to deploy attention effectively, they will be even more reliant on heuristics, and so more likely to exhibit the delusions and other disorders of thought that reflect the operation of judgmental heuristics.

Moreover, because schizophrenia tends to run in families, these cognitive biases and shortcomings are likely to be shared by other individuals around him or her. This means that a young schizophrenic has a social environment that provides lots of opportunities to pick up delusional explanations through social learning—by example, if not precept. This factor, of course, is what saves us from the possibility that judgmental biases and shortcomings are not as prevalent as claimed. Nobody asserts that human judgment and inference are perfectly rational, and unerringly follow the rules of normative inference. All the argument requires is that people fall short at least a little—a tendency that could be magnified by schizophrenia.

SOME NEW DIRECTIONS FOR RESEARCH

On the basis of our analysis, we can offer some directions for studying the nature of delusions. First, to return to the title of this chapter, there is the use of hypnosis and other special states of consciousness as laboratory models for the study of the formation of delusions and other symptoms of psychopathology. Hypnosis is of special interest here, because it seems to afford, in hypnotizable subjects, a means of inducing subjectively compelling anomalies in experience, thought, and action. The research of Zimbardo et al. (1981) opens up a new avenue of approach to experimental work on the delusional process, using hypnotic and posthypnotic suggestion as a laboratory model. Of course, the success of the model is determined wholly by the degree to which hypnotic subjects are denied access to correct explanations for their experiences. In fact, hypnosis permits just such a denial of information. For example, posthypnotic responses can occur outside the experimental setting in which they were suggested, and even in the absence of the hypnotist. This reduces the likelihood that subjects will (correctly) attribute their anomalous experiences to some prior hypnotic session. The likelihood is reduced still further by the fact that subjects' memories for the suggestion can be controlled by means of suggestions for amnesia. If the attributional explanation is correct, delusions should form, as they did in the Zimbardo experiment, when subjects are amnesic for the hypnotic suggestion that is the true source of their experience; but they should drop the delusion as soon as the amnesia suggestion is canceled, and memory restored.

Other sorts of advantages accrue to the use of hypnosis as a laboratory model. For example, posthypnotic suggestions and their accompanying amnesias can remain in effect over a considerable period of time. This would allow the investigator the opportunity to watch delusions evolve and solidify over time. Moreover, the use of explicit hypnotic suggestions gives the investigator a great deal of control over the nature of the anomaly to be induced. For example, it would be possible to disrupt perception, memory, voluntary action, or any combination of the three, and see if delusions changed accordingly. It would also be possible, as the Zimbardo experiment shows, to induce anomalies of varying degrees of subtlety. Finally, the effects of hypnotic suggestion are easily reversible, so that it should be possible to observe the fate of the delusion when the true source of the anomalies and discontinuities is made known to the subject.

Next, of course, there is the study of deluded individuals themselves. Beginning with the work of Von Domarus, Goldstein and Scheerer, and others, there has been a long tradition of the study of thought disorder in schizophrenic individuals (Chapman & Chapman, 1973). The judgmental heuristics approach puts a new perspective on schizophrenic thought disorder by providing a new theoretical perspective and a new set of experimental tasks. We may look forward to a host of studies in which the paradigms now used to study normal judgment and inference are applied to the pathological case (for analogous expectations in the domains of perception and attention, see Kihlstrom, 1983). Of particular interest would be the longitudinal study of people who are at risk for the kinds of syndromes in which delusions appear. It should be possible to inoculate such people against delusions, even if it is not possible to prevent them from suffering the primary psychological deficits.

Moreover, there is the continued study of the shortcomings of normal judgment and inference. As Hastie (1983) and Sherman and Corty (1984) have noted, the judgmental heuristics approach is currently incomplete. We know relatively little about such matters as the conditions that invoke heuristic as opposed to normative inference procedures, or the types of tasks in which one heuristic will be employed as opposed to another. Experimental psychopathology will advance only with improved theoretical understanding of normal cognitive, social, developmental, and psychobiological processes.

REFERENCES

Abramson, L.Y., Seligman, M.E.P., & Teasdale, J.D. (1978). Learned helplessness in humans: Critique and reformulation. *Journal of Abnormal Psychology*, *87*, 49–74.

Albright, J.S., & Kihlstrom, J.F. (1986). *Motivation, visual perspective, and the self-other difference in causal attributions: A study of autobiographical memory.* Unpublished manuscript.

Anderson, J.R. (1983). *The architecture of cognition.* Cambridge, MA: Harvard University Press.

Bleuler, E. (1950). *Dementia praecox, or the group of schizophrenias.* New York: International Universities Press. (Original work published 1911.)

Blum, G.S. (1961). *A model of the mind: Explored by hypnotically controlled experiments and examined for its psychodynamic implications.* New York: Wiley.

Blum, G.S. (1967). Hypnosis in psychodynamic research. In J.E. Gordon (Ed.), *Handbook of clinical and experimental hypnosis.* New York: Macmillan.

Blum, G.S. (1975). A case study of hypnotically induced tubular vision. *International Journal of Clinical and Experimental Hypnosis*, *23*, 111–119.

Blum, G.S. (1979). Hypnotic programming techniques in psychological experiments. In E. Fromm & R.E. Shor (Eds.), *Hypnosis: Developments in research and new perspectives.* New York: Aldine.

Bowers, K.S. (1976). *Hypnosis for the seriously curious.* Monterey, CA: Brooks/Cole.

Brown, R. (1985). *Social psychology* (2nd ed). New York: Free Press.

Brown, R., & Fish, D. (1980). The psychological causality implicit in language. Unpublished manuscript, Harvard University.

Cantor, N., Mischel, W., & Schwartz, J. (1982). Social knowledge: Structure, content, use, and abuse. In A. Hastorf & A. Isen (Eds.), *Cognitive social psychology.* New York: Elsevier-North Holland.

Chapman, L.J., & Chapman, J.P. (1973). *Disordered thought in schizophrenia.* Englewood Cliffs, NJ: Prentice-Hall.

Coe, W.C., & Sarbin, T.R. (1977). Hypnosis from the standpoint of a contextualist. In W.E. Edmonston (Ed.), *Conceptual and investigative approaches to hypnosis and hypnotic phenomena. Annals of the New York Academy of Sciences*, *277*, 2–13.

Cooper, L.M. (1979). Hypnotic amnesia. In E. Fromm & R.E. Shor (Eds.), *Hypnosis: Developments in research and new perspectives.* New York: Aldine.

Crawford, H.J., Macdonald, H., & Hilgard, E.R. (1979). Hypnotic deafness: A psychophysical study of responses to tone intensity as modified by hypnosis. *American Journal of Psychology*, *92*, 193–214.

Cunningham, P.V., & Blum, G.S. (1982). Further evidence that hypnotically induced color blindness does not mimic congenital defects. *Journal of Abnormal Psychology*, *91*, 139–143.

Damaser, E.C. (1964). *An experimental study of long-term posthypnotic suggestion.* Unpublished doctoral dissertation, Harvard University, Cambridge, MA.

Dixon, N.F. (1971). *Subliminal perception*. New York: McGraw-Hill.

Dixon, N.F. (1981). *Preconscious processing*. Chichester: Wiley.

Dywan, J., & Bowers, K.S. (1983). The use of hypnosis to enhance recall. *Science, 222,* 184–185.

Erdelyi, M.H. (1974). A new look at the new look: Perceptual defense and vigilance. *Psychological Review, 81,* 1–25.

Erdelyi, M.H. (1984). *Psychoanalysis: Freud's cognitive psychology*. San Francisco: Freeman.

Erickson, M.H., & Erickson, E.M. (1983). The hypnotic induction of hallucinatory color vision followed by pseudo-negative afterimages. *Journal of Experimental Psychology, 22,* 501–588.

Evans, F.J. (1968). Recent trends in experimental hypnosis. *Behavioral Science, 13,* 477–487.

Finke, R.A. (1980). Levels of equivalence in imagery and perception. *Psychological Review, 87,* 113–132.

Fischoff, B., & Beyth-Marom, R. (1983). Hypothesis testing in Bayesian perspective. *Psychological Review, 90,* 239–268.

Frieze, I.H., & Weiner, B. (1971). Cue utilization and attributional judgments for success and failure. *Journal of Personality, 39,* 591–605.

Geiselman, R.E., Fisher, R.P., MacKinnon, D.P., & Holland, H.L. (1985). Eyewitness memory enhancement in the police interview: Cognitive retrieval mnemonics versus hypnosis. *Journal of Applied Psychology, 70,* 401–412.

Goodwin, D.W., & Guze, S.B. (1984). *Psychiatric diagnosis* (3rd ed.). New York: Oxford University Press.

Greenwald, A.G. (1980). The totalitarian ego: Fabrication and revision of personal history. *American Psychologist, 35,* 603–618.

Greenwald, A.G., & Pratkanis, A.R. (1984). The self. In R.S. Wyer & T.K. Srull (Eds.), *Handbook of social cognition* (Vol. 3). Hillsdale, NJ: Erlbaum.

Harvey, M.A., & Sipprelle, C.N. (1978). Color blindness, Perceptual interference, and hypnosis. *American Journal of Clinical Hypnosis, 80,* 189–193.

Hasher, L., & Zacks, R.T. (1979). Automatic and effortful processes in memory. *Journal of Experimental Psychology: General, 108,* 365–388.

Hastie, R. (1983). Social inference. *Annual Review of Psychology, 34,* 511–542.

Hastie, R. (1985). Causes and effects of causal attribution. *Journal of Personality and Social Psychology, 46,* 44–56.

Heider, F. (1944). Social perception and phenomenal causality. *Psychological Review, 51,* 358–374.

Heider, F. (1958). *The psychology of interpersonal relations*. New York: Wiley.

Hilgard, E.R. (1965). *Hypnotic susceptibility*. New York: Harcourt, Brace, & World.

Hilgard, E.R. (1973). A neodissociation interpretation of pain reduction in hypnosis. *Psychological Review, 80,* 396–411.

Hilgard, E.R. (1975). Hypnosis. *Annual Review of Psychology, 26,* 19–44.

Hilgard, E.R. (1977). *Divided consciousness: Multiple controls in human thought and action,* New York: Wiley-Interscience.

Hilgard, E.R. (1979). Divided consciousness in hypnosis: The implications of the hidden observer. In E. Fromm & R.E. Shor (Eds.), *Hypnosis: Developments in research and new perspectives.* New York: Aldine.

Hilgard, E.R. & Hilgard, J.R. (1983). *Hypnosis in the relief of pain* (New ed.). Los Altos, CA: Kaufman.

Hilgard, J.R. (1970). *Personality and hypnosis: A study of imaginative involvement.* Chicago: University of Chicago Press.

Hilgard, J.R., & LeBaron, S. (1984). *Hypnotherapy of pain in children with cancer.* Los Altos, CA: Kaufman.

Holender, D. (1986). Semantic activation without conscious identification in dichotic listening, parafoveal vision, and visual masking: A survey and appraisal. *Behavioral and Brain Sciences, 9,* 1–66.

Hoyt, I.P., & Kihlstrom, J.F. (1986). *Posthypnotic and waking instruction.* Unpublished manuscript.

Huston, P.E., Shakow, D., & Erickson, M.H. (1934). A study of hypnotically induced complexes by means of the Luria technique. *Journal of General Psychology, 11,* 65–97.

Jacoby, L.L. (1982). Knowing and remembering: Some parallels in the behavior of Korsakoff patients and normals. In L.S. Cermak (Ed.), *Human memory and amnesia.* Hillsdale, NJ: Erlbaum.

Jacoby, L.L., & Dallas, M. (1981). On the relationship between autobiographical memory and perceptual learning. *Journal of Experimental Psychology: General, 110,* 306–340.

James, W. (1980). *Principles of psychology.* New York: Holt.

Jaspers, K. (1962). *General psychopathology.* Chicago: University of Chicago Press. (Original work published 1923.)

Johnson, M.K., & Raye, C.L. (1981). Reality monitoring. *Psychological Review, 88,* 67–85.

Johnson, W.G., Ross, J.M., & Mastria, M.A. (1977). Delusional behavior: An attributional analysis of development and modification. *Journal of Abnormal Psychology, 86,* 421–426.

Jones, E.E. (1979). The rocky road from acts to dispositions. *American Psychologist, 34,* 107–117.

Jones, E.E., & Davis, K.E. (1965). From acts to dispositions: The attribution process in person perception. In L. Berkowitz (Ed.), *Advances in experimental social psychology* (Vol. 2). New York: Academic Press.

Jones, E.E., & Nisbett, R.E. (1972). The actor and the observer: Divergent perceptions of the causes of behavior. In E.E. Jones, D.E. Kanouse, H.H. Kelley, R.E. Nisbett, S. Valins, & B. Weiner (Eds.), *Attribution: Perceiving the causes of behavior.* Morristown, NJ: General Learning Press.

Kahneman, D. (1973). *Attention and effort.* Englewood Cliffs, NJ: Prentice-Hall.

Kahneman, D., Slovic, P., & Tversky, A. (Eds.) (1982). *Judgment under uncertainty: Heuristics and biases.* Cambridge: Cambridge University Press.

Kahneman, D., & Tversky, A. (1972). Subjective probability: A judgment of representativeness. *Cognitive Psychology, 3,* 430–454.

Kahneman, D., & Tversky, A. (1973). On the psychology of prediction. *Psychological Review, 80,* 237–251.

Kahneman, D., & Tversky, A. (1982). The simulation heuristic. In D. Kahneman, P. Slovic, & A. Tversky (Eds.), *Judgment under uncertainty: Heuristics and biases.* New York: Cambridge University Press.

Kelley, H.L. (1967). Attribution theory in social psychology. In D. Levine (Ed.), *Nebraska symposium on motivation* (Vol. 15). Lincoln: University of Nebraska Press.

Kelley, H.L. (1972). Attribution in social interaction. In E.E. Jones, D.E. Kanouse, H.H. Kelley, R.E. Nisbett, S. Valins, & B. Weiner (Eds.), *Attribution: Perceiving the causes of behavior.* Morristown, NJ: General Learning Press.

Kelley, H.H., & Michela, J.L. (1980). Attribution theory and research. *Annual Review of Psychology, 31,* 457–501.

Kihlstrom, J.F. (1977). Models of posthypnotic amnesia. In W.E. Edmonston (Ed.), *Conceptual and investigative approaches to hypnosis and hypnotic phenomena. Annals of the New York Academy of Sciences, 296,* 284–301.

Kihlstrom, J.F. (1979). Hypnosis and psychopathology: Retrospect and prospect. *Journal of Abnormal Psychology, 88,* 459–473.

Kihlstrom, J.F. (1980). Posthypnotic amnesia for recently learned material: Interactions with "episodic" and "semantic" memory. *Cognitive Psychology, 12,* 227–251.

Kihlstrom, J.F. (1982). Hypnosis and the dissociation of memory, with special reference to posthypnotic amnesia. *Research Communications in Psychology, Psychiatry, and Behavior, 7,* 181–197.

Kihlstrom, J.F. (1983a). Instructed forgetting: Hypnotic and nonhypnotic. *Journal of Experimental Psychology: General, 112,* 73–79.

Kihlstrom, J.F. (1983b). Mental health implications of information processing: Studies of perception and attention. In National Institute of Mental Health, *Behavioral sciences research in mental health: An assessment of the state of the science and recommendations for research directions* (Vol. 2). Rockville, MD: Alcohol, Drug Abuse, and Mental Health Administration.

Kihlstrom, J.F. (1984). Conscious, subconscious, unconscious: A cognitive perspective. In K.S. Bowers & D. Meichenbaum (Eds.), *The unconscious reconsidered.* New York: Wiley.

Kihlstrom, J.F. (1985a). Hypnosis. *Annual Review of Psychology, 36,* 385–418.

Kihlstrom, J.F., (1985b). Posthypnotic amnesia and the dissociation of memory. In G.H. Bower (Ed.), *The psychology of learning and motivation* (Vol. 19). New York: Academic Press.

Kihlstrom, J.F., & Cantor, N. (1984). Mental representations of the self. In L. Berkowitz (Ed.), *Advances in experimental social psychology* (Vol. 17). New York: Academic Press.

Kihlstrom, J.F., & Cantor, N. (1986). Information processing and the study of the self. In L. Berkowitz (Ed.), *Advances in experimental social psychology* (Vol. 20). New York: Academic Press.

Kihlstrom, J.F., & Evans, F.J. (1979). Memory retrieval process in posthypnotic amnesia. In J.F. Kihlstrom & F.J. Evans (Eds.), *Functional disorders of memory.* Hillsdale, NJ: Erlbaum.

Klatzky, R.L. (1984). *Memory and awareness: An information-processing perspective.* San Francisco: Freeman.

Laurence, J.-R., & Perry, C. (1981). The "hidden observer" phenomenon in hypnosis: Some additional findings. *Journal of Abnormal Psychology, 90,* 334–344.

Laurence, J.-R., & Perry, C. (1983). Hypnotically created memory among highly hypnotizable subjects. *Science, 222,* 523–524.

Laurence, J.-R., Perry, C., & Kihlstrom, J.F. (1983). "Hidden observer" phenomena in hypnosis: An experimental creation? *Journal of Personality and Social Psychology, 44,* 163–169.

Leibowitz, H.W., Lundy, R.M., & Guez, J.R. (1980). The effect of testing distance on suggestion-induced visual field narrowing. *International Journal of Clinical and Experimental Hypnosis, 28,* 409–420.

Leibowitz, H.W., Post, R.B., Rodemer, C.S., Wadlington, W.L., & Lundy, R.M. (1981). Roll vection analysis in hypnotically induced visual field narrowing. *Perception and Psychophysics, 28,* 173–176.

Levitt, E.E. (1967). *The psychology of anxiety.* Indianapolis: Bobbs-Merrill.

Levitt, E.E., & Chapman, R.H. (1979). Hypnosis as a research method. In E. Fromm & R.E. Shor (Eds.), *Hypnosis: Development in research and new perspectives.* New York: Aldine.

Loftus, E.F. (1979). *Eyewitness testimony.* Cambridge, MA: Harvard University Press.

Luria, A.R. (1932). *The nature of human conflicts.* London: Liveright.

McArthur, L.Z. (1972). The how and what of why: Some determinants and consequences of causal attribution. *Journal of Personality and Social Psychology, 22,* 171–193.

McConkey, K.M., & Sheehan, P.W. (1981). The impact of videotape playback of hypnotic events on posthypnotic amnesia. *Journal of Abnormal Psychology, 90,* 46–54.

McConkey, K.M., Sheehan, P.W., & Cross, D.G.. (1980). Posthypnotic amnesia: Seeing is not remembering. *British Journal of Social and Clinical Psychology, 19,* 99–107.

MacCracken, P.J., Gogel, W.C., & Blum, G.S. (1980). Effects of posthypnotic suggestion on perceived egocentric distance. *Perception, 9,* 561–568.

McGuigan, F.J. (1966). Covert oral behavior and auditory hallucinations. *Psychophysiology, 3,* 421–428.

Maher, B.A. (1974). Delusional thinking and perceptual disorder. *Journal of Individual Psychology, 30,* 98–113.

Maher, B.A., & Ross, J.S. (1984). Delusions. In H.E. Adams & P.B. Sutker (Eds.), *Comprehensive handbook of psychopathology.* New York: Plenum Press.

Mandler, G. (1984). *Mind and body: Psychology of emotion and stress.* New York: W.W. Norton.

Marcel, A.J. (1980). Conscious and preconscious recognition of polysemous words: Locating the selective effect of prior verbal context. In R.S. Nickerson (Ed.), *Attention and performance* (Vol. 8).

Marcel, A.J. (1983a). Conscious and unconscious perception: Experiments on visual masking and word recognition. *Cognitive psychology, 15,* 197–237.

Marcel, A.J. (1983b). Conscious and unconscious perception: An approach to the relation between phenomenal experience and perceptual processes. *Cognitive Psychology, 15,* 238–300.

Marshall, G.D., & Zimbardo, P.G. (1979). Affective consequences of inadequately explained physiological arousal. *Journal of Personality and Social Psychology, 37,* 970–988.

Maslach, C. (1979). Negative emotional biasing of unexplained arousal. *Journal of Personality and Social Psychology, 37,* 953–969.

Maslach, C., Zimbardo, P., & Marshall, G. (1979). Hypnosis as a means of studying cognitive and behavioral control. In E. Fromm & R.E. Shor (Eds.), *Hypnosis: Developments in research and new perspectives.* New York: Aldine.

Miller, R.J., & Leibowitz, H.W. (1976). A signal detection analysis of hypnotically induced narrowing of the peripheral visual field. *Journal of Abnormal Psychology, 85,* 446–454.

Mineka, S., & Kihlstrom, J.F. (1978). Unpredictable and uncontrollable events: A new perspective on experimental neurosis. *Journal of Abnormal Psychology, 87,* 256–271.

Mischotte, A. (1963). *The perception of causality.* New York: Basic.

Moscovitch, M. (1982). Multiple dissociations of function in amnesia. In L.S. Cermak (Ed.), *Human memory and amnesia.* Hillsdale, NJ: Erlbaum.

Nisbett, R.E., & Ross, L. (1980). *Human inference: Strategies and shortcomings of social judgment.* Englewood Cliffs, NJ: Prentice-Hall.

Nogrady, H., McConkey, K.M., Laurence, J.-R., & Perry, C. (1983). Dissociation, duality, and demand characteristics in hypnosis. *Journal of Abnormal Psychology, 92,* 223–235.

Norman, D.A., & Bobrow, D.G. (1975). On data-limited and resource-limited processes. *Cognitive Psychology, 7,* 44–64.

Orne, M.T. (1951). The mechanisms of hypnotic age regression: An experimental study. *Journal of Abnormal and Social Psychology, 46,* 213–225.

Orne, M.T. (1959). The nature of hypnosis: Artifact and essence. *Journal of Abnormal and Social Psychology, 58,* 277–299.

Orne, M.T. (1970). Hypnosis, motivation, and the ecological validity of the psychological experiment. In W.J. Arnold & M.M. Page (Eds.), *Nebraska symposium on motivation.* Lincoln: University of Nebraska Press.

Orne, M.T. (1979). The use and misuse of hypnosis in court. *International Journal of Clinical and Experimental Hypnosis, 27,* 311–341.

Orne, M.T., Soskis, D.A., Dinges, D.F., & Orne, E.C. (1984). Hypnotically induced testimony. In G.L. Wells & E.F. Loftus (Eds.), *Eyewitness testimony.* Cambridge: Harvard University Press.

Perry, C., & Walsh, B. (1978). Inconsistencies and anomalies of response as a defining characteristic of hypnosis. *Journal of Abnormal Psychology, 87,* 574–577.

Posner, M.I., & Snyder, C.R.R. (1975). Attention and cognitive control. In R.L. Solso (Ed.), *Information processing and cognition.* Hillsdale, NJ: Erlbaum.

Reed, G. (1974). *The psychology of anomalous experience: A cognitive approach.* Boston: Houghton Mifflin.

Reeder, G.D., & Brewer, M.B. (1979). A schematic model of dispositional attribution in interpersonal perception. *Psychological Review, 86,* 61–79.

Register, P.A., & Kihlstrom, J.F. (1987). Hypnotic effects on hypermnesia. *International Journal of Clinical and Experimental Hypnosis, 35,* 155–170.

Reyher, J. (1967). Hypnosis in research on psychopathology. In J.E. Gordon (Ed.), *Handbook of clinical and experimental hypnosis.* New York: Macmillan.

Ross, L. (1977). The intuitive psychologist and his shortcomings: Distortions in the attribution process. In L. Berkowitz (Ed.), *Advances in experimental social psychology* (Vol. 10). New York: Academic Press.

Ross, M., & Fletcher, G. (1985). Attribution and social perception. In G. Lindzey & A. Aronson (Eds.), *Handbook of social psychology* (3rd ed., Vol. 2). Reading, MA: Addison-Wesley.

Rozin, P. (1976). The psychobiological approach to human memory. In M.R. Rosenzweig & E.L. Bennett (Eds.), *Neural mechanisms of learning and memory.* Cambridge: MIT Press.

Sacks, M.H., Carpenter, W.T., & Strauss, J.S. (1974). Recovery from delusions. *Archives of General Psychiatry, 30,* 117–120).

Sanders, G.S., & Simmons, W.L. (1983). Use of hypnosis to enhance eyewitness accuracy: Does it work? *Journal of Applied Psychology, 68,* 70–77.

Sarbin, T.R. (1958). Contributions to role-taking theory: I. Hypnotic behavior. *Psychological Review, 57,* 255–270.

Sarbin, T.R., & Coe, W.C. (1972). *Hypnosis: A social psychological analysis of influence communication.* New York: Holt, Rinehart & Winston.

Sarbin, T.R., & Coe, W.C. (1979). Hypnosis and psychopathology: Replacing old myths with fresh metaphors. *Journal of Abnormal Psychology, 88,* 506–526.

Schacter, D., & Tulving, E. (1982). Amnesia and memory research. In L.S. Cermak (Ed.), *Human memory and amnesia*. Hillsdale, NJ: Erlbaum.

Schneider, K. (1959). *Clinical psychopathology*. New York: Grune & Stratton.

Schneider, W., & Shiffrin, R.M. (1977). Controlled and automatic human information processing: 1. Detection, search, and attention. *Psychological Review, 84,* 1–66.

Sheehan, P.W. (1969). Artificial induction of posthypnotic conflict. *Journal of Abnormal Psychology, 74,* 16–25.

Sheehan, P.W. (1979). Hypnosis and the processes of imagination. In E. Fromm & R.E. Shor (Eds.), *Hypnosis: Developments in research and new perspectives*. New York: Aldine.

Sheehan, P.W. (1982). Imagery and hypnosis: Forging a link, at least in part. *Research Communications in Psychology, Psychiatry, and Behavior, 7,* 257–272.

Sheehan, P.W. (1985, August). *Memory bias in hypnosis*. Paper presented at the 10th International Congress of Hypnosis and Psychosomatic Medicine, Toronto.

Sheehan, P.W., Obstoj, I., & McConkey, K.M. (1976). Trance logic and cue structure as supplied by the hypnotist. *Journal of Abnormal Psychology, 85,* 459–472.

Sheehan, P.W., & Perry, C. (1976). *Methodologies of hypnosis: A critical appraisal of contemporary paradigms of hypnosis*. Hillsdale, NJ: Erlbaum.

Sherman, S.J., & Corty, E. (1984). Cognitive heuristics. In R.S. Wyer & T.K. Srull (Eds.), *Handbook of social cognition*. (Vol. 1). Hillsdale, NJ: Erlbaum.

Shevrin, H., & Dickman, S. (1980). The psychological unconscious: A necessary assumption for all psychological theory? *American Psychologist, 35,* 421–434.

Shiffrin, R.M., & Schneider, W. (1977). Controlled and automatic human information processing: 2. Perceptual learning, automatic attending, and a general theory. *Psychological Review, 84,* 127–190.

Shor, R.E. (1959). Hypnosis and the concept of the generalized reality orientation. *American Journal of Psychotherapy, 13,* 582–602.

Shor, R.E. (1962). Three dimensions of hypnotic depth. *International Journal of Clinical and Experimental Hypnosis, 10,* 23–38.

Shor, R.E. (1970). The three-factor theory of hypnosis as applied to the book-reading fantasy and to the concept of suggestion. *International Journal of Clinical and Experimental Hypnosis, 18,* 89–98.

Shor, R.E. (1979). A phenomenological method for the measurement of variables important to an understanding of hypnosis. In E. Fromm & R.E. Shor (Eds.), *Hypnosis: Developments in research and new perspectives*. New York: Aldine.

Silverman, L. (1976). Psychoanalytic theory: Reports of my death are greatly exaggerated. *American Psychologist, 31,* 621–637.

Smith, M.C. (1983). Hypnotic memory enhancement of witnesses: Does it work? *Psychological Bulletin, 94,* 387–407.

Snyder, M., & Swann, W.B. (1978). Hypothesis testing processes in social interaction. *Journal of Personality and Social Psychology, 36,* 1202–1212.

Spanos, N.P. (1986). Hypnotic behavior: A social psychological interpretation of amnesia, analgesia, and "trance logic." *Behavioral and Brain Sciences, 9,* 449–502.

Spanos, N.P., deGroot, H.P., Tiller, D.K., Weekes, J.R., & Bertrand, L.D. (1985). Trance logic, duality, and hidden observer responding in hypnotic, imagination control, and simulating subjects: A social psychological analysis. *Journal of Abnormal Psychology, 94,* 611–623.

Stanley, S.M., Lynn, S.J., & Nash, M.R. (1986). Trance logic, susceptibility screening, and the transparency response. *Journal of Personality and Social Psychology, 50,* 447–454.

Stern, J.A., Brown, M., Ulett, G.A., & Sletten, I. (1977). A comparison of hypnosis, acupuncture, morphine, valium, aspirin, and placebo in the management of experimentally induced pain. In W.E. Edmonston (Ed.), *Conceptual and investigative approaches to hypnosis and hypnotic phenomena. Annals of the New York Academy of Sciences, 296,* 175–193.

Sutcliffe, J.P. (1958). *Hypnotic behavior: Fantasy or simulation?* Unpublished doctoral dissertation, University of Sydney, Sydney, Australia.

Sutcliffe, J.P. (1960). "Credulous" and "skeptical" views of hypnotic phenomena: A review of certain evidence and methodology. *International Journal of Clinical and Experimental Hypnosis, 8,* 73–101.

Sutcliffe, J.P. (1961). "Credulous" and "skeptical" views of hypnotic phenomena: Experiments in esthesia, hallucination, and delusion. *Journal of Abnormal and Social Psychology, 62,* 189–200.

Sutcliffe, J.P. (1972). Afterimages of real and imaged stimuli. *Australian Journal of Psychology, 24,* 275–289.

Taylor, S.E., & Fiske, S.T. (1978). Salience, attention, and attribution: Top of the head phenomena. In L. Berkowitz (Ed.), *Advances in experimental social psychology* (Vol. 11). New York: Academic Press.

Tellegen, A., & Atkinson, G. (1974). Openness to absorbing and self-altering experiences ("absorption"), a trait related to hypnotic susceptibility. *Journal of Abnormal Psychology, 83,* 268–277.

Trope, V., & Bassok, M. (1982). Confirmatory and diagnostic strategies in social information gathering. *Journal of Personality and Social Psychology, 43,* 22–34.

Tulving, E., & Pearlstone, Z. (1966). Availability versus accessibility of information in memory for words. *Journal of Verbal Learning and Verbal Behavior, 5,* 381–391.

Tversky, A., & Kahneman, D. (1973). Availability: A heuristic for judging frequency and probability. *Cognitive Psychology, 5,* 207–232.

Tversky, A., & Kahneman, D. (1974). Judgment under uncertainty: Heuristics and biases. *Science, 185,* 1124–1131.

Tversky, A., & Kahneman, D. (1982). Judgments of and by representativeness. In D. Kahneman, P. Slovic, & A. Tversky (Eds.), *Judgment under uncertainty: Heuristics and biases.* New York: Cambridge University Press.

Watson, D. (1982). The actor and the observer: How are their perceptions of causality different? *Psychological Bulletin, 92,* 682–700.

Weiner, B., Frieze, I., Kukla, A., Reed, L., Rest, S., & Rosenbaum, R.M. (1972). Perceiving the causes of success and failure. In E.E. Jones, D.E. Kanouse, H.H. Kelley, R.E. Nisbett, S. Valins, & B. Weiner (Eds.), *Attribution: Perceiving the causes of behavior*. Morristown, NJ: General Learning Press.

Weitzenhoffer, A. (1963). "Credulity" and "skepticism" in hypnotic research: A critical examination of Sutcliffe's thesis and evidence. *American Journal of Clinical Hypnosis, 6,* 137–162.

Weitzenhoffer, A. (1964). "Credulity" and "skepticism" in hypnotic research: a critical examination of Sutcliffe's thesis and evidence. Part II. *American Journal of Clinical Hypnosis, 6,* 241–268.

White, R.W. (1941). A preface to the theory of hypnotism. *Journal of Abnormal and Social Psychology, 36,* 477–505.

Williamsen, J.A., Johnson, H.J., & Eriksen, C.W. (1965). Some characteristics of posthypnotic amnesia. *Journal of Abnormal Psychology, 70,* 123–131.

Zimbardo, P.G., Andersen, S.M., & Kabat, L.G. (1981). Induced hearing deficit generates experimental paranoia. *Science, 212,* 1529–1531.

CHAPTER 5

Standard Utilization and the Social-Evaluative Process: Vulnerability to Types of Aberrant Beliefs

E. TORY HIGGINS and MARLENE M. MORETTI

New York University   University of Waterloo

Aberrant beliefs and delusions occur in a variety of medical and psychological conditions (World Health Organization, 1973). Despite the contributions of many outstanding theoreticians and researchers (Bleuler, 1950; Kraepelin, 1919/1971; Freud, 1923/1961; Sullivan, 1953), an empirically based and clearly conceptualized model of these symptoms has failed to emerge. The limited theoretical and research development of the field is reflected by the fact that several fundamental issues remain unresolved. Researchers continue to debate on the primary characteristics that distinguish an unusual or aberrant belief from a delusion. A related question concerns the possible etiological and phenomenological heterogeneity of delusional symptoms. In addition, researchers continue to struggle in their attempts to understand the relation between types of delusional symptoms and various forms of psychopathology.

In the midst of this uncertainty, clinicians and researchers continue to recognize that delusional symptoms tend to occur in particular types of psychological disorders and are indicative of severe psychological disturbance. The Research Diagnostic Criteria (RDC) (Spitzer, Endicott, & Robins, 1978) list eight "active phase" symptoms in schizophrenia, of which

Preparation of this manuscript was supported in part by Grant MH39429 from the National Institute of Mental Health to the first author and by a Canada Council Postdoctoral Fellowship to the second author.

four refer to delusional features. In the *Diagnostic and statistical manual of mental disorders* (DSM-III) (American Psychiatric Association [APA], 1980), delusional symptoms are represented in three of the six active phase criteria for schizophrenic disorders. Although less diagnostic, delusional symptoms may also be present in affective disorders.

In light of the continued attention that clinicians and researchers pay to these symptoms and to the difficulty they present in treatment, the need for the development of new models that can provide a framework for understanding empirical findings and clinical observations has been raised in several reviews (see Arthur, 1964; Winters & Neale, 1983). In the current chapter we propose a potential framework derived from a model of social evaluation recently developed by Higgins and his colleagues (see Higgins, 1987; Higgins, Bond, Klein, & Strauman, 1986; Higgins, Strauman, & Klein, 1986a).

Normative Standard Utilization and the Formation of Beliefs

The DSM-III (APA, 1980) defines a delusion as:

> A false personal belief based on incorrect inference about external reality and firmly sustained in spite of what almost everyone else believes and in spite of what constitutes incontrovertible and obvious proof or evidence to the contrary. The belief is not ordinarily accepted by other members of the person's culture or subculture (i.e., it is not an article of religious faith).
>
> When a false belief involves an extreme value judgment, it is regarded as a delusion only when the judgment is so extreme as to defy credibility.

(p. 356)

Note that delusional ideation is confined to a context in which clearly incongruent information is readily available. Hence, by definition, the development and maintenance of the aberrant belief or delusion cannot be traced to some qualitative differences in the nature of available information. While unusual beliefs may indeed arise when an individual is confronted with insufficient or unusual types of information, this is by no means a common characteristic in the genesis of aberrant beliefs or delusions (see Chapman & Chapman, this volume). In addition, unusual beliefs that arise from unusual or insufficient information are often relinquished in the face of additional or clarifying information (Johnson, Ross, & Mastria, 1977). This mutability does not characterize aberrant beliefs or delusions. Clinical observation suggests that individuals who hold such beliefs do not perceive available information as incongruent with their beliefs. In fact, information that is presented to them in an attempt to alter their beliefs (i.e., information that others would perceive as highly incongruent), is often assimilated in a peculiar manner as additional evidence supporting the aberrant belief.

Although by definition aberrant beliefs and delusions do not arise from the atypical quality of available information, they could nevertheless arise from the atypical manner in which this information is evaluated. We propose that aberrant beliefs and delusions reflect atypical or nonnormative *judgments* and *interpretations* of information. Further, we suggest that judgments and interpretations will be deviant to the extent that normative considerations have been violated in the *selection* and the *application* of standards during information processing.

Deviations from normative standard utilization may occur along two dimensions. First, deviations in standard utilization may occur along a dimension of normativeness in *standard selection*. Individuals may deviate in selecting a nonnormative *type of standard* for processing information. In this case, the content of the standards in themselves may not be unusual or peculiar, but their use to evaluate particular events is nonnormative. Deviations in standard selection will be predictive of the nature of the distortion constituting the aberrant belief or delusion; that is, whether the belief reflects an enhanced (positive distortion) or a devalued (negative distortion) perception of the self. Negative distortion arising from nonnormative standard selection is illustrated in the following example: In evaluating one's own artistic creativity and skill, an individual may select a standard based on the creativity and skill demonstrated in the works of a renowned artist. The selection of this standard by an individual who has dedicated a good deal of time and energy to their development as a professional artist may be appropriate and normative. The selection of this standard by an individual who has only recently been introduced to the study of art, however, would be nonnormative and could possibly contribute to the formation of negative beliefs and expectations about their current skills and potential for artistic development. In this case, a more appropriate or normative standard would be the average performance of others who are at a similar point in training.

Deviations in standard utilization may also occur along a dimension of normativeness in *standard application*. That is, individuals may deviate in the extent to which standards are *applied at nonnormative stages* during information processing. Here, the standard selected to evaluate an event may be normative but its application at a given stage of processing violates normative rules. As we pointed out in our previous example, for some individuals the evaluation of artistic creativity and ability based on a standard of the works produced by a renowned artist is normative. Normatively this standard would be applied to *appraise* one's performance. An individual may interpret his or her work as successful based on how it compares to the work of other artists with comparable training, but may appraise his or her work as poor because it fails to approach the work of a great artist. The premature application of this standard for *interpreting* whether one's work is a success or a failure is nonnormative and could possibly lead to overly negative evaluations of one's artistic creativity and potential. Deviations in the stage at which standards are applied will be predictive of the degree of deviation or severity of distortion reflected in the aberrant belief or delusion. Of course, individuals may demonstrate both forms of deviation in standard utilization.

When individuals' judgments and interpretations are based on nonnormative standard utilization, they are nevertheless judged by others as if they were based on normative standard utilization (unless explicit or implicitly specified otherwise), and hence are perceived as atypical or even bizarre. It is important to note that individuals need not be aware and often are not aware of the standards they employ during information processing. In addition, social evaluations based on nonnormative standard utilization may become dissociated from the context in which they were derived, just as judgments based on normative standard utilization can become contextually dissociated, and this may lead to distortions in subsequent memory and judgments (Higgins & Stangor, 1987).

The analysis we propose is most useful for understanding aberrant self-evaluative beliefs and delusions. Aberrant beliefs or delusions that are not primarily self-evaluative in nature are not easily explained within this model. The current analysis assumes that both the content and utilization of standards vary culturally and historically (see Heise, this volume). Thus, the correctness of standard selection and application is a matter of social consensus. We also assume that all judgments and interpretations vary along a

TABLE 5.1.   Aberrant Beliefs and Delusions as a Function of Standard Use in Social Evaluation

---

Assumption. The atypical use of standards leads to unusual (strange, out of the ordinary, bizarre) judgments and interpretations of social stimuli.

Hypothesis 1. The greater an individual's deviation in the use of standards from what is typical for the individual's community, the greater the likelihood that the individual's judgments and interpretations will be perceived as aberrant or delusional.

Corollary H_1. There are *quantitative differences* in the severity of deviance reflected in a belief that parallel the extremity of deviation in the use of standards.

Hypothesis 2. The nature of the aberrant belief or delusion an individual displays is a function of the *type* of deviation in the individual's use of standards from what is typical for the individual's community.

Corollary H_2. There are *qualitatively different* types of aberrant beliefs and delusions that reflect the type of nonnormative *selection of standards* and/or the type of nonnormative *application of standards.*

---

continuum of normativeness in standard utilization. This assumption is consistent with growing evidence that a wide range of ideational distortions is found in both psychiatric and nonpsychiatric populations (Chapman & Chapman, this volume; Strauss, 1969). An outline of our perspective, basic assumptions, and hypotheses is provided in Table 5.1.

Standards as Determinants of Social Experience

Psychologists have been concerned with the consequences of standard utilization for many years. Sherif (1936) and Lewin (1951) state that judgments and experiences of success and failure take place within some frame of reference, where the frame of reference can be the interiorization of the norms and values of one's culture, the achievements of others, one's own level of aspiration (i.e., one's personal goals), or one's own past performance. The literature on reference groups, in which judgments are anchored to membership and nonmembership groups, describes two basic kinds of social group influence on individuals' self-judgments (e.g., Hyman, 1942; Kelley, 1952; Merton & Kitt, 1952; Newcomb, 1952; Sherif, 1948). First, there are social groups that serve as a comparison point against which a person can evaluate himself or herself (considered to be a "perceptual" standard). Second, there are norm-setting and norm-enforcing social groups whose code defines the acceptability or propriety of a person's behavior (considered to be a "motivational" standard). In addition to social groups, it has been suggested that particular individuals can serve as standards for evaluation (see Festinger, 1954; Freud, 1923/1961; Mead, 1934; Merton & Kitt, 1952), either because the individual is salient or emotionally significant in one's life or because the individual's attributes permit a valid assessment of one's ability (see Goethals & Darley, 1977).

Different self-concepts or ego states have also been proposed as functioning as standards for self-evaluation, such as James' (1890/1948) ideal social self and spiritual self, Freud's (1923/1961) superego, and Rogers' (1961) ideal self (see Higgins et al., 1986a, for a review of these kinds of standards). Bandura (1982) distinguishes between such personal standards and the social referential comparison standards described earlier. Recently, it has been suggested that self-evaluation can even involve comparisons to constructed or imaginary standards, such as mental simulations (Kahneman & Tversky, 1982), constructed norms and alternatives to reality (Kahneman & Miller, 1986), or possible selves (Markus & Nurius, 1987), which can consist of dreams and fantasies as well as logical possibilities (see also Freud's (1923/ 1961) discussion of the ego-ideal).

From even this brief review, it is evident that many different kinds of standards for self-evaluation have been identified in the literature. The framework proposed by Higgins (1987) systematically organizes and distinguishes among these, and other varieties of standards have been proposed (Higgins, Strauman, & Klein, 1986a). In the next section we provide a brief overview of two major types of standards—*factual points of reference* and *acquired guides*. This will be followed by a discussion of the consequences of nonnormative selection of standards.

Factual Points of Reference

One major type of standard involves the evaluator's belief about the actual performance of attributes of one or more persons that is used as a point of reference relative to which the evaluator judges his or her own attributes or performance—factual points of comparison. It must be noted that although the point of reference is subjectively or phenomenologically factual, this does not imply that it is objectively accurate. There are four basic kinds of factual reference points—social category, meaningful other, autobiographical, and social context comparison points.

Social Category Reference Point

A social category reference point is a factual standard defined by the average performance of attributes (e.g., mean, median, modal, prototypic) of the members of some social category or group. The evaluator may or may not be a member of the group and may or may not have any direct social interaction with the group members (see Merton & Kitt, 1952; Newcomb, 1952). Moreover, the size of the social category or group can vary greatly, from "people in general" to "closest friends." Changes in the social category to which one compares one's performance have been shown to influence one's self-evaluation (Hyman, 1942), as well as one's evaluations of others (Higgins & Lurie, 1983).

Meaningful Other Reference Point

A meaningful other reference point is a factual standard defined by the performance or attributes of another individual who is meaningful to the evaluator either because of the relevance or appropriateness of the individual's attributes for social comparison (see Bernstein & Crosby, 1980; Festinger, 1954; Goethals & Darley, 1977) or because of his or her emotional significance or importance to the evaluator. The meaningful other may or may not be a personal acquaintance of the evaluator (e.g., movie star) and may or may not be currently alive (e.g., one's deceased father). Comparison to a meaningful other can influence judgments about the self (Merton & Kitt, 1952) as well as judgments about others (see Higgins & King, 1981; Nisbett & Ross, 1980; Sarbin, Taft, & Bailey, 1960).

Autobiographical Reference Point

An autobiographical reference point is a factual standard defined by the evaluator's own past performance or attributes. It can represent a single instance or a distribution of instances, and can be recent or remote. There is evidence that use of an autobiographical reference point can lead to relatively positive self-evaluation when skill acquisition shows rapid advancement (Ruble, 1983; Suls & Mullen, 1982; Veroff, 1969). Different self-evaluations can occur depending on whether an individual uses a recent or remote autobiographical comparison point.

Social Context Reference Point

A social context reference point is a factual standard defined by the performance of the immediate context of persons to whom the evaluator is currently exposed (and notices). The social context can be one or more persons. Morse and Gergen (1970), for example, found that people will evaluate themselves more highly after exposure to a person with undesirable characteristics. A social context reference point is distinct from a social category reference point in that the former is a momentary stimulus event rather than a preestablished or defined social construct that is represented in, and retrieved from, memory.

Acquired Guides

Individuals also rely on another type of standard to assess the acceptability or excellence of their performance—guides for behavior. Acquired guides differ from factual points of reference in that the former represent internalized standards or valued self end-states while the latter refer to standards that are based on beliefs about the actual performance of self and others.

Self-discrepancy theory (Higgins, 1986) outlines two dimensions that underlie the different kinds of acquired guides. First, self-discrepancy theory distinguishes between three domains of the self—the *actual self*, the *ideal self*, and the *ought self*. The actual self consists of those attributes that someone (self or other) believes the person actually posesses (i.e., the self-concept); the ideal self refers to those attributes that someone (self or other) would ideally like the person to possess (i.e., hopes or wishes the person would possess); and the ought self refers to those attributes someone (self or other) believes the person should or ought to possess (i.e., believes it is the person's duty or obligation to possess).

The second dimension proposed by self-concept discrepancy theory is *standpoints on the self*. Standpoint is a point of view or position from which a person is judged, reflecting a set of attitudes or values. Each of the domains of the self can be viewed from one's *own* standpoint, or from the standpoint of the *other*. Each individual can, and often does, have multiple "other" standpoints on his or her self that are meaningful or relevant (e.g., mother, father, older brother, best friend, spouse, boss, colleague).

Combining across these two dimensions of the self (domains by standpoints) yields six potentially different perspectives on the self: *Actual/Own*, *Actual/Other*, *Ideal/Own*, *Ideal/Other*, *Ought/Own*, and *Ought/Other*. The actual/own self-state, and to a lesser extent the actual/other self-state, are analogous to what is typically meant by a person's "self-concept" (Wylie, 1979). The four remaining self-states may be selected and applied as guides in the evaluation of one's performances.

Nonnormative Selection of Standards

Earlier we identified two classes of nonnormative standard utilization that increase the probability that one's judgments and interpretations will deviate from what is typical given a particular culture or subculture—nonnormative standard selection and nonnormative standard application. We will now review the consequences of nonnormative standard selection with reference to the type of standards we have outlined.

Nonnormative Selection of Factual Points of Reference

Individuals may be deviant in their selection of both factual reference points or acquired guides. Factual standards may seem to be more firmly based in reality than are acquired guides and therefore their use might be construed as less likely to lead to unusual or bizarre judgments or interpretations. It must be recalled, however, that the content of the standards in themselves is of little importance. What is critical is that selection occurs within normative considerations. One can easily imagine the consequences of the nonnormative selection of social category and meaningful other reference points. Consider, for example, a graduate student who evaluates her knowledge of the field against the knowledge of the first-year undergraduate students she tutors. This nonnormative selection of a social category reference point would lead to a heightened evaluation of performance. The expression of this evaluation *without specific mention of nonnormative standard selection* (i.e., "I know so much about statistics.") may be considered grandiose precisely because others interpret this evaluation as if it were based on normative standard selection (i.e., "I know so much more about statistics than my fellow graduate students do."). Similarly, consider the graduate student who evaluates his accomplishments and contributions to the field against that of the renowned experts (nonnormative selection of a social category reference point), or against that of an individual professor he perceives as outstanding is his field (nonnormative selection of a meaningful other reference point). This deviation from normativeness may lead him to underestimate his performance. In fact, an extreme deviation in the selection of a meaningful other reference point—for example, comparing oneself to Napoleon—may lead to bizarre self-evaluations.

Similar examples readily come to mind when we consider the consequences of the nonnormative selection of autobiographical reference points. Selecting a relatively recent autobiographical reference point would be nonnormative for evaluating one's progress on a very difficult task that requires considerable effort and typically shows slow gains. For example, individuals who have suffered damage to verbal or motor abilities through accidents or illnesses may apply recent autobiographical reference points based on their performance prior to the accident or illness in evaluating their progress in rehabilitation. The selection of this reference point will lead to highly negative evaluations of progress and a sense of hopelessness. Indeed, in such cases it is often helpful to discuss the importance of selecting other factual points of reference in performance evaluation.

Acknowledging but failing to apply social context reference points may also lead to negative evaluations of oneself rather than to the recognition that one's experiences are common within a particular group of individuals. For example, even though a new mother may acknowledge that initial feelings of anxiety, depression, and insecurity are common among other first-time mothers in the same hospital room (social context reference point), she may disregard this standard and evaluate her feelings and performance against the happiness and confidence with which her close friend appears to embrace the role of being the mother of three children. Her continued disregard for this social context reference point may lead her to feel guilty about her negative feelings and to believe she lacks the skills necessary to cope in her new role.

It should be recalled that in all of these examples nonnormative standard utilization leads to evaluations of the self that if expressed to others may be considered biased. What is more important is that these evaluations also become personal realities—even with equivalent performances one individual may come to view himself or herself as a great success while another comes to view himself or herself as a terrible failure.

Nonnormative Selection of Acquired Guides

The relative accessibility or readiness with which acquired guides are applied during information processing may vary across individuals and across events depending on what is normative for a particular context. Indeed, it is more difficult to establish a baseline of normativeness in the selection of acquired guides than in the selection of factual points of reference. In some situations, estimates of normativeness in guide selection may be drawn from contextual information. For example, if a student finds that he or she has received a grade of 60% on an examination, it would be difficult to evaluate whether the application of an acquired guide (ideal or ought) is normative. If the student was informed that this mark was well beyond the mean grade (social context reference point), however, the application of an ideal or ought guide would seem inappropriate to interpret his or her basic success or failure on the exam.

Normativeness in the selection of acquired guides can also be evaluated in terms of the extent to which the application of a particular guide *pervades* the evaluation of one's attributes or performances across contexts. The importance of this chronic individual difference in understanding vulnerability to aberrant beliefs and delusions will be discussed more fully in a later section of this chapter. Let us now turn to the second parameter of the social evaluation theory proposed by Higgins et al. (1986a)—the stages in the process of social evaluation. This will be followed by a discussion of the consequences of nonnormative application of standards.

Normative Standard Application in Social Evaluation

Social evaluation involves a multi-stage process in which each stage can have emotional consequences. Higgins et al. (1986a) propose that there are four basic stages in the process of social evaluation: stimulus representation, identification, interpretation, and general appraisal.

Stimulus Representation

The stage of stimulus representation involves registration and representation of the details and features of the attribute or performance-related stimulus (i.e., action, event, performance-related outcome, etc.). This stage is restricted to describing or encoding the salient aspects of the stimulus information. Although inferential processes can be involved even at this stage (e.g., inferring that turned up corners of the mouth is a smile and not a grimace) and the judgment can be influenced by concomitant circumstances, neither the evaluative standards described earlier nor causal attributions are typically utilized at this stage.

Identification

The stage of identification involves designating the attribute or performance-related stimulus as being a particular type of entity or event. This stage involves recognizing that an attribute or performance is an instance of some previously established action class or event class (e.g., an instance of greeting behavior). Like the stimulus representation stage, neither the evaluative standards described earlier nor causal attributions are likely to be involved at this stage. Of course, this is not to say that inference or identification does not involve comparing the degree of match or similarity between the stimulus and alternative stimulus classes (see Rosch, 1978; Tversky & Gati, 1978). This stage is more likely to produce an emotion.

Interpretation

The stage of interpretation involves inferring or construing the personal meaning or implications of an attribute or performance-related stimulus. In contrast to stimulus identification, interpretation necessarily involves the utilization of some standard of evaluation. Standards utilized in the interpretation stages are typically factual points of reference. More than either the stimulus representation stage or the identification stage, the interpretation stage is likely to have emotional consequences because interpretation of one's performance necessarily has personal, self-evaluative significance.

General Appraisal

The stage of general appraisal involves an overall estimation of the worth or value of the attribute or performance-related stimulus. Standards used in the general appraisal stage are typically acquired guides. Even more than the interpretation stage, the general appraisal stage is inherently evaluative with direct emotional impact.

Nonnormative Application of Standards

Violations of normative considerations in the applications of standards during information processing can produce a range of ideational distortions from mild distortions in the evaluation of performance to gross misconstructions and hallucinations regarding the very nature of the attribute and performance-related stimuli.

The application of acquired guides at the stage of interpretation is probably the mildest and most common form of nonnormative standard utilization. In such cases, the stimulus and its event class are correctly (normatively) identified, but an acquired guide rather than a factual point of reference is applied at the stage of interpretation. For example, a student may correctly *represent* his or her grade as 80 percent and correctly *identify* this event as a "pass," but may *interpret* it as an unsuccessful performance because an acquired guide (Ideal/Own or Ought/Other), such as "I would like to get over 90%," rather than a factual guide (e.g., social context reference point, such as "the average grade on the exam was 70%") is applied. The negative distortions that result from the premature application of acquired guides are similar in type and severity to the systematic negative distortions that Beck (1967, 1976) described as characterizing depression.

The application of acquired guides prior to the stage of interpretation would severely disturb the normative identification and evaluation of events. Using the previous example, application of an acquired guide at the stage of identification may result in preservation of the stimulus representation—the grade is seen as 80 percent—but the stimulus event is misidentified—it is identified as a "fail" rather than a "pass."

The application of acquired guides at the stage of stimulus representation may result in gross disturbances of perception. It is important to note that guides applied at the stages of identification, interpretation, and appraisal operate in an evaluative capacity. However, when guides or standards are applied at the earlier stage of stimulus representation, they perform a distinctly different function of *organizing perception* in much the same way as a construct organizes perception. That is, the negative psychological situation represented by the discrepancy may be projected into the perception of events. For example, a student applying a guide at the stage of stimulus representation may experience distortions in the perception of stimuli—a grade of 80 percent is *perceived* as a grade of 30 percent. That is, the discrepancy standard organizes the perception of the stimulus.

VULNERABILITY TO NONNORMATIVE STANDARD UTILIZATION

Up to this point we have discussed the potential consequences of violating normative considerations in the utilization of standards on judgments and interpretations. Specifically, we have focused on the consequences of deviations in standard utilization along the dimensions of standard selection and the stage of standard application. We now turn our attention to the consideration of vulnerability factors that may predispose an individual to utilize standards in a nonnormative fashion.

In our previous discussion we noted that there exist several acquired guides or self-directive standards that individuals may utilize to evaluate their performances: Ideal/Own, Ideal/Other, Ought/Own, and Ought/Other. Self-discrepancy theory (Higgins, 1987) proposes that when the self-concept (Actual/Own or Actual/Other self-state) is perceived as discrepant from acquired guides, individuals will experience psychological discomfort, and they will be motivated to reduce this state of discrepancy. Further, the theory predicts that different types of discrepancies between actual self-states and acquired guides will have different psychological consequences. The negative psychological situation reflected in a discrepancy represents an individual's beliefs about the consequences or significance of possessing self-attributes (actual self-state) that are discrepant from acquired guides, and this negative psychological situation has significant emotional and motivational consequences.

As we noted earlier, the relative accessibility or readiness with which acquired guides are applied in the process of evaluation is influenced by both contextual and individual difference factors. Individuals need not be aware, and are often not aware, of the contextual factors that "prime" the accessibility of standards or guides (see Higgins & King, 1981; Higgins et al., 1986a). Frequent activation of a particular acquired guide, and hence of a self-discrepancy, may lead to a state of chronic accessibility that is easily activated in response to ambiguous life events (see Higgins, King, & Mavin, 1982).

Chronic use of ideal guides for self-evaluation can create a negative psychological situation in which the attributes of the perceived self (i.e., Actual/Own) are highly discrepant from the attributes that one wishes or desires to possess (Ideal/Own) or that significant others ideally wish or desire one to possess (Ideal/Others). Individuals with such chronic ideal self-discrepancies believe that they are unable to obtain their own goals (Ideal/Own) or unable to fulfill the hopes and desires that others have for them (Ideal/Other). They are, therefore, vulnerable to the negative motivational state of experiencing an absence of (or inability to effect) positive outcomes. They feel dissatisfied with themselves, disappointed, and dejected (Ideal/Own), or shameful (Ideal/Other).

Chronic use of ought guides for self-evaluation can create a negative psychological situation in which the attributes of the perceived self are highly discrepant from the attributes that one believes one ought to possess (Ought/Own) or significant others believe one ought to possess (Ought/Other). Individuals with such chronic ought self-discrepancies believe that they have failed to uphold their duties and obligations as prescribed by themselves (Ought/Own) or as put forth by others (Ought/Other) and thus expect sanctions to be applied to them. They are, therefore, vulnerable to the negative motivational state of expecting the presence of (or inability to avoid) negative outcomes. They feel guilty and worthless (Ought/Own) or fearful and apprehensive (Ought/Other).

The extent to which an individual comes to believe through significant interpersonal relations that care and affection or punishment and criticism are contingent upon their living up to and pursuing the ideals or oughts held by themselves or by significant others will determine the psychological consequences of a self-discrepancy. If this interpersonal-outcome contingency is high (i.e., a strong belief that failing to meet ideals or oughts has significant implications for the absence of positive outcomes or the presence of negative outcomes in their interpersonal relationships), psychological distress and the motivation to reduce the state of self-discrepancy will also be high.

Predictions based on self-discrepancy theory receive support from a review of past literature. The failure to meet one's own ideal standards has been associated with dissatisfaction and disappointment (e.g., Adler, 1964; Allport, 1955; Duval & Wicklund, 1972; Horney, 1950; James, 1890/1948; Rogers, 1961), while the failure to meet the ideal guides of significant others has been associated with shame (e.g., Cooley, 1902/1964; Erikson, 1950/1963; James, 1890/1948; Lewin, 1935; Lewis, 1979). In contrast, the failure to meet one's own standards of duty and obligation has been associated with feelings of guilt and worthlessness (e.g., Erikson, 1950/1963; Freud, 1923; Horney, 1950; James, 1890/1948; Lewis, 1979), while the failure to meet the standards of duty and obligation set forth by a significant other (Ought/Other) has been associated with apprehension and insecurity (e.g., Erikson, 1950/1963; Freud, 1923/1961; Sullivan, 1953).

Higgins, Klein, and Strauman (1985) found direct support for the predictions of self-discrepancy theory in the self-reports of undergraduates: Actual self-ideal guide (Ideal/Own; Ideal/Other) discrepancies were more closely associated with dejection-related emotions (e.g., dissatisfaction, shame, feeling blue) than with agitation-related emotions (e.g., guilt, panic, fear). The reverse was true of actual self-ought guide (Ought/Own; Ought/Other) discrepancies. In another study (Higgins, Klein, & Strauman, 1987) the predictive value of type of self-discrepancy for future development of depression and anxiety symptoms was evaluated. As predicted, the magnitude of discrepancy between subjects' actual self and ideal guides was a significantly better predictor of depressive symptoms at two months follow-up than was the magnitude of discrepancy between their actual self and ought guides. Similarly, the magnitude of discrepancy between subjects' actual self and ought guide was a significantly better predictor of anxiety symptoms at follow-up than was the magnitude of discrepancy between their actual self and ideal guides.

In their most recent studies, Higgins, Bond, Klein, and Strauman (1986) found that type and magnitude of self-discrepancy predicted subjects' responses to either positive or negative psychological events. Specifically, subjects with high actual-ideal discrepancies but low actual-ought discrepancies and subjects with high actual-ought discrepancies but low actual-ideal discrepancies were asked to imagine either a positive event (received a grade of "A" in a course; just spent an evening with someone they admired for some time) or a negative event (received a grade of "D" in a course; a lover just left them). Subjects with high actual-ideal discrepancies who imagined a negative event experienced greater dejection and demonstrated more psycho-motor retardation (reduced writing speed) than did either subjects with high actual-ideal discrepancies who imagined a positive event or subjects with high actual-ought discrepancies who imagined a negative event. Subjects with high actual-ought discrepancies who imagined a negative event experienced greater agitation and psychomotor excitation (increased writing speed) than did either subjects with high actual-ought discrepancies who imagined a positive event or subjects with high actual-ideal discrepancies who imagined a negative event.

In a second experiment reported in the same paper, Higgins, Bond, Klein, and Strauman (1986) demonstrated that increasing the accessibility of different *types* of discrepancy (either actual-ideal or actual-ought) in subjects with *both* high actual-ideal and high actual-ought discrepancy produced different types of emotional responses: Priming aimed at increasing the accessibility of actual-ideal discrepancy produced dejection-related emotions whereas priming aimed at increasing the accessibility of actual-ought discrepancy produced agitation-related emotions. Priming in subjects with low actual-ideal and low actual-ought discrepancy failed to produce these emotions.

Chronic Self-Discrepancy as a Vulnerability Factor

How might the negative psychological situation of chronic self-discrepancy predispose an individual to violate normative consideration in the utilization of acquired guides? As previously noted, when an individual comes to believe that care, affection, or punishment are contingent on meeting particular standards, they will be motivated to monitor and evaluate their experiences in terms of these standards. The strength of this belief will vary between individuals as a function of situational factors such as the termination of an important relationship or the loss of a job, and the degree to which individuals have acquired this belief through their early relationships with parents or significant others (see Strauman, Higgins, & Klein, 1986). The stronger this belief, the stronger the motivation will be to monitor experiences in terms of salient guides so as to prevent the loss of positive outcomes (e.g., loss of love, affection) or to avoid the occurrence of negative outcomes (e.g., disapproval, punishment). In addition, the affective consequences of perceived discrepancy will add to the motivation to monitor and evaluate performance against significant guides with the goal of reducing the discrepancy. Thus, as suggested by James (1890/1948), and more recently by proponents of control theory and cybernetics (e.g. Miller, Galanter, & Pribram, 1960; Wiener, 1948), self-guides or standards are an integral component of self-regulatory behavior. Individuals with a chronic history of self-discrepancy who adhere strongly to the belief that significant outcomes are contingent on meeting particular guides will be extremely motivated to apply these guides in the evaluation of their performance.

One consequence of chronic self-discrepancy, and the associated increase in motivation to apply particular guides in self-evaluation, is the selection of a particular guide for the evaluation of an *increasing range* of events or performances. In other words, the selection of a guide for performance evaluation will become increasingly determined by its chronic accessibility and the motivational state of self-discrepancy, and there will be a correspondent reduction in reliance on or sensitivity to contextual and stimulus information.

A second consequence of chronic self-discrepancy will be the introduction of particular guides at *successively earlier stages* of information processing. That is, as the accessibility and magnitude of a discrepancy increases, there will be an increase in psychological discomfort and the motivation to reduce the state of discrepancy. The introduction of acquired guides prior to the stage of appraisal—a nonnormative form of standard utilization—will lead to unusual, aberrant, and possibly quite bizarre beliefs.

In the next section we outline the specific consequences of chronic ideal self-discrepancies and chronic ought self-discrepancies on the utilization of guides with respect to (1) the selection of particular guides for the evaluation of an increasing range of events and performances; and (2) the introduction of guides at successively earlier stages of information processing.

Chronic Ideal Self-Discrepancy

Range of Utilization

The use of ideal guides in the evaluation of some types of events and performances serves to provide important feedback information about the level of performance and motivates individuals in the pursuit of goals. With the development of chronic ideal self-discrepancy, however, the use of ideal guides becomes pervasive in the process of evaluation. Ideal guides are used to evaluate both events for which the use of ideal guides is normative and events for which the use of ideal guides is clearly nonnormative.

In tracing the consequences of chronic ideal self-discrepancy on the formation of beliefs let us consider the following example. A young man has developed a chronic ideal self-discrepancy with respect to the attribute of intellectual competence or intelligence; he experiences his actual self as intellectually limited or "slow" but wishes to be extremely bright and witty (Ideal/Own). For this individual, his Ideal/Own self-guide may come to be applied in the evaluation of events that are not normatively evaluated in these terms. Social interactions may become increasingly dominated by the need to demonstrate and evaluate wit or intellectual competence. Despite these attempts, and perhaps impervious to the positive responses of others, he may be disappointed in his comments and believe his opinions are unsatisfactory and inadequately formed.

Our second example is that of a young woman who had developed a chronic ideal self-discrepancy with respect to the attribute of social adequacy or interpersonal skill. She experiences her actual self as unable to attract the attention of others and lacking in social graces, and she believes that her parents would ideally like her to be entertaining and socially skilled (Ideal/Other). Not only will this self-guide be significant in the evaluation of interactions with friends and acquaintances in social situations, but it may also come to be applied in the evaluation of performances in contexts that are not primarily social in nature. Performance at work may come to be evaluated in terms of how well she feels she gets on with her superiors rather than feedback about the quality of her work per se. For example, despite her supervisor's praise of her work, she may feel she has failed because her supervisor does not stop to chat when passing in the hall.

Stage of Application

Previously we noted that the application of acquired guides at the stage of appraisal was normative. It should be noted, however, that the *chronic* or *exclusive* application of a particular ideal guide even at this stage of information processing violates normative considerations and may lead to unusual judgments about events or performance. For example, some individuals may apply normative guides at the stages of identification (e.g., performance is correctly identified as acceptable) and interpretation (performance is interpreted as a success), but *chronically* apply a particular ideal guide at the stage of appraisal. Consequently they may feel that they are continually falling short of their goals.

The application of ideal guides prior to the stage of appraisal is nonnormative. When discrepant ideal guides are chronically applied at the stage of interpretation, judgments and evaluations about events and performance are likely to be mildly to moderately deviant and highly negative. With respect to our first case example, we would predict the application at interpretation of an ideal guide regarding intellectual competence to result in negative performance evaluation because although performance is correctly (normatively) identified as adequate, it is interpreted as unsuccessful (evidence of intellectual incompetence hence confirming the discrepancy) because it fails to meet the ideal standard. With respect to our second case example, we would predict the application of an ideal guide regarding social competence to result in the correct (normative) identification of social performance as appropriate, but the interpretation of performance as unsuccessful (evidence of social ineptitude hence confirming the discrepancy) because it falls short of the ideal guide. The chronic application of ideal guides at the stage of interpretation is likely to lead to a highly negative and distorted evaluation of oneself.

As we have already noted, Higgins and his colleagues have found that the emotional consequences of chronic ideal discrepancy include a sense of disappointment, dejection, and despair. A secondary emotional consequence of chronic ideal-self discrepancy may be the development of a general state of frustration-anger. The relation between type of self-discrepancy and feelings of frustration-anger and resentment-anger was examined in a recent study by Higgins, Strauman, and Klein (1986b). Partial correlations controlling for ought self-discrepancy and resentment-anger toward others indicated ideal self-discrepancy was associated with frustration-anger toward the self, $r(63) = .30$, $p < .02$. However, ideal self-discrepancy was *not* associated with resentment-anger toward others when controlling for ought self-discrepancy and frustration-anger toward the self, $r(63) = -.11$, $p > .05$. As we point out in the next section, the pattern of results that emerged for ought self-discrepancy was strikingly different.

In conjunction with the selection of ideal standards for the evaluation of an increasing range of events, the nonnormative application of an ideal guide at interpretation could lead to a generalized and highly negative view of the self. This type of negative self-evaluation is consistent with numerous studies indicating that even though depressed individuals do not differ from nondepressives in performance on many tasks, they consistently evaluate their performance more negatively than do individuals who are not depressed (Beck, 1976; Dobson & Shaw, 1981; Lobitz & Post, 1979; Loeb, Beck, & Diggory, 1971; Smolen, 1978; Wollert & Buchwald, 1979; Zarantello, Johnson, & Petzel, 1979).

When discrepant ideal guides are chronically applied even at the earlier stage of identification, self-evaluation will be extremely distorted and highly negative. Again, using our example of the young man experiencing high ideal self-discrepancy with respect to the attribute of intellectual competence, we would expect the application of this ideal guide at the stage of identification to result in extreme negative distortion in the meaning of stimulus events— even though a particular performance is represented accurately, the individual *identifies* it as failing. Application of ideal guides at this stage would lead the young woman experiencing high ideal self-discrepancy with respect to the attribute of social adequacy to identify her social gestures as inappropriate (failure) even though others may respond favorably to her. Hence, even in the face of contradictory evidence, both individuals may persist in their highly aberrant beliefs of personal inadequacy. These types of judgments and beliefs about the self are likely to be viewed as highly aberrant or delusional.

The emotional consequences of applying ideal guides at this stage of information processing will be an extreme sense of disappointment and dejection. Negative beliefs about the self or delusions of self-deprecation that arise as a consequence of applying ideal guides at the stage of identification may be found in cases of major depression with mood-congruent psychotic features.

The application of ideal guides at the stage of stimulus representation will lead to gross disturbances of perception (hallucinations). Application of ideal guides at this stage would lead the individual with high ideal self-discrepancy regarding the attribute of intellectual competence to distort the stimulus representation; clear positive feedback about performance is *seen* or *encoded* as negative feedback. Similarly, the application of ideal guides at this stage would lead the individual with high ideal self-discrepancy regarding social adequacy to grossly misperceive or hallucinate with respect to the quality of her behavior with others, or to experience auditory hallucinations with deprecatory content. Running negative self-commentary about inadequacy or failure may also occur. The young woman may report hearing the voice of her mother or of others telling her that she is always saying the wrong thing; that she is inadequate, and that no one will ever come to accept her.

The recent findings of Higgins, Strauman, and Klein (1986b) support the unique relation between ideal self-discrepancy and ideal-outcome contingency with symptoms of depression but not with symptoms of anxiety. In this study, subjects' self-discrepancies were measured weeks prior to completing measures of depression and anxiety. Results indicated that high self-discrepancy in conjunction with the belief that not meeting ideal standards had significant negative implications for interpersonal relationships (i.e., failure to meet standards results in the withdrawal of love and approval—the absence of positive outcomes) and predicted self-reports of depression on both the Beck Depression Inventory, $R^2(70) = .39$, $p < .001$, and the Hopkins Symptom Checklist, $R^2(70) = .27$, $p < .001$. In contrast, controlling for ought self-discrepancy, the relation between ideal self-discrepancy and self-reports of anxiety and paranoid ideation on the Hopkins Symptom Checklist was not significant.

Chronic Ought Self-Discrepancy

Range of Utilization

As with ideal guides, the use of ought guides in the evaluation of some types of events and performances serves several important functions. That many needs are primarily expressed and met within a social context necessitates that behavior be monitored and controlled to meet at least some of the demands set out by significant others (e.g., parents). The application of ought guides provides individuals with feedback information so that they may alter their behavior in this regard.

With the development of chronic ought self-discrepancy the application of ought guides becomes pervasive in the process of evaluation. In tracing the consequences of chronic ought self-discrepancy on the formation of beliefs, let us take the following two cases as examples. A young man has developed a chronic actual-ought discrepancy with respect to the attribute of being responsible, he experiences his actual self as irresponsible and unreliable and believes he should be an outstanding example of responsibility (Ought/Own). A young woman has developed a chronic ought self-discrepancy with respect to the attribute of morality; she experiences her actual self as immoral and believes that significant others (i.e., her parents) feel she should be moral and virtuous (Ought/Other). For both individuals, the presence of chronic self-discrepancy may lead to the use of ought guides for the evaluation of performances in an increasing range of contexts. In the first case, the ought guide of responsibility becomes salient in the evaluation of work, interpersonal relations, and so on. He may feel it is his responsibility to ensure that *all* his workers get along well, or he may walk away from meeting a casual acquaintance, berating himself for failing to offer his help in finding the individual a job or helping him to move. In the second case, the question of moral integrity and virtuousness enters in the evaluation of behavior in a wide range of contexts. She may feel nervous when she finds herself attracted to a particular individual or she may feel apprehensive if she has lunch with a married male coworker despite the fact that the lunch was clearly work-related.

Stage of Application

As with ideal guides, the *chronic* or *exclusive* application of a particular ought guide at the stage of appraisal is nonnormative and can lead to unusual or atypical judgments about events and performances. With reference to our two cases, even though both individuals may apply normative guides at the stages of identification and interpretation, they would be predisposed to chronically apply ought guides at the stage of appraisal. The chronic application of ought guides at the stage of appraisal would result in persistent mild anxiety associated with the evaluation of oneself as failing to act as one should.

The application of ought guides prior to the stage of appraisal is nonnormative. The application of ought guides at the stage of interpretation predisposes individuals to form judgments and beliefs that are mildly to moderately deviant and negative in nature. With reference to our first case, we would predict the application of the ought guide regarding responsibility at the stage of interpretation to result in negative self-evaluation. Even though performance is correctly (normatively) identified as acceptable, it is interpreted as inadequate or failing to meet a level of responsibility that one should display. Similarly, in reference to our second case, we would predict the application of ought guides regarding morality at the stage of interpretation to result in negative self-evaluation because even though behavior is correctly (normatively) identified as acceptable, it is interpreted as improper or failing to meet a level of moral integrity that others believe she ought to demonstrate.

As we pointed out, negative emotional consequences of chronic ought self-discrepancy are quite distinct from the negative emotional consequences of chronic ideal self-discrepancy. Higgins and his colleagues have documented that the emotional consequences of chronic ought self-discrepancy include a sense of guilt, worthlessness, apprehension, and fear. A secondary emotional consequence of chronic ought self-discrepancy may be the development of a general state of irritability (Ought/Own), or resentment directed toward specific others because they are perceived as exerting inordinate demands and threatening punishment for failure (Ought/Other). The results of Higgins, Strauman, and Klein (1986b) support the relation between ought self-discrepancy and resentment-anger. Partial analyses controlling for ideal self-discrepancy and frustration-anger toward the self revealed that ought self-discrepancy correlated with resentment-anger toward others, $r(63) = .26$, $p < .05$. Ought self-discrepancy was *not* associated with frustration-anger toward the self when controlling for ideal self-discrepancy and resentment-anger toward others, $r(63) = -.09$, $p > .05$.

In conjunction with the selection of ought guides for the evaluation of an increasing range of events, the nonnormative application of ought guides at the stage of interpretation could lead to a pervasively negative view of the self and a mild to moderate sense of anxiety and irritability. This constellation of symptoms is typically found in cases of anxiety disorder (Beck, Emery, & Greenberg, 1985).

The application of ought guides at the stage of identification will result in the distortion of stimulus meaning and will lead to the formation of highly negative and distorted self-evaluations. In our first case, we would predict the application of ought guides regarding responsibility at the stage of identification to result in the failure to normatively identify stimulus meaning. Even though he may receive clear indication that he has acted responsibly in a particular situation, he will *identify* his behavior as irresponsible and inadequate. Hence, even in the face of clear contradictory evidence, he will persist in his belief that he has failed to act as he believes he should have. Similarly, in our second case we would predict the application of ought guides regarding morality at the stage of identification to result in distortion of stimulus meaning. Even though she may receive clear indications that her behavior has been morally acceptable and entirely appropriate, she may persist in identifying her behavior as violating rules of morality.

The emotional consequences of applying ought guides at the stage of identification will include an extreme sense of guilt or sin and associated apprehension and vigilance. Intense resentment over others' sanctions may develop as a secondary emotional consequence. Beliefs and negative self-evaluations that arise from the application of ought standards at the stage of identification may be classified as delusions of guilt or sin, delusions of persecution, and delusions of being controlled.

When ought guides are applied at the stage of stimulus representation there may be gross disturbances of perception (hallucinations). With reference to our first case, for example, the application of ought guides regarding responsibility may result in auditory hallucinations of self-reprimands and running commentary about his irresponsibility and inadequacy. In our second case, the application of ought guides regarding morality may produce auditory hallucinations of others reprimanding her for her sins and indicating that she should be punished.

The relation between ought self-discrepancy and ought-outcome contingency with symptoms of anxiety is supported by the recent findings of Higgins, Strauman, and Klein (1986b). Subjects' self-discrepancies were measured weeks prior to their completing measures of depression and anxiety. High ought self-discrepancy in conjunction with the belief that not meeting the standards prescribed by oneself or by others will have significant negative implications for interpersonal relationships (i.e., result in punishment—the presence of negative outcomes) predicted self-reports of anxiety and paranoid ideation on the Hopkins Symptom Checklist, $R^2 (70) = .22$, $p < .01$ and $R^2 (70) = .24$, $p < .01$, respectively. In contrast, the relation between ought self-discrepancy and self-reports of depression on the Beck Depression Inventory was not significant. Similarly, controlling for ideal self-discrepancy, the relation between ought self-discrepancy and self-reports of depression on the Hopkins Symptom Checklist was not significant.

The Continuum of Vulnerability to Aberrant Beliefs

In this chapter we have outlined a framework for understanding the formation of atypical inferences. We identified two continua or dimensions along which deviations from normative standard utilization may occur. Deviations may occur along the continuum of normativeness in *standard selection* and along the continuum of normativeness in *standard application* at stages of the social evaluative process. Greater deviations from normativeness along either or both dimensions will increase the likelihood that atypical or aberrant beliefs will be formed.

In addition, we identified a vulnerability factor—chronic self-discrepancy—that predisposes individuals to violate normative considerations in the utilization of standards. This individual difference factor influences both the *selection* of standards and the *application* of standards at different stages of the social evaluative process (see Table 5.2).

When chronic self-discrepancy exists together with the belief that the absence of positive outcomes or the presence of negative outcomes is contingent upon failing to meet particular standards, we would predict that the psychological consequences of self-discrepancy will be profound. In these cases, the state of self-discrepancy will be accompanied by extreme psychological distress and heightened motivation to monitor performance in terms of standards with the goal of reducing the discrepancy.

This model assumes that over the course of time individuals may vary in the degree to which they violate normative standard utilization, depending on the magnitude and accessibility of individuals' self-discrepancies and their

TABLE 5.2.   Normative and Nonnormative Application of Standards

	Normative Application of Standards	Nonnormative Application of Standards in Chronic Self-Discrepancies
Stage of the Social Evaluative Process		
Stimulus Registration	Registration and representation of attribute feature	Chronic application of guides may occur, resulting in gross disturbances of perception
Identification	Recognition of attribute as an instance of a class or category	Chronic application of guides may occur, resulting in distortion of stimulus meaning and in the formation of extremely negative self-evaluations and delusions
Interpretation	Application of factual guides	Chronic application of guides may occur, resulting in the formation of negative self-evaluations and aberrant beliefs
Appraisal	Application of various acquired guides	Chronic application of a particular acquired guide resulting in mildly negative self-evaluation

beliefs concerning the interpersonal consequences of failing to reduce them. The *type* of deviation they demonstrate, however, will remain relatively stable. Thus, we would predict that there should be some degree of similarity within individuals between the nature of their aberrant beliefs prior to a psychotic episode and the nature of their delusional beliefs during psychosis. Indeed, this prediction of a continuous relation between nonpsychotic aberrant beliefs and psychotic delusions is supported by the reports of several clinicians and researchers (Chapman & Chapman, this volume; Harrow, Rattenbury, & Stoll, this volume; Strauss, 1969).

One of the strengths of the current model is that it takes into consideration clinical and empirical findings regarding the formation of beliefs. The model integrates our current understanding of cognitive processes that underlie the formation of judgments and beliefs (both normative and nonnormative), as well as our understanding of individual differences in cognitive, motivational, and affective states that influence the formation of judgments and beliefs.

A second strength of the model is that it is readily open to empirical evaluation. In the current chapter we have presented preliminary results regarding the emotional consequences of self-discrepancy. Future research might examine the value of self-discrepancy in identifying individuals who may be prone to the development of aberrant beliefs or delusions; or examine the effect of changing the accessibility of self-discrepancy (e.g., by priming) on normative and nonnormative standard utilization.

We would like to point out, however, that there are several limitations of this framework. First, the explanatory power of the model seems limited to the arena of self-evaluative or self-referential aberrant beliefs. As previously noted, the self-discrepancy model is most applicable to understanding negative aberrant beliefs or delusions—self-deprecation, guilt, or sin, and delusions of persecution or being controlled. However, aberrant beliefs or delusions that are not self-evaluative and delusions of grandiosity are not well explained in the context of self-discrepancy theory.

One possibility is that delusions are not homogeneous with respect to etiology. Another possibility is that some aberrant beliefs (e.g., grandiose beliefs) involve the nonnormative application of standards within the context of social comparison. That is, some aberrant beliefs may arise because different standards are applied to the self than are applied to others. Recall our example of a graduate student who evaluates her knowledge of the field against the knowledge of the first-year undergraduates she tutors.

It would be interesting to speculate on the cognitive and motivational processes that differentiate between individuals who apply guides that lead to overly negative self-evaluation from those who apply guides that lead to overly positive self-evaluation; or that cause an individual to change the type of guides that they apply in the evaluation of their performance. The continued investigation of cognitive, affective, and motivational factors that contribute to the formation of self-discrepancies and to the utilization of standards during self-evaluation may provide a theoretical and empirical basis from which to address these issues.

REFERENCES

Adler, A. (1964). *Problems of neurosis.* New York: Harper & Row.

Allport, G.W. (1985). *Becoming.* New Haven, CT: Yale University Press.

American Psychiatric Association. (1980). *Diagnostic and statistical manual of mental disorders* (3rd ed.). (DSM-III). Washington, DC: Author.

Arthur, A.Z. (1964). Theories and explanations of delusions: A review. *American Journal of Psychiatry, 121,* 105–115.

Bandura, A. (1982). The self and mechanisms of agency. In J. Suls (Ed.), *Psychological perspectives on the self* (Vol. 1). Hillsdale, NJ: Erlbaum.

Beck, A.T. (1967). *Depression: Causes and treatment.* Philadelphia: University of Pennsylvania Press.

Beck, A.T. (1976). *Cognitive therapy and the emotional disorders.* New York: International Universities Press.

Beck, A.T., Emery, G., & Greenberg, R.C. (1985). *Anxiety disorders and phobias.* New York: Basic Books.

Bernstein, M., & Crosby, F. (1980). An empirical examination of relative deprivation theory. *Journal of Experimental Social Psychology, 16,* 442–456.

Bleuler, E. (1950). *Dementia praecox or the group of schizophrenias.* New York: International Universities Press.

Cooley, C.H. (1964). *Human nature and the social order.* New York: Schocken Books. (Original work published 1902.)

Dobson, K.S., & Shaw, B.S. (1981). The effects of self-correction on cognitive distortion in depression. *Cognitive Therapy and Research, 1,* 311–329.

Duval, S., & Wicklund, R.A. (1972). *A theory of objective self-awareness.* New York: Academic Press.

Erikson, E.H. (1963). *Childhood and society* (2nd ed.). New York: W.W. Norton. (Original work published 1950.)

Festinger, L. (1954). A theory of social comparison processes. *Human Relations, 1,* 117–140.

Freud, S. (1961). The ego and the id. In J. Strachey (Ed. and Trans.), *The standard edition of the complete psychological works of Sigmund Freud* (Vol. 19). London: Hogarth. (Original work published 1923.)

Goethals, G.R., & Darley, J.M. (1977). Social comparison theory: An attributional approach. In J.M. Suls & R.L. Miller (Eds.), *Social comparison processes: Theoretical and empirical perspectives.* Washington, DC: Hemisphere.

Higgins, E.T. (1987). Self-discrepancy: A theory relating self and affect. *Psychological Review, 94,* 319–340.

Higgins, E.T., Bond, R.N., Klein, R., & Strauman, T. (1986). Self-discrepancies and emotional vulnerability: How magnitude, accessibility and type of discrepancy influence affect. *Journal of Personality and Social Psychology, 51,* 5–15.

Higgins, E.T., & King, G. (1981). Accessibility of social constructs: Information processing consequences of individual and contextual variability. In N. Cantor & J. Kihlstrom (Eds.), *Personality, cognition and social interaction.* Hillsdale, NJ: Erlbaum.

Higgins, E.T., King, G., & Mavin, G.H. (1982). Individual construct accessibility and subjective impressions and recall. *Journal of Personality and Social Psychology, 43,* 35–47.

Higgins, E.T., Klein, R., & Strauman, T. (1985). Self-concept discrepancy theory: A psychological model for distinguishing among different aspects of depression and anxiety. *Social Cognition, 3,* 51–76.

Higgins, E.T., Klein, R., & Strauman, T. (1987). Self-discrepancies: Distinguishing among self-states, self-state conflicts, and emotional vulnerabilities. In K. Yardley & T. Honess (Eds.), *Self and identity: Psychosocial perspectives.* New York: Wiley.

Higgins, E.T., & Lurie, L. (1983). Context, categorization and memory: The "change-of-standard" effect. *Cognitive Psychology, 15,* 525–547.

Higgins, E.T., & Stangor, C. (1987). Context-driven social judgment and memory: When "behavior engulfs the field" in reconstructive memory. In D. Bar-Tel & A. Kruglanski (Eds.), *Social psychology of knowledge.* Cambridge, England: Cambridge University Press.

Higgins, E.T., Strauman, T., & Klein, R. (1986a). Standards and the process of self evaluation: Multiple affects from multiple stages. In R.M. Sorrentino & E.T. Higgins (Eds.), *Handbook of motivation and cognition: Foundations of social behavior.* New York: Guilford Press.

Higgins, E.T., Strauman, T., & Klein, R. (1986b). *Affect as a function of magnitude, type, and perceived consequences of actual-self: Self-guide discrepancy.* Unpublished manuscript, New York University, New York.

Horney, K. (1950). *Neuroses and human growth.* New York: W.W. Norton.

Hyman, H.H. (1942). The psychology of status. *Archives of Psychology, 269,*

James, W. (1948). *Psychology.* New York: World. (Original work published 1890.)

Johnson, W.G., Ross, J.M., & Mastria, M.A. (1977). Delusional behavior: An attributional analysis of development and modification. *Journal of Abnormal Psychology, 86,* 421–426.

Kahneman, D., & Miller, D.T. (1986). Norm theory: Comparing reality to its alternatives. *Psychological Review, 93,* 136–153.

Kahneman, D., & Tversky, A. (1982). The simulation heuristic. In D. Kahneman, P. Slovic, & A. Tversky (Eds.), *Judgments under uncertainty: Heuristics and biases.* New York: Cambridge University Press.

Kelley, H.H. (1952). Two functions of reference groups. In G.E. Swanson, T.M.

Newcomb, & E.L. Hartley (Ed.), *Readings in social psychology* (2nd ed.). New York: Holt, Rinehart & Winston.

Kraepelin, E. (1971). *Dementia praecox and paraphrenia.* New York: Kreiger. (Original work published 1919.)

Lewin, K. (1935). *A dynamic theory of personality.* New York: McGraw-Hill.

Lewin, K. (1951). *Field theory in social science.* New York: Harper.

Lewis, H.B. (1979). Shame in depression. In C.E. Izard (Ed.), *Emotions in personality and psychopathology.* New York: Plenum Press.

Lobitz, W.C., & Post, R.D. (1979). Parameters of self-reinforcement and depression. *Journal of Abnormal Psychology, 88,* 33–41.

Loeb, A., Beck, A.T., & Diggory, J. (1971). Differential effects of success and failure on depressed and nondepressed patients. *Journal of Nervous and Mental Disease, 152,* 106–114.

Markus, H., & Nurius, P.S. (1986). Possible selves. *American Psychologist, 41,* 954–969.

Mead, G.H. (1934). *Mind, self and society.* Chicago: University of Chicago Press.

Merton, R.K., & Kitt, A.S. (1952). Contributions of the theory of reference-group behavior. In G.E. Swanson, T.M. Necomb, & E.L. Hartley (Eds.), *Readings in social psychology* (2nd ed.). New York: Holt, Rinehart & Winston.

Miller, G.A., Galanter, E., & Pribram, K.H. (1960). *Plans and the structure of behavior.* New York: Holt, Rinehart & Winston.

Morse, S.J., & Gergen, K.J. (1970). Social comparison, self-consistency, and the concept of self. *Journal of Personality and Social Psychology, 16,* 148–156.

Newcomb, T.M. (1952). Attitude development as a function of reference group: The Bennington study. In G.E. Swanson, T.M. Newcomb, & E.L. Hartley (Eds.), *Readings in social psychology* (2nd ed.). New York: Holt, Rinehart & Winston.

Nisbett, R.E., & Ross, L.D. (1980). *Human inference: Strategies and shortcomings of informal judgment.* Englewood Cliffs, NJ: Prentice-Hall.

Rogers, C.R. (1961). *On becoming a person.* Boston: Houghton Mifflin.

Rosch, E. (1978). Principles of categorization. In E. Rosch & B.B. Lloyd (Eds.), *Cognition and categorization.* Hillsdale, NJ: Erlbaum.

Ruble, D.N. (1983). The development of social comparison processes and their role in achievement-related self-socialization. In E.T. Higgins, D.N. Ruble, & W.W. Hartup (Eds.), *Social cognition and social development: A socio-cultural perspective.* New York: Cambridge University Press.

Sarbin, T.R., Taft, R., & Bailey, D.E. (1960). *Clinical inference and cognitive theory.* New York: Holt, Rinehart & Winston.

Sherif, M. (1936). *The psychology of social norms.* New York: Harper.

Sherif, M. (1948). *An outline of social psychology.* New York: Harper.

Smolen, R.C. (1978). Expectancies, mood, and performance of depressed and nondepressed inpatients on chance and skill tasks. *Journal of Abnormal Psychology, 87,* 91–101.

Spitzer, R.L., Endicott, J., & Robins, E. (1978). *Research diagnostic criteria (RDC) for a selected group of functional disorders.* New York: Biometrics Research.

Strauman, T., Higgins, E.T., & Klein, R. (1986). *Emotional vulnerability as a function of self-discrepancies and their perceived interpersonal significance.* Unpublished manuscript, New York University, New York.

Strauss, J.S. (1969). Hallucinations and delusions as points on a continua function: Rating scale evidence. *Archives of General Psychiatry, 21,* 581–586.

Sullivan, H.S. (1953). *The collected works of Harvey Stack Sullivan* (Vol. 1). Edited by H.S. Perry & M.L. Gavel. New York: W.W. Norton.

Suls, J., & Mullen, B. (1982). From the cradle to the grave: Comparison and self-evaluation across the life-span. In J. Suls (Ed.), *Psychological perspectives on the self* (Vol. 1). Hillsdale, NJ: Erlbaum.

Tversky, A., & Gati, I. (1978). Studies in similarity. In E. Rosch & B.B. Lloyd (Eds.), *Cognition and categorization.* Hillsdale, NJ: Erlbaum.

Veroff, J. (1969). Social comparison and the achievement motivation. In C.P. Smith (Ed.), *Achievement-related motives in children.* New York: Russell Sage Foundation.

Wiener, N. (1948). *Cybernetics: Control and communication in the animal and the machine.* Cambridge, MA: MIT Press.

Winters, K.C., & Neale, J.M. (1983). Delusions and delusional thinking in psychotics: A review of the literature. *Clinical Psychology Review, 3,* 227–253.

Wollert, R.W., & Buchwald, A.M. (1979). Subclinical depression and performance expectations, evaluations of performance, and actor performance. *Journal of Nervous and Mental Disease, 167,* 237–242.

World Health Organization. (1973). *The international pilot study of schizophrenia.* Geneva: Author.

Wylie, R.C. (1979). *The self-concept.* Lincoln: University of Nebraska Press.

Zarantonello, M.W., Johnson, J.E., & Petzel, T.P. (1979). The effects of ego involvement and task difficulty on actual and perceived performance of depressed and nondepressed college students. *Journal of Clinical Psychology, 5,* 273–281.

CHAPTER 6

Defensive Functions of Manic Episodes

JOHN M. NEALE

State University of New York, Stony Brook

There are many reasons for studying delusions. Since the beginnings of descriptive psychiatry, delusions have played an important role in the diagnosis of psychotic conditions. Delusions have also been thought to be of significance for *differential* diagnosis, for example, Schneider's proposals concerning the relevance of first rank symptoms to schizophrenia. The study of delusions is also of relevance to other areas of general interest in psychology, notably belief formation and change. Finally, studying delusions provides an alternative research strategy to the more usual practice of psychological deficit research and yields some distinct advantages in this context.

The study of psychological deficits in various psychoses has a long tradition. In a recent paper, Neale, Oltmanns, and Harvey (1985) argued that this research is often conceptually unfocused. For example, much of the psychological deficit research in schizophrenia has been directed at thought disorder, at least implicitly. Few researchers, however, have taken the additional step of actually examining the relationship between their measure of deficit and thought disorder per se. Neale, Oltmanns, and Harvey addressed this issue by reporting data examining the correlation between a referential communication task developed by Kagan and Oltmanns (1981) and measures of language disorder. In a sample of adult psychiatric patients the referential communication task was unrelated to several measures of language disorder as assessed by Andreasen's (1979) Scale for Thought, Language and Communication Disorders. Similarly, in a sample of high-risk children, the referential communication task did not correlate with measures of cohesion and reference used by Rochester and Martin (1979) in their studies of schizophrenic discourse.

Results such as these further the argument that at least some of our efforts in the realms of both research and theory should be more directly oriented toward symptoms. The principal advantage is that theories are forced to become more explicit. It is no longer possible to get away with vague statements linking a less than adequately defined diagnostic label (e.g., schizophrenia) to a dysfunction in attention or dopamine excess.

The two symptoms that have received the most attention are delusions and hallucinations. Even here, though, the literature is relatively sparse, particularly at the level of empirical findings. Delusions have been widely written about but little researched. In a recent review of models of delusions, Winters and Neale (1983) identified two themes that cut across existing theories. The first theme was motivational. Theories of this kind propose a specific motivating force that leads to the delusion. Examples are the delusions constructed to explain unusual perceptual experiences (Maher, 1974) and delusions that seem to reduce or provide relief from states of psychological discomfort. A second major theme is that delusions result from a fundamental defect in cognitive processes. The best known example here is the Von Domarus principle, wherein schizophrenics were proposed to conclude that two things were identical based on equality of predicates.

In general, explanations of delusions have either considered them as a single class or have focused specifically on paranoid delusions. But delusional beliefs vary widely on many dimensions: content, pervasiveness, persistence, bizarreness, and so forth. This great variability makes it desirable to focus efforts at theory building on a specific type of delusion. Distinctly different mechanisms may be involved in the production of different types of delusional beliefs. For example, Cameron's (1959) account of the development of the pseudocommunity remains a plausible, if largely unvalidated, theory of the development of paranoid delusions. Maher's (1974) theory seems best suited to handling a subclass of delusions wherein an actual physiological sensation or hallucinated experience demands explanation. Some bizarre delusions may represent attempts to gain attention or to keep the focus of an interview away from more distressing material. And some delusions, as noted by several representatives of the Heidelburg school, may be inexplicable using any of the concepts available in the current literature.

This chapter, therefore, will focus on one type of delusion and will propose a theory of its development. The grandiose delusions characteristic of mania are the type that will be discussed. Several factors led to this choice. First, there has been very little psychological theorizing about bipolar disorder in general and about grandiose delusions in particular. Although psychological theories of depression have gained widespread currency in recent years, bipolar disorder has been left largely to the physiologically oriented theorist. This chapter, therefore, begins to fill a gap in psychological theory. Second, Winters and Neale (1985) have already conducted a study testing one aspect of the traditional psychodynamic account of grandiose delusions.

The results of that study, to be described fully later, provided an important stimulus for the work discussed here.

GRANDIOSE DELUSIONS IN MANIA

Delusions of grandiosity are common in bipolar disorder and also predictive of the diagnosis. For example, in the International Pilot Study of Schizophrenia (World Health Organization, 1973) 92 percent of patients with grandiose delusions were given a diagnosis of manic psychosis, and Carlson and Goodwin (1973) reported that 75 percent of their bipolar patients had delusions during a manic episode. These delusions are usually regarded as mood congruent, although empirical support for this idea does not seem to be available. Leff, Fischer, and Bertelsen (1976) offered the following classification of the content of grandiose delusions in mania:

1. Special abilities: The patient is an inventor, a great athlete, a world-renowned businessman.
2. Grandiose identity: The patient claims to be a reincarnation of some famous historical figure or a descendant of a famous figure.
3. Wealth: The patient is a millionaire, the "true" owner of all oil in the Middle East.
4. Special mission: The patient has been chosen to solve the problem of war and bring peace to the world or to save the young prostitutes in the Times Square area of New York City.

Even when full-blown grandiose delusions are not present in the manic, grandiose ideation is likely. Among bipolar patients in the Stony Brook high-risk project, for example, over 90 percent show grandiosity. As noted previously by Strauss (1969), data such as these may indicate the presence of a continuum from the milder forms of grandiosity to true delusional beliefs. Therefore, grandiosity and grandiose delusions will not be sharply distinguished in this chapter.

It is likely that the grandiosity of the manic can be differentiated from that of the paranoid schizophrenic, although few available data are directly relevant to the point. On an empirical level, Carpenter, Strauss, and Bartko (1974) have shown that delusions are more circumscribed in mania than in schizophrenia. Furthermore, although data are not available, the delusions of the manic may be more plausible and less likely to be judged as bizarre than those of the paranoid schizophrenic.

PSYCHOLOGICAL THEORIES OF GRANDIOSITY

As noted earlier, there has been little psychological theorizing concerning bipolar disorder and grandiose delusions. The theories that do exist are principally psychodynamic in orientation. Rooted in the theories of delusions identified by Winters and Neale (1983), these accounts are clearly motivational in nature. Furthermore, the theories are usually not specifically relevant to grandiose delusions per se but are accounts of bipolar disorder in general. However, grandiosity plays an important role; these theories are therefore of considerable relevance.

In the first psychoanalytic paper on the topic Karl Abraham (1911/1927) described one of the basic tenets of the psychodynamic approach: "A manic . . . appears very cheerful on the surface . . . however, both phases are dominated by the same complexes . . . In the depressive state he allows himself to be weighed down by his complex . . . in the manic state he treats the complex with indifference." The point being made here is that the same process underlies both mania and depression. The two phases of the disorder are different reactions to the same enduring difficulty.

In Freud's (1917/1950) celebrated *Mourning and Melancholia*, Abraham's ideas were extended. Freud basically agreed with Abraham that depression and mania were attempts to deal with the same complex. In a tentative way he also suggested a reason for the appearance of a manic episode: "The ego must have surmounted the loss of the object . . . whereupon which the whole amount of anticathexis which the painful suffering of the melancholia drew from the ego and 'bound' becomes available."

Both Freud and Abraham saw bipolar disorder as a result of loss and introjection of the ambivalent feelings toward the lost object. Melancholia results when anger is directed against the ego, which has incorporated the lost object. These feelings of anger emanate from the superego, which continuously reproaches and acuses the ego. (The concept of the superego and its relations to mania are more fully presented in *Group Psychology and Analyses of the Ego*, Freud, 1921.)

The theory was developed further by Rado (1928). One important addition was a clear description of a predisposition to bipolar disorder—an intense narcissism that renders the person vulnerable to events that threaten self-esteem. Self-esteem is therefore regarded as unstable and based entirely on "external supplies." As in earlier theories, Rado claimed that the lost object was introjected not once but twice. The "good" object is introjected into the superego and the "bad" object into the ego. The "task" of melancholia is to destroy the bad object so the ego can regain the love of the good object. This end is achieved in mania.

Subsequent analytic writers have expanded and modified the theory in many ways, but those changes have not altered its basic structure. Klein (1968), for example, proposed that mania was an attempt to escape from both melancholia and paranoia. In the manic state, denial handles the anxiety associated with the introjected object and a sense of omnipotence develops for the purpose of controlling and mastering objects. Similarly, Jacobsen (1953) emphasized the failure of denial in melancholia and its success in mania.

To summarize, a psychoanalytic theory that incorporates the views of the most prominent writers on the topic would include the following points:

1. A predisposition to bipolar disorder is a state of unstable self-esteem. Because the person's feelings about the self are totally dependent on the external world, self-esteem fluctuates with variations in life experience.

2. Events that precipitate depression or mania are those that threaten this vulnerable sense of self-esteem.

3. Hostility/anger toward the frustrating object is redirected at the ego (introjected). The anger enlists on the side of the superego and attacks the ego. The sometimes delusional self-reproach of melancholics is therefore an attempt to attack the introjected object.

4. In mania, the ego attains what it is striving for, that is, narcissistic supplies of complete approval, acceptance, affection, and the like. The ego attains complete control and the superego becomes powerless. The grandiosity, increased self-esteem, and seeming imperviousness to external threats to self-esteem are all examples of this process. The manic state results from the triumph of the ego and release of energy that was bound in the depressive struggle. The fears of the superego are, however, not entirely overcome but are being successfully defended with denial, reaction formation, and overcompensation.

The theory to be developed in this chapter draws heavily on these psychodynamic formulations, on clinical experience, and on psychological research. Before describing the theory a clinical case will be described that is relevant to the original psychoanalytic formulation and that stimulated the author's interest.

Doug was 38 when he entered treatment for a manic episode. He had experienced at least one episode of major depressive disorder in the past and perhaps several minor depressive episodes as well. By his own description and that of his wife (his third) and family it was likely that he had also experienced several episodes of hypomania. Currently he was in a full-blown manic state that had begun several weeks previously, at the beginning of December. At that time he had begun a frantic flurry of activity centered around establishing a new business. He stayed up to all hours, writing letters and making phone calls about his plan to surpass both Rockefeller and Getty in the business world. His mood was elated and he drank heavily. At Christmas dinner, with his wife and grandparents, he became drunk and obnoxious and ultimately stormed out of the house before the meal had ended. He smashed his car on the way home, was hospitalized for possible injuries, and then committed.

The tantalizing aspect of the case lies in the link between the content of the manic episode and its grandiose delusion and the patient's prior life history. In fact, Doug could best be described by an outside observer as a failed businessman. Although he would not assent to such a description, the fact was that his father had loaned him money several times to start up a new company only to see it fall into bankruptcy. Indeed, at least part of Doug's striving toward success seemed to be a way of trying to compete with his highly successful father. His past episodes of minor depression had generally occurred during periods of impending business failures and his most recent business venture had gone under during the past fall.

Clearly this case seems to illustrate well the defensive function of grandiose delusions that have been described by psychodynamic theory. Doug's self-esteem was based in large part on his economic success and ability to match his father. His failures elicited episodes of both depression and mania and the content of his grandiose delusion was obviously linked to the source of his distress. The theory, however, has had little impact on general psychology and has elicited almost no research.* Part of this neglect is no doubt due to the lack of general appeal of psychoanalytic constructs such as primary narcissism, the ego and superego, introjection, and defense mechanism. Also omitted from this description of psychoanalytic accounts are those aspects that are likely to be even less appealing than the ones already described—for example, Klein's assertion that the manic defense is actually established during childhood when the infant fears that the aggressive id will destroy the mother's breast. Certain parts of the theory are, however, promising and are amenable to empirical investigation. Drawing on cases like Doug's, on psychodynamic theory, and on the psychological literature, some ideas on the development of bipolar disorder and grandiosity will now be presented. Both bipolar disorder and grandiosity will be discussed because there seems to be

---

*One exception is research on the supposed inner directed aggression of the depressive (e.g., Beck & Ward, 1961). There is, however, virtually no empirical work on the mania aspect of the theory.

a true symptom cluster here. Unlike schizophrenia, wherein diverse symptoms are not strongly related to one another, the grandiose ideation, inflated self-esteem, elated mood, and behavioral excesses of the bipolar patient form a coherent cluster the various parts of which are difficult to discuss independently of one another. Although it will be argued that the cognitive manifestations of the disorder are primary, there is in fact no direct clinical evidence to support this postulate.

THE THEORY

Predisposition

In agreement with several psychodynamic writers, it is proposed that unstable self-esteem is the psychological predisposition to bipolar disorder and to grandiose delusions. Although a relatively large literature exists on self-esteem and self-concept, the area suffers from failures to define adequately the concept and deal fully with measurement issues. Most research on self-esteem has taken a trait approach, with self-esteem measured by a single self-report questionnaire. The trait measures of self-esteem are then typically related to other personality traits. As a trait, self-esteem does show moderate test-retest correlations over a one-year period, typically in the .50 to .60 range (Hoge & McCarthy, 1983).

Little research has been completed on the correlates of the stability of trait measures of self-esteem. In the few studies that have been reported, however, stability of self-esteem has proven to be an interesting variable. In a study of college students Brownfain (1952) found that stable self-esteem was associated with feelings of comfort, absence of tension, and psychological adjustment. More recently, Kugle, Clements, and Powell (1983) found that stability of self-esteem was related to academic achievement and the accuracy of self descriptions of ability in elementary-school-age children. Interestingly, level of self-esteem did not predict either criterion variable and was also unrelated to self-esteem stability.

These data, however, are not quite on the mark for the concept of self-esteem stability being considered here. Self-esteem is proposed to be a relatively enduring and consistent set of self-attitudes, but situational variables can yield momentary or relatively transient changes in it. Instability of self-esteem occurs when the variance in self-esteem due to transient environmental change becomes very large.

There is very little information concerning point assessments of self-esteem. In a one-week longitudinal study, Savin-Williams and Demo (1983) studied point ratings of the self-concept obtained six to eight times per day in a relatively small sample of adolescents. Considerable variation was observed in the ratings, and in a small subset of the group, good and poor self-concepts even showed an alternating pattern. These data suggest that point assessments of self-esteem do vary. Furthermore, in these normal adolescents the point ratings did not predict trait measures of self-esteem (Demo, 1985). This, too, is expected because relatively stable traitlike measures of self-esteem should not be strongly related to varying point assessments unless the point assessments are aggregated.

It is important to stress again that the predisposing factor is not simple low self-esteem. Such a view would be inconsistent with what scant data we have on people at risk for bipolar disorder or on interepisode adjustment of bipolars. Depue et al. (1981) have reported on several characteristics of the behavior of individuals identified by a questionnaire as prone to bipolar disorder. The key characteristic of these cyclothymic individuals is variability—in mood, behavior, and even cortisol levels. In the theory being described here, fluctuations in self-esteem are regarded as the cause of the variability in mood and behavior displayed by cyclothymes. A consistent low level of self-esteem would not be a viable explanatory factor for these data. Similarly, information on interepisode adjustment of bipolars does not fit well with the hypothesis that they have a consistently low level of self-esteem. While some behavioral indicants reflect problems (e.g., marital discord, occupational problems), data from various personality questionnaires show no significant maladjustment (e.g., McVane, Mange, Brown, & Zayat, 1978).

Related to this instability of self-esteem is a special need to succeed in specific life spheres. It is presumed that early life experiences make success in certain life areas particularly important. In other words, the person's "ideal self" contains unrealistic standards for success, setting the stage for unfavorable comparisons between actuality and ideal and making the person's self-esteem vulnerable to even minor life experiences that threaten or suggest failure. Furthermore, because of the extremely salient nature of this internalized standard, the usual defense that can be employed here—overestimating the importance of one's strengths and underestimating the importance of one's weaknesses (Lewicki, 1984)—does not succeed. (See Higgins & Moretti, this volume, for a discussion of related issues.)

Another hypothesized aspect of the predisposition to grandiose delusions lies in the characteristic use of pleasant fantasies and/or activities as a means of coping with daily stress. Because the use of pleasant activities is limited by physical, realistic constraints, fantasy predominates. This proved to be the case with Doug. While in therapy he described how frequently he daydreamed about great business successes and that he had well-developed fantasies in this area. In Stone and Neale's research on daily coping, some of the coping mechanisms observed could fall into this category (Stone &

Neale, 1984),* indicating that coping is sometimes accomplished with these means. With unstable self-esteem, it would be presumed that fantasies would be used often. Over time, a set of detailed scenarios is constructed that the bipolar can easily draw upon. Frequent use of pleasant fantasies to distract oneself from unpleasant events or cognitions may make the fantasies more accessible and may heighten their reality. Johnson, Raye, Wang, and Taylor (1979), for example, have shown that there can be confusion in deciding when a memory has been elicited by an external source and when it is self-generated. The more one thinks about a stimulus, the greater the estimates of the frequency with which it was actually presented (see Johnson, this volume, for more details). Therefore, frequent "fantasy trials" may blur the distinction between these cognitions as fantasies versus memories of actual events. Furthermore, over many trials the fantasies are likely to become more elaborated and detailed. These increased details can serve to further increase the reality (i.e., sensory-based nature) of the fantasy. Finally, the repeated trials could make the elicitation of the fantasy more automatic, thus reducing the experience of generation, another cue for distinguishing memories from fantasies (see Johnson & Raye, 1981). In sum, fantasies that occur frequently and become more realistic set the stage for the later development of grandiosity and delusion.

Precipitants

Episodes of both mania and depression can be elicited by stressful life events. The extent of the contribution of life events is, however, less in bipolar than in unipolar depression, and among bipolars, less for an episode of mania than for an episode of depression (see Depue & Monroe, 1978). The relevance of these stressful life events is that they would be expected to activate feelings of low self-esteem in a person with unstable self-regard. Activation of these feelings is hypothesized as the immediate cause of an episode of either depression or mania.

Clearly, though, the *majority* of episodes of mania are not preceded by major life stressors. Given the assumption of unstable self-esteem, however, major life stress is not a necessary precipitant. Daily, more minor stressors of the type that Stone and Neale (1982) have been studying would be sufficient to intensify feelings of low self-esteem. Unfortunately, longitudinal studies of the relevance of these daily stressors for episodes of either mania or depression have not been conducted.

---

*Unfortunately, none of the coping styles in the Stone and Neale study are directly analogous to what is being discussed here. Engaging in pleasant fantasies or activities could, however, be reported in several of the categories that appear in the assessment device.

A relatively large proportion of manic episodes may be preceded by neither major nor minor life event stressors. The precipitant may be a cognitively produced intensification of low self-regard produced either by thoughts of anticipated failures or negative events or by accessing memories of past failures. Both of these mechanisms would seem plausible if we regard unstable self-esteem as a schema that guides cognitive processes such as access of self-referent information (e.g., Markus, 1977). Such a viewpoint would also be consistent with the high correlation between bipolar disorder and alcohol abuse (Reich, Davies, & Himmelhoch, 1974), with the primary effect of alcohol viewed in the cognitive context of Hull's (1981) theory.

According to Hull, alcohol decreases the sense of self-awareness by interfering with cognitive processes that are relevant to it. The theory is based on Duval and Wicklund's (1972) model, which posits that self-awareness is a state of self-focused attention in which the real and ideal selves are compared. Negative affect is the result of an unfavorable comparison and yields either avoidance of the self-awareness state or attempts to reduce the real-ideal self-discrepancy. Alcohol is postulated as a method of reducing the negative affect caused by unfavorable comparison of real and ideal selves. In a series of studies Hull and his colleagues have gathered support for the theory and shown that alcohol does interfere with the cognitive processes related to self-awareness and that it reduces negative self-evaluation following failure.

Clearly, these effects are totally consistent with the description of the bipolar that is being proposed here. Excessive alcohol use in bipolars is a method of dealing with the negative affect associated with unstable self-esteem. Interestingly, the manic episode itself exemplifies the second mechanism that Duval and Wicklund (1972) proposed as a means of reducing the negative affect associated with an unfavorable real-ideal self-comparison. The grandiose delusion in paticular could be viewed as a strategy for achieving congruence between real and ideal selves.

The Defensive Role of the Manic Episode

At issue here is the likely success of a manic episode in keeping distressing cognitions and currently distressing life events out of consciousness. At the outset, it might be noted that the various aspects of mania are not without their costs. In the long run, of course, the manic's behavioral excesses often yield unpleasant consequences—institutionalization, loss of job and friends, depletion of financial resources. Importantly, however, these are long-term consequences and may therefore have little impact as the episode develops. But what of more short-term effects, particularly those linked to the grandiose decision? First, it might be supposed that publicly talking about grandiose material would elicit negative reactions from the environment. That is possible, but it does not occur often. More typical responses are likely to be ignoring or humoring the patient. Second, it might be proposed that the grandiose delusion cannot be achieved, so failure is inevitable. While this point is correct, the argument does not consider whether failing to exceed Rockefeller, the Pope, or Hank Aaron is diagnostic, that is, yields information about the self (e.g., Carver, Antoni, & Scheier, 1985). With such extreme concepts built into the delusion, failure becomes irrelevant and nondiagnostic. Returning to Doug, the case described earlier, failing to match Rockefeller and Getty is not truly important because he is really in competition with his father.

The grandiose delusion is well suited for keeping distressing memories and distressing cognitions about current life experiences out of consciouness. First, there is a substantial literature showing the effect of distracting cognitions on pain. Performing a distracting task or engaging in distracting cognitive activity can lead to as much pain reduction as that observed in highly hypnotizable subjects given suggestions of analgesia (Spanos, McNeil, Gwynn, & Stam, 1984). Research on schema-based processing and memory is also relevant here. Although there are many controversies in this literature, a portion of it is consistent with the notion that an activated schema can direct current processing of stimuli from the environment and recall of memories. The grandiose delusion could clearly be considered as an activated schema, guiding current cognitive activity away from distressing material. Therefore, by distracting the person, guiding information processing, or occupying the limited processing capacity of conscious awareness, the grandiose delusion may function as an avoidance response, reinforced by the reduction of distress.

Grandiose delusions may have yet another function in that they produce the elated mood of the manic. Elated mood could make it less likely that the manic will access distressing cognitions from memory, an effect similar to the one discussed for alcohol. Experiments demonstrating this possibility have been reported by Bower (1981). In his studies, different moods have been hypnotically induced so that the influence of mood on recall can be studied. The research shows a congruence effect similar to the results of older research on state-dependent learning. That is, memories stored while in one mood state are recalled best when the recall trials occur while the subject is in the same mood as when he or she was learning the material. Recall declines when mood during learning and mood during recall do not match. Therefore, the positive mood of the manic episode is expected to make "positive" memories more accessible.

Is there any evidence to suggest that bipolars are defensive? Winters and Neale (1985) have found that bipolar patients in remission score the same as

TABLE 6.1. Mean Scores (and Standard Deviations) on Self-Esteem, Social Desirability, and Self-Deception

	Remitted Bipolars	Remitted Depressives	Normals
Self-esteem	233.8 (18.7)	187.0 (10.6)	240.0 (17.1)
Social Desirability	90.6 (14.8)	81.1 (10.7)	80.5 (7.9)
Self-deception	50.8 (7.9)	44.6 (3.9)	42.5 (6.4)

normals on the Epstein/O'Brien self-esteem scale. The data were complicated, however, by the fact that bipolars scored higher than both normals and a group of remitted depressives on the Marlowe-Crowne Social Desirability Scale (Crowne & Marlowe, 1964), as well as Sackeim and Gur's (1979) Self-Deception Questionnaire (see Table 6.1). Furthermore, for the bipolars the correlations between self-esteem and social desirability (.60) and between self-esteem and self-deception (.58) were highly significant while for the other two groups these correlations were much lower and were nonsignificant. The overall pattern of data, therefore, indicates that bipolars are highly defensive and that their reports of "normal" levels of self-esteem may be inaccurate.*

The Winters and Neale study also included a novel assessment of self-esteem using a pragmatic inference task. A pragmatic inference is merely a conclusion that is drawn by an individual from stated information; however, the conclusion consists of information that was not stated directly and need not logically follow from the original statement (Harris & Monaco, 1978). While people can distinguish between given information and inferred information under detailed immediate questioning, such distinctions generally are lost at later recall. This confusion between stated and inferred information is consistent with the view that people go beyond the information given and make tacit assumptions about causality, actors, instruments, and actions (Johnson, Bransford, & Solomon, 1973). Furthermore, there is growing evidence to suggest that cognitive schemas can affect information processing in such a task (e.g., Markus, 1977).

The pragmatic inference paradigm was used to investigate patterns of causal attributions in remitted manics. A causal attribution, which is merely the assignment by a person of a cause to some event (such as a good or bad

---

*Unfortunately, the data were not analyzed with the Marlowe-Crowne scale broken down into its two components, the alpha and gamma factors. These factors have been identified as reflecting self-deception and impression management (Paulhus, 1984). However, the fact that the same pattern of data was obtained with Sackeim and Gur's Self-Deception Questionnaire would be most consistent with an interpretation of these data in terms of self-deception.

event), is a form of pragmatic inference; a low self-esteem attributional pattern was defined as assigning external factors (e.g., luck) to the cause of positive events and assigning internal factors (e.g., self) to the cause of negative events. In the study, a pragmatic inference task was utilized in which subjects were read aloud short scenarios characterized by ambiguous causal attributions of events and characters. Subjects were required to make inferences about causal attributions implied within the story. It was hypothesized that remitted manics would be more likely than other subjects to infer that positive events are due to external factors and negative events to internal ones.

An example of one item is presented in Table 6.2 and the results in Table 6.3. As can be seen in the top panel, there are no between-group differences in recall of facts that were part of the inference task. The groups did, however, differ in their inferences for the failure scenarios. Both the bipolars and depressives chose more internal causes for failure than normals.

In their original report, Winters and Neale interpreted these data in the context of unreported feelings of low self-esteem. Remitted bipolars scored the same as normals and higher than remitted depressives on self-esteem, scored higher than both groups on social desirability and self-deception, and, like the remitted depressives, attributed significantly more negative events to internal causes than normals. Insofar as the tendency to infer that failures are due to internal causes reflects an underlying cognitive schema of low

---

TABLE 6.2.   An Example of One Failure Scenario from the Pragmatic Inference Task

You have been seen looking unsuccessfully for a job as a factory worker. Unemployment is a problem in the economy, especially in your field. Sales have been hurt because of foreign imports. You decide to talk to a friend about the situation, who reminds you that you've had difficulties with management because of tardiness and a poor performance record. Indeed, the last job in which you were laid off almost ended earlier when the boss threatened to fire you. Your search for a job is frustrating and you go four weeks without one.

1. With whom do you discuss your situation? (factual)
   A. A relative
   B. A friend
2. In what type of field were you previously employed? (noncausal inference)
   A. Automobile industry
   B. Computer industry
3. How long do you go without finding work? (factual)
   A. Four weeks
   B. Four months
4. Why do you have trouble finding work? (causal inference)
   A. Poor work record
   B. Poor job market

TABLE 6.3. Means (and Standard Deviations) on the Pragmatic Inference Task

	Remitted Bipolars	Remitted Depressives	Normals
Recall of Stated Facts			
Success	5.8 (1.5)	5.7 (2.0)	5.9 (.8)
Failure	5.6 (2.6)	5.8 (1.4)	6.0 (.0)
Low Self-Esteem			
Success	2.8 (.9)	2.3 (1.0)	2.6 (1.1)
Failure	3.3 (.8)	3.0 (.6)	2.3 (.8)

self-esteem, it can be inferred that remitted bipolars, like remitted depressives, have feelings of low self-esteem. The theoretical perspective developed in the present chapter suggests another interpretation. These findings may be viewed as evidence for the presumed unstable self-esteem of bipolars. The testing context, a clinic linked to their last hospitalization, and the failure cues in the task, may be sufficient to activate these feelings. The absence of between-group differences in the success stories would also be consistent with such a view.

Terminating the Episode

Some consideration needs to be given to how the episode of mania stops. It is clear that the majority of episodes of mania and depression are self-limiting, even if untreated. Why does this periodicity exist? In general, satisfactory answers to this question do not exist, nor do they exist for theories of unipolar depression.

One answer to the question lies in considering the manic episode itself in the context of the theory being considered here. The manic episode is viewed as a defense against low self-esteem, but the instability of self-esteem and the unrealistic aspects of the ideal self are still present. Therefore, over time, the defense may weaken and ultimately be shattered. Two mechanisms may be at work here. On the one hand, the bipolar may simply run down physically—the prolonged increase in activity level and little sleep for several weeks catch up with the patient. Simultaneously, as the episode progresses the manic is likely to encounter more and more negative events in the environment. This piling up of negative experience may break the defense.

Why Mania or Depression?

What accounts for whether a manic or depressive episode is elicited at a particular time? One possibility lies in the severity and cause of the negative effect that is to be avoided. Life events are more likely to precede an episode of depression than mania. Perhaps obvious life stress is more difficult to handle with a cognitive defense mechanism. In contrast, cognitive sources of negative affect that are more likely to precede a manic episode may be more readily avoided with inherently cognitive defenses. In a similar vein, the feelings of low self-esteem may be more severe before a depressive than a manic episode. The manic defenses may, therefore, be able to effectively deal with only a moderate level of low self-esteem.

Another interpretation is suggested by Wortman and Brehm's (1975) reactance hypothesis. According to their model, reactance is the initial reaction to a helplessness induction. Effort and activity are increased as the person strives to regain control. If, however, these initial efforts are unsuccessful, the typical helplessness effects ensue. The relevance of Wortman and Brehm's model lies in the possible identification of reactance and a manic episode. The manic defenses discussed earlier may indeed be the first attempts at mastering stress. If they fail, they are abandoned and a depressive episode results. If they succeed initially, they are intensified, and the manic episode results. Two further pieces of evidence are relevant. First, Wortman and Brehm's reactance theory is based principally on laboratory studies employing helplessness inductions in normal college students. It is important to note, however, that reactance effects occur only among students who are low in self-esteem (Brockner, 1979). Furthermore, high levels of self-consciousness, produced experimentally or assessed via a questionnaire, are also associated with strong reactance effects (Brockner et al., 1983). The unstable self-esteem of the manic, therefore, suggests that reactance may be a probable result of exposure to negative experiences.

CONCLUSIONS AND NEEDED DATA

In this chapter evidence has been marshaled for a theory of bipolar disorder that ascribes a defensive function to grandiose delusions. Clearly, little direct evidence supports the theory but it seems sufficiently promising to warrant data collection. What kinds of data would be most relevant?

1. Self-esteem needs to be assessed longitudinally, probably with a method that would bypass defensiveness. Two kinds of data are required. First, global self-esteem needs to be studied so that the instability can be directly demonstrated. Second, point assessments of self-esteem are needed to demonstrate the extent to which manics are reactive to life events in their self-regard. Both types of studies could be done on both remitted bipolars and persons at risk for the disorder.

2. The theme of the grandiose delusion needs to be related to the principal concerns that are part of a depressive episode as well as general, thematic life concerns. Such data would allow evaluation of a central part of the theory—that the grandiose delusion is indeed defending against some enduring area of life difficulty. Therefore the content of grandiose delusions should be congruent with enduring life concerns and themes that are a prominent part of depressive episodes. Some evidence already exists for this congruence hypothesis. Forgus and DeWolfe (1974) categorized delusions according to Murray's formulations and then compared these themes to data obtained from Guilford and Heopfner's (1971) consequences test. Support was obtained for a congruence hypothesis in general, although the data were not focused on the specific concept of congruence being considered here. Tentative support for the congruence hypothesis has also been offered by the data presented in this volume by Harrow et al.

3. Studies of cognitive processes in people at risk for bipolar disorder or in remitted patients could test their use of fantasy. Naturalistic recording of fantasies could be undertaken using Hurlbert's (1979) random time sampling procedure. In Hurlbert's method subjects carry a small boxlike device in their pockets with a wire leading to a hearing aid earplug. The device emits sounds on a random basis and the tones signal a time for subjects to describe their thoughts at the moment. Subjects could also prospectively record stressful experiences and their efforts to cope with them, particularly the use of fantasy. In addition, the articulated thoughts paradigm (Davison et al., 1984) could be used to examine cognitive processes during various experimental manipulations. In the procedure, subjects are first trained to verbalize their thoughts and then can be placed in experimental contexts to allow thoughts to be studied in response to different conditions.

In summary, the ideas presented in this chapter have clearly been speculative. Bipolar disorder, however, has been long neglected by psychological researchers and it is hoped that some of the ideas presented herein may act as a stimulus for further research.

REFERENCES

Abraham, K. (1927). Notes on the psychoanalytical investigation and treatment of manic-depressive insanity and allied conditions. In E. Jones (Ed.), *Selected papers of Karl Abraham*. London: Hogarth. (Original work published 1911.)

Andreasen, N.C. (1979). Thought, language, and communication disorders-II. Diagnostic significance. *Archives of General Psychiatry, 36,* 1325–1330.

Beck, A.T., & Ward, C.H. (1961). Dreams of depressed patients: Characteristic themes in manifest content. *Archives of General Psychiatry, 5,* 462–467.

Bower, G.H. (1981). Mood and memory. *American Psychologist, 36,* 129–148.

Brockner, J. (1979). The effects of self-esteem, success, failure, and self-consciousness on task performance. *Journal of Personality and Social Psychology, 37,* 1732–1741.

Brockner, J., Gardner, M., Bierman, J., Mahan, T., Thomas, B., Weiss, W., Winters, L., & Mitchell, A. (1983). The roles of self-esteem and self-consciousness in the Wortman-Brehm model of reactance and learned helplessness. *Journal of Personality and Social Psychology, 45,* 199–209.

Brownfain, J.J. (1952). Stability of the self-concept as a dimension of personality. *Journal of Abnormal and Social Psychology, 47,* 597–606.

Cameron, N. (1959). The paranoid pseudo community revisited. *American Journal of Sociology, 65,* 52–56.

Carlson, G.A., & Goodwin, F.K. (1973). The stages of mania: A longitudinal analysis of the manic episode. *Archives of General Psychiatry, 28,* 221–228.

Carpenter, W., Strauss, J., & Bartko, J. (1974). Use of signs and symptoms for the identification of schizophrenic patients. *Schizophrenia Bulletin, 2,* 37–49.

Carver, C.S., Antoni, M., & Scheier, M.F. (1985). Self-consciousness and self-assessment. *Journal of Personality and Social Psychology, 48,* 117–124.

Crowne, D.P., & Marlowe, D. (1964). *The approval motive.* New York: Wiley.

Davison, G.C., Feldman, P.M., & Osborn, C.E. (1984). Articulated thoughts, irrational beliefs, and fear of negative evaluation. *Cognitive Therapy and Research, 8,* 349–362.

Demo, D.H. (1985). The measurement of self-esteem: Refining our methods. *Journal of Personality and Social Psychology, 48,* 1490–1502.

Depue, R.A., & Monroe, S.M. (1978). The unipolar-bipolar distinction in the depressive disorders. *Psychological Bulletin, 85,* 1001–1030.

Depue, R.A., Slater, J.F., Wolfstetter-Kausch, H., Klein, D., Gopelrud, E., & Farr, D. (1981). A behavioral paradigm for identifying persons at risk for bipolar depressive disorder: A conceptual framework and five validation studies. *Journal of Abnormal Psychology, 90,* 381–437.

Duval, S., & Wicklund, R.A. (1972). *A theory of objective self-awareness.* New York: Academic Press.

Forgus, R.H., & DeWolfe, A.S. (1974). Coding of cognitive input in delusional patients. *Journal of Abnormal Psychology, 83,* 278–284.

Freud, S. (1921). *Group psychology and the analysis of the ego.* London: Hogarth.

Freud, S. (1950). Mourning and melancholia. In *Collected papers* (Vol. 4). London: Hogarth. (Original work published 1917.)

Guilford, J., & Hoepfner, J.P. (1971). *The analysis of intelligence.* New York: McGraw-Hill.

Harris, R.J., & Monaco, G.E. (1978). Psychology of pragmatic inference: Information processing between the lines. *Journal of Experimental Psychology, 107,* 1–22.

Hoge, D.R., & McCarthy, J.D. (1983). Issues of validity and reliability in the use of real-ideal discrepancy scores to measure self-regard. *Journal of Personality and Social Psychology, 44,* 1048–1056.

Hull, J.D. (1981). A self-awareness model of the causes and effects of alcohol consumption. *Journal of Abnormal Psychology, 90,* 586–600.

Hurlbert, R.T. (1979). Random sampling of cognitions and behavior. *Journal of Research in Personality, 13,* 103–111.

Jacobson, E. (1953). Contribution to the metapsychology of cyclothymic depression. In P. Greenacre (Ed.), *Affective disorders.* New York: International Universities Press.

Johnson, M.K., Bransford, J.D., & Solomon, S.K. (1973). Memory for tacit implications of sentences. *Journal of Experimental Psychology, 98,* 203–225.

Johnson, M.K., Raye, C.L. (1981). Reality monitoring. *Psychological Review, 88,* 67–85.

Johnson, M.K., Raye, C.L., Wang, A.Y., & Taylor, T.H. (1979). Fact and fantasy: The role of accuracy and variability in confusing imagination with perceptual experiences. *Journal of Experimental Psychology: Human Learning, and Memory, 5,* 229–240.

Kagan, D.L., & Oltmanns, T.F. (1981). Matched tasks for measuring single-word referential communications: The performance of patients with schizophrenic and affective disorders. *Journal of Abnormal Psychology, 90,* 204–212.

Klein, M. (1968). A contribution to the psychogenesis of manic-depressive states. In W. Gaylin (Ed.), *The meaning of despair.* New York: Science House.

Kugle, C.L., Clements, R.O., & Powell, P.M. (1983). Level and stability of self-esteem in relation to academic behavior of second graders. *Journal of Personality and Social Psychology, 44,* 201–207.

Leff, J.P., Fischer, M., & Bertelsen, A.C. (1976). A cross-national epidemiological study of mania. *British Journal of Psychiatry, 129,* 428–442.

Lewicki, P. (1984). Self-schema and social information processing. *Journal of Personality and Social Psychology, 47,* 1177–1190.

McVane, J.R., Mange, J.D., Brown, W.A., & Zayat, M. (1978). Psychological functioning of bipolar manic-depressives in remission. *Archives of General Psychiatry, 35,* 1351–1354.

Maher, B.A. (1974). Delusional thinking and perceptual disorder. *Journal of Individual Psychology, 30,* 98–113.

Markus, H. (1977). Self-schemata and processing information about the self. *Journal of Personality and Social Psychology, 35,* 63–78.

Neale, J.M., Oltmanns, T.F., & Harvey, P.D. (1985). The need to relate cognitive deficits to specific behavioral referents of schizophrenia. *Schizophrenia Bulletin, 2,* 286–291.

O'Brien, E.J. (1980). *The self-report inventory.* Unpublished manuscript, University of Massachusetts.

Paulhus, D.L. (1984). Two-component models of socially desirable responding. *Journal of Personality and Social Psychology, 46,* 598–609.

Rado, S. (1928). The problem of melancholia. *International Journal of Psychoanalysis, 90,* 420–438.

Reich, L.H., Davies, R.K., & Himmelhoch, J.M. (1974). Excessive alcohol use in manic-depressive illness. *American Journal of Psychiatry, 131,* 83–89.

Rochester, S.R., & Martin, J.R. (1979). *Crazy talk.* New York: Plenum Press.

Sackeim, J.A., & Gur, R.C. (1979). Self-deception, other deception, and self-reported psychopathology. *Journal of Consulting and Clinical Psychology, 47,* 213–215.

Savin-Williams, R.C., & Demp, D.H. (1983). Situational and transsituational determinants of adolescent self-feelings. *Journal of Personality and Social Psychology, 44,* 824–833.

Stone, A.A., & Neale, J.M. (1982). Development of a methodology for assessing daily experiences. In A. Baum & J. Singer (Eds.), *Advances in environmental psychology* (Vol. 4). Hillsdale, NJ: Erlbaum.

Stone, A.A., & Neale, J.M. (1984). Development of a method for assessing daily coping. *Journal of Personality and Social Psychology, 46,* 892–906.

Strauss, J. (1969). Hallucinations and delusions as points on a continua function. *Archives of General Psychiatry, 21,* 581–586.

Spanos, N.P., McNeil, C., Gwynn, M.I., & Stam, H.J. (1984). Effects of suggestion and distraction on reported pain in subjects high and low on hypnotic susceptibility. *Journal of Abnormal Psychology, 93,* 277–284.

Winters, K.C., & Neale, J.M. (1983). Delusions and delusional thinking in psychotics: A review of the literature. *Clinical Psychology Review, 3,* 227–253.

Winters, K.C., & Neale, J.M. (1985). Mania and low self-esteem. *Journal of Abnormal Psychology, 94,* 252–290.

World Health Organization. (1973). *The international pilot study of schizophrenia.* Geneva: Author.

Wortman, C.B., & Brehm, J. (1975). Responses to uncontrollable outcomes: An integration of reactance theory and the learned helplessness model. In L. Berkowitz (Ed.), *Advances in experimental social psychology* (Vol. 8). New York: Academic Press.

CHAPTER 7

On the Experimental Psychopathology of Delusions

MILTON E. STRAUSS

The Johns Hopkins University

The empirical study of paranoid disorders—where delusional thinking is the core feature—has a long history. These disorders are among the most extensively studied forms of psychopathology, beginning with Freud's (1911/1957) famous case of the jurist Schreber. There is a large literature of both clinical psychiatric and experimental psychopathological research (cf. Schooler & Feldman, 1967; Wolowitz & Shorkey, 1969). Over the years, the approaches taken to the study of delusions by experimental psychopathologists have varied. Those most prominent at any point in time reflect the prevailing conceptual structure of psychology in that period.

The first and longest lived theory of delusional thinking—Freud's—emphasized unconscious motivational processes. Not surprisingly, the earlier empirical studies attempting to garner support for this hypothesis of a homoerotic basis of paranoid delusions used clinical records and, later, projective techniques (cf. Wolowitz, 1971). These methods have limited acceptability among experimentally oriented investigators, who point to a lack of empirical support for psychodynamic hypotheses (e.g., Oltmanns, this volume). However, there is interesting empirical work on the psychodynamics of delusions that falls more within the mainstream of experimental psychopathology.

Wolowitz (1965) was interested in the question of the motivational basis of the delusions of persecution and of grandeur seen in male paranoid schizophrenics. His study is an ingenious test of the neo-Freudian hypothesis that paranoid symptomatology is based on an attraction and repulsion to

Preparation of this chapter was supported in part by the Scottish-Rite Schizophrenia Research Program and National Institute of Mental Health Grant MH31536-06. I thank Ms. Casey Camponeschi for her editorial advice.

power in like-sexed persons. His experiment made use of the concepts and methods of general experimental psychology, in particular Miller's then prominent stimulus-response approach-avoidance conflict model.

Wolowitz (1965) had paranoid and nonparanoid schizophrenic men place pictures of men and women at the distance at which each "looked best." According to Miller (cited in Wolowitz, 1965), the strength of approach and avoidance tendencies toward an object varies as a function of distance from that object. The model also proposes that the strength of avoidance tendencies increases more rapidly than the strength of approach tendencies with nearness to a goal object, and that these tendencies interact algebraically to determine the distance a male places between himself and a conflictual goal. The neo-Freudian hypothesis leads to the prediction of a correlation between the distance at which the male paranoids place pictures of males and independently obtained ratings of perceived power; conversely, the hypothesis predicts that there should be no such relationship for photos of females. The results were consistent with this idea and not with the hypothesis of more undifferentiated homoerotic conflicts among paranoids.

Wolowitz's (1905) study is particularly pertinent because, like many of the contributors to this volume, he approaches a problem of clinical interest from an experimental-psychological perspective. This approach permits a more direct operationalization of concepts and more explicit tests of hypotheses than do clinically based frameworks alone. Other examples of such research in the psychodynamic tradition can certainly be found. Zamansky (1958), for example, studied the homoerotic hypothesis of paranoia by measuring the amount of time patients looked at photos of males or females in a size discrimination task. Wolowitz and Shorkey (1966, 1969) further explored the neo-Freudian power hypothesis in analyses of TAT stories using a validated measure of power motivation.

The experimental-psychological study of psychodynamic hypotheses, however, has not made distinctions that more contemporary experimentally oriented investigators believe are critical. Maher's analysis, for one, stresses the importance of separately treating questions about content and form (Maher, 1974; Maher & Ross, 1984; see also Maher, this volume). The distinction between content and form is often unclear in psychodynamically grounded research and theory. Wolowitz's (1965) study, described above, seems more pertinent to the themes of paranoid delusions than to their origins—that is, to the questions of why it is that a person has a delusion at all. Psychodynamically oriented investigators seem more interested in understanding the themes of delusions than in the mechanisms that give rise to the symptom (cf. Wolowitz's 1971 review).

The emphasis on motivational processes stands in contrast with the more recent literature. Maher (1974), for example, emphasizes perceptual factors in accounting for the origins of delusions. This is in keeping with a general shift from motivational concepts toward cognitive concepts in psychology. Recall for a moment the "new look" in preception of the 1950s, particularly the phenomena of perceptual defense and subception. Motivational concepts were proposed as explanations, prompting much research, but, as Dixon's (1981) recent monograph summarizes, these phenomena proved more tractable when approached in terms of cognitive processes and mechanisms, their dynamic appearance notwithstanding (cf. Dixon, 1981).

Maher would offer that the same is true for understanding delusions (Maher, 1974; Maher & Ross, 1984; see also Maher, this volume). He makes the case for both the perceptual or attributional basis of delusions, and their grounding in the proclivity of humans to make sense of things—particularly the inclination to see causality in covariation or coincidence. These proclivities are well documented in the recent literature of cognitive and social psychology. Judging from Anderson's (1980) text, it seems that, indeed, normal adults do not sharply differentiate deduction from induction.

It is also evident from that text that our understanding of how people draw conclusions has far to go. Hemsley and Garety (1986) have recently suggested that a Bayesian normative perspective on normal belief formation and maintenance may be a useful framework within which to study the relations between cognitive processes and perceptual distortions, such as hallucinations, or moods in the genesis of delusions. The further development of theories about how people ascribe meaning to experience may make possible more specific or detailed empirical tests of the idea that in delusions normal cognitive processes are applied to unusual data. It is a promising hypothesis, but only that.

The working hypothesis of "normal processes applied to unusual data," like other accounts, however, can be criticized from a number of points of view. There is a risk that cognitive psychological models may be construed too narrowly. Johnson's work (this volume), though consistent with Maher's viewpoint, describes the difficulty that sometimes occurs in separating perception and imagination. Gjerde (1983), in a recent review of theories of attentional dysfunction in schizophrenia, voiced concern that the cognitive psychology of schizophrenia is about "cold" cognition. Cognitive processing of motivationally significant information ("hot" cognition) would seem understudied in that field, and there is the risk of underemphasis in the contemporary experimental psychopathology of delusions as well. Neale's (this volume) analysis of delusions in mania underscores the continued importance of "dynamic" or motivational concepts in the empirical study of delusions.

Currently available evidence for the attributional or perceptual basis of delusions is only correlational, but this should not be of great concern at this stage in the development of the model. Though the potential falsifiability of a theory is critical, demonstration studies are important early on. Clinical studies such as that done by Johnson, Ross, and Mastria (1977) are of great value in deciding whether a theoretical view has any promise. These authors reported the treatment of a patient with a monosymptomatic delusion of having intercourse with a "warm form." Their observations of the behavior of the patient suggested that he was misattributing sensations associated with subtle masturbatory activity. A reattributional treatment program based on this supposition was effective. Although not probative, reports such as this one are encouraging of a misattributional formulation.

Demonstrations are sometimes much more to the point than experiments because they may stay closer to the phenomena of interest. The details of phenomena like delusional ideas are important in the absence of a well-grounded model. For that reason, there is less relevance for an experimental-psychological theory of delusions in, for example, the Zimbardo, Andersen, and Kabat (1981) *experiment* than in the Nielsen *demonstration* (cited in Maher, 1974; see also Maher, this volume). The behavior, self-report, and personality test responses of Zimbardo's experimental subjects do not include delusional thinking, while the behavior of Nielsen's apparently does. The characterization of the subjects in the Zimbardo et al. published report is reminiscent of the paranoid character, as described by David Shapiro (1965), rather than delusional disorder. It would seem important to clearly differentiate between delusion as a specific symptom and as a personality pattern, although, as Shapiro (1965) argues, there may be relationships between them.

An analog experiment establishes the plausibility of a hypothesis. The likely importance of a plausible hypothesis, however, depends on the adequacy or reasonableness of the analog as a model. The evaluation of that would seem to require the integration of experimental research with clinical studies.

The existence of an association between characteristics should not be taken to imply similar mechanisms or a direct causal link. Perhaps, as Maher (this volume) implies, the observed correlation between unappreciated sensory loss and paraphrenic delusions reflects a causal association. However, it is not likely to be a simple or direct effect, for the correlation itself is not simple. The occurrence of paraphrenia in conjunction with deafness seems to be moderated by social history and personological characteristics, including some of the traits studied by Zimbardo et al. (1981; cf. Kay & Roth, 1961). It is probably safe to assume that there are many more people with undiagnosed deafness with paranoid-like traits than with full-blown delusional disorders. Identifying individual differences in the proclivity to develop delusions, whether due to experiential anomalies or coincidence thinking, remains a problem for research and theory.

Classical, more clinically based analyses of the development of paranoid disorders have focused on psychodynamic and experiential variables in accounting for individual differences (e.g., Heilbrun & Bronson, 1975; Shapiro, 1965). On the other hand, the experiences of "relief" or "significance" and the "delusional mood" in Maher's (1974, see also this volume) cognitive-perceptual account are assumed to have neural bases. A focus on neural or physiological variables as individual differences factors would seem in keeping with the increasingly psychobiological perspective that can be seen in experimental psychology, although analyses in terms of self-perception and self-evaluation are plausible as well (see Higgins & Moretti, this volume).

What the biological factors might be is not yet clear. Perhaps, akin to the way earlier experimental psychopathological research was influenced by dynamic personality psychology, current work will become influenced by ideas in neuropsychology and behavioral neurology. Baer (1979), for example, describes a concept of sensory-limbic hyperconnectiveness in developing ideas about the propensity of temporal lobe epileptics, particularly those with left hemisphere foci, to impute particular significance to trivial stimuli, that is, to say things that are seen by clinicians as having paranoid delusional qualities.* Although speculative, the extension of these ideas to a more general set of hypotheses about corticolimbic interactions in cognitive and affective processes (Baer, 1983) might provide a plausible neurological model of vulnerability to the development of delusions. Of course, the diversity of medical and psychiatric disorders in which delusions may be seen (Maher & Ross, 1984; see also Maher, this volume) and their diverse form make unlikely the hypothesis of a single common cause (see Neale, this volume).

That delusions occur in a variety of disorders has methodological as well as theoretical implications. A review of the psychological literature on delusions would probably show that few studies examine the characteristics of delusional patients as such. Instead, groups in which delusions are common are compared with groups in which delusions are not common or predominant symptoms. This is a limited and unsuitably indirect approach. The modal contrast ought not to be of paranoid schizophrenics, nonparanoid schizophrenics, and controls. By studying delusions in schizophrenia, and often only indirectly, we are unduly restricting our focus and introducing the confounding variables of that particular disorder. As Maher (this volume) suggests, it may well be more useful to study the relation of delusions to other attributes, categorizing patients in terms of the formal characteristics of their delusions, rather than in terms of their illness or condition.

---

*I thank Jason Brandt for bringing this work to my attention.

The empirical study of delusions began in the evaluation of the psychoanalytic theory of paranoia. At the conclusion of the case used to illustrate the theory—that of Schreber—Freud (1911/1959, pp. 465–466) wrote: "It remains for the future to decide whether there is more delusion in my theory than I should like to admit, or whether there is more truth in Schreber's delusion than other people are as yet prepared to believe."

It turned out, in fact, that there was more truth in Schreber's delusion (MacAlpine & Hunter, 1953; Niederland, 1963) than Freud could know. Contemporary experimental psychopathologists would suggest that there turned out to be less truth in Freud's beliefs. Future empirical work and developments in psychological theory will undoubtedly permit a similar decision about contemporary experimental psychological analyses of delusions.

REFERENCES

Anderson, J.R. (1980). *Cognitive psychology and its implications*. San Francisco: Freeman.

Baer, D.M. (1979). The temporal lobes: An approach to the study of organic behavioral changes. In M.S. Gazzaniga (Ed.), *Handbook of behavioral neurobiology: Vol. 2. Neuropsychology*. New York: Plenum Press.

Baer, D.M. (1983). Hemispheric specialization and the neurology of emotion. *Archives of Neurology, 19*, 195–202.

Dixon, N.F. (1981). *Preconscious processing*. New York: Wiley.

Freud, S. (1957). Psychoanalytic notes upon an autobiographical account of a case of paranoia (*dementia paranoides*). In A. Strachey & J. Strachey (Eds.), *Sigmund Freud Collected Papers* (Vol. 3). New York: Basic Books. (Original work published 1911.)

Gjerde, P.F. (1983). Attentional capacity dysfunction and arousal in schizophrenia. *Psychological Bulletin, 93*, 57–72.

Heilbrun, A.B., Jr., & Bronson, N. (1975). Fabrication of delusional thinking in normals. *Journal of Abnormal Psychology, 84*, 422–425.

Hemsley, D.R., & Garety, P.A. (1986). The formation and maintenance of delusions: A Bayesian analysis. *British Journal of Psychiatry, 149*, 51–56.

Johnson, W., Ross, J., & Mastria, M. (1977). Delusional behavior: An attributional analysis of development and modification. *Journal of Abnormal Psychology, 86*, 421–426.

Kay, D.W.K., & Roth, M. (1961). Environmental and hereditary factors in the schizophrenia of old age ("Late Paraphrenia") and their bearing on the general problem of causation in schizophrenia. *Journal of Mental Science, 107*, 649–686.

MacAlpine, I., & Hunter, R.A. (1953). The Schreber case. *Psychiatric Quarterly, 22*, 238–268.

Maher, B.A. (1974). Delusional thinking and perceptual disorder. *Journal of Individual Psychology, 30,* 98–113.

Maher, B.A., & Ross, J.S. (1984). Delusions. In H.E. Adams & S.B. Sutker (Eds.), *Comprehensive handbook of psychopathology.* New York: Plenum Press.

Niederland, W.G. (1963). Further data and memorabilia pertaining to the Schreber case. *International Journal of Psychoanalysis, 44,* 208–212.

Schooler, C., & Feldman, S.E. (1967). *Experimental studies of schizophrenia.* Goleta, CA: Psychonomic Press.

Shapiro, D. (1965). *Neurotic styles.* New York: Basic Books.

Wolowitz, H.M. (1965). Attraction and aversion to power: A psychoanalytic conflict theory of homosexuality in male paranoids. *Journal of Abnormal Psychology, 70,* 360–370.

Wolowitz, H.M. (1971). The validity of the psychoanalytic theory of paranoid dynamics evaluated from the available experimental evidence. *Psychiatry, 34,* 358–377.

Wolowitz, H.M., & Shorkey, C. (1966). Power themes in the TAT stories of paranoid schizophrenic males. *Journal of Projective and Personality Assessment, 30,* 591–596.

Wolowitz, H.M., & Shorkey, C. (1969). Power motivation in male paranoid children. *Psychiatry, 32,* 459–466.

Zamansky, H.S. (1958). An investigation of the psychoanalytic theory of paranoid delusions. *Journal of Personality, 26,* 410–425.

Zimbardo, P.G., Andersen, S.M., & Kabat, L.G. (1981). Induced hearing deficit generates experimental paranoia. *Science, 212,* 1529–1531.

PART 2

Descriptions and Definitions

CHAPTER 8

The Genesis of Delusions

LOREN J. CHAPMAN and JEAN P. CHAPMAN

University of Wisconsin-Madison

Delusions occur in a surprisingly wide range of clinical conditions. Manschreck (1979) and Maher and Ross (1984) have pointed to more than 75 different clinical conditions that are accompanied by delusions. Nevertheless, the psychological processes involved in the development and maintenance of delusions are still a matter of controversy.

We will present evidence on two issues concerning the genesis of delusions. First, we will discuss the relationship between the delusions of psychotic patients and the less deviant but still aberrant beliefs that they held before they became psychotic. Then, more speculatively, we will discuss the relationship of delusions to anomalous perceptual experiences and to thought disorder. We will attempt to specify the nature of the thought disorder that makes delusions possible.

We studied 162 college students who scored deviantly high (2.0 or more standard deviations above the mean) on one or both of two scales that were intended to measure proneness to schizophrenia. Our deviant subjects were less disturbed, on the average, than most delusional persons, although many were found to have either delusions or aberrant beliefs. We define aberrant beliefs as delusionlike ideas, that is, attenuated forms of delusions.

We interviewed these subjects on two occasions, 25 months apart, in the context of a broader prospective investigation of the characteristics of hypothetically schizophrenia-prone individuals. About half of the subjects qualified for the *Diagnostic and Statistical Manual of Mental Disorders* (DSM-III) (American Psychiatric Association [APA], 1980) diagnosis of schizotypal personality disorder at their initial interview, although most of

This research was supported by a Research Grant (MH-31067) from the National Institute of Mental Health, United States Public Health Service.

The authors are indebted to Terry Fujioka, Laurie Frost, John Allen, and Rebecca Laird for their critical comments on an earlier draft of the manuscript.

them had not received any clinical attention. The second interview was conducted to determine if any of the subjects had been treated for psychosis during the 25-month interim.

We have used several screening instruments in this work but will focus here on subjects identified by the Perceptual Aberration Scale (Chapman, Chapman, & Raulin, 1978) and the Magical Ideation Scale (Eckblad & Chapman, 1983). The Perceptual Aberration Scale consists of 35 true-false items designed to measure distortions in the perception of one's own body and distortions in the perception of one's environment. These items ask about episodes such as feeling that parts of one's body are detached, experiencing difficulty in distinguishing where one's body ends and other objects begin, and having feelings that one's body is altered, dead, unreal, or not one's own. The 30-item Magical Ideation Scale is designed to measure belief in forms of causation that by conventional standards in our culture are invalid, such as thought transmission, psychokinetic effects, precognition, and the transfer of psychical energies between people. The Magical Ideation Scale has obvious face validity for identifying persons with delusional beliefs, but the Perceptual Aberration Scale identifies them as accurately. Because the two scales correlate around .70 and identify similar subjects (Chapman, Chapman, & Miller, 1982), we treat high scores on either of the two scales as a single group in most of our research.

The interview we used was a modified version of the Schedule for Affective Disorders and Schizophrenia-Lifetime Version (SADS-L) (Spitzer & Endicott, 1977). The modifications consist of the addition of questions about attenuated forms of many of the same symptoms that are used in the SADS-L to diagnose psychosis. These symptoms are (1) transmission of thoughts, (2) passivity experiences, (3) auditory hallucinations, (4) thought withdrawal, (5) delusions, and (6) visual hallucinations. Each of the six symptom classes and their attenuated forms are scored for deviancy on a continuum of 1 to 11. Rating values for each of 80 types of deviant experience were obtained from a panel of six well-known psychopathologists and were averaged to construct a rating manual (Chapman & Chapman, 1980). The manual gives rating values for each type of deviant experience with the proviso that values one point higher or one point lower than the listed value are given for experiences that are more deviant or less deviant than the average experience of that type. Variations in deviancy are judged by bizarreness of content, amount of time preoccupied with the experience, frequency and duration of the experience, and amount of cultural support for the experience. A score of 1 is for a normal experience, that is, a nondeviant experience. Rating of 2 to 5 are for experiences that are judged to be psychoticlike but are not sufficiently deviant to be labeled psychotic. Ratings of 6 to 11 are for experiences that are judged to be of psychotic severity, that is, resembling the experiences of clinical psychotics. (This rating does not mean, however, that the subject should be diagnosed as psychotic, because much more disorder than an occasional psychotic experience is required for such a diagnosis.)

The dimension of delusions and their attenuated form, aberrant beliefs, is of special interest here. We score as deviant only those beliefs that have a personal flavor—that is, are related to oneself—because most delusions of psychotics have personal relevance. For example, a belief that some people can hypnotize others merely by a glance of the eyes would not qualify as deviant, but a subject's belief that he does this himself would qualify, as would a belief that someone else hypnotizes him in that manner. Firm belief in aberrant ideas is scored higher than mere suspicion or wavering belief. Reports of nonbizarre ideas of reference, of mistreatment, or of being observed are not severely delusional and therefore receive a modal score of 4. For example, if a woman reports that she sometimes gets the idea that all her professors are out to flunk her and then realizes that it isn't true, the belief is scored 4. If a man reports that for three months after arriving in town he felt that strangers on the street were staring at him, the score is 5. When a man reports that he is always getting the idea that people are saying derogatory things about him, but realizes later that it isn't true, or that when he walks into a room, he frequently believes that everyone is talking about him but then later realizes that it isn't true, the score is 3.

At the other end of the severity dimension is a bizarre delusional belief. Here the term *bizarre* is defined by DSM-III (APA, 1980) standards as a belief that could not possibly be true, is absurd or fantastic, and receives no direct support from the person's religious or subcultural background. An example is the suspicion by one of our subjects that some of his alien thoughts were injected into his head by a hypodermic needle while he slept. We scored this as a 7 rather than a 10 or 11 because the subject merely suspected that this happened rather than believing it firmly. Scores in the range of 4 to 6 are given for delusional beliefs that are logically consistent with the tenets of the subject's religious or cultural group, although the belief would be decisively rejected by most members of that group. An example is the belief by an only mildly religious subject of Protestant background that an evil spirit visited her in an attempt to possess her (score of 6).

Delusions and other personally relevant aberrant beliefs constitute only one of six classes of symptoms or experiences that the interviewers inquired about. The other five classes of symptoms were usually scored as deviant only if the subject reported having had an aberrant belief or delusion concerning the experience. The deviancy of the belief largely determined the score. For example, if a man has violent sexual thoughts that he experiences as not his own, and his explanation is that he is being influenced by his roommate who talks a lot about violent sex, the experience is scored as only slightly deviant (a score of 2). On the other hand, if he suspects that the devil forced him to have those thoughts or feelings, the score is in a range of 3 to 5, the exact score depending on the subject's religious background. If he is certain, rather than merely suspicious, that the devil is responsible, the experience is scored in the range of 5 to 7. If he believes that another human being seized control of his body or mind to think these thoughts, the score is 10.

We interviewed 162 subjects identified as psychosis prone on the basis of the two scales and 158 control subjects on two occasions about 25 months apart. At the initial interview, psychotic experiences (scored 6 to 11) were reported by 8 percent of the identified subjects (perceptual aberration-magical ideation subjects) and less than 1 percent of the control subjects. Psychoticlike experiences in the range of scores from 3 to 5 were reported by 55 percent of the perceptual aberration-magical ideation subjects and 14 percent of the control subjects. Almost all of these deviant experiences involved aberrant beliefs, although the experiences were usually scored in one of the other categories of symptoms. For example, some subjects reported the experience and belief that other people put thoughts into their heads by action at a distance. Other subjects reported the experience, with belief, that other people heard their thoughts. We scored the first kind of experience as a passivity experience and the second as thought transmission, although an aberrant belief was an integral feature of both kinds of experience.

THE CONTINUITY OF ABERRANT BELIEFS AND DELUSIONS

The aberrant beliefs of our subjects seemed to be continuous with full-fledged delusions both in content and in degree of deviancy. The aberrant beliefs had themes similar to those of psychotic delusions. For example, many of our subjects believed their thoughts were read, a belief that seems similar to but less deviant than the psychotic delusion that one's thoughts are broadcast. Other subjects reported recurrent unrealistic beliefs of being talked about—beliefs similar to, but milder than, more fully developed delusions of reference. Our subjects reported symptoms at all degrees of deviancy between mildly deviant beliefs and full-fledged psychotic delusions, but reported the mildly deviant beliefs much more often. Plotting the frequency of such beliefs on a continuum of deviancy, one finds that the more deviant the belief, the more uncommon it was. Although we have gathered data on this matter systematically only for these hypothetically psychosis-prone subjects and control subjects, our own clinical experience indicates that the same phenomenon holds true for schizophrenics also. Among schizophrenics, aberrant beliefs of nonpsychotic deviancy are, we believe, even more common than full-fledged delusions. However, the literature on schizophrenia has paid little attention to the presence or frequency of these nonpsychotic aberrant beliefs because the more grossly delusional beliefs are more important for diagnosis.

Another sense in which delusions are continuous with aberrant beliefs is that many of the nonpsychotic aberrant beliefs in the premorbid period are similar to the same patient's psychotic delusional beliefs in later psychotic episodes. Strauss (1969) has reported this on the basis of his clinical experience, as have Gillies (1958) and James Chapman (1966). We have observed a similar phenomenon in our subjects. Between the first and second interview, three of our perceptual aberration-magical ideation subjects, but none of the control subjects, received their first clinical treatment for psychosis. Our subjects had, of course, passed through only a very small portion of their total risk for psychosis during this 25-month period. One subject had become a DSM-III (APA, 1980) chronic schizophrenic, another was suffering from a bipolar disorder with psychotic features, and the third had been treated on an outpatient basis for a paranoid delusion. All three of these subjects reported at their first interview, before they became psychotic, aberrant experiences and beliefs that were somewhat similar in content to the psychotic experiences and delusions that they exhibited later when they were treated for their psychoses.

The subject who developed a chronic schizophrenic disorder reported at the first interview that he had a frequent inner voice that commented on his behavior by giving him moral admonitions. He interpreted the voice as that of an archangel. (We score both outer voices and inner voices, but we label an inner experience as a voice only if the subject states, in response to questioning, that the experience was more like a voice than like thoughts, that he could distinguish between this kind of experience and his usual thoughts, and, in addition, that the experience was more like being talked to than like thinking to oneself.) The subject also reported occasional outer voice experiences. For example, on one occasion, when he was in the basement of his parents' home, he heard a voice that seemed to come from the corner of the room say, "Life is more meaningful than it seems." At the time it seemed to him that the voice might be that of his paternal grandfather whom he had never seen. The subject justified this interpretation by explaining that he had always been involved with the supernatural. Both of these voice experiences are on the margin between psychoticlike and psychotic and received scores of 5 or 6 in our scoring system. When he later was treated for psychosis, this man was having much more frequent external voice experiences, and he had deviant ideas about the messages. For example, he heard the picture of Christ in his local church speaking to him as an outer voice.

He believed the experience was veridical and, in response to the hallucinated instruction, the subject ran naked through the snow. This hallucination received the very deviant score of 8, in part because of the deviancy of the subject's delusional belief about his perceptual experience. He heard many other voices as well, some of which he attributed to human persons and some to spirits. He also reported having believed that the police who arrested him for public nakedness were devils who were taking him to Satan to be tortured (score of 8 for delusional belief). All of these delusions had the same religious flavor as his prepsychotic aberrant belief that his voice of conscience was that of an archangel. During this psychotic episode, however, he also had another delusion that the world was coming to an end, a belief that had little similarity to his reported prepsychotic aberrant beliefs.

The subject who developed a bipolar disorder also reported at her first interview attenuated versions of the same kinds of symptoms and beliefs that she showed more fully when she was clinically psychotic. At her first interview, she related that she sometimes heard a variety of sounds, noises, and what she called "musical pictures" as both inner and outer experiences. She said that she could hear them whenever she shut everything else out, and that she heard them without trying to do so a couple of times a week. Because she had never believed that the sounds were veridical, these experiences were not scored. At the second interview she reported that during her psychosis, she had heard a great deal of buzzing and music. She also heard external voices that, at the time of the experience, she regarded as veridical. She reported that she held conversations with the voices, although she wasn't able to tell us afterward who she believed the people were (score of 8 for auditory hallucination). The delusional belief in the reality of the voices was necessary for receiving the score.

Our paranoid patient, at her first interview, described herself as being overly sensitive to the possibility that other people were prejudiced against her because she was Jewish. She reported that every week or two something would happen that she would misinterpret as evidence of an anti-Semitic bias, although later she would realize there had been little or no justification for that interpretation. She used the term "paranoid" to describe her problem. These beliefs were only mildly psychoticlike and earned a 3 for aberrant beliefs. At her follow-up interview she related having had a full-fledged persecutory delusion, but with somewhat different content. She believed that two scientists had placed her in her local community in order to watch her and test her behavior on a day-to-day basis and were plotting to do her harm (score of 9). Nevertheless, she recognized these concerns as deviant and sought therapy for them.

Nine other perceptual aberration-magical ideation subjects who were not treated for psychosis also reported at the second interview isolated psychotic symptoms with delusions that were more deviant than, but rather similar to, symptoms they had reported at the first interview. We speculate that these subjects may be moving toward overt psychosis. For example, one female subject at her first interview entertained tentatively the possibility that other people could read her mind. When asked how they could do this, she explained that it was by the expression on her face or by her eyes, although it seemed to her when it happened that it might be thought reading (score of 3). At her second interview, she related several recent instances of the more deviant experience and belief that other people heard her thoughts through their ears. She said that they heard her thoughts just as though she was saying them out loud, and she fully believed in the validity of the experience (score of 8).

A similar change occurred in this subject's voice experiences. She initially reported two mildly deviant voice experiences. One was hearing her own voice as an inner voice of conscience criticizing her (score of 2) and the other was an outer voice of someone occasionally speaking her name a single time (no score—we do not judge the hearing of one's name as deviant enough to be scored unless it occurs as many as three times within an hour). In the follow-up interview, she described two inner voices, one of which was good and one bad, although the voices sometimes deceived her as to which was which. She believed that the good voice might be that of God but was uncertain about the identity of the bad voice (score of 6). Moreover, she reported an outer voice that not only called her name but occasionally admonished her as to proper behavior. When asked for her explanation of that voice, she said that she never thought about where it came from or who it was (score of 6).

The same subject showed an increased deviancy of paranoid beliefs. At the first interview, she described intense concern as often as once a week that someone whom she encountered was talking about her (score of 3). At the second interview, she continued to have these concerns but also described the fear that one or another person wanted to kill her, and that the man for whom she worked was out to get her (score of 5). Later follow-up will enable us to determine if she and the other of these nine subjects are truly decompensating into clinical psychosis.

THE ROLE OF ANOMALOUS EXPERIENCES IN THE GENESIS OF DELUSIONS

Psychopathologists do not agree about how anomalous experiences contribute to the genesis of delusions. Maher has offered the suggestion both in this volume and in earlier papers (Maher, 1974; Maher & Ross, 1984) that all delusions can be understood as responses to anomalous experience. An anomalous experience is one that seems inexplicable in terms of normal principles of causation. We would suggest that examples include hearing voices when no source of the voice is evident, or experiencing thoughts without awareness of participating in the act of thinking those thoughts. Maher contends that delusions are rational and systematic explanations of anomalous experiences and, given the intensity of those experiences, are reasonable conclusions. He believes the explanations are arrived at by the same process that scientists use to account for their observations. Like scientists, delusional patients investigate alternative interpretations before settling on a delusional one. Maher (1974) suggests that the anomalous experience that forms the basis of the delusion may arise in part from the defect in attentional focusing described by McGhie and Chapman (1961). The patient is unable to distinguish relevant from irrelevant data and cannot select the stimuli to which he or she responds. Instead, Maher (1974, p. 103) stated, the patient is "impressed with the significance of various discrete stimuli as they gain momentary control of his attentional focus," and responds accordingly. In the present volume, Maher suggests additional reasons why some patients may select inappropriate data. Maher's emphasis on the reasonableness of delusional interpretations of available data seems to imply that anyone who had such experiences would interpret the experiences in a delusional way.

We believe that the subjects interviewed in the present study are a useful source of data on this issue. Because they were less deeply disturbed than clinical psychotics, they were able to give a better account of the reasons for their beliefs than can clinical psychotics. Some of these beliefs were sufficiently deviant to be termed delusional while others were merely aberrant. We believe that the same principles account for both delusions and aberrant beliefs.

The Relation of Delusions and Aberrant Beliefs to Anomalous Experiences

If delusions are reasonable interpretations of anomalous experiences, subjects with similar experiences should have similar beliefs. We examined the relationship of beliefs to experiences in our subjects and found that subjects responded to similar experiences with beliefs that ranged from the normal to the fully delusional. We found some cases in which a delusion was the clear result of an anomalous perceptual experience because acceptance of the veridicality of the experience demanded, or almost demanded, a delusional belief. Other subjects reported delusions or aberrant beliefs that had no apparent relationship to any unusual experiences. Still others reported delusions that had some relation to their unusual experiences, but yet were not necessary, or even reasonable, interpretations of those experiences.

Among those whose aberrant beliefs clearly reflected anomalous experiences were subjects who actually felt thoughts leaving their heads and going to the ears or to the minds of other people. The belief in thought transmission directly reflected this perceptual experience. Indeed, the belief was required if the subject accepted the experience as veridical. Another subject observed bad thoughts in her mind without experiencing herself as a participant in thinking them. Her interpretation that an evil spirit had seized control of her mind might be viewed as a reasonable interpretation of that experience.

Far more common, however, were anomalous experiences that did not demand any particular interpretation, and in response to which subjects differed widely in the deviancy of their beliefs about the event. The subject's interpretation of the experience determined its deviancy. One good example is voice experiences, which can be interpreted in either a deviant or nondeviant manner. Many of our subjects described vivid inner voices that criticized their behavior. These voice experiences must be viewed as anomalous sensory events. Yet, there was a striking variation in beliefs about these voices. The most common interpretation, even by subjects who felt tormented by the voices and who did not recognize the voice as their own, was that the voice represented their own conscience or represented the incorporation of parental admonitions (score of 2). A few subjects, however, believed that the voices truly represented the intercession of other people. For example, one young woman, from a different series of subjects, heard the voices of her deceased father and paternal grandmother argue about whether or not the subject should purchase an automobile or go on a trip. The subject interpreted the experience as the helpful intercession of these dead relatives to help her solve her day-to-day problems (score of 8). Other subjects attributed the voices, with varying degrees of certainty, to God, to the devil, or to both (scores of 3 to 6 depending on the subject's religion and degree of conviction). A few subjects had outer voices. Again, some subjects recognized these outer voices as the product of their own minds while others developed delusional beliefs concerning their origins. A typical subject who lacked delusional beliefs reported hearing the voice of his or her mother or boss, but then added, "I knew it couldn't really be true." Thus, the individual's interpretation of an anomalous experience is what determines the presence or absence of a delusion.

As we see it, the processes by which subjects reach delusional or nondelusional interpretations of anomalous experiences are not equally reasonable. The reasonableness of a belief should be judged in part by the range of evidence considered and by the weights given the various bits of evidence. The nondelusional person takes the usual step of considering more information about the world than the anomalous experience itself, while the delusional person responds to the experience as if it were the only datum available. One's life experience concerning causal relationships will usually rule out such events as spirit influences and will suggest alternative explanations of the anomalous experience. We will elaborate on this theme later in the chapter.

A delusional interpretation of an anomalous experience can also be adopted from other people. One of our subjects who hallucinated an outer voice reported that he never came to a conclusion about its origin until a cult group interpreted it for him. This magical ideation subject, from another series of subjects (Eckblad & Chapman, 1983), claimed to have a spirit guide who constantly accompanied him, whispering messages in his ear. For example, the spirit guide might say, "Go back and turn off the gas." The subject said that he had heard this voice for many years but did not know what it was until he encountered members of an organization that encourages and interprets psychic experiences. The members of this group explained to him that the voice was a spirit guide, a belief that he happily adopted, feeling pleased that he had this special gift.

The data from these several subjects clearly indicate that a voice experience is subject to radically different interpretations ranging from the normal to the slightly aberrant to the delusional. One might contend that the subjects with delusional interpretations of the voice experiences were responding to more vivid perceptual events than those subjects with nondelusional interpretations. The reports of our subjects do not, however, seem to support this interpretation in that some subjects reported intensely vivid voice experiences yet continued to believe themselves to be responsible. One such subject reported that she was tormented for three months by hearing her boss's voice as an outer voice when she was away from the office, but insisted that she never suspected that the experience was veridical.

Evidence against the requirement of an anomalous experience for forming a delusion is a finding that some subjects develop delusional or aberrant beliefs in response to experiences that would not be considered anomalous by most people. For example, two subjects reported episodes in which they interpreted shadows at night as indicating the actions of spirits. Another common experience that only some subjects interpreted aberrantly or delusionally was that of someone else having the same thoughts as oneself. For example, when the subject is at a party with a friend and wants to go home, the friend may say unexpectedly "Let's go home." Most people do not infer thought transmission or mind reading from this kind of experience, but many of our subjects did. Some of them concluded that the friend picked up thought waves and actively read their minds. A number of our subjects were preoccupied with these experience of their minds being read. One young man whose girlfriend usually guessed when he would telephone her objected to her mind reading as an intrusion on his privacy. One can never know the subjective vividness of a perceptual event, but in the light of our subjects' reports, we feel unconvinced that all those subjects who reached delusional conclusions about their experiences of shadows or of shared thoughts had had more intense perceptual experiences than those who did not.

In some instances, a deviant belief seems to give rise to an anomalous perceptual experience instead of the experience giving rise to the deviant belief. Some of our subjects reported seeing auras around other people. An aura is a glow of light seen around the head or body of another person, and the color of the glow is usually interpreted as telling something about the individual. These subjects believe in the existence of auras and belong to cults or are on the fringes of cults that encourage belief in auras. It seems likely that the shared belief system helps to sustain the perception of auras, or even to facilitate the initial perceptual experience of the aura.

The Role of Formal Thought Disorder in Delusional Beliefs

Formal thought disorder, or its attenuated form, cognitive slippage, may also contribute to some delusional beliefs. It is well known that many groups of patients who have delusional symptoms, such as schizophrenics, also have thought disorder. Because schizophrenics reason so badly about most problems in their lives, it would surely be unexpected if they reasoned more accurately about delusional topics. Maher's (1974) description of delusional persons as reasoning in a normal way about their anomalous perceptual experiences has its greatest appeal for describing patients who do not show formal thought disorder, such as persons with pure paranoia.

In our own research, all of our interviewers were struck by our subjects' upsurge of cognitive slippage when they began to talk about psychotic and psychoticlike experiences, including delusions and aberrant beliefs. The subjects began to express themselves vaguely, became tangential, jumped inappropriately from one topic to another, had difficulty finding the right choice of words, and expressed themselves inexactly. For example, when asked for an explanation of his deviant experiences, a subject may, instead of answering directly, talk about his acceptance of other paranormal beliefs, such as horoscopes and the Bermuda triangle. Some of this vagueness and circumlocution could merely be a defensive response to the questioning, but some other subjects showed more serious verbal deviances. One subject said, in describing her inner voices, which she sometimes believed or suspected were veridical, that she heard the voice of an "analogue of a person," but could not explain what she meant by that term. Another subject, when asked whether her voice was an inner voice or an outer voice, said that it was more a revelation than a voice, as if revelation and voice were meaningful alternatives. She also said, "The voices are a sort of power that is transmitted between people." (We were careful not to infer deviant beliefs on the basis of such vague statements, but instead required fully explained examples to score deviant beliefs.) Apparently the subject's consideration of deviant experiences stimulated the cognitive slippage, but regardless of how the cognitive slippage and deviant experiences are related, the subjects did not seem to reason and speak clearly about their aberrant beliefs.

To investigate whether the same kinds of subjects show cognitive slippage and aberrant beliefs, Chapman, Edell, and Chapman (1980) judged the presence or absence of cognitive slippage and found that perceptual aberration subjects, who had more delusional and aberrant beliefs than control subjects, also had more cognitive slippage than control subjects. (This sample of subjects is different from that discussed above.) However, this cognitive slippage primarily appeared in the subjects' discussion of symptoms. In another study we rated cognitive slippage shown by subjects in their discussion of nonpathological anxiety-laden experiences, such as problems in dating, and found no difference in cognitive slippage between perceptual aberration-magical ideation subjects and control subjects. We have been successful in finding evidence of verbal deviancy of these perceptual aberration-magical ideation subjects in laboratory tasks. Miller and Chapman (1983) found that members of this group gave more deviant word associations than control subjects on the Continuous Word Association Test, and Martin and Chapman (1982) found that these subjects were more deviant in communication as measured by the Rosenberg and Cohen (1966) Word Communication Task. Nevertheless, the deviancies in discourse of our perceptual aberration-magical ideation subjects are clearly most striking in their discussions of their other symptoms.

The Cognitive Deviancies in Delusions

But what is the nature of the deviant thinking that characterizes the formation of delusions and aberrant beliefs? We believe there is a useful lead in Maher's statement (Maher, 1974; Maher & Ross, 1984) that delusional patients, given the experiences available to them, reason like scientists in building theories based on their observations. Scientists who build theories are notorious for selectively attending to supporting data and ignoring data that conflict with their theory. We believe that one may reasonably infer from this analogy that delusional patients constrict the information that they consider in reaching a conclusion. The delusional person ignores or gives inadequate weight to data from his or her other experiences, some of which may contradict the delusional belief. A person who interprets shadows as reflecting spirit influences is failing to incorporate the fact that shadows are commonplace and result from the play of light on objects. The subject who suspected that thoughts had been injected into his head with a hypodermic needle was failing to consider his accumulated experience and knowledge, which would contradict the physical possibility of such a mode of transmission of thoughts. Delusional patients, in general, show a loss of the benefit of their accumulated life experience as to common causal relationships and the range of physical possibilities. But this defect does not account for the content of delusional beliefs; it instead accounts for the failure to reject delusional beliefs as unrealistic.

The defect can be illustrated by some delusions of schizophrenic patients. One patient, whom one of us knew many years ago, heard the sound of the water rushing down the pipe while draining the washbasin after washing her face and hands one morning. She interpreted the sound of the rushing water as being the voice of her mother and came running out of the washroom in a panic, asking for help. She believed that her mother had gone down the drain. Clearly, this patient was having the anomalous experience of hearing her mother's voice come from the drain. However, a nonpsychotic person with the same experience would consider other information when interpreting the experience, such as the physical impossibility of an adult person's body fitting into the narrow drain pipes, as well as the unlikelihood that her mother, who had not been at the hospital that day, would suddenly appear. As a result, the nonpsychotic person would investigate more reasonable explanations of the experience, for example, that the voice was that of someone else nearby. The patient's delusion could not be entertained without a constriction of the information taken into account. Or, consider Maher's patient (in this volume), who, on finding himself at a #11 street address at 11:00 on Armistice Day, concluded that he was responsible for World War I. To reach this conclusion the patient had to exclude as evidence his prior knowledge concerning his relationships with governmental authorities.

But are these thought processes of delusional patients really different from those of scientists? Although it is clear that scientists, like delusional patients, ignore contradictory evidence in reaching their conclusions, it is also clear that delusional patients ignore far more obvious and clearly relevant information than do scientists. Delusional patients deny well-established facts of physical reality that they and others have experienced all their lives. In this respect, delusional patients do not show a qualitatively unique kind of error, but instead accentuate a normal error tendency to the point of gross deviancy.

Support for the role of incomplete information in the formation of delusions is provided by observations of the effects of incomplete information on the formation of grossly erroneous beliefs by nonpsychotic persons. People who lack access to relevant information readily interpret events in ways that would look delusional were it not for their lack of information. For example, in World War II, the natives of New Guinea responded inappropriately when they saw cargo planes arriving with supplies for the warring troops. Many of the natives constructed crude replicas of the airplanes on the ground as decoys to attract other cargo-laden planes so that the planes would land and disgorge their riches (Harris, 1974). A person in the United States who did such a thing would be viewed as grossly delusional because of his or her failure to use information that is readily available to all members of the society. But the natives responded on the basis of incomplete information about the airplanes and about the arrangements that led to their arrival with supplies. The New Guinea natives were not delusional, or even unreasonable, given the information that was available to them. Harris (1974) argued persuasively that their behavior made good sense in the context of their cultural tradition of cargo cults, and the available information, including their awareness of the inequity of distribution of wealth between the natives and their foreign visitors. The natives' inappropriate methods of attempting to obtain cargo clearly reflected the insufficiency of their information about both airplanes and the Western economic system.

We wish to suggest an alternative to Maher's (1974) principle concerning the stimuli to which delusional persons respond. He suggested that they fail to select the stimuli to which they respond. As he put it, for these patients "Everything is 'figure' and hence significant" (p. 103). We suggest, instead, that delusional patients focus more often on stimuli that are strong or prominent by normal standards, neglecting weaker stimuli. By the term *stimuli*, we include inner events such as emotions and thoughts as well as external events. One such strong stimulus is a person's own emotional responses to the environment. Delusional patients also focus, we believe, on other kinds of stimuli that are strong, immediate, and personally salient by normal standards and they ignore stimuli that are weaker or less immediately compelling.

We have previously reported a series of studies demonstrating excessive reliance of schizophrenics on strong stimuli in their interpretation of words (Chapman & Chapman, 1965; Chapman, Chapman, & Miller, 1964). Schizophrenics constrict their interpretations of the meanings of words to meanings that are strongest by normal standards, ignoring weaker meanings that are more appropriate to the context. For example, in one task of one of our studies, schizophrenic and normal subjects were asked to sort a series of cards, each bearing the name of one object, into two boxes. The cards naming things that have a head were to go into one box and the cards naming things that do not have heads were to go into a second box. The cards named animate things that have a head—like dog, mouse, and horse— as well as inanimate things that have a head—like pin, hammer, and arrow. The schizophrenics, unlike the normal subjects, excluded the inanimate objects from the category of things that have a head, but did not exclude the animate objects. Separate data showed that normal subjects, when presented with the word *head* without context and without examples, interpreted it primarily in terms of its animate meaning. Yet, normal subjects were able to use the weaker meaning of the word *head* when that meaning was appropriate in the context of the question being asked. In contrast, the schizophrenics narrowed their interpretation of the word *head* to the meaning that is strongest for normals when presented without context, regardless of the appropriateness of that strong meaning when the word is presented in a context. They were unable to use the weaker meaning when that weaker meaning was appropriate in the context of the problem at hand. As a result, the patient says, "No, a nail doesn't have a head," even though information to the contrary has been available to the patient since early childhood.

We suggest now, rather speculatively, that one may extend this principle from the interpretation of the meanings of words to the interpretation of evidence. Schizophrenics seem to be unable to select and weigh appropriately all the information that is needed to arrive at reasonable interpretations of events in their environments. They overrespond to stimuli that are stronger, more immediate, or compelling at the moment and tend to ignore or give inadequate weight to information that is less so.

There is danger of circularity in this formulation in that we infer a difference in strength of stimuli from the choice of stimuli to which schizophrenics respond. We have not developed independent measures of strength, like those in our studies of word usage, to test whether the information that the delusional patient neglects is the weaker or less immediately compelling information by normal standards. Examples of delusions, however, seem consistent with this principle. For the subjects who interpreted shadows as spirit influences, knowledge of the origin of shadows does not seem to have been a strong stimulus at the moment of seeing shadowy objects at night. For the patient who believed that her mother had gone down the drain, the voice from the drain would seem to have been a stronger stimulus than knowledge of the limitations of the size of the drains. This interpretation—that delusions show an excessive response to strong stimuli and a neglect of weaker stimuli—is a statement that the delusional person shows an accentuation of a normal response bias.

We do not wish to imply that schizophrenic reasoning is normal. Schizophrenic delusions are clearly abnormal in that they reflect a constriction of the evidence considered, a constriction far in excess of that shown by nonpsychotics. Delusions are also characterized, we believe, by an abnormal neglect of weaker stimuli.

In summary, delusions of psychosis are often more deviant versions of aberrant beliefs that were held by patients before they became psychotic. The relationships between delusions, anomalous experience, and thought disorder can reasonably be construed as ones of mutual augmentation. Among patients who have all three of these abnormalities, each of the three seems to enhance the other two. None of the three uniformly occurs first in a causal sequence. None of the three seems necessary for the occurrence of another; instead, all three are probably direct expressions of the psychosis.

REFERENCES

American Psychiatric Association. (1980). *Diagnostic and statistical manual of mental disorder* (3rd ed.) (DSM-III). New York: Author.

Chapman, J. (1966). The early symptoms of schizophrenia. *British Journal of Psychiatry, 112,* 225–251.

Chapman, L.J., & Chapman, J.P. (1965). Interpretation of words in schizophrenia. *Journal of Personality and Social Psychology, 1,* 135–146.

Chapman, L.J., & Chapman, J.P. (1980). Scales for rating psychotic and psychotic-like experiences as continua. *Schizophrenia Bulletin, 6,* 476–489.

Chapman, L.J., Chapman, J.P., & Miller, E.N. (1982). Reliabilities and intercorrelations of eight measures of proneness to psychosis. *Journal of Consulting and Clinical Psychology, 50,* 187–195.

Chapman, L.J., Chapman, J.P., & Miller, G.A. (1964). A theory of verbal behavior in schizophrenia. In B.A. Maher (Ed.), *Progress in experimental personality research* (Vol. 1). New York: Academic Press.

Chapman, L.J., Chapman, J.P., & Raulin, M.L. (1978). Body-image aberration in schizophrenia. *Journal of Abnormal Psychology, 87,* 399–407.

Chapman, L.J., Edell, W.A., & Chapman, J.P. (1980). Physical anhedonia, perceptual aberration, and psychosis proneness. *Schizophrenia Bulletin, 6,* 639–653.

Eckblad, M., & Chapman, L.J. (1983). Magical ideation as an indicator of schizotypy. *Journal of Consulting and Clinical Psychology, 51,* 215–225.

Gillies, H. (1958). The clinical diagnosis of early schizophrenia. In T.F. Rodger, R.M. Mowbray, & J.R. Roy (Eds.), *Topics in psychiatry.* London: Cassell.

Harris, M. (1974). *Cows, pigs, wars and witches.* New York: Random House.

McGhie, A., & Chapman, J. (1961). Disorders of attention and perception in early schizophrenia. *British Journal of Medical Psychology, 34,* 103–116.

Maher, B. (1974). Delusional thinking and perceptual disorder. *Journal of Individual Psychology, 30,* 98–113.

Maher, B., & Ross, J. (1984). Delusions. In H.E. Adams & P.B. Sutker (Eds.), *Comprehensive handbook of psychopathology.* New York: Plenum Press.

Manschreck, T.C. (1979). The assessment of paranoid features. *Comprehensive Psychiatry, 20,* 370–377.

Martin, E.M., & Chapman, L.J. (1982). Communication effectiveness in psychosis-prone college students. *Journal of Abnormal Psychology, 91,* 151–156.

Miller, E.N., & Chapman, L.J. (1983). Continued word association in hypothetically psychosis-prone college students. *Journal of Abnormal Psychology, 92,* 468–478.

Rosenberg, S., & Cohen, B.D. (1966). Referential processes of speakers and listeners. *Psychological Review, 73,* 208–231.

Spitzer, R.L., & Endicott, J. (1977). *Schedule for affective disorders and schizo-phrenia-lifetime version (SADS-L).* New York: New York State Psychiatric Institute.

Strauss, J.S. (1969). Hallucinations and delusions as points on continua function: Rating scale evidence. *Archives of General Psychiatry, 21,* 581–586.

CHAPTER 9

Schizophrenic Delusions: An Analysis of Their Persistence, of Related Premorbid Ideas, and of Three Major Dimensions

MARTIN HARROW, FRANCINE RATTENBURY, and FRANK STOLL

Michael Reese Medical Center and The University of Chicago

Delusional ideation, a central feature of psychosis, is recognized as a major characteristic of schizophrenia and of schizoaffective disorders. Despite the centrality of this psychotic symptom, there has been a lack of systematic longitudinal research on the nature and course of delusions. At present, there are large gaps in our understanding of the nature of psychotic symptoms of any kind. The major focus of the current research involves an attempt to further knowledge about psychotic symptoms by an investigation of three major dimensions of delusional ideation in a sample of hospitalized schizophrenic and nonschizophrenic patients. The chapter also presents data concerning the course of delusions over time, and concerning whether the content of patients' preepisode ideas is related to the content of their subsequent acute phase delusions.

Recent investigations have begun to examine delusions from several vantage points. These approaches include attempts to determine whether delusions form a continuum with normal beliefs (Strauss, 1969; Chapman & Chapman, 1980; Harrow & Silverstein, 1977), and to analyze stages that occur as patients enter into and emerge from delusional states (Bowers,

This research was supported, in part, by Grant No. MH-26341 from the National Institute of Mental Health, and research grants from the John D. and Catherine T. MacArthur Foundation, the Irving B. Harris Foundation, and the Four Winds Research Fund. Portions of this work were conducted while the second author was a Clinical Research Training Fellow in Adolescence (funded by National Institute of Mental Health training grant # 5 T32 MH14668-10) in the Department of Psychiatry, Michael Reese Hospital and Medical Center in a program also sponsored by the Department of Behavioral Sciences (Committee on Human Development), The University of Chicago.

1974; Carr, 1983; Docherty, Van Kammen, Siris, & Marder, 1978; McGlashan, Levy, & Carpenter, 1975; Sacks, Carpenter, & Strauss, 1974). They also include studies of the course of delusions and their prognostic significance (Gift, Strauss, Kokes, Harder, & Ritzler, 1980; Harrow, Carone, & Westermeyer, 1985; Harrow & Silverstein, 1977; Silverstein & Harrow, 1978, 1981; Strauss & Carpenter, 1974, 1977; Zubin, Sutton, Salzinger, Burdock, & Peretz, 1961), as well as attempts to assess other factors that might be involved in delusions (Heilbrun & Heilbrun, 1977; Hole, Rush, & Beck, 1979; Kendler, Glazer, & Morgenstern, 1983; Rudden, Gilmore, & Frances, 1982; Stoll, Harrow, Rattenbury, DeWolfe, & Harris, 1980).

Over the years, a number of general theories of delusions have been proposed by major investigators in the field (Bleuler, 1911/1950; Freud, 1911/1958; Jaspers, 1923/1963). Less frequently seen than these overall theories of delusions, however, are analyses of the specific dimensions that are important in delusional ideation. This area has just recently begun to be the subject of systematic research (Hole et al., 1979; Kendler et al., 1983; Rudden et al., 1982; Stoll et al., 1980). Further empirical analysis of specific characteristics of delusional thinking could advance our understanding about the nature of psychosis in the major functional disorders.

For the purposes of the present research, delusions were viewed as false beliefs that persist despite evidence to the contrary, and that are not ordinarily shared by other members of an individual's culture or subculture. This view of delusions is consistent with those adopted in instruments widely used to assess major psychopathology (e.g., Endicott & Spitzer, 1978).

The current research analyzes three basic aspects that we have proposed as important dimensions of patients' delusional ideation (Stoll et al., 1980): (1) patients' belief-conviction about the delusion, (2) their perspective on the delusion, and (3) their emotional commitment to the delusion.

The first of these dimensions, belief-conviction, refers to the extent of the patient's delusional belief, or how certain the patient is about the reality or accuracy of his or her consensually deviant ideas. The degree of conviction the patient maintains regarding the validity of the false belief has been widely recognized as a principal aspect of delusional ideation (Redlich & Freedman, 1966; Hole et al., 1979; Kendler et al., 1983). The above research suggests that delusions are not unidimensional phenomena and that in most cases other dimensions are important in understanding the mechanisms of delusional thinking and in determining whether or not a patient is flagrantly psychotic. The current research, conducted on a sample of primarily young early-course psychotic patients, studies the extent of patients' belief-conviction in their delusions over several phases during their psychotic episodes, and explores the relationship between these patients' belief-conviction and other dimensions of delusions.

The second of these major dimensions of delusional ideation is the patient's perspective about how others will view his or her delusional beliefs. This refers to how aware a patient is that other people will view his or her delusional beliefs as aberrant, implausible, or crazy, and is based on the patient's awareness of social norms as they apply to his or her particular beliefs and behavior. Normal individuals are generally able to maintain perspective on and to recognize the adequacy of their beliefs from the standpoint of their society. Thus, normals have internalized consensual standards of belief and behavior and usually do not publicly verbalize beliefs that conflict grossly with widely held standards of social appropriateness and plausibility (Berger & Luckman, 1966). In contrast, our recent research with psychotic patients suggests that an impairment in perspective is a prominent characteristic of abnormal cognition (Harrow & Miller, 1980; Harrow & Quinlan, 1985). In this research schizophrenics and other patients with thought pathology demonstrated poor perspective in judging the inappropriateness of their own disordered speech and thinking. These patients were, nevertheless, significantly better able to judge the inappropriateness of bizarre verbalizations produced by *other* patients than they were able to judge the inappropriateness of their *own* bizarre verbalizations (Harrow & Miller, 1980). The present research systematically assesses the degree to which severely delusional patients are able to recognize that other people regard their delusional ideas as strange or deviant.

A third major dimension of delusional thinking studied in the current research involves emotional commitment—the immediacy, importance, or urgency the patient attaches to his or her delusional ideas. We have proposed that this dimension may be a crucial factor in determining whether delusional individuals will be able to function competently in society despite the fact that they maintain some degree of belief-conviction about the truth of their aberrant ideas (Stoll et al., 1980). In clinical practice we have observed a number of delusional patients who were able to function adequately outside the hospital for many years, despite their fixed delusional conviction. These patients, however, did not show strong emotional commitment in that they did not attach great urgency to these beliefs. The current research assesses the level and persistence of hospitalized patients' emotional commitment to their delusional ideas and the relationship of emotional commitment to other aspects of delusional thinking and overt behavior.

We would propose that the first dimension, the extent of belief in one's delusional ideation, is a central feature of delusional ideation, but one that would not account fully either for the development of an acute delusional episode or for recovery from an acute delusional episode. Our clinical observations suggest that a firm belief in the reality of one's delusion may be a necessary but not a sufficient condition to produce the kind of flagrantly delusional behavior that requires hospitalization. Consequently, it becomes important to understand the role that each of the three factors plays at different stages in the delusional episode and how the factors interact with one another.

The current research, focusing on three dimensions of delusional ideation, addresses the following specific questions:

1. How firm are psychotic patients' belief-convictions in the reality of their delusions? Does the extent of conviction provide evidence about whether delusions form a continuum with normal beliefs?

2. Is an impairment in patients' perspective about how others regard their unreal ideas an important feature of a delusional episode? Are delusional patients able to recognize how others regard their delusional beliefs after a month's hospitalization?

3. Is strong emotional commitment to their delusions an important dimension for psychotic patients? Is there a reduction in emotional commitment after a month in the hospital and if so, does diminished commitment relate to whether patients need continued hospitalization?

RESEARCH STRATEGY AND MEASUREMENT PROCEDURES

Patients

The subjects were 34 hospitalized patients from Michael Reese Hospital (MRH) and the Illinois State Psychiatric Institute (ISPI). These patients, selected for intensive study of delusional ideation, form part of the Chicago Followup Study (Harrow, Grinker, Silverstein, & Holtzman, 1978; Harrow & Quinlan, 1977, 1985; Harrow, Silverstein, & Marengo, 1983; Pogue-Geile & Harrow, 1985). The sample was selected from patients who showed evidence of delusions at hospital admission, as assessed by one of the following structured interviews: the Schedule for Affective Disorders and Schizophrenia (SADS) (Endicott & Spitzer, 1978), administered at MRH, or a modified version of the Present State Examination (PSE) (Wing, Cooper, & Sartorius, 1974), administered at ISPI. Diagnoses were made prospectively, using the Research Diagnostic Criteria (RDC) (Spitzer, Endicott & Robbins, 1978). The sample consisted of 14 schizophrenics, 11 schizoaffective patients, and 9 patients with other types of major psychotic disorders (e.g., psychotic depressives).

The single most prominent delusion of each patient in the sample was selected for evaluation. In terms of types of delusion, the current sample included 10 patients with prominent persecutory delusions, 5 with referential delusions, 7 with grandiose delusions, 4 with delusions that other people could read their minds, and 8 with various other types of delusions (e.g., somatic, religious, or delusions of guilt or sin).

The mean age of the sample was 24.4 years, and the mean educational level was 12.7 years. The mean raw Information Subtest score on the Wechsler Adult Intelligence Scale (Wechsler, 1955) was 15.34, which lies within the average range of intelligence. Age, intelligence, and education of the sample patients were not significantly related to the results found on any of the three main dimensions studied in the research.

Sixty-eight percent of the sample were receiving neuroleptics at the time of the hospital interview. Analyses of differences between neuroleptically treated and nonneuroleptically treated patients on the major dimensions of delusions studied are described in the Results section.

Assessment Procedures

The Personal Ideation Inventory (PII) (Rattenbury, Harrow, Stoll, & Kettering, 1984), administered to all patients in the sample, is a semistructured interview designed to focus on major dimensions and components of patients' prominent delusions. The PII consists of 71 items that assess various aspects of the content of a delusion, including its relationship to premorbid concerns and the extent of a patient's conviction, commitment, and perspective about his or her central delusion. Less than the full sample of 34 patients was included in several of the analyses because of insufficient information for some patients on a few of the variables. The present research focuses on three major dimensions of delusional thinking.

The first dimension studied is the patients' belief-convictions about their delusions, or how strongly they believe that their delusional ideas are real or true. This variable is rated on a three-point scale, with a score of 1 assigned for no belief in the delusion, 2 for partial, and 3 for full belief-conviction.

The second dimension is the patients' perspective about whether others will regard their delusional ideas as strange or implausible. Perspective, as we have used the term, refers to the individuals' recognition of social norms as they apply to their particular beliefs and behaviors (Harrow & Miller, 1980). In the present case, perspective refers to whether patients were able to recognize that others regarded their beliefs as delusional. In this scale, a score of 1 was assigned for good perspective, 2 was assigned for partial perspective, and 3 was assigned for poor perspective. To inquire about patients' perspective, questions such as the following were asked: "How do other people feel about your idea that ... ?" "What is their reaction?" "Do they agree with it?"

The third major element is the patients' emotional commitment to their delusional beliefs. Emotional commitment, as discussed in the Introduction, refers to the immediacy of the belief, or how impelling and important it feels to the patient. Emotional commitment contains both behavioral and cognitive components. Thus, the measure of emotional commitment to a delusional belief was based on (1) *cognitive* signs of commitment (time spent thinking about the delusion and ability to stop attending to it), and on (2) *behavioral* signs (extent to which the delusion influenced daily activities). Both cognitive and behavioral aspects of commitment were rated on a five-point scale that varied from a score of 0 for none to 4 for very high emotional commitment. The final score was a composite score used to represent the extent of the patients' emotional commitment. It was based on the more extreme sign of commitment to the delusion (i.e., the higher score on either the cognitive or behavioral ratings of commitment).

Satisfactory interrater reliabilities were obtained based on separate evaluations made by two raters who listened independently to the same 14 taped interviews. Interrater reliability coefficients obtained for belief-conviction, perspective, and emotional commitment were $r = .82$, $r = .81$, and $r = .77$, respectively.

The following case example, from the current sample studied, provides an illustration of the manner in which belief-conviction, perspective, and emotional commitment were rated.

At the height of her delusional episode, four months prior to the hospital interview, a 23-year-old schizoaffective (manic type) female student, who was having frequent arguments with her mother, experienced a paranoid delusion that her family, friends, and others were trying to poison her (the target delusion studied). She became so obsessed with this idea that she had to be apprehended by the police for screaming paranoid accusations at people in a hotel lobby. She experienced a number of major difficulties, among which were elated and irritable mood, pressured speech, insomnia, reckless spending, and other provocative behavior, as well as auditory hallucinations, visual hallucinations, grandiose delusions, and other psychotic symptoms. At the height of her episode, she was fully convinced of the reality of her belief that others were trying to poison her (a score of 3 for full belief-conviction). She showed partial perspective (a score of 2) in that she thought strangers might regard the paranoid idea as "crazy," although she felt confident that her own friends would believe her. A high degree of emotional commitment to the delusion was demonstrated cognitively by her constant preoccupation with paranoid ideation and behaviorally by her screaming paranoid accusations to strangers (leading to a score of 4 for very high emotional commitment).

After little more than a month in the hospital (medicated with lithium), her belief-conviction had moderated to the extent that she was able to express some doubt about the validity of her delusion. She had also regained adequate perspective, recognizing that others did not believe her ideas. Thus, she showed a reduction of belief-conviction (her partial belief led to a score of 2), and she had good perspective (a score of 1). Her emotional commitment remained high, however, as evidenced by her continued preoccupation with her paranoid idea as well as withdrawn and paranoid behavior on the unit (maintaining a score of 4 for her emotional commitment).

Patients were interviewed, using the PII, a median of 26 days following hospital admission. The PII was administered orally and individually by trained interviewers blind to diagnosis. The interviews were tape-recorded for subsequent rating. The semistructured interview included questions referring to the status of the patients' delusions both at the time of the hospital interviews and at the height of their delusional episodes. The median length of time from the height of the delusional episode to the time of the hospital interview was 1.8 months.

PREMORBID IDEAS AND DELUSIONS AT FOLLOWUP

As a first step toward advancing knowledge about delusions, prior to our analyses of the three dimensions outlined above, we analyzed material on the persistence and importance of delusions in schizophrenia, and on background factors that might influence the content of delusions. The data in these two areas are presented in this section and the following section.

The Persistence and Importance of Delusions

Our evaluation of the importance of delusions was based on an analysis of a separate sample of 34 DSM-III (American Psychiatric Association, 1980) schizophrenic patients we have studied prospectively as inpatients and then followed up at a mean of 2.4 and then 4.8 years after their hospital discharge (Harrow et al., 1985). Table 9.1 presents the data from the two successive follow-ups of this sample of 34 schizophrenics. This aspect of our research has focused on determining whether delusional beliefs persist past the acute phase in schizophrenia, and, when studied after the acute phase, whether they predict the subsequent functioning of patients. Recent proposals have suggested that negative symptoms are important and have prognostic significance for schizophrenics, but that positive symptoms such as delusions may not persist in schizophrenia and are not predictive of subsequent functioning. The data in Table 9.1 from the sample of 34 schizophrenics indicate that between 55 percent and 60 percent of these patients showed evidence of at least some delusional activity at each of the two follow-up

TABLE 9.1.   Course of Delusions in DSM-III Schizophrenics
Delusions at Index and at Two Successive Posthospital Assessments

	Delusions Absent	Delusions Marginal or Equivocal	Delusions Present
Index ($N = 34$)	12%	3%	85%
First Follow-up ($N = 34$)	41%	12%	47%
Second Follow-up ($N = 34$)	44%	18%	38%

assessments. Thus, for instance, at the second follow-up 38 percent of the schizophrenics showed clear evidence of delusional activity and another 18 percent showed marginal or equivocal evidence of delusional activity.

In addition, a separate analysis of data we collected on the functioning and adjustment of the schizophrenics at the two follow-ups indicates that the schizophrenics with delusions at the first follow-up showed significantly poorer functioning at the second follow-up than the schizophrenics who did not show delusional activity at the first follow-up (Pogue-Geile & Harrow, 1985). These data suggest that the presence of delusions in schizophrenics *after the acute phase* predicts subsequent poor functioning.

Overall, the follow-up data from a sample of schizophrenics we have assessed at the acute phase and then followed up and reassessed twice point to the prominence and importance of delusional activity in schizophrenic patients. Other preliminary data suggest, however, that delusional activity may be less persistent among initially psychotic patients who are not schizophrenic.

Background Ideation Influencing the Content of the Delusions

An analysis of the above data from a separate sample of 34 patients indicated that delusions are persistent and important in some groups of psychotic patients (e.g., in schizophrenics). We next analyzed data from the current sample on the background ideation from which the content of delusions arise. Namely, from 27 of the current sample of psychotic patients, we analyzed data obtained from the PII concerning whether the content of most of these patients' delusional ideation was related to the content of nondelusional ideas or concerns of theirs that predated the onset of the delusions the patients were experiencing. Table 9.2 presents these data.

The data from 19 of the 27 patients (70 percent) suggested that their delusional ideation was related to nondelusional ideas or concerns that predated the onset of the delusion under inquiry (see Table 9.2). Thus, in most

TABLE 9.2.   **Relationship of Delusional Content to
Preexisting Ideation**

Delusions Related to Preexisting Ideation	19 (70%)
Delusions Unrelated to Preexisting Ideation	8 (30%)

cases, the delusional idea was not an entirely foreign one, but may have developed out of normal, preexisting concerns. Some of these earlier ideas or concerns originated a number of years ago, while others arose more recently.

The following examples illustrate cases in which background ideation was related to the content of current delusions.

A 28-year-old single, unemployed depressed patient was fully convinced of multiple somatic delusions when interviewed. Although no medical basis for his somatic complaints could be found, he believed that he possessed a weak circulatory system, leading to frequent chills and a fear of prolonged activity. He also believed that he had a heart murmur that was responsible for a frequent sensation of blood "slipping back" into his heart. He stated that the initial onset of these beliefs had occurred at age 16, and that since early childhood he had worried about the possible medical significance of coldness in his extremities.

A 22-year-old married homemaker, diagnosed as schizoaffective, was convinced at admission that her thoughts had been taken over by the devil. This belief had begun suddenly, four weeks before admission. When interviewed in the hospital seven weeks later, the patient expressed doubt about the validity of her belief, stating that she could be just imagining it. She revealed that approximately six months prior to onset of the belief, she had seen a movie about devil possession and had been wondering about the extent of the devil's powers.

When these data were looked at diagnostically, there was a slightly stronger tendency in this sample for the content of the delusions of the nonschizophrenics to be related to past ideation (78 percent) than for the schizophrenics. Slightly more of the schizophrenics' delusions showed content that almost seemed to come "out of the blue" than was the case for nonschizophrenics. Even within the schizophrenics, however, the data suggested that approximately half (56 percent) of their central delusions were related to prior concerns.

These data on the background of the delusional ideation were also analyzed in terms of whether the presence of preexisting ideation plays a role in the short-term persistence of the delusion. The results of this analysis are

TABLE 9.3.   Relatedness of Delusional Content to Preexisting Ideation as an Influence on Length of Hospitalization

	Length of Hospitalization		
	1–2 Months	3 Months	4 Months or Longer
Delusions Related to Preexisting Ideation ($N = 18$)	6 (33%)	5 (28%)	7 (39%)
Delusions Unrelated to Preexisting Ideation ($N = 8$)	3 (38%)	4 (50%)	1 (13%)

$t = 1.39$, $p < .20$ (t = test based on full range of scores for number of months hospitalized).

presented in Table 9.3. As can be seen in Table 9.3, 88 percent of the patients with unrelated delusions, or delusions that almost seemed to arise out of the blue, were discharged within four months of hospital admission, compared with only 61 percent of those with related delusions. Statistical comparison of the number of months in the hospital for the current episode revealed a minor nonsignificant trend for the group with unrelated delusions to have briefer hospitalizations ($p < .20$). Though the results in this area are nonsignificant, these data leave open the possibility that delusions that are a more central part of the patient's life could persist longer.

A comparison of level of emotional commitment indicated no significant difference between the patients with related and unrelated delusions. The lack of significant difference on emotional commitment occurred at both the height of the episode and at the time of the hospital interview.

Overall, the results regarding the relationship of delusional content to preexisting ideation suggest that the psychotic ideation of most (but not all) of these patients was related to ideas about which they had shown some concern or consideration in the past. Although these data were obtained from already-hospitalized patients reporting on their previous experience, they are consistent with Chapman and Chapman's (this volume) prospective observations of delusional content in initially nonhospitalized college students. These authors observed that many nonpsychotic beliefs are similar in content to the same subjects' psychotic beliefs in later delusional episodes.

In addition, our data did not support the notion of a unique, premorbid schizophrenic preoccupation that leads such patients to become delusional. Although the content of more than half of the schizophrenic delusions in the present study were predated by normal ideation of similar content, a slightly greater proportion of nonschizophrenic delusions also rose from the elaboration or distortion of preexisting ideas or concerns. The current data also suggest that delusional ideas that arise "out of the blue," with no apparent connection to prior concerns, may have a slight tendency to predict better short-term outcomes. Such "foreign" ideas may be less central to the patient's overall ideation, and thus less persistent.

THREE DIMENSIONS OF DELUSIONAL BELIEFS

Belief-Conviction in Delusions

The data on the degree of patients' belief-conviction about the reality of their delusions at the hospital interview and at the height of their disorders are reported in Table 9.4. As noted earlier in our description of the method, assessments of both current status and status at the height of the episode were made during the same index interview.

1. The results in Table 9.4 on the extent of the patients' beliefs about their delusional ideas indicate that at the height of their disorder 82 percent of the patients were fully convinced of the accuracy or reality of their ideas. Only 18 percent indicated some limited degree of doubt about the reality of their delusions.

2. The results in Table 9.4 on the extent of the patients' beliefs at the time of the hospital interview indicate that 44 percent of the patients were still fully convinced of the reality of their delusions, and another 44 percent demonstrated at least partial or wavering belief about their delusions. Thus, even after a month in the hospital, only 12 percent completely rejected their delusional beliefs as false.

3. A comparison of the extent of patients' belief-conviction about their delusions at the height of the episode to their belief-conviction at the time of the hospital interview reveals a marked and statistically significant reduction in the extent of their belief at the hospital interview ($p < .001$). A reduction in the extent of belief-conviction was shown by approximately 50 percent of the patients who had originally shown full belief in their delusions, with most of these patients shifting to partial belief in their delusions at the time of the hospital interview.

TABLE 9.4. Belief-Conviction Concerning Delusion

	Belief-Conviction		
	None	Partial	Full
Height of Episode ($N = 34$)	0	6 (18%)	28 (82%)
One Month in Hospital ($N = 34$)	4 (12%)	15 (44%)	15 (44%)

The outstanding feature in this area was the continuing strength of delusional conviction displayed by many patients even after a month's hospitalization. This belief in delusions persisted despite the fact that during hospitalization the patients were subjected to considerable social disapproval for their delusions, intended to cast serious doubt on the validity of their beliefs, from hospital staff, friends, and relatives. Thus, although patients showed a statistically significant reduction in the extent of their beliefs after a month in the hospital, most patients still maintained some or substantial levels of belief concerning their delusions. These results support many clinicians' anecdotal reports suggesting that delusions are among the most enduring features of psychosis, which for some patients can persist for a considerable period (Harrow et al., 1985; Harrow & Silverstein, 1977) despite vigorous negative feedback.

Perspective on Delusions

The data regarding the level of the patients' perspective on their delusions at the hospital interview and at the height of the delusional episode are reported in Table 9.5. As we noted earlier, we use the term *perspective* to refer to the patients' ability to recognize how *other* people would assess the validity of their delusional beliefs and to judge accurately how their beliefs would correspond with consensual social norms (Harrow & Quinlan, 1985; Stoll et al., 1980).

1. The data on perspective in Table 9.5 indicate that at the height of their disorders 23 percent of the patients had very poor perspective (were completely unaware that others might view their beliefs as aberrant or implausible), and another 74 percent had partial perspective (indicating partial or wavering recognition of the lack of consensual approval for their beliefs). Only 3 percent (1 female patient) showed full perspective and was able to judge that other people would regard her delusional belief as strange, unreal, or crazy.

2. The results in Table 9.5 indicate that the patients' perspective had shifted somewhat at the time of the hospital interview (after one month's

TABLE 9.5. Perspective on Delusion

	Perspective		
	Full	Partial	None
Height of Episode ($N = 31$)	1 (3%)	23 (74%)	7 (23%)
One Month in Hospital ($N = 34$)	5 (15%)	24 (71%)	5 (15%)

hospitalization). The data suggest that at that point 15 percent of these delusional patients had very poor perspective. Another 71 percent showed partial perspective after a month in the hospital, and 15 percent showed good perspective, recognizing that others would reject their beliefs as implausible or crazy.

3. A comparison of perspective scores for the 31 patients with data available at both of the assessment periods revealed a modest but statistically significant improvement in patients' perspective from the height of their disorders to the hospital interview ($p < .05$). Further examination of the data show that although 13 percent of the patients demonstrated some degree of improvement in perspective, 90 percent still continued to exhibit at least some residual impairment in perspective at the time of the hospital interview. This can be seen in the following example from the current sample:

At the height of his delusion three months prior to admission, a 25-year-old, single, white college-educated male schizophrenic, who had quit his job and become increasingly withdrawn over the preceding year, began to experience paranoid ideation that his family, neighbors, and people in the street were conspiring to murder him. This resulted in considerable conflict with his parents and in his refusal to leave the house for fear of attack. At that time he was fully convinced of the truth of his idea (3 on belief), although he only showed partly impaired perspective, believing that others might or might not believe that his delusion was true (a score of 2 on perspective). His strong emotional commitment to the paranoid belief was shown by his constant mental preoccupation with the idea and eventually in his need to flee his home state in order to escape this imagined persecution. After one month's hospitalization and treatment with thorazine, he became less convinced of the reality of the idea (2 on belief), but he showed no change in perspective (2 on perspective). With regard to emotional commitment, he still found it difficult to put the thought out of his mind, but was now able to keep his thought to himself and not let it affect his actions.

The overall results lend support to our hypothesis that delusional patients show some impairment in their ability to maintain perspective on consensual views regarding the validity of their own delusional beliefs. While a degree of impairment in perspective about their own beliefs persisted even after a month in the hospital, there was also evidence of a moderate but statistically significant improvement in patients' perspective-taking from the time of the height of their psychotic episodes to the hospital interview.

Emotional Commitment to Delusions

The data on emotional commitment, or the importance, immediacy, or urgency that the patients attach to their delusional ideas, are presented in Table 9.6. These data are reported both for the height of their delusional episodes and at the hospital interview. Entries in the "None" column indicate the percentage of patients who showed no evidence of delusional ideation at that particular time.

The results from the composite index, based on the highest level of emotional commitment (manifested as either overt behavioral activity or mental preoccupation with the idea), indicate the following:

1. At the height of their disorder, 82 percent of the patients showed evidence of very high emotional commitment (were never able to put their delusional ideas out of their minds, and/or acted overtly and publicly in accordance with the delusional belief), and another 11 percent showed a high level of commitment (frequently thought about delusional ideas, but were sometimes able to put their ideas out of their minds, and/or showed their commitment behaviorally by speaking about the delusion in private to a few other people). At this most acute period, when emotional commitment was at its most intense, only 8 percent of the sample showed either a minimal or moderate level of commitment to the delusion (they were frequently or always able to put their delusional ideas out of their minds, and their activities were never influenced by their delusional ideation: or, at worst, they acted privately in accordance with their delusional beliefs in such a way that others did not know about the ideas).

2. Even after a month in the hospital, 69 percent of the patients experienced a high or very high degree of emotional commitment. By that time, however, a number of psychotic patients no longer showed intense emotional commitment. Thus, 31 percent of the patients showed evidence of no commitment or only mild levels of emotional commitment.

TABLE 9.6.   Emotional Commitment to Delusion

	Emotional Commitment				
	None	Minimal	Moderate	High	Very High
Height of Episode ($N=28$)	0	1 (4%)	1 (4%)	3 (11%)	23 (82%)
One Month in Hospital ($N=29$)	4 (14%)	5 (17%)	0	7 (24%)	13 (45%)

3. A comparison of emotional commitment at the two time periods revealed a statistically significant overall reduction by the time of the hospital interview ($p < .01$). Analysis of the individual cognitive and behavioral components indicated that both of these aspects of emotional commitment diminished significantly after a month in the hospital. Overall inspection of the data indicates that 46 percent of these delusional patients showed at least some improvement from their initial level on the composite index, even though there were still a number of patients experiencing a very high degree of emotional commitment to their delusions after a month in hospital.

An example of a patient with a high level of emotional commitment can be seen in the following report from a patient in the current sample:

At the height of his delusional episode three months prior to hospitalization, a 20-year-old single, white schizoaffective (depressed type) male college student, who had been reared in a strict religious household, reported audible thoughts, as well as several mood-incongruent and mood-congruent delusions. One of the latter was the belief that he had become possessed by the devil. This patient was also suffering from depressed mood, self-reproach, weight loss, anhedonia, and suicidal ideation. At the height of his episode, he was fully convinced that the devil had taken possession of his soul and was influencing his actions (belief-conviction = 3). He also showed a partial impairment in perspective in that he recognized that while some might question the plausibility of his delusion, he also felt that other people would believe in it (perspective = 2). His high emotional commitment to his delusional idea led him, behaviorally, to withdraw from school because he felt the need to conceal what he considered his moral corruption from his classmates. Cognitively, he found himself continually thinking about it and unable to put the thought out of his mind (emotional commitment = 4).

At the time of the interview after a month's hospitalization and treatment with phenothiazines, this patient showed decreased belief-conviction concerning the validity of his idea of being possessed by the devil (belief-conviction = 2) and admitted that he might just be imagining it. However, there was no significant corresponding improvement in his perspective (score of 2). The patient continued to show a high although somewhat diminished level of emotional commitment to his delusion (a score of 3). But he still reported speaking about his idea to a few others and having difficulty putting the thought out of his mind.

This patient was also followed up one year after hospital discharge. At that time he had been readmitted to the hospital for severe depression and suicidal ideation, although he no longer reported this delusion or any other signs of psychosis.

While emotional commitment can manifest itself in either cognitive or behavioral modes, in the hospital most patients showed a more rapid reduction in behavioral than in cognitive modes of emotional commitment. This may be due in part to the fact that hospitals are restrictive settings that, when compared to the environment outside the hospital, tend to limit patients' opportunities to act overtly on their delusions. Although a few hospitalized patients still managed to act publicly on their delusions, most hospitalized patients tended to show their emotional commitment in cognitive rather than in behavioral terms (i.e., they had difficulty putting their delusions out of their minds).

Relations Among Different Dimensions of Delusions

The following results emerged with respect to the intercorrelations of the three dimensions of delusions at the time of the hospital interviews.

1. There were strong and significant relationships between belief-conviction and the two other dimensions (perspective, $r = .58$, and emotional commitment, $r = .51$) at the time of the hospital interview.
2. The relationship between perspective and emotional commitment at the hospital interview was not significant, $r = .21$, $p = NS$.

These data could support the view that belief-conviction is a core dimension of delusional experience. For hospitalized patients, at least a moderate level of belief-conviction is, in most cases, a necessary but insufficient condition for them to manifest impaired perspective about their delusions and to show high emotional commitment to their false beliefs. On the other hand, the lack of a significant relationship between perspective and emotional commitment indicates that among hospitalized psychotic patients there is either a minor relationship between these two dimensions of delusions, or they are unrelated to each other.

Overall, while the findings indicated moderately strong relationships between the patients' beliefs and the other two dimensions of delusions studied, there was also evidence that within a sample of psychotic patients some other dimensions of delusions may be partly or completely independent of one another. The low relationship between perspective and emotional commitment is in agreement with our own recent conclusions and those of several other researchers (Hole et al., 1979; Kendler et al., 1983; Stoll et al., 1980) that delusions are multidimensional phenomena. Because of the recency of these findings, the multidimensional nature of delusions has not yet been given proper attention in standard assessment procedures that treat delusions as unitary phenomena.

DIMENSIONS OF DELUSIONS AND OTHER CLINICAL CONSIDERATIONS

Neuroleptic Treatment and the Dimensions of Delusions

To assess the effects of medication, patients being treated with neuroleptics were compared with those not being treated with neuroleptics at the time of the hospital interview. For the analysis, 68 percent of the patients were receiving therapeutic doses of neuroleptics at the time of the interview, and these patients were compared to the other 32 percent of the sample with respect to their level of belief in their delusions, their level of perspective, and the extent of their emotional commitment. The results showed a minor, nonsignificant trend for the psychotic patients being treated with neuroleptics to show *less* belief in their delusions ($p < .20$). The neuroleptically treated patients also showed slightly better perspective and slightly less emotional commitment as well, but these latter differences did not approach statistical significance. The use of neuroleptics has been shown in numerous studies to have antipsychotic and antidelusional effects (e.g., Cole, Klerman, & Goldberg, 1964), and the current data on belief-conviction could fit in with these previous findings. However, caution must be exercised in interpreting these results concerning neuroleptics since the patients were not assigned to the medication groups on a random basis.

Diagnostic Categories and the Dimensions of Delusions

Analyses were conducted to assess potential differences among RDC (1) schizophrenics, (2) schizoaffective patients, and (3) the combined group of patients with other types of major psychotic disorders, with regard to key dimensions of delusions. Among this overall sample of psychotic patients, no significant differences were found among the different diagnostic groups on the level or extent of psychopathology manifested on the three dimensions studied. The absence of any significant differences held true both at the hospital interview and at the height of the delusional episode.

Overall, the results suggest that, during early phases of a major psychotic episode, patients of various diagnostic types who are delusional show similarities in the extent of psychopathology on certain dimensions of their delusions. It is still an open question as to whether patients with different diagnoses would also be comparable as time elapsed and they moved further into the recovery phase. It is possible that some diagnostic types would improve more rapidly at a later stage in the recovery process with respect to pathology on these three dimensions. Other data we have recently collected on positive symptoms and psychosis during the posthospital period suggest that diagnostic differences could appear after patients emerge from the acute phase (Harrow, Marengo, & McDonald, 1983; Harrow et al., 1985).

Hospital Discharge and the Dimensions of Delusions

In order to obtain construct validity on the dimensions of delusions we have studied, we have begun to assess their relationships to other variables, and other types of behavior and events. Within this framework we explored whether the hospitalized patients who maintained higher levels of emotional commitment to their delusions took longer to be discharged from the hospital than patients with lower levels of emotional commitment. Table 9.7 presents data on the relationship of emotional commitment to length of hospitalization.

When assessed after one month in the hospital, 13 of the 29 patients with complete data in this area still maintained full emotional commitment to their delusions (a score of 4 on the emotional commitment scale). The data indicated that none of these 13 patients with full emotional commitment were discharged from the hospital within the next month after their hospital assessment. Among the other 16 patients, eight (or 50 percent) were discharged from the hospital within the next month. This difference in rapidity

TABLE 9.7. 7A. Relationship of Emotional Commitment to Length of Hospitalization

Emotional Commitment After One Month in the Hospital	Subsequent Length of Hospitalization	
	Less than One Month	One Month or More
None to High	8 (50%)	8 (50%)
Very High	0	13 (100%)

7B. Relationship of Perspective to Length of Hospitalization

Perspective After One Month in the Hospital	Subsequent Length of Hospitalization	
	Less than One Month	One Month or More
Good	2 (40%)	3 (60%)
Partial or Poor	6 (21%)	22 (79%)

of discharge between patients from the sample with a score of 4 versus those with a score of 3 or less on emotional commitment was significant ($p < .05$). These data are in accord with our formulation that one of the factors leading to delusional patients' hospitalization and/or slower hospital discharge is the extent of their emotional commitment to their delusions.

In contrast, the data on both belief-conviction and on perspective indicated a lower relationship between both the extent of belief-conviction and perspective and the length of time until hospital discharge. Although hospital discharge is related to a number of factors, one interpretation of these results is that they may highlight the potential importance of a high level of emotional commitment to delusions as one factor that tends to extend the length of hospitalization.

IMPLICATIONS

We have presented results on several different aspects of delusions, but in the subsequent discussion we will focus on our main theme in the current chapter, our data on dimensions of delusions.

In the present research we have studied three major dimensions associated with delusions in psychotic patients. In the past, theory and empirical research on delusions have usually focused on the extent of patients' belief-conviction about their delusional ideas, although recently several other investigators and our own research group have begun to conduct more detailed analyses of other major dimensions of delusions (Hole et al., 1979; Kendler et al., 1983; Rudden et al., 1982; Stoll et al., 1980).

We have attempted to isolate and study three dimensions of false beliefs for purposes of empirical and conceptual analysis, although these different aspects of delusional ideation occur in vivo as interrelated parts of patients' delusional experiences. These dimensions clearly interact with and influence one another to shape delusional patients' experiences. Moreover, the extent of psychopathology on these dimensions may be influenced by some of the underlying factors. In our analysis, the three dimensions studied showed some relationship to one another. However, the data indicated that these variables can also be studied as separate dimensions. Thus, two of the three dimensions did not correlate highly with each other. In addition, their role as separate variables worthy of independent study was supported by data indicating that at the time of the hospital interview there was often improvement in one dimension without corresponding improvement in the other dimension.

Belief-Conviction and Double Awareness

With regard to the specific dimensions analyzed here, the extent of patients' belief-conviction about their delusions is probably still the central factor about which all other aspects of delusions revolve. Thus, as we have noted, without belief in their delusions, patients cannot be considered delusional.

The current study addressed several major issues concerning the nature of delusional belief systems. Delusions have traditionally been regarded as discrete and discontinuous entities, clearly separate from normal ideation (Jaspers, 1923/1963). However, the present data, indicating that over 40 percent of the patients showed a partial or wavering belief about the accuracy of their delusions after a month in the hospital, are in accord with the more recent reports of Sacks, Carpenter, and Strauss (1974), of Chapman and Chapman (1980), and our own report (Harrow & Silverstein, 1977). Sacks, Carpenter, and Strauss describe this phenomenon as a state of double awareness, in which the patient partly believes and partly does not believe his or her delusion. The present results bear on views about double awareness, since they suggest the presence of a middle ground between discrete categories of delusional and normal thinking. The presence of this middle ground also supports positions that regard delusions as points on a continuum extending from normal ideation to extremely unrealistic beliefs (Chapman & Chapman, 1980; Harrow & Silverstein, 1977; Strauss, 1969). As observed by Chapman and Chapman (this volume) in a study of nonhospitalized, psychosis-prone individuals, aberrant beliefs are reported at all degrees of deviancy, from mildly unusual to blatantly psychotic.

The current research also addresses the question of whether or not delusions are fixed ideas that are not susceptible to disconfirmation or subject to modification over time (Jaspers, 1923/1963). While some research (Rokeach, 1964) has found delusions to be relatively fixed entities, more recent studies suggest that many delusions are not as irreversible as was previously thought (Hole et al., 1979; Rudden et al., 1982). The results indicate that for some or many patients, the strength of their delusional belief-conviction diminishes over the course of their episodes. However, most patients continued to show some persistence of delusional beliefs, often at lower levels of intensity, even after a month's hospitalization, despite strong societal pressure in the direction of reality testing. This finding tends to cast doubt on the view that delusional conviction is easily or rapidly reversible for the majority of psychotic patients over a short-term period. Other recent follow-up research of ours also indicates the persistence of delusions over time for many schizophrenics, usually at reduced levels of intensity (Harrow et al., 1985).

Perspective

When we isolate the three dimensions we have studied and look at them separately, we can see that the patients' perspectives about whether other people would regard their delusional ideas as strange can be treated as an independent dimension to study in reviewing major aspects of the delusional status of the patients. At the height of their disorder almost all of the patients had at least a partial impairment in perspective, although most of these patients had a degree of intact perspective or a suspicion that their beliefs may seem "off" to other people. A partial or full impairment in perspective can be viewed as an important dimension of the delusional experience, since patients with impaired ability to judge how odd and inappropriate their delusions must seem to others would be less likely to question the accuracy of their own delusional beliefs.

The results indicating that delusional patients have impaired perspective about their unreal beliefs would fit in with our previous research suggesting that impaired perspective is a factor often involved in positive thought disorder (Harrow & Miller, 1980; Harrow & Quinlan, 1985). The results of the present study, combined with other research, tentatively could support a view that impaired perspective is an important common factor that is involved in diverse types of psychotic phenomena such as delusions, hallucinations, and severe positive thought disorder.

It should be noted, however, that many patients who were fully convinced of the truth of their delusions, and who had strong emotional commitment to their delusional beliefs, nevertheless showed at least a limited capacity for partial perspective about the social inappropriateness of their beliefs. Thus, data indicating partial perspective by a number of delusional patients even at the height of their disorder, and data indicating major psychopathology on the other two dimensions, suggest that factors other than perspective (i.e., emotional commitment) are at least as important, and may be more important, in delusional behavior.

Emotional Commitment and Hospitalization

Systematic data on the extent of emotional commitment to their delusions by schizophrenic and other psychotic patients have not been available before, although other investigators are beginning to explore this dimension. The current data indicate a very high level of emotional commitment at the height of the patients' disorders. This should not be surprising, since this was a sample of patients who were subsequently hospitalized. The data indicating a high level of emotional commitment at the height of their episode, and the data presented in Table 9.7, could fit in with our view that the emotional commitment of patients to their delusions is an important factor in their acute psychosis, and in their ultimate hospitalization.

The nearly uniformly high degree of emotional commitment to delusions shown by patients at the height of their delusions, and the large number who still maintained some degree of commitment after a month of hospital treatment, indicate that the immediacy, urgency, or dominating force to them of their delusions is not a transient matter for many *hospitalized* delusional patients. At the same time, however, the intense emotional commitment of a large number of patients does begin to diminish after a month in the hospital. As we have noted, our observations have led us to believe that a reduction of emotional commitment to a lower level is a key factor in determining how patients are viewed by others. With the reduction in emotional commitment patients are more likely to be viewed as being in partial or complete remission, even though they may still maintain some belief in their delusions. As a consequence of their reduced emotional commitment, professional staff often regarded them as able to leave the hospital. The current data support this hypothesis, suggesting the importance of emotional commitment, and we are beginning to study this variable with a new sample of delusional patients.

In relation to emotional commitment, other follow-up data of ours on patients studied after the acute phase indicate that a number are able to live outside of the hospital with partial or full belief-conviction in their delusions (Harrow & Silverstein, 1977; Harrow et al., 1985). However, such individuals generally do not show strong emotional commitment to their delusions. Our informal observations suggest that potential rehospitalization becomes an important issue at the point when (as the result of some mechanism that is presently unknown) their emotional commitment to their delusions becomes stronger and their delusions begin to dominate their thinking and their behavior. At that point they often act overtly on their delusions, and friends and relatives become extremely alarmed. Thus, an increase in the emotional commitment of an already delusional patient who has been able to maintain some minimal level of self-sufficiency outside of the hospital can result in a situation in which his or her delusions become a central part of his or her life, rather than only a peripheral one. Our observations thus far suggest that rehospitalization is often required in such cases.

Since the current research is based on patients who have been recently hospitalized—a factor that could influence the data on emotional commitment—we are now conducting a study of psychotic patients living in the community. Thus we will have an opportunity to observe whether a similar relationship between pronounced emotional commitment and subsequent hospitalization can be observed in delusional patients studied prospectively.

Diagnostic Nonspecificity of the Dimensions of Delusions

The current research has focused on major dimensions of delusions to provide a more complete picture of the nature and severity of psychopathology on these dimensions and to begin to explore their consequences, rather than focusing on which type of patients are delusional. Thus, the current research did not focus on the frequency of delusions in different diagnostic groups.

Though not the prime focus, we also have analyzed the diagnostic groups to study whether patients' scores on the three dimensions of delusions differed according to whether the patients had a schizophrenic, schizoaffective, or other type of psychotic disorder. One issue concerning diagnosis is whether certain characteristics of delusions, such as extreme emotional commitment to delusions or grossly impaired perspective, are specific to schizophrenics or are instead characteristic of delusional nonschizophrenics as well.

The results showed no significant differences between diagnostic groups, indicating that once a patient is delusional and disordered severely enough to be hospitalized, there are no major diagnostic differences on the dimensions studied. Thus although these dimensions are relevant and important in understanding major characteristics of patients' delusions, the extent of psychopathology on each is not diagnosis-specific.

These data fit in with recent empirical studies providing evidence that psychotic phenomena such as delusions, hallucinations, and even first rank symptoms are not specific to schizophrenia during either the acute in-hospital phase or the posthospital phase of disorder (Pope & Lipinski, 1978; Silverstein & Harrow, 1978, 1981; Strauss & Carpenter, 1974; Taylor, Gaztanaga, & Abrams, 1974). Some of these symptoms, however, are more frequently manifested among schizophrenics and are more likely to persist past the acute phase among schizophrenics (Harrow & Silverstein, 1977). Fitting in with this, recent findings on other major types of psychopathology that may be related to psychosis indicate that severe thought pathology is also not specific to schizophrenia (Andreasen, 1979b; Andreasen & Powers, 1974; Harrow & Quinlan, 1977, 1985; Harrow, Grossman, Silverstein, & Meltzer, 1982; Marengo & Harrow, 1985; Oltmanns, Murphy, Berenbaum, & Dunlop, 1985; Rattenbury, Silverstein, DeWolfe, Kaufman, & Harrow, 1983). It should be noted, however, that although we have analyzed the presence, extent, and shifts in frequency of three dimensions of patients' delusional ideas and found that they are not diagnosis-specific, it is possible that other aspects or dimensions of delusional ideation may differ according to diagnostic type (e.g., whether a patient is schizophrenic as opposed to some other type of psychotic disorder).

Recovery on Major Dimensions of Delusions

The current results concerning the patients' status at the height of their episodes and one month after hospitalization suggest a tentative view of the early course of delusional episodes. The data indicate that during the height of their episodes one typically finds in psychotic patients (who will be *hospitalized*) full belief-conviction about their delusions, intense emotional commitment to them, and at least moderate (but not necessarily complete) impairment in perspective about how society would view their delusions. These are probably accompanied by, and interact with, other factors not studied in the current research, such as acute upset and disturbance, and a high level of emotional turmoil.

The results indicate a significant decrease in patients' beliefs about their delusions and in their emotional commitment, as well as a significant, though smaller, improvement in perspective after a month in the hospital. The results indicating a reduction, but not complete elimination, of belief-conviction for many psychotic patients are of special theoretical interest, and are in accord with other recent research (Harrow et al., 1985; Sacks et al., 1974).

SUMMARY

This chapter presents results concerning the course of delusions over time, reports data concerning whether the content of patients' preepisode ideation is related to the content of their subsequent acute phase delusions, and analyzes data on three major dimensions of delusions. These three dimensions of delusions are (1) patients' belief-conviction about their delusions, (2) patients' perspective about whether other people will regard their ideas as aberrant or unrealistic, and (3) patients' emotional commitment to their delusions.

The data support formulations about the importance of delusions in schizophrenia, indicating that the delusions of many schizophrenics persist into the posthospital phase. Evidence also was found that the content of many patients' delusions can be traced back to their premorbid concerns.

The results of an analysis of the three dimensions of delusions noted above, studied in a combined sample of 34 schizophrenic, schizoaffective, and other psychotic patients, showed that psychotic patients had high levels of belief-conviction in their delusions at the height of their episodes. A relatively high level of belief-conviction in their delusions was maintained by many (but not all) of these psychotic patients after a month in the hospital, despite a significant overall reduction in delusional beliefs. An intermediate stage of "double awareness" was found among many delusional patients as they recovered from acute delusional episodes. Patients showed relatively poor perspective about whether most other people would regard their delusional ideation as unrealistic, although most showed at least a limited degree of recognition in this area.

At the acute phase patients showed strong emotional commitment or feelings of immediacy and urgency about their delusions. Their emotional commitment to their delusions declined significantly after a month in the hospital. Other data indicated that patients with low emotional commitment were subsequently discharged significantly more rapidly from the hospital. These data support formulations about the importance of emotional commitment in delusional states. They fit in with hypotheses that the extent of emotional commitment by a patient who is delusional is a major factor in acute psychosis, hospitalization, and subsequent hospital discharge, and contributes to others' perception of the patient as being in partial or complete remission.

REFERENCES

American Psychiatric Association. (1980). *Diagnostic and statistical manual of mental disorders* (3rd ed.) (DSM-III). New York: American Psychiatric Association.

Andreasen, N. (1979a). Thought, language and communication disorders. I. Clinical reassessment, definition of terms, and evaluation of their reliability. *Archives of General Psychiatry, 36,* 1315–1321.

Andreasen, N. (1979b). Thought, language and communication disorders. II. Diagnostic significance. *Archives of General Psychiatry, 36,* 1325–1330.

Andreasen, N.C., & Powers, P.S. (1974). Overinclusive thinking in mania and schizophrenia. *British Journal of Psychiatry, 125,* 452–456.

Berger, P.L., & Luckman, T. (1966). *The social construction of reality: A treatise on the sociology of knowledge.* Garden City, NY: Doubleday.

Bleuler, E. (1950). *Dementia praecox or the group of schizophrenias* (U. Zinkin, Trans.). New York: International Universities Press. (Original work published 1911.)

Bowers, M.B., Jr. (1974). *Retreat from sanity: The structure of emerging psychosis.* New York: Human Sciences Press.

Carr, V.J. (1983). Recovery from schizophrenia: A review of patterns of psychosis. *Schizophrenia Bulletin, 9,* 95–125.

Chapman, L.J., & Chapman, J.P. (1980). Scales for rating psychotic and psychotic like experiences as continua. *Schizophrenia Bulletin, 6,* 476–480.

Cole, J.O., Klerman, G.L., & Goldberg, S.C. (1964). Phenothiazine treatment in acute schizophrenia. *Archives of General Psychiatry, 10,* 246–261.

Docherty, J.P., Van Kammen, D.P., Siris, S.G., & Marder, S.R. (1978). Stages of onset of schizophrenic psychosis. *American Journal of Psychiatry, 135,* 420–426.

Endicott, J., & Spitzer, R. (1978). A diagnostic interview. The schedule for affective disorders and schizophrenia. *Archives of General Psychiatry, 35,* 837–844.

Freud, S. (1958). Psycho-analytic notes on an autobiographical account of a case of paranoia (dementia paranoides). *Standard edition. Complete psychological works* (Vol. 12). London: Hogarth. (Original work published 1911.)

Gift, T.E., Strauss, J.S., Kokes, R.F., Harder, D.W., & Ritzler, B.A. (1980). Schizophrenia: Affect and outcome. *American Journal of Psychiatry, 137,* 580–585.

Harrow, M., Carone, B.J., & Westermeyer, J. (1985). The course of psychosis in early phases of schizophrenia. *American Journal of Psychiatry, 142,* 702–707.

Harrow, M., Grinker, Sr., R.R., Silverstein, M., & Holzman, P. (1978). Is modern-day schizophrenic outcome still negative? *American Journal of Psychiatry, 135,* 1156–1162.

Harrow, M., Grossman, L.S., Silverstein, M.L., & Meltzer, H.Y. (1982). Thought pathology in manic and schizophrenic patients: Its occurrence at hospital admission and seven weeks later. *Archives of General Psychiatry, 39,* 665–671.

Harrow, M., Marengo, J.T., & McDonald, C. (1986). The early course of schizophrenic thought disorder. *Schizophrenia Bulletin, 12,* 208–224.

Harrow, M., & Miller, J.G. (1980). Schizophrenic thought disorders and impaired perspective. *Journal of Abnormal Psychology, 89,* 717–727.

Harrow, M., & Quinlan, D. (1977). Is disordered thinking unique to schizophrenia? *Archives of General Psychiatry, 34,* 15–21.

Harrow, M., & Quinlan, D. (1985). *Disordered thinking and schizophrenic psychopathology.* New York: Gardner Press.

Harrow, M., & Silverstein, M. (1977). Psychotic symptoms in schizophrenia after the acute phase. *Schizophrenia Bulletin, 3,* 608–616.

Harrow, M., & Silverstein, M.L. (1980). Cognitive processes during the postacute phase of schizophrenia. In S.B. Sells, R. Crandall et al. (Eds.), *Human functioning in longitudinal perspective.* Baltimore: Wilkins.

Harrow, M., Silverstein, M., & Marengo, J. (1983). Disordered thinking: Does it identify nuclear schizophrenia? *Archives of General Psychiatry, 40,* 765–711.

Heilbrun, A.B., Jr., & Heilbrun, K.S. (1977). Content analysis of delusions in reactive and process schizophrenics. *Journal of Abnormal Psychology, 86,* 597–608.

Hole, R.W., Rush, A.J., & Beck, A.T. (1979). A cognitive investigation of schizophrenic delusions. *Psychiatry, 42,* 312–319.

Jaspers, K. (1963). *General psychopathology* (J. Hoenig & Hamilton, Trans.). Chicago: University of Chicago Press. (Original work published 1923.)

Kendler, K.S., Glazer W., & Morgenstern, H. (1983). Dimensions of delusional experience. *American Journal of Psychiatry, 140,* 466–469.

Marengo, J., & Harrow, M. (1985). Thought disorder: A function of schizophrenia, mania, or psychosis? *The Journal of Nervous and Mental Disease, 173,* 35–41.

McGlashan, T.H., Levy, S.T., & Carpenter, W.T. (1975). Integration and sealing over: Clinically distinct recovery styles from schizophrenia. *Archives of General Psychiatry, 32,* 1269–1272.

Oltmanns, T.F., Murphy, R., Berenbaum, H., & Dunlop, S.R. (1985). Rating verbal communication impairment in schizophrenia and affective disorders. *Schizophrenia Bulletin, 11,* 292–299.

Pogue-Geile, M.F., & Harrow, M. (1985). Negative symptoms in schizophrenia: Their longitudinal course and prognostic importance. *Schizophrenia Bulletin, 11,* 427–439.

Pope, H., & Lipinski, J. (1978). Diagnosis in schizophrenia and manic-depressive illness. *Archives of General Psychiatry, 35,* 811–828.

Rattenbury, F.R., Harrow, M., Stoll, F.J., & Kettering, R.L. (1984). *The personal ideation inventory: An interview for assessing major dimensions of delusional thinking.* New York: Microfiche Publications.

Rattenbury, F.R., Silverstein, M.L., DeWolfe, A.S., Kaufman, C.F., & Harrow, M. (1983). Associative disturbance in schizophrenia, schizoaffective disorders, and major affective disorders: Comparisons between hospitalization and one-year follow up. *Journal of Consulting and Clinical Psychology, 51,* 621–623.

Redlich, F.C., & Freedman, D.X. (1966). *The theory and practice of psychiatry.* New York: Basic Books.

Rokeach, M. (1964). *The three Christs of Ypsilante: A psychological study.* New York: Alfred Knopf.

Rudden, M., Gilmore, M., & Frances, A. (1982). Delusions: When to confront the facts of life. *American Journal of Psychiatry, 139,* 929–932.

Sacks, M.H., Carpenter, W.T., & Strauss, J.S. (1974). Recovery from delusions. *Archives of General Psychiatry, 30,* 117–120.

Silverstein, M., & Harrow, M. (1978). First-rank symptoms in the postacute schizophrenia: A follow-up study. *American Journal of Psychiatry, 135,* 1481–1486.

Silverstein, M.L., & Harrow, M. (1981). Schneiderian first rank symptoms in schizophrenia. *Archives of General Psychiatry, 38,* 288–293.

Spitzer, R., Endicott, J., & Robins, E. (1978). Research diagnostic criteria. *Archives of General Psychiatry, 35,* 773–782.

Stoll, F., Harrow, M., Rattenbury, F., DeWolfe, A., & Harris, S.O. (1980, September). The role of perspective in schizophrenic delusions. Paper presented at the 88th Annual Meeting of the American Psychological Association, Montreal.

Strauss, J. (1969). Hallucinations and delusions as points on continua function. *Archives of General Psychiatry, 21,* 581–586.

Strauss, J.S., & Carpenter, W.T. (1974). Characteristic symptoms and outcome in schizophrenia. *Archives of General Psychiatry, 30,* 429–434.

Strauss, J.S., & Carpenter, W.T., Jr. (1977). Prediction of outcome in schizophrenia: III. Five year outcome and its predictors. *Archives of General Psychiatry, 34,* 159–163.

Taylor, M.A., Gaztanaga, P., & Abrams, R. (1974). Manic-depressive illness and acute schizophrenia: A clinical, family history, and treatment response study. *American Journal of Psychiatry, 131,* 678–682.

Wechsler, D. (1955). *Wechsler adult intelligence scale manual.* New York: Psychological Corp.

Wing, J.K., Cooper, J.E., & Sartorius, N. (1974). *The measurement and classification of psychiatric symptoms.* London: Cambridge University Press.

Zubin, J., Sutton, S., Salzinger, S., Burdock, E.I., & Peretz, D. (1961). A biometric approach in schizophrenia. In P.H. Hoch & J. Zubin (Eds.), *Comparative epidemiology in the mental disorders.* New York: Grune & Stratton.

CHAPTER 10

Some Cross-Cultural Aspects of Delusions

JOSEPH WESTERMEYER

University of Minnesota

Clinical disciplines, including the psycho-behavioral ones, are seeking hypotheses that are valid across all, or at least most, cultures. This cross-cultural approach to understanding human behavior and psychology is often termed *etic* (from the linguistic term *phon*etic, referring to sounds that are common to many languages). Etic discoveries enable the development of an international science of psychology and behavior and facilitate psychological assessment and psychiatric treatment across cultural boundaries. If psycho-behavioral disciplines remain intracultural in theory building, conclusions drawn will not have cross-cultural validity. Such non-generalizable or iso-cultural results can be termed *emic* (from the linguistic term *phon*emic, referring to meanings of sounds or words that are language specific). Emic findings are of historical and geographical interest, but do not contribute to a more general scientific understanding of the human condition.

If psycho-behavioral theories are emic in nature, they may entail certain problems. If they are mistaken to be etic when they are not, the behavior and psychology of those from other cultures may be grossly misunderstood. This can lead to considerable frustration in clinical settings, as well as in social, economic and political relationships between groups. It is also possible that academic or professional persons in other societies may erroneously assume that American findings have etic relevance for their societies, when they in fact do not. Those who mistakenly propose that their emic conclusions are etic may be justly accused of academic imperialism—that is, trying to impose their own culture-bound explanations on others.

Cross-cultural study of delusions may aid in pointing up some of the emic-etic dimensions of these psychological phenomena. This type of study provides an opportunity to test theories in order to assess the degree to which they have etic validity. Analysis of delusional material of those from other cultures can contribute to an understanding of delusions in general. The observation of marked differences in delusions across cultural boundaries would favor sociocultural explanations with strong culture-specific or emic features. If there are considerable similarities in delusions across cultural boundaries, biopsychological causation of an etic nature would be likely. Should there be a mix of similarites and differences in delusions across cultural boundaries, it would be reasonable to conclude that both sociocultural and biopsychological factors are operative (i.e., that delusions are etic in some ways and emic in other ways).

This chapter is based on three sources of information. First, the literature on cultural aspects of delusions is reviewed. Second, field notes and clinical research notes from former studies of psychopathology among American Indians, Southeast Asians (studied in Asia), foreign-born patients, and Hmong refugees in the United States are reviewed. These data come from an International Clinic conducted by the author over the last 15 years at the University of Minnesota Hospitals and Clinics, from four years of field work in Asia, and from several studies of culture and psychopathology conducted in the United States. Third, case data regarding delusions for patients and subjects being studied in current projects are reviewed.

CULTURAL VARIATIONS IN DELUSIONAL CONTENT

To what extent are delusions influenced by culture? Do delusions always evidence cultural attitudes and values? Do demographic factors with cultural implications, such as age, education, or social class, affect whether an individual's delusions are culture bound? The literature on these issues, though sparse, dates back 30 years, and may provide some notions about these questions.

Opler (1959) compared 40 Irish-American and 37 Italian-American male schizophrenics. These samples were remarkably similar with regard to age, course of illness, education, IQ, years of illness, and marital status. Despite these demographic and clinical similarites, there were differences in their delusional systems. The Irish-Americans were more apt to manifest disordered thinking with regard to sexuality and sin and guilt preoccupations. The Italian-Americans had more fixity in their delusion systems and more hypochondriacal delusions. The delusions of the Irish-Americans indicated more compliant attitudes toward authority, while those of the Italian-Americans manifested more rejecting attitudes toward authority. Similarly overdetermined delusional content has been observed in many other cultural groups. East Indian schizophrenics demonstrated more negativism as compared to schizophrenics elsewhere (Wittkower, Murphy, Fried, & Ellenberger, 1960). African schizophrenics demonstrated less aggressive content (Benedict & Jacks, 1954), while Iraqi schizophrenics have shown more aggressiveness (Bazzouli & Al-Issa, 1966). Weinstein (1962) studied the content of psychotic delusions in the Virgin Islands. He found that the content of delusions correlated strongly with local cultural values and symbols. Delusional themes with culture-bound features included issues of identity, family organization, sex roles, interpersonal relationships (in particular the parent-child dyad), language, and religion.

There is some indication that delusional content is not only culture bound, but also perhaps bound to particular historical periods. Klaf and Hamilton (1961) found that, among nineteenth-century patients in London's Bedlam Royal Hospital, delusional themes focused more on religion and less on sex as compared to the themes of twentieth-century patients in the same facility. The same observation was made in Zurich, where delusions among psychotic patients of 1912 were compared with those of 1973 (Steinbrunner & Scharfetter, 1976). A diminution of religious and magic themes was evident in delusional content observed over the six-decade period.

CLINICAL DETERMINATION OF DELUSIONS ACROSS CULTURES

If culture-bound aspects of delusions (i.e., content, as suggested in the previous section) were overriding, one might conclude that clinicians would often be unable to ascertain whether culture-bound thoughts expressed by someone from an unfamiliar culture were delusional. Conversely, if the structure of delusions were the critical element, clinicians would always recognize and correctly identify delusions in patients from unfamiliar cultures. Alternatively, if both viewpoints were partially valid, one would expect some interrater reliability among psychiatrists of all cultures, but greater interrater reliability among psychiatrists who are of the same culture, or who are at least familiar with the patient's culture. Does the literature indicate whether the etic dimensions of delusions (i.e., form or structure) are sufficient to permit adequate cross-cultural assessment of delusions? Or do the emic dimensions of delusions (i.e., culture-bound aspects of content) preclude such cross-cultural assessment? Several studies from the last 15 years may help to clarify these issues.

In the early seventies, a cross-cultural study of schizophrenia diagnosis was begun under the auspices of the World Health Organization, focusing on diagnostic criteria among various countries. This study showed that psychiatrists from different countries applied the same or fairly similar diagnostic criteria to patients in their own societies (Carpenter, Strauss, & Bartko, 1973). Some differences were observed among American psychiatrists in the early 1970s; Americans applied the schizophrenia diagnosis when psychiatrists from other countries used the bipolar diagnosis—a difference that has largely disappeared in recent years (Tsuang, 1976; United States-United Kingdom Cross-National Project, 1974). Despite this difference, a study undertaken around the same time, in which British, American, and Swiss psychiatrists were asked to make diagnoses based on videotapes of American patients, showed a high diagnostic agreement for the major categories of schizophrenia, affective disorder, and organic syndromes (Surawicz & Sandifer, 1970).

Leff (1974) studied nine psychiatrists from technically developed countries and four psychiatrists from developing countries. Using videotapes of 26 patients from both developing and developed countries, he observed that all psychiatrists showed good diagnostic agreement for the patients from developed societies. Moreover, psychiatrists from the developing countries showed good agreement with one another on patients from the technically developing countries. However, psychiatrists from technically developed countries showed poor agreement for patients from developing countries. Leff concluded that psychiatrists from the developing countries were more perceptive with both kinds of patients because they had had experience with patients from both developed and developing countries (usually during their training in technically developed countries), while psychiatrists from the technically developed countries usually had had experience only with patients from their own type of society. (Another possibility is that psychiatrists from developing countries might be more familiar with similar categories of culture-bound ideas—such as those regarding sorcery, ghosts, and animistic forces in nature—whereas psychiatrists from developed countries are not as familiar with these.)

Westermeyer and Sines (1979) studied five clinicians trained in the West, including four psychiatrists (one Asian-born) and one clinical psychologist. These cases consisted of 35 subjects identified as *baa*, or "insane," in Laos. Three of the clinicians had had extensive psychiatric experience in Asia, and two had not. Using the Kappa score (Fleiss, 1971) to compare diagnoses, the authors found that ratings by the "Asia experienced" raters versus the "Asia inexperienced" raters were essentially the same. Their ratings showed the highest interrater reliability for organic psychosis, the second highest for schizophrenia, and the lowest for affective psychosis.

The patient's cultural orientation has also been studied as a factor in delusional content. In a study of 69 patients at the University of Kuwait, local and largely traditional Kuwaiti patients (with only recent foreign influences) were compared with Arab patients from other Arab countries (El-Islam & Malasi, 1985). The Kuwaiti patients were found to have significantly more delusions centered around supernatural phenomena (e.g., sorcery, devil [*Shaitan*], or spirits [*Jinn*]). This difference held both for men

TABLE 10.1.   Social Class and Number of Patients with
Religious and Secular Delusions

Class	Religious Content	Secular Content
Low	33	28
Middle	8	22
High	3	16

($p < .02$) and for women ($p < .05$) in the sample. Contrary to expectations, delusional level or history of residence abroad was not related to delusional content. It was concluded that family and school socialization during childhood were the critical factors in determining delusional content. Jimens, Oritiz-de Zorate, and Antonio (1979), in a review of this topic, also concluded that religious, magical, and mythical beliefs tend to appear in delusional content when these beliefs are prevalent in culturally supported institutions.

In a study of 110 paranoid or schizophrenic persons in Eygpt, social class was found to influence delusional content (El Sendiony, 1976). As in other studies, males and females did not show a significant difference. Those in the lower social classes were more apt to manifest religious content (e.g., thinking that one is Mohammed, God, a saint, a great prophet, or is controlled by sorcery), while those in the upper classes displayed more secularized content (e.g., thinking that one is under the influence of computers, that x-rays or electricity are going through the body, or that one is being spied upon or watched by the government). The data are shown in Table 10.1 [χ^2 (2 d.f., $N = 110$) = 9.86].

Data from Laotian psychotic persons (mostly schizophrenic, with some affective and organic psychosis) indicated a relatively low level of culture-bound delusional content. The sample included 35 persons surveyed in villages and a town in Laos (Westermeyer & Sines, 1979). Delusion assessment in this group is given in Table 10.2. The three subjects (all schizophrenics)

TABLE 10.2.   Types of Delusions in Psychotic Laotian Patients

Delusional Status	Number of Subjects
No current delusions	2
Probable delusions, but patient mute or nonsensical	7
Secular delusions	23
Culture-bound delusions	3

with culture-bound delusions also had non-culture-bound delusions as follows:

1. A 33-year-old single man, living on the grounds of a temple, expected the imminent arrival of his deceased relatives, who would fly from heaven back to Laos in order to assist him. This relatively optimistic delusion was countered by two distressful delusions: that metal pieces had gotten into his abdomen and were causing him pain, and that communists and other political activists were plotting against him.

2. A 45-year-old divorced male expressed fear of ghosts, who might come out of the forest and kill him. On the "direction of a spirit," he ate only once a day. He believed that he was a professor whose task in life was to teach people traditional Lao myths. Episodically he feared that others in the village were against him and wanted to harm him.

3. A 22-year-old single man was chronically afraid that certain spirits and deceased ancestors wanted to kill him. He heard the threatening voices of these spirits and at times conversed or argued with them. He accused others in his village of sending the police after him and of "putting electricity" into his body. At times he would act on these paranoid delusions and had to be restrained.

One man had secular delusions of a somatic and nihilistic type (diagnosis was recurrent psychotic depression). However, he dealt with these in a highly traditional and religious fashion:

4. A 43-year-old single man believed that his disorder was due to his own sinfulness from childhood, and his past disobedience toward his now-deceased parents. In order to make amends for his delusional sinfulness, he had established a large shrine for propitiation to the Lord Buddha and his parents. He had spent the previous two decades constructing an extensive shrine with scores of concrete figures up to 50 feet high.

In another case, described elsewhere (Westermeyer, 1972, 1973), secular delusions also resulted in traditional behavior, albeit with a modern adaptation:

5. A 26-year-old was publicly reprimanded at a temple festival for dancing in a nontraditional style. He angrily left the festival, returning later with a grenade, which he flung into the group, killing 16 and wounding 20. Rather than escaping, he jumped into the middle of the chaos, shouting that he had done it and had no remorse about it. (While

traditional *amok* with bladed weapon was known under such circumstances, this man innovatively employed a modern rather than a traditional weapon.)

Of interest, the cases with culture-bound delusions or delusion-dominated culture-bound behavior involved the so-called functional psychoses (i.e., schizophrenia, affective psychosis, paranoia) rather than organic psychoses (in which delusions as well as consequent behavior were secular).

Little can be concluded from such a small number of subjects with religious or culture-bound delusional content. Perhaps the very sparseness of such content may point to the practical or secular nature of these Laotians, most of whom were illiterate or barely literate peasants. In contrast to other studies, there were only four men with religious delusions in the sample, although 16 of the 35 subjects were women (a difference that has only borderline significance at the .07 level, using the hypergeometric probability distribution of Lieberman & Owen, 1971). The predominance of men in this small sample may be due to the fact that in Lao society virtually all men went to the Buddhist temple for instruction in their faith during childhood, whereas virtually no women did so (at least during childhood).

Despite these marked differences in delusional content across cultures, it should be emphasized that the form or structure of delusions remains remarkably constant. Regardless of culture, the delusional form of psychotic persons includes such themes as grandiosity, paranoia, nihilism, negativism, somatism, guilt, and shame.

Summing up, the following conclusions may be drawn from the available literature on delusions and culture:

1. The structure of delusions varies little, if any, across cultures, whereas the content may be influenced by culture.
2. In developing countries, culture-bound aspects of delusional content involve principally religious and traditional culture-bound world views, especially those that are being undermined by modern secular society.
3. Elements of culture-bound content in delusions seem to be acquired during childhood in the home and elementary school, rather than later, during advanced education or experience in other cultures.
4. Males and females generally show similar delusional content, although content may differ when socialization experiences differ greatly as a function of gender. Rudden, Sweeney, Francis, and Gilmore (1983) have also described certain differences in delusional content between men and women in the United States, involving mostly affective and sexual material. (Further work is needed on this point.)

5. Culture-bound (i.e., emic) and secular (i.e., etic) delusional content are not mutually exclusive, but may coexist in the same individual.
6. Delusional content can be quite etic, or secular, and yet still give rise to behaviors that are highly culture bound or emic (such as building a religious shrine or undertaking *amok*-type violence).

Westermeyer and Zimmerman (1981) also compared the folk diagnosis of *baa* ("crazy" or "insane") with the psychiatric diagnosis of psychosis. The same five clinicians and case studies were used as in the study described above. In this study the "Asia experienced" psychiatrists showed high Kappa scores—that is, good reliability—with villagers (i.e., .63, .63, and .68), while the "Asia inexperienced" raters showed much lower Kappa scores (.21 and .52).

In most studies of cross-cultural diagnosis, the culturally inexperienced clinicians demonstrated both overdiagnoses and underdiagnoses. That is, at times they did not recognize delusions (when others thought they were present), and at other times they labeled certain ideas as delusional (when others thought the ideas were culturally consistent and normal). This problem, as well as methods for coping with it, has been detailed elsewhere (Westermeyer, 1987).

Difficulties can arise when the delusions expressed are supported by the patient's reference group. For example, the family of the third subject described in the section above believed that the spirit of a deceased relative (and perhaps other spirits) were speaking to the subject, even though they could not hear the voices. Further, they believed that these spirits had malevolent intentions—perhaps even intentions of death—against their relative. However, they also believed that he was *baa* (Lao for "insane") because he killed two small animals, ran away from home occasionally, could not work, and wrongfully accused fellow villagers of wanting to harm him. Thus, the family accepted the voices and *some* of the delusions as true phenomena, while interpreting other false ideas as delusions and interpreting the person's behavior as insane. (In fact, they blamed the spirits for making him insane—a notion similar to some traditional Christian notions of demon possession.) Murphy (1967) has labeled such rare but difficult clinical examples as "delusionary cultural belief" (i.e., "receives general acceptance within a cultural unit but which appears . . . to be improbable, to lack objective verification or even to be objectively disprovable") (p. 684). El Sendiony (1976) has also addressed this issue, referring to such cases as "diagnostic difficulties in intercultural situations." He opines that in these special situations "only a close knowledge of the cultural conditions" (p. 201) will permit adequate psychiatric assessment. At the same time he acknowledges that even then it may be difficult to distinguish strongly held, eccentric, culturally inconsistent ideas (often with religious or political overtones) from delusional thinking, although presence of other psychopathological characteristics and deterioration, from fixed ideas to loose association, usually aids in clarifying the situation.

Research findings at this time permit the following generalizations regarding cross-cultural assessment of delusions:

1. Both the structure and the content of most delusions are not culture-bound and can be readily identified across cultural boundaries.

2. Where the content of the expressed idea is culture bound, the structure of the idea (e.g., grandiose, paranoid, nihilistic) becomes relatively more important. Especially when religious or political themes are involved, it behooves the clinician to seek further clarification or consultation (e.g., from a clinician familiar with the cultural group, an anthropologist, or a cultural peer of the patient).

3. There will still be a small residuum of cases, usually mild or early cases of mental disorder or socially eccentric or revolutionary persons, in whom the determination of delusions is difficult. Consultation and discussion among culturally experienced clinicians can usually resolve the difficulty, although at times one must still apply "the test of time" and follow the person's course over an extended period.

SOCIOCULTURAL FACTORS AND PARANOIA

The previous two sections, which have addressed differences in delusional content across cultures, indicate that delusional structure (e.g., grandiosity, paranoia, nihilism) is constant and recognizable by clinicians across cultural boundaries. Another important question is whether cultural factors affect the distribution of delusional structure in a population of psychotic persons. It would be useful to know whether some cultures are more apt to produce grandiose delusions; other cultures, paranoid delusions; and so forth. Unfortunately, the data available do not permit even a tentative response to this question. A large body of information does exist, however, on the effects of sociocultural change on delusional structure, with reference to paranoia in particular.

Over the last 50 years clinicians have described a high rate of paranoid symptomatology among migrants in general (Odegaard, 1932), but especially among refugees who become psychiatric patients (Murphy, 1955). This type of delusional structure accompanies a variety of diagnostic entities, including depression, mania, schizophrenia, and various paranoid disturbances (Pedersen, 1949; Kino, 1951; Williams & Westermeyer, 1986). This high percentage of paranoid symptoms was first observed among Eastern

European refugees who relocated to Western Europe following World War II, and was later described among Indochinese refugees arriving in the United States during the 1970s and 1980s.

Is this high rate of paranoid symptoms *in patients* a function of individual maladjustment and the various factors involved in becoming a patient? Or is some general culture-wide suspiciousness merely exaggerated in those who become patients? If the former were the case, then the paranoid structure of a migrant's paranoia would be due to individual environment differences. If the latter were the case, the cultural group might be influencing the psychopathology of the refugee—an example of culture affecting the structure of delusions. The following paragraphs describe a project in which the author and his colleagues have sought to clarify this question.

In a sample of nonpatient Hmong refugees from Laos, the paranoid symptomatology item of the Symptom Checklist Scale (SCL) did not get the highest score on the 90-item checklist (Derogatis, Rickels, & Rock, 1976). Depression, Interpersonal Sensitivity, and Obsessive Compulsiveness scales all were higher. Over a period of time, these other elevated scales fell in the direction of normality, however, while the Paranoia scale remained elevated (Westermeyer, Neider, & Vang, 1984). The items on which the self-rated Paranoia scale is based are as follows:

Feeling others are to blame for most of your troubles (SCL-8);

Feeling that most people cannot be trusted (SCL-18);

Feeling that you are watched by or talked about by others (SCL-43);

Having ideas or beliefs that others do not share (SCL-68);

Feeling that others do not give you proper credit for your achievements (SCL-76);

Feeling that people will take advantage of you if you let them (SCL-83).

TABLE 10.3. **Scores on the Paranoia Scale for Nonpatient Hmong Refugees**

Symptom Checklist (SCL) Item		Mean Score		
		1977–1978 (n = 93)	1979–1980 (n = 89)	1983–1985 (n = 97)
Blames others	SCL-8	.59	.41	.53
Cannot trust others	SCL-18	1.39	1.57	1.30
Watched/talked about	SCL-43	1.01	.84	.77
Ideas not shared by others	SCL-68	.76	.71	.67
No proper credit	SCL-76	.94	.81	.92
Taken advantage of	SCL-83	1.11	.76	.98
SCL-Paranoia (all six scales)		.96	.83	.86

TABLE 10.4. Paranoia Rating Based on Interviews with
Nonpatient Hmong Refugees

Item	Number of Subjects
No paranoid symptoms	50 (52%)
Some trouble trusting others	22 (23%)
Suspicious of others	20 (21%)
Ideas of reference	3 (3%)
Delusions of reference or persecution	2 (2%)
	97 (101%)*

*Percent exceeds 100 due to rounding off.

These items (translated into Hmong and Hmong-dialect Lao) were scored by the individual as follows: 0 = not at all, 1 = a little bit, 2 = moderately, 3 = quite a bit, 4 = extremely. Despite some initial statistically insignificant improvement, the scores in these subjects remained high (see Table 10.3).

In addition to the self-rated SCL scale, the author also rated paranoia based on individual interviews from 1983 to 1985. Data for this rating were obtained during interviews lasting 1.5 to 2.0 hours. Of the 102 subjects in the sample, 97 permitted the interview. Number of subjects by category is shown in Table 10.4. This global rating, made without access to the subject's self-rating, revealed a group distribution similar to that obtained by the self-rated SCL Paranoia scale items.

These findings indicate high levels of mistrust and suspiciousness among refugees generally, amounting to about 50 percent of the group. Thus, it seems that the few individuals reaching clinical awareness with more severe paranoid symptoms fall at the extreme and along a spectrum for the entire group, rather than representing an entirely separate or bimodal distribution. Anecdotally, this conclusion is supported by the fact that many refugees (and not just refugee patients) have experiences that might elicit mistrust and suspiciousness. These include being the object of hostility by natives, being taken advantage of, not realizing their expectations in the new country, not understanding the new language and culture, and projection of hostile feelings at having their own lives so completely disrupted.

FOLK DESCRIPTIONS OF DELUSIONS

One problem in ascertaining the presence or absence of delusions in cross-cultural contexts involves language. One must phrase questions to the subject in a culturally appropriate fashion in order to elicit possible delusions. Then, in order to determine if the idea is culturally consistent, one must ask the subject's peers about the rationality or appropriateness of the idea. Some examples of strategies for the latter are presented below.

There are no technical terms for delusions in the Lao language. Villagers do use the following terms, however, for beliefs that we would term delusional: "foolish thoughts," "wrong ideas," or "false beliefs" (Westermeyer & Wintrob, 1979). Examples include the following:

He says that someone stole his wife and children, but he has never been married and has no children.

He thinks that people have put an electric current into him and that they are trying to poison him. He also thinks that people are sending the police after him to harm him.

He thinks that he might be killed by others, especially at night. So he keeps a knife by his bed, and he keeps the lamp on all night long. He stays awake and vigilant until sunrise.

Informants mentioned foolish thoughts, wrong ideas, or false beliefs as criteria for *baa* ("insane" or "crazy") for 25 of the 35 subjects who were studied in Laos. More than 25 of these subjects had delusional ideas in the author's judgment, but informants mentioned folk evidence of the *baa* disorder in only 25 of the 35 cases. Other common folk criteria included danger to self (26 subjects), nonviolent but socially disruptive behavior (27 cases), incomprehensible or nonsensical speech (26 cases), dysfunctional behavior—behavior viewed as strange, unexpected, or embarrassing (34 cases)—social isolation (29 cases), and inability to work (27 cases).

In sum, *delusion* is a technical term that can have several synonyms in the daily or common language of a people. For example, the Lao used three phrases to describe ideas not consistent with their own cultural reality. Once informants described the particular idea they categorized as *baa*, it was usually obvious (in the context of the case) whether delusions were present. Six other abnormal characteristics of mentally ill persons were named more often than false beliefs by villagers as folk criteria for *baa*, suggesting that social behavior was a more important consideration than the individual's disturbed psychological processes.

DELUSION OR CULTURALLY SYNTONIC BELIEF: *KORO* AND HEART ATTACK

Clinicians often interpret unfamiliar belief systems as delusional, especially when the systems do not fit known pathological entities or when they seem highly unlikely. In fact, such belief systems may or may not be evidence of delusions.

Koro provides us with an example. This is an Asian folk syndrome in which the penis is thought to be shrinking up into the abdomen; total disappearance into the abdomen is believed to be followed by immediate death. *Koro* can exist as a nondelusional accompaniment of various psychiatric disorders. For example, an Asian patient in the midst of a panic attack may fear impending doom as a result of imminent *koro*. Such a patient may not believe that his penis is shrinking or has shrunk, but rather that it *might* shrink and thus cause death. This contrasts with the *koro* patient who believes that his penis has already begun to shrink into his abdomen, and that death is imminent. The patient suffering from the panic attack is much like the North American patient with a panic attack who fears death from a heart attack in association with chest pain, dyspnea, acute anxiety, and so forth. The *koro* patient resembles the North American patient who is convinced that he is dying of cancer. The patient suffering from panic believes that he *might* have a heart attack or *koro* in association with panic, whereas the other type of patient is convinced that he *has koro* or cancer and death will inevitably ensue.

Recently a depressed Vietnamese refugee woman told a resident and the author that she feared death because the spirit of her deceased mother had been appearing in her dreams. The resident believed that this represented a delusional misinterpretation of the patient's dreams, and concluded that she was psychotically depressed. He recommended hospitalization, with neuroleptic and antidepressant medication. The author believed that the patient's dream was consistent with her cultural beliefs, because certain dreams (such as seeing a deceased person) are considered harbingers of death. Moreover, dreams are seen by many Asian peasant and tribal people as actual events rather than merely as psychological phenomena, so that her mother's spirit was, to her, actually traveling from the after-life back to this life in order to communicate with her. The author recommended psychotherapy (given the other elements of the case), supplemented by antidepressant medication if the patient failed to improve within a session or two. On the latter regimen the patient recovered uneventfully.

These examples underscore the need to clarify the meaning of unfamiliar material expressed by patients from other cultures. This is especially true when unfamiliar notions represent the patient's *interpretations* of actual events or symptoms (e.g., anxiety symptoms, dreams) as opposed to more typical delusional themes (e.g., paranoia, grandiosity, nihilism).

DELUSIONS IN THE SERVICE OF THE COMMUNITY

On several occasions during field work in rural areas of Asia, the author has observed otherwise intact individuals undergo time-limited experiences that they viewed as preternatural. We might view these as brief psychotic episodes. These events often occurred in the context of extraordinary family or communal stress. The following is an example.

A Lao man, the author's friend and former Lao language instructor, had graduated from high school and attended the East-West Center at the University of Hawaii for two years. He lived in the national capital, Vientiane, but on weekends he would return to the village where he had been born and raised. Still in his midtwenties, he was viewed by villagers as a burgeoning leader by virtue of his knowledge and experience regarding the world outside the village. Prior to the event he related, he had been distressed as a result of a conflict within the village. One of the villagers was planning to cut down a huge tree and sell it for a princely sum—approximately the amount of money that it would take a villager two years to earn. This decision had come about because of new private property laws stating that large trees on a privately owned plot of land belonged to the individual personally. This constitutional law was at odds with the traditional law. Traditionally, large village trees were seen as belonging to the entire village, or at least to the many houses for which a tree provided shade from the hot midday sun. Further, large trees were believed to possess their own spirits. These spirits might prove beneficial to the villagers if the trees received proper care, but could cause damage and harm if the sanctity of the tree was not respected. The village chief had been unable to solve this problem, which occurred at the intersection between traditional mores and modern constitutional law. Villagers had then sought the advice of the author's friend, who had spoken to government authorities. The latter indicated that the government would have to support the man who was planning to cut down his tree. Thus, there seemed to be no means by which the traditional communal law might hold sway. Bicycling home at dusk to his village, the author's friend was passing by the tree in question when—according to him—a blinding light leaped out of the tree and struck him to the ground. There then came a voice from the tree indicating that the speaker was the spirit of the tree. The spirit threatened to "eat a village child" if the tree were cut down. The author's friend was found rolling on the ground and moaning in the midst of the village, unable to walk and obviously agitated. A healer was summoned, and interpreted the events as indicating that a village child would die if the tree were cut down. Further, the healer indicated that the person responsible for the death of the next child would be the tree owner. Now greatly alarmed, the entire village threatened the tree owner that he would be responsible for the murder of this unnamed child if he proceeded with cutting down the tree. At this point, he announced publicly that the tree would not be cut down. A series of healing rituals were held on Saturday for the author's friend, and he had recovered entirely by Sunday afternoon so that he was able to return to his work in the city.

What do such cases have to tell us regarding hallucinations and delusions? Certainly the man was highly stressed by this sequence of events. On the one hand he wanted to see the community resolve its problem, regardless of what decision was made—the tree itself did not hold a lot of meaning for him since he spent relatively little time in the village. If anything, as a modern Lao he was more committed to constitutional law than to traditional law. His role as a developing village leader, one who understood the nuances of the changing society and could interpret them to villagers, was also a powerful influence to him. All of this produced considerable pressure. By the same token, his preternatural experience with the tree spirit began and ended at times that were convenient to his work schedule back in town. His hallucinatory and delusional content was highly slanted toward an outcome that would resolve this community dilemma. Yet in recounting the story he was apparently completely amazed by the sequence of events. While one might describe the event as hysterical, the man did not demonstrate other concomitants of hysteria in his personality or day-to-day behavior.

Such cases occur not only in illiterate Asian village people, but also among college graduates. In the case of the author's friend, for example, the man had been socialized as a child in his traditional culture and had retained many attitudes and values consistent with that culture, despite exposure to higher education and modern influences. Events such as the one that he experienced tend to be highly time limited and to serve family or communal ends.

Was this person delusional? From the perspective of his fellow villagers, no. They believed that the great tree did possess a spirit, that the spirit had every reason to be angry, and that tree spirits were capable of making themselves known to individuals—even to the extent of knocking them off their bikes, or killing them. Did he have hallucinations and delusions from a technical perspective? Yes, he did. But is this question relevant? The man did not present to a clinical facility; he was not impaired; and he did not need or want any ministrations. At the same time he was sufficiently in awe of the experience to describe it to a foreign friend whom he knew to be interested in his culture and in such unusual events. How does one resolve this apparent discrepancy between folk and professional perspectives with regard to delusions? Perhaps it might be better to ask whether one should even try to resolve the discrepancy between the two systems. Folk and professional systems also differ with regard to such categories as heart problems, pregnancy, and fracture. The two systems have different purposes, although it seems likely that folk concepts affect professional concepts as well as vice versa (Kroll, 1973; Tseng, 1974; Westermeyer & Wintrob, 1979a,b). The two systems provide explanations of mental and behavioral phenomena that arouse fear and anxiety, anger and remorse. While the two systems can be complementary to an extent, each inevitably reflects its own orientation, assumptions, method of information acquisition, and analytic techniques.

Fortunately, delusions in the service of the community do not produce mischief in clinical settings, because they are rarely referred for treatment. They do provide a challenge, however, for attempts to understand delusions, along with their genesis, neurophysiology, and psychology. In certain respects these phenomena resemble short-lived, drug-precipitated psychoses—but with community-induced stress as a precipitant rather than a drug.

SUMMARY

Are delusions emic or etic phenomena? Most often, delusions are etic in both structure and content. This is true even in highly traditional societies, where people are socialized to have a world view strongly influenced by religion. Culture has a great influence on the content of delusional material. In cases of emic delusional content, childhood socialization experiences seem to weigh most heavily. Cultural change seems to foster increases in the proportion of paranoid delusions—the one example cited here of culture affecting delusional structure. Like the broad-based socialization experiences, the paranoia of the refugee or migrant has its correlates in the reference group at large (rather than being merely idiosyncratic to a few particular patients).

In most cross-cultural instances, it is quite feasible for experienced clinicians to ascertain the presence or absence of delusions with a high degree of reliability. Collateral informants can be helpful in this process. Clinicians should be especially cautious in labeling the patient's interpretation of a physical or physiological symptom as delusional. It is necessary to take into account the health beliefs prevalent in the patient's culture in the formulation of such judgments.

REFERENCES

Bazzouli, W., & Al-Issa, I. (1966). Psychiatry in Iraq. *British Journal of Psychiatry, 112*, 827–832.

Benedict, P.K., & Jacks, J. (1954). Mental illness in primitive societies. *Psychiatry, 17*, 377–389.

Carpenter, W.T., Strauss, J.S., & Bartko, J.J. (1973). A flexible system for the diagnosis of schizophrenia. Report from the WHO International Pilot Study of Schizophrenia. *Science, 182*, 1275.

Derogatis, L.R., Rickels, K., & Rock, A.F. (1976). The SCL-90 and the MMPI: A step in the validation of a new self-report scale. *British Journal of Psychiatry, 128*, 280–289.

El-Islam, M.F., & Malasi, T.H. (1985). Delusions and education. *Journal of Operational Psychiatry, 16,* 29–31.

El Sendiony, H.F.M. (1976). Cultural aspects of delusions: A psychiatry study of Egypt. *Australia New Zealand Journal of Psychiatry, 10,* 201–207.

Fleiss, J.L. (1971). Measuring nominal scale agreement among many raters. *Psychological Bulletin, 76,* 378–382.

Jimens, L., Oritiz-de Zorate, A., & Antonio, P. (1979). Brain delusions and myths. *Revista Psiquiatria Psicologia Medica, 14,* 113–122.

Kino, F.F. (1951). Refugee psychosis in Great Britain: Aliens paranoid reaction. *Journal of Mental Science, 87,* 589–594.

Klaf, F.S., & Hamilton, J.G. (1961). Schizophrenia—A hundred years ago and today. *Journal of Mental Science, 107,* 819–827.

Kroll, J. (1973). A reappraisal of psychiatry in the Middle Ages. *Archives of General Psychiatry, 29,* 276–283.

Leff, J.P. (1974). Transcultural influence on psychiatrists' rating of verbally expressed emotion. *British Journal of Psychiatry, 125,* 336.

Lieberman, G.J., & Owen, D.B. (1971). *Tables of the hypergeometric probability distribution.* Stanford, CA: Stanford University Press.

Murphy, H.B.M. (1955). *Flight and resettlement.* Paris: United Nations Educational, Scientific and Cultural Organization.

Murphy, H.B.M. (1967). Cultural aspects of delusion. *Stadium Generale, 20,* 684–692.

Odegaard, O. (1932). Emigration and insanity. *Acta Psychiatrica Scandinavica, Supplementum IV,* 9–206.

Opler, M.K. (1959). Cultural differences in mental disorders: An Italian and Irish contrast in the schizophrenia—U.S.A. In M.K. Opler (Ed.), *Culture and mental health.* New York: Macmillan.

Pedersen, S. (1949). Psychopathological reactions to extreme social displacements (refugee neuroses). *Psychoanalytical Review, 36,* 344–354.

Rudden, M., Sweeney, J., Francis, A., & Gilmore, M. (1983). A comparison of delusional disorders in women and men. *American Journal of Psychiatry, 140,* 1575–1578.

Steinbrunner, S., & Scharfetter, C. (1976). Changes in delusional psychosis—A historical transcultural comparison. *Archiv fur Psychiatrie und Nervenkrankheitan, 222,* 47–60.

Surawicz, F.G., & Sandifer, M.G. (1970). Cross cultural diagnosis: A study of psychiatric diagnosis, comparing Switzerland, the United States and the United Kingdom. *International Journal of Psychiatry, 16,* 232.

Tseng, W.S. (1974). The development of psychiatric concepts in traditional Chinese medicine. *Archives of General Psychiatry, 29,* 569–575.

Tsuang, M.T. (1976). Schizophrenia around the world. *Comprehensive Psychiatry, 17,* 477–481.

United States-United Kingdom Cross-National Project: The diagnosis and psychopathology of schizophrenia in New York and London. (1974). *Schizophrenia Bulletin, 1,* 80–102.

Weinstein, E.A. (1962). *Cultural aspects of delusion.* New York: Free Press.

Westermeyer, J. (1972). A comparison of amok and other homicide in Laos. *American Journal of Psychiatry, 129,* 703–709.

Westermeyer, J. (1973). On the epidemicity of amok. *Archives of General Psychiatry, 28,* 873–876.

Westermeyer, J. (1985). Psychiatric diagnosis across cultural boundaries. *American Journal of Psychiatry, 142,* 798–805.

Westermeyer, J. (1987). Clinical considerations in cross cultural diagnosis. *Hospital and Community Psychiatry, 38,* 160–165.

Westermeyer, J., Neider, J., & Vang, T.F. (1984). Acculturation and mental health: A study of Hmong refugees at 1.5 and 3.5 years postmigration. *Social Science Medicine, 18,* 87–93.

Westermeyer, J., & Sines, L. (1979). Reliability of cross-cultural psychiatric diagnosis with an assessment of two rating contexts. *Journal of Psychiatric Research, 15,* 199–213.

Westermeyer, J., & Wintrob, R. (1979a). "Folk" criteria for the diagnosis of mental illness in rural Laos: On being insane in sane places. *American Journal of Psychiatry, 136,* 755–761.

Westermeyer, J., & Wintrob, R. (1979b). "Folk" explanations of mental illness in Laos. *American Journal of Psychiatry, 136,* 901–905.

Westermeyer, J., & Zimmerman, R. (1981). Lao folk diagnoses for mental disorder: Comparison with psychiatric diagnosis and assessment with psychiatric rating scales. *Medical Anthropology, 5,* 425–443.

Williams, C., & Westermeyer, J. (1986). *Refugee mental health resettlement countries.* New York: Hemisphere Press.

Wittkower, E.D., Murphy, H.B., Fried, J., & Ellenberger, H. (1960). A cross-cultural inquiry into the symptomatology of schizophrenia. *Annals of the New York Academy of Sciences, 84,* 854–863.

CHAPTER 11

Delusions: Culture, Psychosis and the Problem of Meaning

ATWOOD D. GAINES

Case Western Reserve University

Delusions are associated with a number of psychiatric conditions of an organic, toxicological, or psychological origin. Examples of each might be senile dementia, amphetamine-induced delusional disorder and schizophrenia, according to the *Diagnostic and Statistical Manual of Mental Disorders* (DSM-III) of the American Psychiatric Association (APA, 1980). The emphasis in American psychiatry is generally on the meaning of the delusional material as seen from some standard of believability. This standard is essentially unspecified yet is somehow unproblematic as, for example, in the case of the diagnostic criteria for schizophrenic disorders (APA, 1980):

1. Bizarre delusions (content is patently absurd and has no possible basis in fact, such as delusions of being controlled, thought broadcasting, thought insertion or thought withdrawal).
2. Somatic, grandiose, religious, nihilistic, or other delusions without persecutory or jealous content.
3. Delusions with persecutory or jealous content if accompanied by hallucinations of any type.

In the anthropology of religion and in cultural (anthropological) psychiatry (Kleinman, 1980a), formerly called comparative (Yap, 1974), transcultural (Wittkower & Prince, 1974) or cross-cultural psychiatry, the problematics of the universality of the criteria delineating the delusional have been raised. In these fields, research has discerned the relativity of material considered in the West to be delusional. There is now recognition that beliefs of particular cultural groups, both at home and abroad, may

---

The author would like to thank Drs. Richard Day and Thomas Oltmanns for their helpful comments and criticisms of drafts of the present chapter.

seem bizarre and delusional in the context of American psychiatry. Simultaneously, it is increasingly difficult to maintain that the perspective of American psychiatry (or psychology) is uniquely capable of universally differentiating normal from pathological ideation.

Recent anthropological research has demonstrated that psychiatry, as a branch of Western professional medicine (called "biomedicine"; see Gaines & Hahn, 1982; Hahn & Gaines, 1985; Weisberg & Long, 1984) is anything but an acultural, scientifically neutral enterprise. In fact, biomedicine, and psychiatry within it, embodies and reflects specific, unique American variants of Northern European Protestant cultural ideology (Gaines, 1982a, 1985a) in its theories, research, and clinical practices (Eisenberg & Kleinman, 1981; Gaines, 1979, 1982a, 1982b, 1985a; Gaines & Hahn, 1982, 1985; Hahn & Gaines, 1985; Hahn & Kleinman, 1983; Johnson, 1985; Mishler et al., 1981; White & Marsella, 1982; Young, 1981).

Anthropological research highlights the problematics of an implicit, putatively objective psychiatric (and psychological) standard of evaluation of credibility in two ways. First, cross-cultural research has provided considerable evidence indicative of the wide variety of beliefs that seem quite fantastic outside of their indigenous cultural contexts. Second, the anthropology of biomedicine (and psychiatry) has demonstrated the cultural basis of both the ideology and praxis of various Western biomedicines (e.g., American, Canadian, English, and German), thus challenging the presumed cultural neutrality of their diagnostic entities and evaluative criteria, especially in psychiatry (Eisenberg & Kleinman, 1981; Gaines & Hahn, 1982; Hahn & Gaines, 1985; Gaines, 1979, 1982a, 1982b; Kleinman & Good, 1985; Mishler et al., 1981; Maretzki & Seidler, 1985).

To advance our understanding of delusions and, it is hoped, to improve clinical psychiatric practice, this chapter adopts three foci: (1) the relationship of delusions to culture (delusions seen here as meaningful discourse), (2) the relationship of delusional content to the individual's cultural affiliation and personal psychocultural conflicts and, (3) the explication and critique of implicit standards of evaluation employed in psychiatry. Overall, this chapter seeks to provide a new cultural perspective on delusions and a new standard for their determination.

CULTURAL BELIEFS AND DELUSIONS

Delusions may be defined for our purposes as ideas and beliefs expressed in an individual's discourse that are indicative of personal theories of cause and effect and of motivation and behavior that are seen by other members of the individual's cultural or subcultural group as being unsupportable, as lacking in credibility. The very definition of delusion presupposes an articulation, a discourse, for otherwise the very existence of a delusion would be impossible to ascertain. Delusions thus may be seen as aspects of a culture's communicative systems, which suggests that such ideation is not beyond the pale of culture. Cross-cultural research argues for a relativist, rather than a universalist, psychiatric or psychological conception of appropriate evaluative standards of the credibility, veracity, and meaningfulness of beliefs.

The relative nature of that which is seen as true, factual, or bizarre may be demonstrated by considering ethnographic data. Cross-cultural research has long demonstrated the widespread existence of beliefs shared by members of particular cultures that appear delusional to the Westerner. Examples of such ideation related to culture-specific mental disorders and beliefs are considered here. Such conditions and beliefs, when found in a plural medical context that includes folk as well as biomedical beliefs, often leads to the mislabeling of ideation in medical contexts (see, e.g., Lyles & Hillard, 1982).

The first folk disorder to be considered is called *koro,* a genital retraction syndrome found among the southern Chinese and the Chinese of the Malay Archipelago (Leng, 1985; Yap, 1965). Individuals suffering from this folk disorder (most often male) believe their genitals are retracting into their bodies. This causes great anxiety and concern and initiates strategies to prevent the retraction. (It is relevant here to note that local folk belief holds that the dead have no genitals.) There have been large epidemics of this disorder in the areas where it occurs, indicating the belief's sharedness. If such a belief were reported to an American physician it would likely be seen as a delusion.

Another disorder found in the cross-cultural literature is that called *grisi siknis,* which is found among the Miskito people of the Altantic coasts of Nicaragua and Honduras (Dennis, 1985). This disorder causes individuals to lose consciousness, during which time the afflicted believe that devils beat them and sexually ravage their bodies. This culturally shared complex of beliefs would probably be seen as psychotic and evidence of some underlying paranoid process in the West.

Windigo, a disorder found among the Northern Algonkian peoples (Ojibwa, Cree Indians) of the northern United States and southern Canada, is named after a monster who, it is believed, possesses individuals, especially during the winter months (Marano, 1985). The windigo monster (also called "witigo") has a "heart of ice," and so has no loyalty, sympathy, or compassion for others, even relatives. Individuals possessed by it develop an intense, compulsive desire to consume human flesh. In some instances this desire may be satisfied through acts of cannibalism waged against the windigo victim's relatives, as these are his or her only close companions during the winter months. Though the story of the Witigo monster is known and validated by many among the Ojibwa, the articulation of these beliefs in the context of American psychiatry would probably be interpreted as paranoid schizophrenic ideation.

In Bali one finds widespread belief in several forms of spiritual entities, witches, and spiritual siblings. The former are known to cause illnesses, and their actions must be counteracted. For the latter, Balinese individuals believe they have four spirit siblings (as well as a guardian spirit). The lives of these invisible brothers and sisters are closely followed; their spirit marriages, children, and other life events are duly noted (Conner, 1982). The intricate histories and characteristics that informants can produce concerning their spirit siblings would surely be seen as delusional material by Western psychiatry, yet in Bali such beliefs are culturally normative.

In the West itself, witches are believed to exist according to local cultural knowledge, as in contemporary France (Favret-Saada, 1980) and other Mediterranean countries. Such beliefs were common to all Europe in the past, as in Scotland (Larner, 1981), where these "enemies of God" were believed to plot against humans and God.

In the United States, one finds beliefs in witches in history as well as on the contemporary scene. Witch beliefs are widely distributed among many U.S. cultures, including Italian-Americans (Foulkes, Freeman, Kaslow, & Mado, 1977), southern American culture bearers (those of European [White] and European and West African [Black] ancestry), Hispanics, and Native Americans (Gaines, 1982a; Hillard & Rockwell, 1978; Lyles & Hillard, 1982; Snow, 1977). Such beliefs are often seen as delusional in clinical practice because American clinicians usually fail to recognize that the beliefs about witches and hexes, for example, are culturally normative (Lyles & Hillard, 1982; Foulkes et al., 1977; Snow, 1977). In addition, generally shared folk beliefs in the American South hold that various sorts of creatures (e.g., frogs, snakes) can "get under the skin" and move about (Snow, 1974). Such beliefs and experiences are interpreted as somatic delusions by psychiatrists who encounter them.

In some recent research in France concerning the patterning of dysphoric affect, attention was focused on a Paris suburb and local community members referred to by others in their community as "saints." Called "visible saints" by the authors (Gaines & Farmer, 1986), these people are copresent contemporaries, rather than historical figures, in the Mediterranean Culture Area (Gilmore, 1982) who lead lives of heroic, exemplary, and public suffering. They are a community's lay saints. Among such people, it is believed that their extraordinary suffering derives from a particular interest and involvement of God in their lives. Misfortune (e.g., miscarriages, difficult spouses, unruly children, money difficulties, and other problems) are seen as deliberately visited upon the individual by God as a divine test; the visible saint's endurance and perseverance are viewed in sacred terms, as being beyond the means of mortals (Gaines, 1986; Gaines & Farmer, 1986).

It is locally believed that those who suffer most are loved most by God. Hence, suffering and misfortune are believed to ennoble the individual and to deepen, thereby creating a "serious" personality, as is the case in Iran, another part of the Mediterranean Culture Area (Good, Good, & Moradi 1985). To outsiders such beliefs may seem like paranoid delusions, tinged with masochism and notions of grandeur, especially in the usually irreligious context of lay or medical professional America (but see Gaines, 1982c, 1985a).

Lest it should seem that only outside of mainstream America are there highly problematic beliefs, it should be noted that most psychiatrists believe in the existence of at least one immaterial spirit (God). Other psychiatrists believe in several different, and sometimes opposed, spirits (e.g., God, Jesus/ Christ, the Holy Ghost, and the devil), as among the Christian psychiatrists whom the author has studied (Gaines, 1982c, 1985a). These individuals were generally evangelical Christians who were also trained psychiatrists or psychiatrists-in-training. They believed that they had an "on-going, personal relationship" with a spirit, Christ. Christ was believed to be a spirit that at one time was made flesh and sacrificed whereas other spirits such as God and the Holy Ghost (or Holy Spirit) have remained immaterial. Their religious beliefs were intentionally manifest in their clinical practices, which included prayer with and for patients, conversion, witnessing, and bible study (Gaines, 1982c, 1985a).

The absence of even the slightest basis in fact for the beliefs in the immaterial spirits must be noted. And though there is much heterogeneity of belief within psychiatry (Gaines, 1979, 1985a), the "secular psychiatrists" in the local southern area of the research (all those not called "Christian psychiatrist," who nonetheless might be very religious), believed the avowedly religious Christian psychiatrists to be at least somewhat delusional (Gaines, 1982c, 1985).

All of the cultural beliefs noted above, beliefs concerning retracting penises, possessing devils, cannibalistic monsters, malign witches, spirit siblings, a loving but slightly sadistic God, relationships with spirits, and so forth, are culturally shared and socially validated. As such, they cannot be classified as delusions. Despite this, all of these ideas seem bizarre and without a basis in fact from the formal professional perspective of American psychiatry and its wider, implicit cultural ideology (Northern European Protestant; Gaines, 1982a, 1985c). The delusional quality of these ideas seems to stem from a lack of familiarity with and acceptability of various culturally normative ideas, not from a lack of credibility or veracity in the face of the application of immutable, universal standards of believability.

The basis for distinguishing the delusional from the nondelusional seems to be the cultural sharedness of the range of articulated semantic units and symbols, (i.e., words, acts, and gestures, or events) (Geertz, 1973). For example, American psychiatrists familiar with Christian ideology would accept as valid beliefs in on-going relationships with a spirit called "Christ," whereas Sinhalese Buddhist psychiatrists would not.

A putatively objective standard of the untrue or the bizarre seems nonexistent. Whether something is bizarre depends entirely upon experience and familiarity. Witches and spirit siblings, after all, are not unusual, anxiety-provoking entities to the Balinese. Rather, such spirits are part of the everyday furniture-of-life, much like Aztec sacrifices, which were intended to replenish and revitalize the sun (see Heise, this volume).

Sharedness of beliefs alone, however, may not be a sufficient criterion. A sharing of beliefs among a small group of individuals such as those noted in Heise (this volume) does not exclude the possibility that the beliefs are delusional. Another criterion, such as extent of sharedness, or *reasonableness* in terms of the culture at large, may be needed to distinguish the delusional from the nondelusional. This point will be taken up in the Conclusion.

CULTURE, MEANING, AND PSYCHOSIS: THREE CASES

In this section, psychotic discourses are considered from the standpoint of cultural semantics (i.e., meaning in culture and the meaningfulness of culture and its constituent elements). Culture is seen here as a system of meanings embodied in symbols (Geertz, 1973). This semantic system is learned, shared, and communicated. It is enacted by individuals through interactions. Interactions are constituted by the flow of meanings carried by symbols brought to and exchanged in interactional encounters (Geertz, 1973; Blumer, 1969; Schutz, 1967). Both social reality and clinical reality (e.g., paranoia and delusions) are constructed in and by the interactions of individuals as they define their situations (Kleinman, 1980b).

One of the interests here is the cultural status—the relationship to culture—of psychotic thoughts, including delusions. Are delusions acultural, outside of culture, rendering those afflicted outcasts from the meaning system of culture? Is it possible to make general statements about delusions and cultural meaning?

The psychotic discourses presented below are analyzed in terms of their coherence, organization, sharedness, and communicability. It is demonstrated that even delusions have more or less cultural or subcultural meanings, and are thus cultural entities. It is further shown that as individuals evidence more psychotic tendencies, delusions lose their cultural grounding, cease to be delusions, and the individual's expressions move beyond culture. There is a point beyond which utterances and thoughts are so privatized or egocentric (Heise, this volume), that they cease to have any real meaning at all. In severe psychotic states, meanings are so idiosyncratic as to be uncontextable; they cannot be placed in normal, expected, shared linguistic and thought contexts. Without context and sharedness, the elements of discourse are cast adrift in an acultural sea of meaninglessness. The fact that delusions can be communicated to others even though the delusional character is recognized suggests that coherence in such phenomena is maintained. But in the severe psychotic, delusion has given way to a jumble of disentangled elements that once conveyed meaning. Organization has dissipated, coherence is negligible, form has given way to formlessness, and communication ceases.

Below, delusional discourses are presented in the form of three cases, those of Mary, Bob, and Peter (all pseudonyms). The first two cases show a progression from coherent, logical utterances the premises of which yet mark them as delusions. Their discourses demonstrate levels of organization, form, and sharedness of meanings. Case 3 shows utterances that are incoherent, illogical, and that have neither premise nor meaning.

These cases and others were collected by the author during 1979 while he was a fellow in psychiatry at the University of Hawaii School of Medicine. The cases are those of ward patients who stayed in a major psychiatric hospital in Honolulu. For each case, a text of the material is first presented. This presentation is followed by interpretations of the meanings of the discourse, delusional or otherwise. In the first case, the material is presented as a story much in the words of the informant, whom we will call Mary. The second and third cases present the thought worlds of Bob and Peter through the medium of interviews.

CASE 1—MARY: MORAL CONFLICTS AND SUBCULTURAL SYSTEM

Mary, a 19-year-old female admitted to Kahala-Kokua General Hospital's (a pseudonym) psychiatric ward, was perceived as an Anglo. Mary was brought to the psychiatric emergency room by some of her college schoolmates. The patient, from New Mexico, was in Hawaii to attend college. She had no previous psychiatric record. Although the patient was calm, orderly, well groomed, and seemingly in complete control of her faculties, she related a number of incidents that had occurred to her that seemed beyond belief. Mary believed that she was the intended victim of a plot directed by the mafia. The plot was aimed at "getting (her) to become a prostitute who would work for them." She described several events that supported her story, including the incidents that precipitated the whole affair.

Mary became very strongly attracted to the singer in a local rock band. The band played evenings and weekends at a local club where college students gathered. For some weeks, she had watched him with great interest. She had come to believe that he was interested in her ("liked her") as well. One evening he asked her to go out with him after the last performance. They went out and had what she felt was a wonderful time, including sleeping together, an event she regarded as very important. She was now sure that he "liked her a lot." A few days later, however, when she saw him again at the club, he was cold and indifferent. After introducing her to another member of the band, he ignored her. Mary went out that evening with the other band member, and she slept with him. She did so, she said, because she thought this must have been what the object of her affection wanted her to do, and, "it might make him happy," leading him to again "pay attention to (her)."

On a subsequent visit to the club, Mary was snubbed by both young men. She was "very hurt," she related, and "could not understand what was happening, what made them act that way." Mary became very unhappy but soon "realized what was happening." She came to believe that both men actually liked her very much and that the singer, her original object, was, in fact, "probably in love with (her)." She felt he was "being kept from paying attention to (her) and from being (involved) with (her)" by external forces. She gradually came to believe that the club was probably "mafia controlled" and that these people had "other plans for (her) and didn't want the singer to interfere" and so had been told to ignore her. Mary said that "other things happened to show" the existence of this plot.

On one occasion, she was awakened by a telephone call at 3 a.m. The caller was a male unknown to her. She believed he was a member of the mafia and that "he knew who (she) really was." He asked if he could come over and she supplied him with her address which, she thought, "he probably knew anyway." She did not want to resist for fear that the man would realize that she knew he was part of the plot. The man arrived and stayed the night and into the next day. She reported that he "raped" her, though when asked, she denied his use of verbal or physical threats or use of any force. She "went along with his" advances because she "didn't want him to suspect her" knowledge of the reason for his presence. The next morning, Mary reported that the man took her to brunch. When asked why she went out with a man who presumably raped her, she replied that she "wanted to see what he would do next." The passive, compliant, go-along-with-the-game stance is not uncommon in paranoia (Gaines, 1978).

Later that day, the man drove Mary to a club in an "out of the way" place on the North Shore where she was "drugged." The drugs, she said, took away her "will power." As a consequence, she was unable to resist the sexual advances of two of the man's friends. Both had sex with her in the car outside of the club. Though she was "aware of what was going on" and she again reported that there were no physical or verbal threats, she "couldn't resist because of the drugs they gave me."

Mary also believed that the *gheckos,* small insectivorous lizards found everywhere in Hawaii, spied on her. *Gheckos* make startlingly loud sounds, given their small size, while they lurk in the corners of windows and window screens waiting for insects to alight. She believed that they reported to the mafia on her movements at home and outside. (It may be noted that *gheckos* are frequently personified in Hawaii, and people generally enjoy their presence.)

These incidents had a coherence for Mary. They were all mafia attempts to make her feel worthless and dirty by "forcing (her) to do bad things." She reasoned that if they could make her feel this way about herself, they could get her to agree to become a prostitute for them; she would "have nothing, no self-respect, to lose."

When asked why she believed the mafia was so interested in her and was spending so much time, money, and effort to enlist her, she replied it was because she had "a cute smile and one heck of a figure," so "they think they can make a lot of money off of me." In this her slightly exaggerated sense of self was expressed. (This seemed to be an amplification of a preexisting theme, as in fact are other aspects of the delusion, as Chapman and Chapman, this volume, suggest often occurs.)

Interpretation

Mary seems to have experienced a severe trauma of a moral nature but also a blow to her particular, perhaps exaggerated, sense of worth and self-esteem. This trauma also occurred within, and was given force and meaning by, the context of an all-or-nothing cultural ideology. For although Mary was assumed to be a WASP ethnic (or *Ha'ole,* see Case 2 below) by staff, the moral tone and the tenor of the story of affection and rejection suggested to the author that a particular Mediterranean moral system of evaluation and punishment was at work. Further questioning in this area revealed that the patient was the daughter of an Anglo father and a Chicano mother and had been raised as a devout Catholic in New Mexico. This upbringing seems to have instilled in her basic aspects of the Mediterranean culture, including a notion of romantic love to which sexual relations were tied, notions of the importance of beauty (another Mediterranean social cynosure) (Gaines & Farmer, 1986), the assumed malevolence of unacquainted others, the antipathy of the sexes, and an all-or-nothing, absolutist moral ideology (i.e., that there are but two kinds of women, "mothers (the virtuous mothers and mothers-to-be) and whores" (all others). There are also other aspects of less importance here (for a fuller account, see Peristiany, 1966; Gilmore, 1982; Gaines, 1982a; Gaines & Farmer, 1986).

Mary fell in love in the unfamiliar and, for her, antithetical subcultural context of pop music. In that context, unknown to her, she was assumed by the musicians to be a "groupie"—a promiscuous camp follower of musicians. Groupies are considered inappropriate partners for other than physical relationships; they are disposable women (and men, since the rise of female rock singers). Mary was apparently unaware of this context and assumed that she was entering into a serious relationship, for she did not take sleeping with men lightly.

When Mary was rejected, she reacted, actually overreacted, by first complying with an unspoken wish of her friend that she saw as a means of placating or pleasing him in order to win him back. Mary's notion of romantic love as unconditional made her actions reasonable, though highly traumatic. For her not to pursue him further, to simply "chalk it up to experience," would have meant she had been taken advantage of; an assault both on her particular moral sense *and* on her sense of self-worth. The act of sleeping with another band member, however, further traumatized her; she not only failed to regain the object of her affections, she also had slept with another man *sans amour* and, hence, without reason.

Mary's delusional system is understandable, and we may see her delusional system as purposeful. Simultaneously, the delusional system explains the reasons for her pain and maintains her high self-esteem, for she is desired and desirable. The delusion also provides punishment for her transgressions in the form of external forces that push her to commit further transgressions. These acts or non-acts are seen as out of her control. Misfortunes are not her fault. She is a victim.

Mary's view of her helpless predicament parallels the cultural *weltanschauung* of the Mediterranean. Her discourse is, in part, the "rhetoric of complaint." This rhetoric is a form of verbal self-presentation in the Mediterranean culture area and its daughter cultures in the New World (Latin/Hispanic) wherein self is seen as lacking control over life events; hence, one is at the mercy of external forces. One's victim status is regularly communicated to others in interaction as a rhetorical means of evoking the pity of others and as a means of deflecting known and unknown others' assumed hostile and jealous intention (Gaines, 1982a; Gaines & Farmer, 1986). Thus the overall form of Mary's presentation is culture specific though it appears in an exaggerated form.

The delusional system allowed Mary to feel that she was not a *mala mujer* (bad woman, a whore) for having slept with the musicians. Nevertheless, she was greatly conflicted because of her all-or-nothing ideology, wherein one mistake is the same as a thousand, for there are "but two kinds of women." Her explanation, her delusion, demonstrated her worth and importance as a person in that her friend had to be "forced" to turn from her, and only a serious threat to his safety could make him give her up. The other acts of self-degradation likewise carried a double message in that they showed that she was wanted (desirable, beautiful, and, therefore, worthwhile) while punishing her for what she feared she might be, a woman without virtue.

The elements of Mary's ideational system—the events and people—have cultural acceptability, cultural reality. They are culturally recognized and shared elements. She does not invoke space creatures, talk with angels or other spiritual entities, nor does she manifest thought insertion or thought broadcasting. Rather, she uses themes, persons, groups, and animals known to her culture-mates (e.g., love, the mafia, prostitution, coercion, drugs, pop musicians, and *gheckos*). The constituent elements of her story are known and understood by culture-mates and her delusional system is coherent. They form a story related in a controlled, orderly fashion. The story has internal consistency, and it employs facets of cultural and subcultural knowledge and understanding in a comprehensible manner. Nonetheless, it is recognizable as a delusional system because its *totality* is beyond belief, beyond commonsense expectations and understandings of how the world works, of human motivation, and value. However, it should be stressed that the how and why of the world, that is, common sense, is itself *culture specific* (Geertz, 1973, 1983).

It may be that Mary developed this system to explain an anomalous event, as Maher (1974; Maher & Ross, 1984) suggests (see also Chapman & Chapman, this volume). But the experience was anomalous only *given* Mary's preexisting definitions of the situation. The delusion, located in the context of her version of a larger cultural value system, was also motivated (i.e., driven) by Mary's fragile yet inflated sense of self-worth and her notion of its measure (desirability). While the delusion may be, in some sense, a response to her experience, there is need to look for a motive in the individual's psychocultural system for the establishment of the delusional system. An implicit drive for cognitive consistency (Maher & Ross, 1984) is an insufficient explanation. It is in the motives that distinctive, unshared notions appear. It is the *premises* upon which a delusional system may be built, not the expressed ideas, that are unshared and overly privatized.

In this brief look at Mary's delusional system, a collision was observed between two systems of meaning. One was Mary's absolutist moral system, within which was couched her exaggerated sense of self-worth. The other was a subcultural system of pop music entertainers, with its antithetical (to Mary) interactional rules and expectations about male-female relationships. In the next case, we shall see a less orderly expression of a delusional system.

Initially we will be at a loss to understand the utterances of Bob Edlax. Ethnographic knowledge will provide the key to unlock Bob's system of meaning. Bob's meanings were more private than Mary's and, as a consequence, considerably more work was required to make sense of his discourse and to understand the meanings he wished to communicate. Unlike Mary's case, evidence of a thought disorder appears in Bob's discourse.

CASE 2—BOB: MUSIC AND IDENTITY*

A 26-year-old male was admitted to the psychiatric unit of Kahala-Kokua General after being found wandering about near Waikiki. The patient, unemployed for some time and without permanent residence or means of support, was the son of a Japanese father and an Okinawan mother. He was born in a city on "the big island" (the Island of Hawaii in the state of Hawaii) and had lived there before coming to Honolulu.

Upon admission, the patient gave his name as Bob Edlax. While his given name seems to have been correct, the family name was an enigmatic fabrication. Bob also presented clinicians with a problem regarding his self-definition of ethnic identity. Bob claimed that he was *Ha'ole* (the local term in Hawaii for Anglos). As he once stated, "I'm *Ha'ole*, not Asian. I hate those Asian bastards. I like those people" (he then pointed to a female *Ha'ole* ward clerk). On subsequent days, Bob got into difficulty for verbally and, on several occasions, physically abusing other patients who were seen as Asian ethnics. These hapless people, not knowing of Bob's existential position, would make what Bob considered mistakes, such as sitting next to or speaking to him. Bob interpreted such acts as declarations by these Asian others that he too was Asian and that "they were claiming (him) as one of their own," an identity he vehemently denied.

Not only did Bob see himself as a Ha'ole but as a special sort of Anglo, a "new creature," as he explained in the following exchange with a medical student:

MEDICAL STUDENT (MS): What is your ancestry?

BOB (B): Ancestry is, uh, oriental's blood; along a Japanese father and an Oakie mother (derogatory slang term for Okinawan).

MS: How do you view yourself?

B: As a new creature.

MS: As a new creature? Could you tell me about that?

B: You, have you ever looked at the back of a pyramid, at the eye?

MS: Huh?

---

*This case is excerpted from Gaines 1982b, pp. 246–253.

B: (On the back of the) dollar bill, I mean.

MS: Oh. Yes.

B: You'll see the Virgin Mary was really an Egyptian God, Osiris. When they came to the planet, they started sucking the humanoid out of the modern man and putting the space creature, the new creature, into it. Once Jim died, he left his legacy for his brothers to follow 'cause he knew they would have a hard time doing that. He had no brothers, I don't know . . . he had friends but he left it for the new creatures, where race does not mean anything; just peace and brotherhood among nations of the world. People like (names a local family) and many prominent families, perhaps in the U.S. of A., who disagree with the ways of rock'n'roll. Once we start realizing who these children are, you know, what's gonna happen? It's going to be anarchy.

MS: These new creatures of yours, they're involved with rock'n'roll?

B: Yeah. Rock'n'roll to the world; yeah; food, Jesus, Krshna, maybe even Krshna will be included.

MS: You said sometimes you feel you're being controlled by others, How?

B: Yes. When I get in contact with new creatures, the immortals to be more exact.

MS: How can you tell you're coming into contact . . . ?

B: I feel peace, content, well-being, happiness in my inner soul; way down inside; and I feel content.

MS: Have you come in contact with new creatures recently?

B: Yes. Mike Snow.

MS: Who is he?

B: Rock'n'roll musician (a personal acquaintance, not a major rock figure), vocalist, child of God, flower child, latterday flower child. We'll record on Swan Song. Bet on contract approval by the corporation.

MS: And you're a rock star or musician?

B: Yes, musician. Everybody is a star, but you have to prove that yourself before they can reap the cake, that was left out in the rain. But we know who we are and we're going to try to make it on Swan Song. (Bob begins to doze off here but continues) Try to understand it. Not all love is in vain. It's not a homosexual relationship either.—(aside) Don't know where that word came from. It's in the media all the time.—It's really more like aspiring towards a cheapened communion between brother and sister. My sister is an Indian girl (gives name) who I look forward to seeing, loving and taking away to Hollywood, once I find her.

Later in the same interview, Bob said:

B: Music is my only friend, (well) not really, (it is) one of my friends.

MS: What other friends do you (have)?

B: Freaks. Not really. Children who grew up in the world until they got burned. Can't explain, revolutionary philosophy from the sixties. Can't explain . . . unless you grew up and listened to records then. (I have) a guardian angel, French. Came to take care of me; compassion and pity for a lesser man. She's been through so much burn. Helped me to take the burn off, to have more rational and compatible behavior for Americans.

When the medical student gave Bob a proverb to interpret, he interpreted it as follows:

MS: Can you tell me what the proverb, "A rolling stone gathers no moss" means?

B: (without hesitation) No sticky connections, no shady connections. It's a groove, but no connections. Shady groove but no shady connections. No sticky fingers, there might be some sticky fingers but there is nothing sticky about it.

Interpretation

Neither the residents nor any other members of the attending or ward staff caring for Bob had any doubt whatsoever about the "character of danger" he manifested. All were certain that he was schizophrenic. One of the clear symptoms of that condition was the frequently verbalized, seemingly delusional ethnic self-ascription of *Ha'ole*. It may be questioned, however, whether his claim was really a delusion and therefore a symptom diagnostic of a schizophrenic condition.

The term "new creature" that Bob used stems from some poetry written by the late Jim Morrison of the Doors—a Los Angeles-based rock group popular in the sixties. The portion of the interview in which it appears gives a view of the major elements of Bob's cognitive world, including severe problems over personal identity, popular music culture, pop culture (Eastern religions), sustenance, money, and spiritual/new creatures. The focus here is on the problem of social identity.

Bob denied being Asian. He claimed instead that he was *Ha'ole*, White, or Anglo, the term he would employ varied. Attending health professionals attributed what they termed this "nonsensical" claim to his illness. In fact,

Bob showed more anthropological understanding of the culture construction of ethnic/social categories than did the people who were trying to help him. This is, of course, a case of being right for some of the wrong reasons.

Ethnic or other social distinctions in societies around the world are actually made on the basis of subjective criteria without regard for putatively objective criteria (Barth, 1969; Blu, 1980; DeVos & Wagatsuma, 1966; Domínguez, 1986; Gaines, 1985b, 1985c). Criteria of significance selected in various societies include religion, caste, residence, history, occupation, physiognomy and skin color, and *race*. For the latter criterion, anthropology recognizes no biophysiologically distinct human races. Research in this area shows that for all biological and physical traits measurable there is massive overlap among supposedly dissimilar groups. Hence, "mankind cannot be subdivided into one group with zero percent and one group with 100 percent frequencies for any one characteristic" (Heirnaux, 1970, p. 36). It is recognized that any system of racial classification, whether it contains seven, nine, or however many races (no agreement has ever been reached on the number of such races in the world) is based upon arbitrary, non-empirical criteria (Boas, 1923; Hiernaux, 1970; Montague, 1970; Stocking, 1968; UNESCO, 1969; Washburn, 1972). As Hiernaux asks, "If any racial classification is arbitrary, for what purpose can it be of any use?" (1970, p. 40). The concept of race, therefore, is seen as useless and misleading as a scientific concept (Washburn, 1972; Montagu, 1970; Hiernaux, 1970). It is to be considered as a folk or ethno-theory, as a culturally specific form of social classification (Blu, 1980; Domínguez, 1977, 1986; Gaines, 1985c).

Thus, Bob inadvertently expressed a more scientifically modern conception of culture as the molder of behavior than did his contemporaries in psychiatry, who evidenced various nineteenth-century notions of racial classification. This understanding allows us to see a critical area of Bob's problem, that of self-identity, which was intimately bound up with the American cultural system of race and racism. His is a case of societal or "cultural delusions" about human reality. But it is also clear that Bob had internalized some of society's prejudices.

Bob apparently was trying unsuccessfully to say that, "While I may look Asian, I am culturally Anglo." After listening to Bob's discourse about self and other, the author asked him directly if this was what he meant by his assertion that he was Anglo. As the question was posed, Bob leaned forward with much interest. When the author had finished, he smiled and enthusiastically responded, "Yes! That's it! That's it exactly!" On subsequent days, Bob was able to articulate this explanation to others and derived some satisfaction from his new ability to explain himself in a way that was understandable to them.

Bob's self-identification was not, as was thought initially, a delusion, a schizophrenic symptom. Moreover, treating it as such deflected attention from the patient's central problem, self-identity. Bob experienced a conflict that was and is culturally constituted; he did not create racism, its attendant stereotyping or discrimination. As a consequence, Bob had ambivalent feelings toward his parents; sometimes he was unsure they were his parents. He no doubt cared for them, but he also felt hatred and contempt for them because they had given him a physical appearance that made it difficult (in America), if not impossible, for him to be accepted as a member of the ethnic group to which he felt he belonged. He also felt that he was a new creature, as indicated in the interviews, and as such was not born of parents as are normal people. And, he felt that his mother was of lower status. For all these reasons, exacerbated by his illness and, no doubt, an unexpressed "family romance" delusion, it was not surprising that Bob would doubt his parentage from time to time.

Some vaguely Langian notion is not here suggested (i.e., that the madman is really the architect of a logical new reality in response to illogical external pressures, or that the mentally ill are actually more in touch with reality). Rather, it is shown here that a patient exhibiting schizophrenic symptoms is less out of touch with reality than initially would seem to be the case. In other respects, Bob's case presents us with a chance to see the use of ethnographic knowledge in a clinical situation. The anthropologist was able to gain rapport with the patient because of some ethnographic knowledge of pop culture that paralleled Bob's own. In the exchange with the medical student, Bob's statements seem to make little sense. An exigesis of Bob's statements from the first excerpt is in order. This will be followed by an examination of the second excerpt, which highlights Bob's focus on a specific cultural domain, that of rock'n'roll.

In the first excerpt, Bob talked of "new creatures," a phrase from the Doors' singer Jim Morrison's poetry. His identity as a new creature in part referred to his freedom from traditional social classifications that made him Asian. He saw himself as a member of the leadership (essentially Anglo and male) of a subculture, rock'n'roll, the members of which are presumably above such invidious distinctions. (The rhetoric clearly outstripped the social realities of the time.) He thus equated rock'n'roll with formulation of a world culture and a decline in racial notions of social classification. This identification of music and social change is not, of course, unique to Bob; he had, in fact, internalized a major message of the 1960s cultural upheaval— social change, freedom, equality, and justice through music (and other art forms).

Two other points are also important to make. First, Bob saw new creatures as being in the vanguard of change. This makes sense of his other statements—that Asians were "stuck, rigid, traditional." "They don't understand rock'n'roll." Bob believed he couldn't be Asian *and* be progressive or revolutionary. This negation in part led him to deny his parents explicitly or implicitly ("I am a new creature," e.g., not the son of a Japanese man and an Okinawan woman). Second, new creatures must of necessity be involved with the revolutionary agent, the music. As a consequence of this last belief, he talked in apparent riddles but was actually using song and album titles, song lyrics, and the names of record labels and rock stars. Thus, much of Bob's discourse would be understandable to another member of the subculture or, as in this case, a student of the subculture, the author.

Bob's concentration on a single subcultural domain appeared again more clearly in the second excerpt. While schizophrenic symptomatology was readily observable, Bob's utterances were not random, disorganized, and formless. Making some sense of his speech required knowledge of the specific domain of his discourse. While ethnographic knowledge was the immediate key to the unraveling of the patient's discourse, the assumption that there *would be a key* and that discourse would be patterned according to *some* cultural criteria or criterion was the necessary starting point for understanding.

Bob talked of particular social categories (e.g., child of God, flower child, latter-day flower child). In this he referred to significant social categories of the sixties scene. The word *latter-day* indicated Bob's awareness that the sixties have indeed passed. (It should be noted that the sixties actually refers to the time between 1964–1965 and 1972–1973.) He referred specifically to that time in U.S. history when rock'n'roll matured into rock and became the dominant form of live and recorded musical entertainment.

In his discourse, Bob was faithful to rock music and made virtually no mention of other musical forms (e.g., opera, country, etc.). He did refer to the blues, however, because the blues serves as the basis for rock but not the other forms of popular music. Thus, all major rock musicians are also blues musicians and employ the blues (i.e., West African) musical scale. The rock world with which Bob identified is that of the Beatles, the Rolling Stones, Cream, Led Zeppelin, the Who, the Doors, Jimi Hendrix Experience, Jefferson Airplane, and others. Bob referred to Jim Morrison of the Doors as well as some of the secular and religious themes current in the sixties. The second excerpt actually focuses almost exclusively on the subcultural domain of rock. The "immortals" to whom Bob referred are the legends of rock who have died and include Jim Morrison, as well as Janice Joplin, Jimi Hendrix, Brian Jones (the Rolling Stones), John Bonham (Led Zeppelin), and Keith Moon (the Who).

Swan Song is the name of a record label begun in 1975 by members of Led Zeppelin. The first and major group signed was led by Briton Paul Rogers and was called Bad Company. Perhaps Bob was attracted to this label because of its home base, Los Angeles, and because bad company is the type of company he felt his parents and disapproving others thought that he kept (e.g., freaks, flower children, burnouts, etc.). The fictitious family name, Edlax, was discovered to refer to two friends, *E*ddie and *D*ale, who, with Bob, would go to Los Angeles to record. The airport designation of LA airport is, of course, LAX.

Bob went on to make the statement that "Everybody is a star." This is the title of a famous song by Sly and the Family Stone and refers to the sixties' notion of the inherent value in everyone. The next statement he made, "Before they can reap the cake, that was left out in the rain" was a quote from the psychedelic song written by Jim Webb entitled "MacArthur Park." This use of a lyric from a song appeared earlier in this excerpt. When Bob said he felt content and a sense of well-being "way down inside," he employed a line from Led Zeppelin's song, "Whole Lotta Love." He did this again later in the excerpt when he repeated the phrase, "(I) Can't explain. . . ." This is the title of one of the Who's early hits (1965).

After Bob used the line from "MacArthur Park," he began to doze off. As he did, he provided a marvelous example of a relaxed ego allowing repressed material to enter consciousness. However, Bob did not need to be drowsy to allow such material to gain access to consciousness. Periodically, Bob would say his father wanted to have sex with him or that he wanted, or was afraid to have sex with his father. He said the same of his mother, and expressed fears that other males had homosexual interests in him. Such beliefs are not unusual in schizophrenia and represent the failure of repression; it is indicative of the fact that the misperceptions of hospital staff were not strictly a function of their lack of ethnographic and cultural knowledge.

After saying, "Try to understand it. Not all love is in vain," he regained full consciousness. He then negated the relationship between himself and his friends who were "going to make it on Swan Song" by saying, "It's not a homosexual relationship either." Then, in an aside, he said, "Don't know where that word came from," and so forth. Even in these statements, Bob drew from the rock idiom. He made use of "Love in Vain," an old (ca. 1930) slow blues song written by legendary bluesman Robert Johnson and made popular with rock audiences about 1970 by the Rolling Stones. In an apparent attempt to further deny any homosexual feelings toward his musician friends, Bob began to talk of a woman he once met.

Bob's use of the kinship terms "brother and sister" was also derived from the rhetoric of the sixties. In that rhetoric (and the worldview it expressed), a cue was taken from Black culture (actually, southern culture, based in fundamentalist Christianity) wherein unrelated individuals are referred to by kinship terms. The usage is logical in the context of the rhetoric of the love generation, the members of which were of one generation (conceptually) and were children of love, peace, God, or rock'n'roll. As members of the same generation and offspring of one or another entity (rock'n'roll, love), members were obviously, if only symbolically, siblings. The Indian sister Bob mentioned was a woman he met whom he felt was compatible with the goals of rock (peace, love). He also mentioned a French guardian angel. The angel was a real person, an older woman and friend of the family with whom Bob communicated from time to time while he was a patient. Here, and at other times, Bob characterized the relationship as more than friendship, perhaps for the same reason he hastened to mention the Indian woman after talking about his relationship with Snow.

The interpretation of the proverb that Bob offered found him thinking concretely about rolling stones. However, Bob was thinking not about just any rolling stones, but about *the* Rolling Stones. Bob's interpretation was, in fact, a string of references to recordings by "the Stones." The phrase "no sticky connections" refers to the Stones' sixties hit, "Connection," and to the title of one of their most successful albums, "Sticky Fingers." "No shady connections" again makes reference to the song "Connection" but also to another album title, "Made in the Shade," and another song title, "Standing in the Shadows." Bob went on to restate these titles in different combinations and added the slang term "groove." This term was used in the sixties but predates that time period. It is a jazz term referring to good or quality music or a catchy musical phrase. Bob also made a pun on "shady grove," which itself was the title of an album by the sixties San Francisco rockers, Quicksilver Messenger Service.

Bob's case was one of a schizophrenic with severe problems over self and sexual identity. The focus here primarily has been on the former. Bob clearly cathected rock music and sixties culture as the essential elements of Anglo identity. Having internalized these over the years as an ardent follower of the alternative life-styles of the sixties, he was disturbed about his rejection, real and potential, as a viable Anglo ethnic. His concern was occasioned by the meanings others imposed on his appearance. His identity as a new creature was intended to divest him of his old racial identity. But others, because of their folk racial theories and discriminatory practices, would not allow him to assimilate, to become a rock star.*

Anthropological theory and ethnographic knowledge of popular culture were employed here not to show that a patient was improperly labeled as schizophrenic, but rather to highlight the problematic nature of implicit

---

*The exclusion of people with Asian ancestry from rock is ebbing. For example there is America's premier rock group, Van Halen, has the eponymous Indonesian/Dutch brothers on guitar and drums, and heavy metal guitarist Jake E. Lee of Ozzy Osbourne, among others.

cultural knowledge invoked to construe the statements of others as beyond belief. Bob's beliefs were seen by caregivers as further evidence of his psychotic condition and served as indicators for clinicians of a severe level of distress. Hence, while Bob was certainly afflicted with schizophrenia, he was not as disturbed as his physicians believed. Caregivers' own folk theories of social classification and their lack of knowledge of the rock domain of U.S. culture led them to misinterpret the meaning of his discourse. The level of Bob's distress was later downgraded based on the ethnographic data presented here.

This case also indicates the means whereby clinical reality (Kleinman, 1980b) is constructed. That is, it is constructed according to implicit extra-professional Western cultural notions about cultural, social, and biological reality. Such notions are called folk theories (Gaines & Hahn, 1982; Hahn & Gaines, 1985) or ethno-theories (Lutz, 1985).

Below, in the third and last case, a striking lack of order and coherence and meaning are demonstrated in the discourse of a patient. Neither a lack of knowledge of particular semantic domains (i.e., sharedness of cultural knowledge) nor a lack of knowledge of folk theories is responsible for the incomprehensibility of Peter's utterances. He gives us speech beyond meaning and culture.

CASE 3—PETER: SENSE AND NONSENSE

A 29-year-old male, raised in Hawaii, was brought to Kahala-Kokua by his father. The father had come to Hawaii from Japan only to find that his son had been living a marginal existence in and around Waikiki for about three years prior to his visit. The patient had been seen previously in the hospital for his current problem. An interview with the patient was held two weeks after his admission to the ward. Peter had been receiving antipsychotic medication since his arrival on the ward. In this interview, the psychiatrist again sought to elicit a "story" (Rittenberg & Simons, 1985) that would explain something of the history of the current problem(s).

PSYCHIATRIST (P): How are you feeling?

PETER (PT): Fine.

P: What are you thinking?

PT: About being alone. (I) went to mainland, came back alone; jumped in the pilot seat.

P: In the pilot seat?

PT: Yeah. That's quite a story.

P: Where do you live?

PT: Kahala-Kokua Hospital; around here. Stone house, wooden top, stone bottom. Went to Japan, exiled by myself. All the rest is girls even in bones, it's only lie (lye?) and girls.

P: Are you pointing to something? (Are they) the sores on your foot?

PT: Yeah. Breaking out. There was a girl cleaning camp fire. Acts fat.

P: Is this the same girl?

PT: Yeah. You can tell by smell. Me and my girls.

P: But you have your brother, don't you?

PT: Smelled like a girl, but looked like my brother. (My) brother died in Viet Nam (untrue). Air travel is restricted by their powers.

P: Okay. I'm going to ask you some questions that we usually ask people around here. What day is it?

PT: No. Old fashioned day.

P: What month is it?

PT: No. Old Houses, like hotel.

P: What year is it?

PT: 1979 (correct).

P: Can you say these numbers?

PT: No.

P: Try; 1, 2, 3.

PT: 1, 2, 3.

P: Repeat this series of numbers; 2, 4, 1, 7, 9, 6.

PT: 2, 4, 1, 7, 9, 6. It just echoes.

P: You did it! How about backwards; 4, 6, 8.

PT: 8, 6, 4.

P: Good. Now, could you explain how you thought things and you thought other people would hear you?

PT: (No answer).

P: You see people when no one's there?

PT: They're there, just hiding.

P: Do you hear voices?

PT: Yeah. I like to walk around.

P: From walking around?

PT: Yeah. Like it, those old Japanese man, this girl.

P: Have you been unhappy?

PT: No.

P: Have you ever had problems?

PT: I had to go to war, in Japan. They smashed my finger.

P: Have you ever felt better off dead?

PT: Rest power won't get you.

P: Do you have a girlfriend?

PT: Bone structure is the same, like Gilligan's Island.

P: Would you like to have a girlfriend and a place to live?

PT: Oh, yeah. But I'm not allowed to go to Tantalus (a nearby mountain) anymore. (The mountain has public roads on it and is open to the public.)

P: Would you like a place?

PT: On the beach—girl there, like her. Not pretty. When you come to it, it smells like a girl.

P: When you talk to girls on the beach, what happens?

PT: They play games; give me toys.

P: Do you get angry from playing games?

PT: Yeah, but they come up like a siren and they have tails. Then I see its plastic and they say, "You see who I am." I say, "okay," and leave them alone.

P: Tell me, when people say really strange things (to you).

PT: Probably two for working. One lying told me that it's hard to get here from Japan; got to save 20 years for fuel.

P: Okay, we will stop now and go back to the ward.

PT: Okay, but I heard it takes 400 hours of fast speed to get to the other islands.

Interpretation

Though the psychiatrist attempted to pose straightforward questions and to bring the patient back to the point when he wandered from it, the listener is unable to make sense of Peter's discourse. His speech was disorganized, reflecting his tangential and disorganized thinking. He was unable even to contradict himself as his statements were not clear enough to contradict. His stories did not hang together. In fact, he had no stories. For example, what were "girls" to him? What did he mean by "smells," "games," or his references to "flying"? How were "bone structure" and "Gilligan's Island" related?

The elements Peter used are known to us. We all know of smells, girls, houses, planes and pilots, but here the words lack shared semantic and interpretive contexts that give them meaning. Peter's meanings are unshared.

Because terms are used without initially shared reference points and meaningful contexts, it may be that the terms had no coherent meaning even for Peter. He did not learn from culture-mates his then current use of words and meanings. And so, he talked but failed to communicate.

Peter, a hebephrenic schizophrenic, was beyond meaning, beyond culture. His condition represented the shattering of meaning, the antithesis of culture. Using the analogy of a mirror, perhaps normality might be viewed as a person gazing into a mirror, self seeing self, a reflexive self. As the individual succumbs to the delusional thinking of psychotic states, one may imagine the person standing before and being reflected in a fun house mirror, with its vertical undulations. Though distorted, the image of the person is still quite discernible. Self can yet see and recognize self. But in severe psychosis, the mirror is shattered; all that remain are tiny, disconnected fragments. The fragments produce no coherent picture. Self can no longer see self. Meaning and coherence are lost. The individual has lost his or her self-orientation, one of the key orientations provided by culture (Hallowell, 1971) and, as a result, is beyond culture.

CONCLUSIONS

In the cases presented here, psychotic material has been analyzed from the standpoint of cultural and personal meaning. The cases were selected to show a continuum and to allow for the placement of delusions within a cultural landscape. In the cases of Mary and Bob, delusions were demonstrated to be meaningful and to use shared cultural symbols. The delusional systems were shown to fall within the domain of culture. These cases clarify for us something of the nature of cultural systems themselves. *Cultures may be seen as continua of meanings*, not rigid, uniform or inflexible systems of belief, behavior, and experience. Within them, personal, as well as subcultural variations of larger cultural wholes, may be seen to exist.

The cases of Mary and Bob show that delusions as discourse embody and communicate personal and cultural meanings and conflicts. Conflicts of a personal nature are built upon and reflect conflicts or contradictions in culture itself. Delusions may, therefore, provide important insights into the logic (or lack thereof) of an individual's culture. *Analyses of delusions may serve as a tool for cultural analysis.*

The case of Mary also demonstrates the relativity of trauma (for the cultural relativity of trauma, see Gaines, 1986). The incident that seemed to trigger the construction of her delusional system would not have caused a moment's pause to many other women. The event was traumatic because of her particular cultural orientation combined with her particular self-conceptions. The personal and the social/cultural levels are intimately linked and germane. Being away from home in a new environment could also have contributed to Mary's sensitivity to the events she experienced, for the vulnerability of certain immigrants or travelers is often noted in psychiatric epidemiology (Good, Good, & Moradi, 1985; Gaines & Farmer, 1986).

Ethnographic knowledge and the cases presented above also suggest that delusional beliefs can be distinguished from normal beliefs only by the invocation of specific cultural knowledge and its attendant semantic contexts. Beliefs about witches and their malevolent work may seem absurd and to have no possible basis in fact to some in the United States of America. But for most people in the world, including many Europeans and Americans, such immaterial beings are quite real. The immateriality of objects of belief seems not to be a genuine factor in determining the presence or absence of delusions, for a belief in the Trinity would not qualify. It seems, then, that *cultural compatibility* is, in fact, the psychiatrist's measure of the delusional in the broadest sense.

In the specific instance of a delusion, such as Mary's or Bob's, the elements in the stories are quite recognizable, but the *premises* are unacceptable. This suggests that delusional thinking abandons accepted folk or ethnotheories (Lutz, 1985). These ethno-theories may concern any number of significant events, states, or experiences. They have been shown to include a range of ideas such as the definition of life as ennobling suffering (Gaines & Farmer, 1986; Good et al., 1985; Jackson, 1985; Obeyesekere, 1985), the unity of emotion and cognition (Lutz, 1985), the appropriateness of open, public expression to others of dysphoric affect (Schieffelin, 1985), the lack of consequences of early traumatic life events (Gaines, 1986), the social nature of problem drinking (Gaines, 1985b), the nature of social identity (Blu, 1980; Domínguez, 1977, 1986; Gaines, 1985c), a believed correspondence between medical language and external reality (Good & Good, 1981), a notion of a universal biology (Gaines, 1987), and, finally, a culture's notions of the nature of self and of person (Geertz, 1973; Gaines, 1979, 1982a, 1985a; Hallowell, 1971; Shweder & Bourne, 1982; White & Marsella, 1982).

The delusional individual, while using culturally acceptable components, fails to explain them in acceptable ways; shared ethno-theories have been replaced by idiosyncratic theories. Such instances must be distinguished from instances in which clinicians and others confront culturally shared but seemingly idiosyncratic theories (i.e., delusions), as for example when one is presented with beliefs about witchcraft, spirit siblings, retracting penises, or monsters with hearts of ice.

The line between the delusional and the nondelusional is more blurred than psychiatrists believe, yet the increasingly plural cultural nature of the

United States of America will pose increasingly greater problems for clinicians. Psychiatry and psychology must become more sophisticated in their understanding of cultural differences and cultural beliefs of relevant client populations, such as those of the new immigrants from Southeast Asia, Latin America, and the Caribbean. Problems are sure to arise from confrontations of cultures, largely because of the assumptions in the fields of medicine and psychology that their diagnostic (Kleinman & Good, 1985) and sociological categories (Hahn & Gaines, 1982; Gaines, 1982b) are universally valid.

One ready solution that the author has observed in use in Hawaii was clinicians' adoption of a limited notion of sharedness. Clinicians who were aware of cultural differences—and it is difficult not to be aware of them in Hawaii—came to the stated position that a patient's sharing of a belief, even among only two other individuals, was indicative of nonpathological ideation. This was one solution to the dilemma, but an incomplete one. The French psychiatric notion of *folie à deux*, for example, suggests that more than one person can hold delusional beliefs, as does other work (e.g., Heise, this volume). Thus we must go beyond a notion of limited sharedness, even though this idea is an advance over universalist notions.

It may be appropriate to invoke a conception of *reasonableness* in which an idea would be considered nondelusional if it seemed reasonable to members of the wider culture, even if those members did not share the belief. That is, individuals in a culture are aware of a number of ideas they do not hold, but they perceive them as *reasonable* for others to hold. An example might be the recognition on the part of irreligious people in the United States of America that many of their country-mates believe in various spirits (e.g., God, the devil, Jesus, the Holy Ghost, and angels). A nondelusional belief would have a currency of sorts among culture-mates ranging from nonbelief to strong belief. But believers and nonbelievers would be cognizant of the beliefs of others and perceive them as situated within the domain of the culturally reasonable.

Delusional thinking seems to be related to and derived from personal, cultural, and subcultural meaning contexts of existence as well as the conflicts—over morality, identity, belonging—that populate those contexts. Complete disorganization in psychosis goes beyond culture, for culture is systematized meaning while psychosis is unsystematized nonmeaning. It may be thus argued that delusional individuals yet remain within the domain of their respective cultures. The analysis of delusions allows us not only to explore delusions themselves, but also to recognize that cultures encompass and shape various degrees of both the normal *and* the abnormal, as well as various levels of order *and* chaos. Both continua, in fact, provide the broad semantic contextual axes within which such distinctions are made and in terms of which meaning is generated, learned, shared, and communicated.

REFERENCES

American Psychiatric Association. (1980). *Diagnostic and statistical manual of mental disorders* (3rd ed.) (DSM-III). Washington, DC: American Psychiatric Association.

Barth, F. (Ed.) (1969). Introduction. In *Ethnic groups and boundaries: The social organization of culture difference.* Bergen, Norway: Universitets Forlaget.

Blu, K. (1980). *The Lumbee problem: The making of an American Indian people.* Cambridge: Cambridge University Press.

Blumer, H. (1969). *Symbolic interactionism.* Englewood Cliffs, NJ: Prentice-Hall.

Boas, E. (1923). *Race, language and culture.* New York: Free Press.

Conner, L. (1982). The unbounded self: Balinese therapy in theory and practice. In A. Marsella & G. White (Eds.), *Cultural conceptions of mental health and therapy.* Dordrecht, Holland: D. Reidel.

Crapanzano, V. (1973). *The Hamadsha: Moroccan ethnopsychiatry.* Berkeley: University of California Press.

Dennis, P.A. (1985). Grisi siknis in Miskito culture. In R.C. Simons & C.C. Hughes (Eds.), *The culture-bound syndromes: Folk illnesses of psychiatric and anthropological interest.* Dordrecht, Holland: D. Reidel.

DeVos, G., & Wagatsuma, H. (Eds.). (1966). *Japan's invisible race: Caste in culture and personality.* Berkeley: University of California Press.

Domínguez, V. (1977). Social classification in creole Louisiana. *American Ethnologist, 4*(4), 589–602.

Domínguez, V. (1986). *White by definition.* New Brunswick, NJ: Rutgers University Press.

Eisenberg, L., & Kleinman, A. (Eds.). (1981). *The relevance of social science for medicine.* Dordrecht, Holland: D. Reidel.

Favret-Saada, J. (1980). *Deadly words: Witchcraft in the Bocage.* Cambridge: Cambridge University Press.

Foulkes, E., Freeman, D., Kaslow, F., & Mado, L. (1977). The Italian evil eye. *Journal of Operational Psychiatry, 8*, 28–34.

Gaines, A.D. (1978). Illness and interaction: A case of paranoia. *Kroeber Anthropological Society Papers, 53–54*, 71–87.

Gaines, A.D. (1979). Definitions and diagnoses. *Culture, Medicine and Psychiatry 3*(4), 381–418.

Gaines, A.D. (1982a). Cultural definitions, behavior and the person in American psychiatry. In A. Marsella & G. White (Eds.), *Cultural conceptions of mental health and therapy.* Dordrecht, Holland: D. Reidel.

Gaines, A.D. (1982b). Knowledge and practice: Anthropological ideas and psychiatric practice. In N. Chrisman & T. Maretzki (Eds.), *Clinically applied anthropology.* Dordrecht, Holland: D. Reidel.

Gaines, A.D. (1982c). The twice-born: 'Christian psychiatry' and Christian psychiatrists. In A. Gaines & R. Hahn (Eds.), *Physicians of Western medicine: Five cultural studies. Culture, Medicine and Psychiatry Special Issue, 6*(3), 305–324.

Gaines, A.D. (1985a). The once- and the twice-born: Self and practice among psychiatrists and Christian psychiatrists. In R. Hahn & A. Gaines (Eds.), *Physicians of Western medicine: Anthropological approaches to theory and practice.* Dordrecht, Holland: D. Reidel.

Gaines, A.D. (1985b). Alcohol: Cultural conceptions and social behavior among urban 'Blacks.' In L. Bennet & G. Ames. (Eds.), *The American experience with alcohol.* New York: Plenum Press.

Gaines, A.D. (1985c). Faith, fashion and family: Religion, aesthetics, identity and social organization in Strasbourg. *Anthropological Quarterly, 58*(2), 47–62.

Gaines, A.D. (1986). Trauma: Cross-cultural issues. In L. Peterson & G. O'Shanick (Eds.), *Advances in psychosomatic medicine, Volume 16: Psychosomatic aspects of trauma.* Basel, Switzerland: Karger.

Gaines, A.D. (1987). Cultures, biologies and dysphorias. *Transcultural Psychiatric Research Review, 24*(1), 31–57.

Gaines, A.D., & Farmer, P.E. (1986). Visible saints: Social cynosures and dysphoria in the Mediterranean tradition. *Culture, Medicine and Psychiatry, 10*(3), 295–330.

Gaines, A.D., & Hahn, R.A. (Eds.). (1982). Physicians of Western medicine: Five cultural studies. *Culture, Medicine and Psychiatry Special Issue, 6*(3).

Gaines, A.D., & Hahn, R.A. (1985). Among the physicians: Encounter, exchange and transformation. In R. Hahn & A. Gaines (Eds.), *Physicians of Western medicine: Anthropological approaches to theory and practice.* Dordrecht, Holland: D. Reidel.

Geertz, C (1973). *The interpretation of cultures.* New York: Basic Books.

Geertz, C. (1983). *Local knowledge.* New York: Basic Books.

Gilmore, D. (1982). Anthropology of the Mediterranean area. In *Annual reviews in anthropology.* Palo Alto, CA: Annual Review.

Good, B., & Good, M.J. (1981). The meaning of symptoms. In L. Eisenberg & A. Kleinman (Eds.), *The relevance of social science for medicine.* Dordrecht, Holland: D. Reidel.

Good, B., Good, M.D., & Moradi, R. (1985). The interpretation of Iranian depressive illness and dysphoric affect. In A. Kleinman & B. Good (Eds.), *Culture and depression.* Berkeley: University of California Press.

Hahn, R.A., & Gaines, A.D. (1982). Physicians of Western medicine: An introduction. In A. Gaines & R. Hahn (Eds.), *Physicians of Western medicine: Five cultural studies. Culture, Medicine and Psychiatry Special Issue, 6*(3), 215–218.

Hahn, R.A., & Gaines, A.D. (Eds.). (1985). *Physicians of Western medicine: Anthropological approaches to theory and practice.* Dordrecht, Holland: D. Reidel.

Hahn, R.A., & Kleinman, A. (1983). Biomedicine as a cultural system. In M. Piattelli-Palmarini (Ed.), *Encyclopedia of the social history of the biomedical sciences.* Milan: Franco Maria Ricci.

Hallowell, A.I. (1971). The self and its behavioral environment. In A.I. Hallowell (Ed.), *Culture and experience*. New York: Schocken. (Original work published 1955.)

Hiernaux, J. (1970). The concept of race and the taxonomy of mankind. In A. Montagu (Ed.), *The concept of race*. New York: Macmillan.

Hillard, J.R., & Rockwell, W. (1978). Disesthesia, witchcraft and conversion reaction. *Journal of the American Medical Association, 240*(6), 1742–1744.

Jackson, S. (1985). Acedia the sin and its relationship to sorrow and melancholia. In A. Kleinman & B. Good (Eds.), *Culture and depression*. Berkeley: University of California Press.

Johnson, T. (1985). Consultation-liaison psychiatry. In R. Hahn & A. Gaines (Eds.), *Physicians of Western medicine: Anthropological approaches to theory and practice*. Dordrecht, Holland: D. Reidel.

Kleinman, A. (1980a). Major conceptual and research issues for cultural (anthropological) psychiatry. *Culture, Medicine and Psychiatry, 4*(3), 3–13.

Kleinman, A. (1980b). *Patients and healers in the context of culture*. Berkeley: University of California Press.

Kleinman, A., & Good, B. (Eds.). (1985). *Culture and depression: Studies in the anthropology and cross-cultural psychology of affect and disorder*. Berkeley: University of California Press.

Larner, C. (1981). *Enemies of God: The witch-hunt in Scotland*. Baltimore: Johns Hopkins University Press.

Leng, G. (1985). *Koro*—A cultural disease. In R.C. Simons & C.C. Hughes (Eds.), *The culture-bound syndromes*. Dordrecht, Holland: D. Reidel.

Lutz, C. (1985). Depression and translation of emotional worlds. In A. Kleinman & B. Good (Eds.), *Culture and depression*. Berkeley: University of California Press.

Lyles, M., & Hillard, J.R. (1982). Rootwork and the refusal of surgery. *Psychosomatics, 23*, 1–4.

Maher, B. (1974). Delusional thinking and perceptual disorder. *Journal of Individual Psychology, 30*, 98–113.

Maher, B., & Ross, J. (1984). Delusions. In *Comprehensive handbook of psychopathology*. New York: Plenum Press.

Marano, L. (1985). Windigo psychosis: The anatomy of an emic-etic confusion. In R.C. Simons & C.C. Hughes (Eds.), *The culture-bound syndromes: Folk illnesses of psychiatric and anthropological interest*. Dordrecht, Holland: D. Reidel.

Maretzki, T., & Seidler, E. (1985). Biomedicine and naturopathic healing. *Culture, Medicine and Psychiatry 9*(4), 383–421.

Mishler, E. et al. (1981). *The social contexts of health, illness, and patient care*. Cambridge: Cambridge University Press.

Montagu, A. (Ed.). (1970). *The concept of race*. New York: Macmillan.

Obeyesekere, G. (1985). Depression, Buddhism and the work of culture in Sri Lanka. In A. Kleinman & B. Good (Eds.), *Culture and depression*. Berkeley: University of California Press.

Peristiany, J.G. (1966). *Honour and shame: The values of Mediterranean society.* London: Weidenfeld & Nichols.

Rittenberg, W., & Simons, R.C. (1985). Gentle interrogation: Inquiry and interaction in brief initial psychiatric evaluations. In R. Hahn & A. Gaines (Eds.), *Physicians of Western medicine.* Dordrecht, Holland: D. Reidel.

Schutz, A. (1967). *Collected papers 1: The problem of social reality* (M. Natanson, Ed.). The Hague: Martinus Nijhoff.

Schieffelin, E. (1985). The cultural analysis of depressive affect: An example from New Guinea. In A. Kleinman & B. Good (Eds.), *Culture and depression.* Berkeley: University of California Press.

Shweder, R., & Bourne, E. (1982). Does the concept of person vary cross-culturally? In A. Marsella & G. White (Eds.), *Cultural conceptions of mental health and therapy.* Dordrecht, Holland: D. Reidel.

Snow, L. (1974). Folk beliefs and their implications for the care of patients. *Annals of Internal Medicine, 81,* 32–96.

Snow, L. (1977). Popular medicine in a Black neighborhood. In E. Spicer (Ed.), *Ethnic medicine in the southwest.* Tuscon: University of Arizona Press.

Stocking, G. (1968). *Race, culture and evolution: Essays in the history of anthropology.* New York: Free Press.

U.N.E.S.C.O. (1969). *Race and science.* New York: Columbia University Press.

Washburn, S.L. (1972). The study of race. In J. Jennings & E.A. Hoebel (Eds.), *Readings in anthropology.* New York: McGraw-Hill.

Weisberg, D., & Long, S. (Eds.). (1984). Biomedicine in Asia. *Culture, Medicine and Psychiatry Special Issue, 8*(2).

White, G., & Marsella, A. (1982). Introduction: Cultural conceptions in mental health research and practice. In A. Marsella & G. White (Eds.), *Cultural conceptions of mental health and therapy.* Dordrecht, Holland: D. Reidel.

Wittkower, E., & Prince, R. (1974). A review of transcultural psychiatry. In *American handbook of psychiatry* (2nd ed.). New York: Basic Books.

Yap, P.M. (1965). *Koro*—A culture-bound depersonalization syndrome. *British Journal of Psychiatry, 111,* 43–50.

Yap, P.M. (1974). *Comparative psychiatry: A theoretical framework* (M. Lau & A. Stokes, Eds.). Toronto: University of Toronto Press.

Young, A. (1981). The creation of medical knowledge: Some problems of interpretation. *Social Science and Medicine, 15B*(3), 379–386.

CHAPTER 12

Delusions and the Construction of Reality

DAVID R. HEISE

Indiana University

Observation and conversation allow us to generate definitions of situations much like another person's, shared culture provides similar concepts for interpreting what we see, and watching another's actions informs us about his or her priorities. Then, knowing the others' conceptual framework and values, we can largely duplicate the other's thinking in our own minds. We understand the other's ideas and the other's goals because they are just what we ourselves produce when we take the role of other.*

Occasionally the duplication process generates products that seem out of contact with reality. The other's ideas seem deluded—not just wrongheaded, but wrong. This is not a matter of the other's logical processes having degenerated so much that we cannot duplicate them at all. In delusions the other's thought processes are coherent (Maher & Ross, 1984) but lead us through a mockery of proper thinking to conclusions that seem unreal.

The critical issue in recognizing a delusion seems to be the question of truth, but I argue here that that cannot be the case because truth varies across acceptable social groups and because essentially the same belief can be judged as a delusion or a nondelusion depending on the social conditions of the believer. Instead, the critical issue is whether a person maintains social commitment by thinking in a way that other people want to share. Individuality in thinking is rejected when it becomes too egocentric. Excessive

---

The points in this chapter are developed within a social constructionist framework (Schneider & Kitsuse, 1984; Gergen, 1985; Georgoudi & Rosnow, 1985). The approach has the annoying feature of turning attention away from a problem and onto those who are trying to deal with the problem. Moreover, the framework's treatment of truth seems so nihilistic that even sociologists complain (Stryker, 1984). I hope I have made amends by suggesting how the results of this kind of analysis can have practical utility for those who work with thought disorders.

*The preconditions for interpersonal understanding are topics of study in the branch of sociology that deals with ethnomethodology (e.g., Cicourel, 1964, 1974; Leiter, 1980).

egocentrism is controlled by treating its mental products as delusions without truth value, denying authenticity to an autistic reality.

RELATIVITY OF KNOWLEDGE

Judgment of delusion evidently relates to the truth and authenticity of a person's subjective reality. Yet reality is not as absolute as it seems. Different epistemologies yield different facts, different truths, different realities.

A basic division in the epistemologies of Western society was identified by sociologist Sorokin.

> On one extreme is a mentality for which reality is that which can be perceived by the organs of sense; it does not see anything beyond the sensate being of the milieu. . . . Those who possess this sort of mentality try to adapt themselves to those conditions which appear to the sense organs. . . . On the other extreme are persons who perceive and apprehend the same sensate phenomena in a very different way. For them they are mere appearance, a dream, or an illusion. True reality is not to be found here; it is something beyond, . . . different from this material and sensate veil which conceals it. . . . Whether [true reality] be styled God, Nirvana, Brahma, Om, Self, Tao, Eternal Spirit, *l'èlan vital,* Unnamed, the City of God, Ultimate Reality, *Ding fur und an sich,* or what not, is of little importance. What is important is that . . . true reality is usually considered supersensate, immaterial, spiritual.
>
> *(Sorokin, 1957, pp. 25–26)*

Sorokin subjectively grouped beliefs in mysticism, empiricism, materialism, and so forth, into the subcultural types he called Sensate and Ideational, and showed oscillation between Sensate and Ideational mentalities over time, using data on the number of European intellectuals during each 20-year period from 540 B.C. to 1900 A.D. Simonton (1976) factor analyzed Sorokin's data and found the two dimensions corresponding to the sensate and ideational subcultures, as shown in Figure 12.1. Analyses based on factor scores showed that during times of low creativity (like the Dark Ages), thinking is mostly Ideational; but "as the number of thinkers in-. . . . creases, philosophers and religious thinkers tend to differentiate into a large number of separate schools or sects—some Sensate and others Ideational" (p. 196).

Contemporary civilization is a highly creative period and contains both kinds of subcultures. Sensate subculture is dominant in the sense that its key institutions—like science—are at the center of societal power. Thus we live in a society that legitimates truth based on sensing a determined material world and the associated ideas of progress, individualism, and utilitarian

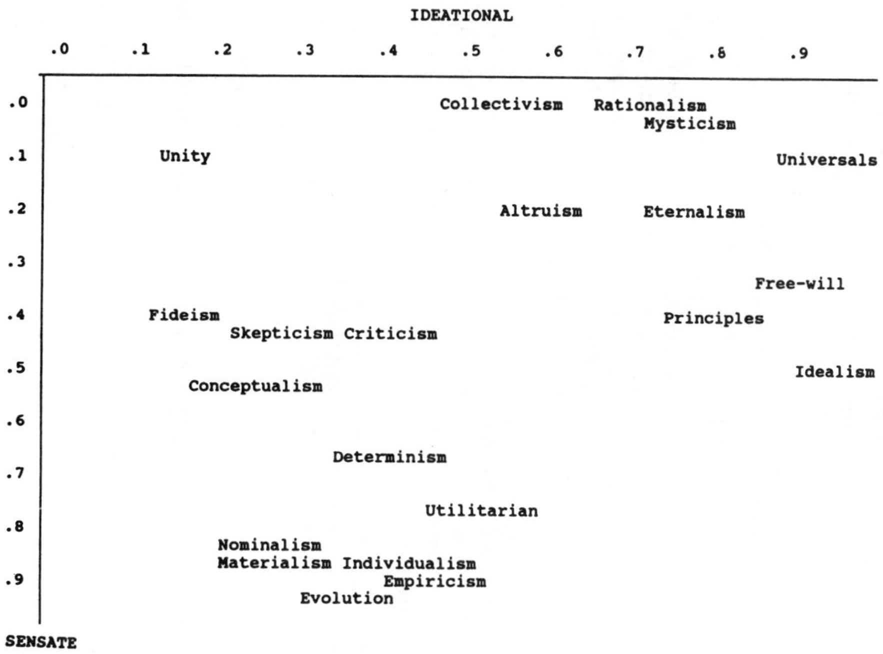

IDEATIONAL

	.0	.1	.2	.3	.4	.5	.6	.7	.8	.9
.0 SENSATE										
.1		Unity				Collectivism		Rationalism / Mysticism		Universals
.2							Altruism	Eternalism		
.3										Free-will
.4		Fideism	Skepticism Criticism					Principles		
.5										Idealism
.6		Conceptualism								
.7					Determinism					
.8		Nominalism / Materialism	Individualism Empiricism			Utilitarian				
.9			Evolution							

KEY

Collectivism = sociological reductionism (universalism)
Rationalism = knowledge based on reason
Unity = individual and society mystically unified (Mystical Unity)
Mysticism = knowledge based on revelation, mystical experience
Universals = universals do exist (Realism)
Altruism = charity (Ethics of Love)
Eternalism = things don't change; there is immutable Being
Free will = (Undeterminism)
Fideism = knowledge is an act of will, blind faith
Skepticism = knowledge is unobtainable
Criticism = reason applied to empirical fact
Principles = ethics of rules, highest values
Idealism = reality exists in spirits or souls
Conceptualism = universals are mental constructs
Determinism = free will doesn't exist
Utilitarian = Ethics of Happiness
Nominalism = universals exist only as constructs, names
Materialism = matter is the basis of reality
Individualism = psychological reductionism (Singularism)
Empiricism = knowledge must be acquired from sensory experience
Evolution = ever changing becoming, progress (Temporalism)

Figure 12.1. Structure of philosophical constructs (based on Simonton, 1976).

ethics. The religious and occult institutions of Ideationism are in the background—for Sundays and for alternative cultures where revelations of an eternal idealistic world give basis to reasoning that individuals are unimportant and behavior based on love is the path to ultimate achievement.

While the Sensate framework is dominant in our society, large numbers of people are involved with Ideational concerns. For example, a 1978 Gallup Poll revealed that 57 percent of Americans believe in unidentified flying objects (UFOs or flying saucers), 54 percent believe in angels, 51 percent believe in ESP, 39 percent believe in devils, 29 percent believe in astrology, and 10 percent or more believe in ghosts and witches (reported in Douglas & Waksler, 1982, p. 370). Moreover, the alternative reality that embraces these concepts is elaborated into a system of knowledge.

When Prophecy Fails (Festinger, Reicken, & Schachter, 1956) reported on a small cult organized around a woman who received revelations via automatic writing. In particular, she prophesied that the world would be destroyed December 21, 1949, and that cult members would be flown to outer space in flying saucers. This classic social psychology study clearly reveals that people on the Ideational side operate within a full-scale reality supported by knowledge that requires years to acquire. The prophet of the group, who became involved in the occult 15 years before she was studied, constructed revelations based on her knowledge of contemporary Ideational subculture.

> [W]e must make it perfectly clear to the reader that the ideology was not *invented*, not created *de novo*, purely in Mrs. Keech's mind. Almost all her conceptions of the universe, the spiritual world, interplanetary communication and travel, and the dread possibilities of total atomic warfare can be found, in analogue or identity, in popular magazines, sensational books, and even columns of daily papers.
>
> The notions of reincarnation and spiritual rarification . . . are likewise echoed in "many modern cults and minority religious movements". . . . The idea that heavenly representatives will visit earth . . . to rescue those whose conduct and beliefs have marked them for salvation is older than Christianity.
>
> . . . . True, Mrs. Keech put together . . . a combination peculiarly well adapted to our contemporary, anxious age—but scarcely a single one of her ideas can be said to be unique, novel, or lacking in popular (though not, for the most part, majority) support.
>
> *(Festinger et al., 1956, 54–55)*

Her key supporters similarly read "widely and eclectically" on mysticism and the occult:

> They studied some of the sacred writings of Hinduism, the Apocrypha, *Oahspe*, and books and pamphlets on theosophy, Rosicrucianism, New

Thought, the I AM movement. . . . The ideas they encountered in this literature, and discussed at length, seem to have opened their minds to possibilities
that many people regard with incredulity. They believed in the existence of a
spirit world, whose masters could communicate with and instruct people of the
earth; were convinced that extrasensory communication and spiritual migra-
tion (without bodily change or motion) had occurred; and subscribed to many
of the more common occult beliefs, including reincarnation.

(pp. 40–41)

A study of a 1970s UFO cult (Balch & Taylor, 1977) presented a similar
finding.

Before they joined, members of the UFO cult shared a metaphysical worldview in which reincarnation, disincarnate spirits, psychic powers, lost conti-
nents, flying saucers, and ascended masters are taken for granted. . . . Within
the metaphysical social world, the seeker is not disparaged as a starry-eyed
social misfit. Instead, he is respected because he is trying to learn and grow.
Members of the cultic milieu tend to be avid readers, continually exploring
different metaphysical movements and philosophies. Whether in a tipi in the
Oregon woods or a mansion in Beverly Hills, their evenings are often spent
with friends and acquaintances discussing metaphysical topics like psychic
research, flying saucers, or Sufi mysticism. A significant part of their lives is
devoted to the pursuit of intellectual growth, however undisciplined that may
be in conventional academic terms.

(p. 850)

The keepers of Ideational knowledge even rely on familiar social mechanisms for safeguarding the integrity of their knowledge. For example,
Festinger et al. (1956) reported confirmation of revelations by references to
periodicals, confirmation of information through independent sources—
spiritualists in this case, assessment of a spiritualist's skill, and appeals to
higher levels of authority.

Scott (1980), in her study of a spiritual growth group and a witchcraft
order, defined 15 basic premises that are common to such groups (spiritual
planes, good and evil spirits, reincarnation, etc.). The manner in which these
forms of knowledge provide a basis for everyday reality is illustrated in the
following incident involving a female novice who was disliked by members of
a witches' coven.

Clovis, who was the most hostile, brought spiritual charges against her. He
claimed he learned psychically that they had been in a group together in a
previous lifetime in the Middle Ages and that she had betrayed the group. He
also claimed that she had come to Earth during this lifetime from another

planet. Since the high priestess and the others considered these charges valid and discussed them seriously, Nancy had little defense. She could only protest that his charges were not true, but there was no rational way to counter his claim. A spiritual charge permitted no rational proofs.

(p. 153)

Ideationalism in contemporary society provides an alternative lay culture that is elaborated and used in much the same way as the materialistic-technological culture that is dominant. The alternative culture offers different bases for knowing about reality and for assessing whether a belief is true. That creates problems for a clinician trying to determine whether a belief is a delusion or not. The belief may seem like nonsense by Sensate standards but not by Ideational standards. Thus the *Diagnostic and Statistical Manual of Mental Disorders (DSM-III)* (American Psychiatric Association [APA], 1980) makes exception for religious beliefs.

Reality Testing

Aside from systems of philosophy, some beliefs seem demonstrably bizarre because they do not accord with simple perception, being held "in spite of what constitutes incontrovertible and obvious proof or evidence to the contrary" to use the words of DSM-III (APA, 1980). However, several problems arise in relying on perceptual testing as a criterion for judging truth and falsity. First, simple perception invokes learned concepts in order to acquire significance (Anderson, 1983; Sowa, 1984), and these concepts may be idiosyncratic. Thus, a man with a belief that he has a misshapen nose may perceptually confirm the idea every time he looks in the mirror, and this is no delusion because he would say the same of anyone who had a nose like his. Johnson (this volume) provides a detailed discussion of frailties in the nexus between perception and conception.

Second, the notion of reality testing presumes a Sensate epistemology—a reliance on evidence of the senses. Evidently, people with Ideational belief systems do make reality tests—they might not be able to survive materially unless they did. The tests lead to discarding some ideas like the failed prophecy studied by Festinger et al., (1956), at least among cultists who lacked social support. In principle, however, people with an Ideational philosophy always can claim that an empirical test constitutes no proof at all.

Third, among those committed to an idea, objective tests are made selectively for their confirmatory value, not in order to disconfirm (Festinger, 1957). Gergen (1985) stated this argument in extreme form as applied to science itself.

Research methods can be used to produce "objectifications" or illustrations useful in advancing the pragmatic consequences of one's work. . . . Although some methods may hold the allure of large samples, others can attract because of their purity, their sensitivity to nuance, or their ability to probe in depth. Such assets do not thereby increase the "objective validity" of the resulting constructions. However, like vivid photographs or startling vignettes drawn from daily life, when well wrought they may add vital power to the pen.

(p. 273)

While we like to think of observations as predetermined and unbiased, they are in fact selected and interpreted within the very framework they are supposed to test. Thus many delusions possibly *are* supported by reality tests, though not the ones *we* think should apply.

Religious beliefs and practices of the Aztecs provide an example of how this might occur. The Aztecs, a cosmopolitan civilization (Pasztory, 1983; Fagan, 1984) that occupied the area around Mexico City from about 1200 A.D. until the Spaniards came and decimated them in 1521, had an extraordinary cosmology.

The sun was born from sacrifice and blood. It is said that the gods gathered in the twilight . . . and one of them . . . threw himself into a huge brazier as a sacrifice. He rose from the blazing coals changed into a sun: but this new sun was motionless; it needed blood to move. So the gods immolated themselves, and the sun, drawing life from their death, began its course across the sky.

This was the beginning of the cosmic drama in which humanity took on the role of the gods. To keep the sun moving on its course, so that the darkness should not overwhelm the world for ever, it was necessary to feed it every day with its food, "the precious water" . . . human blood. Sacrifice was a sacred duty towards the sun and a necessity for the welfare of men: without it the very life of the world would stop. Every time that a priest on the top of a pyramid held up the bleeding heart of a man . . . the disaster that perpetually threatened to fall upon the world was postponed once more. Human sacrifice was an alchemy by which life was made out of death.

(Soustelle, 1961, pp. 96–97)

Perhaps as many as 20,000 humans were sacrificed by the Aztecs each year: "The Mexica did indeed offer up victims to the gods on a scale unparalleled in any other society, but they did so with the conviction that the continued existence of the cosmos depended on it" (Fagan, 1984, pp. 228–289).

The Aztec belief that the flow of human blood would keep the sun rising was stupid by our standards of knowledge, as well as a grisly mental construction. Yet, it was confirmed by reality testing every day. Hearts were torn out yesterday, and sure enough the sun rose today. We say that was the wrong reality test—they should have stopped killing and seen the sun rise anyway, but that is a test that adds vital power to our belief, not theirs. Furthermore, that particular reality test was totally impractical from the Aztec viewpoint, like America testing the Soviet Union's peaceful intent through unilateral disarmament, or like a paranoid approaching his enemies to see if they really want to kill him.

As a criterion for assessing delusion, testing against facts is more problematic than we would like to believe. It depends on what is known and what can be known, both of which are socially variable, and reality tests commonly buttress what already is believed.

Truth and Delusion

Truth is a will-o'-the-whisp once one allows for different systems of knowledge based on different epistemologies. Beliefs that are asinine in one framework are taken-for-granted reality in another framework. Facts do not absolutely credit one belief or another, because facts themselves derive their validity from a system of knowledge, and facts are social constructions as much as representations of nature, even in science: "Although we speak of the resolution of scientific controversies as if it were a matter of the facts closing the case, . . . what actually happens is that scientists close the case and then attribute their action to the existence of facts" (Aronson, 1984, p. 7). Beyond that, facts often are obtained indirectly by communication from others and have to be weighed as a historian evaluates hearsay evidence (McCullagh, 1984). Moreover, people are so subject to social influence (Asch, 1956) that determination of fact has to be suspect when it is supported by an authoritative group. Countering these problems is no simple matter. Institutions like science, law, and scholasticism that winnow facts usually depend on group conflict and social confrontation to do the job.

Thus it is nearly hopeless for a lone clinician to try to judge whether a belief is a delusion or not by determining its truth value. Whatever we ourselves think, the other may be correctly employing truths other than our own. Truth and fact are mercurial constructs that cannot be criteria for resolving controversies across different individual realities. Rather, it must be the case that a judgment about a person's thought processes precedes assessment of truth. Then the truth value of the person's beliefs is a consequence of classification, not its source.

DELUSIONS AND SOCIAL CONTROL

Judgment of delusion is intrinsically social, involving a comparison of minds in which one is treated as authoritative and the other as deficient. The judgment is relativistic—each party is certain about the validity of his or her mental productions and sure that the other is wrong, and no absolute basis exists for settling the matter once alternative realities are admitted. Thus, sociologically, delusions are a form of cognitive deviance—the violation of "rules of what one is expected to believe and not believe, to take as true and as false" (Douglas & Waksler, 1982, p. 388, italics removed). The thinking of one party is reified, the thinking of the other party is stigmatized, and the selection of which is which gets settled in a contest of social power, with the loser subject to social control. "What emerges as truth in [ideological] conflicts is established not on the basis of truth itself but rather on the basis of who has the power to decide what truth is" (Douglas & Waksler, 1982, p. 367). "Diverse interpretations of the world . . . when their social background is uncovered, reveal themselves as the intellectual expressions of conflicting groups struggling for power" (Mannheim, 1936, p. 269).

This sociological perspective raises a different question about delusions—not why or how people reach false conclusions, but rather, what kinds of thinking are being controlled and discouraged in the process of judging delusion? One answer to this question is that accusations of delusion are an aspect of conflict between groups dedicated to Ideational and Sensate philosophies.

People in the Ideational subculture derogate Sensate beliefs. For example, Mrs. Keech (Festinger et al., 1956) advised her followers to cease thinking (p. 47) and referred to nonbelievers as "the scientists" led by Lucifer (p. 52). Scott (1980, p. 14) notes that one of the basic premises of this subculture is that growth can be achieved only by disciplines that "open up the subconscious, intuitive, nonlogical mind and turn off the rational conscious mind." In turn, the believers think that they may be persecuted for their orientations, and they resort to secrecy—even the use of aliases—to protect themselves (e.g., Festinger et al., 1956; Scott, 1980). Festinger et al. (1956) provided good evidence that the antagonism goes in both directions, and the Ideationals do have reason to fear persecution.

> A special PTA meeting was held to discuss means of restraining [Mrs. Keech's] influence on the children and she was finally warned, she claimed, to stop her talks to the children or she would be taken before "a psychiatric examining board." This threat, apparently from the police, proved effective for it terrified her.

(p. 88)

Dr. Armstrong [Mrs. Keech's key supporter] was asked to resign from his position on the college Health Service staff. The reason given him was candid: there had been complaints from parents and students that he was using his position to teach unorthodox religious beliefs and was "upsetting" some students (pp. 85–86). [Later Armstrong's sister] filed a petition to have the two adult Armstrongs declared insane and to obtain custody of their children and their estate.

(p. 232)

By continuing her participation in the movement, [Bertha, a secondary prophet in the group] risked an investigation of her sanity; her husband declared that, if she had not voluntarily given up all connection with the group by January 1, he was going to send her to a psychiatrist and destroy all the books and writings associated with the movement.

(p. 124)

These examples suggest that lay judgments of madness arise in conflicts over what constitutes a valid reality in the everyday world. Those who stray too far from conventional and socially supported truths risk having their beliefs turned into delusions and their character reduced to insanity. Judging people to be mad and their beliefs to be delusions serves as a means of socially controlling cognition, and in contemporary Western society it serves as a mechanism for protecting everyday Sensate reality.

However, those are lay tactics, not the work of psychiatrists. True, Ideational premises do seem to characterize beliefs that are labeled delusions by psychiatrists. Ideas of reference and external control, of mystical power, of persecution, asceticism, and possession are common themes in the Ideational subculture, as they are in delusions. Maher and Ross (1984, p. 401), in discussing a study of 25 amphetamine abusers with delusions of persecution, report that "an increase in philosophical and religious concerns, the revelation of sudden insights, and an acute concern with the meaning of trivial details are described in these patients and are to be found in much the same progression in Schreber's memoirs." However, this correspondence between Ideational concerns and delusion is merely a correlation with exceptions. For example, Dr. Armstrong finally was examined by two court-appointed psychiatrists: "They declared that, although the doctor might have some unusual ideas, he was 'entirely normal'" (Festinger et al., 1956, p. 252). Nor are beliefs from the Sensate system inviolate: The delusion presented in detail by Maher and Ross (1984) is constructed largely from concepts out of scientific culture.

While laypeople use accusations of delusion and madness to protect the preeminence of the Sensate knowledge system and its corresponding reality, psychiatrists do not join in this crusade. Psychiatrists' diagnoses of delusion are not administered in the service of one system of knowledge over another.*

Psychiatric Criteria

Basically the DSM-III (APA, 1980) definition treats delusions as ideas that are (1) false and (2) without social currency. Truth and falsity cannot be assessed without taking an epistemological stand, and since psychiatric diagnoses do not take a position in the social conflict between the competing knowledge systems, practicing psychiatrists cannot logically be using falsity as a criterion of thought disorders. This suggests that social currency is the fundamental basis for a psychiatric judgment that someone is deluded. The credibility of this claim is enhanced by reconstructing cases of nondelusional thinking that already have been considered.

A woman sits alone in her room writing messages from outer space all day, and the messages say she alone is to be saved in a coming world cataclysm. This woman seems a good candidate for psychiatric concern. The Mrs. Keech studied by Festinger et al. (1956) removed herself from such candidacy by basing her beliefs on an accepted body of knowledge and by sharing her revelations and her fate with others. Bo and Peep (Balch & Taylor, 1977) had similar ideas; they were the objects of sociological study rather than psychiatric treatment because they, too, devoted themselves to the social activity of creating a cult.

A man claims that he is receiving secret mental messages that he was married to his wife in a prior life: the information he has is that she was unfaithful to him then, as she is unfaithful to him now: moreover, she is not even a true human. This seems a clear enough case of thought disorder. What makes it different from Clovis' story (Scott, 1980) is that no one wants to hear it. Clovis' story was believable to all the witches in the coven in terms of the knowledge base that they shared, it was relevant to the group, and it had important implications for others.

A man is convinced that his continued existence depends on killing another person each day and tearing out the heart. He surely would be considered dangerously deluded in psychiatric terms. Yet this judgment does not apply to the Aztecs. In a morbid way, the Aztecs' similar belief, and the practices it engendered, support the contention that the Aztecs were "one of the most religious civilizations ever developed by humankind" (Fagan, 1984, p. 209).

---

*Freud may not have been so impartial—as suggested by this statement in *Totem and Taboo:* "Spirits and demons were nothing but the projection of primitive man's emotional impulses; ... quite like the ingenious paranoic Schreber, who found the fixations and detachments of his libido reflected in the fates of the 'God-rays', which he invented" (Freud, 1938, p. 878).

Thus their belief is removed from the arena of psychiatric concern. The hundreds of thousands of Aztecs did not all have a delusion by psychiatric standards because their belief had a religious nature—it was shared and socially supported.

On the other hand, textbook delusions fall out of the psychiatric realm if we give the believer social commitment and modify the belief so it has social significance. For example, here is how some major types of delusions have been, or could be, turned into sociopolitical movements of no direct concern to psychiatrists. *Being controlled:* The mass media is perverting our sexual appetites with subliminal stimulation, and we must seek legislation to prevent this from happening (Key, 1974). *Bizarre:* Everyone who undergoes surgery in New Haven has electrodes implanted in his or her head—the plot is documented by reference to a book (Delgado, 1969) and concerned citizens are calling for an official investigation. *Poverty:* Marxists are attempting to foment a revolution so that the belongings of the wealthy can be given to the underclass. *Jealousy:* Black men have to be intimidated and oppressed because by nature they lust after White women and are devilishly successful in seducing them (a common belief in the traditional U.S. South).

One of the key missions of clinical psychologists and psychiatrists in contemporary civilization is to maintain the population in a reasonable balance between social commitment and individuality. American psychiatry is a liberal profession in that it does not make judgments of delusion on the basis of a patient's alignment with a deviant sociocultural system, as long as constructed beliefs have relevance for others—regardless of how strange the beliefs may be—and approval and confirmation is sought from a group. Rather, psychiatrists are vested with authority to define the limits of individuality, the breakdown of social commitment, the development of excessive egocentricity. The diagnosis of delusion is one means by which they do this. A belief becomes a delusion when the psychiatrist judges that no one wants to hear it and that the patient does not care to adjust the belief in the direction of social value. Factuality is not part of the diagnostic process; rather, a judgment of falsity is part of the control process—removing authenticity from the patient's reality.

Delusions are mental constructions so egocentric that they have no social currency. The judgment of delusion occurs when someone is creating a reality that no one else wants to share, and the believer is not responding to this social isolation. Assessments of these conditions can be made with substantial levels of confidence. Indeed, the objectivity of diagnosing the state associated with delusion probably would improve if the concern for factuality of belief were discarded and the focus on sociality sharpened. This approach would make extrainterview information even more important than it is now—not to check the factuality of a client's beliefs but to check explicitly for a social circle that supports the believer's thinking.*

REFERENCES

American Psychiatric Association. (1980). *Diagnostic and statistical manual of mental disorders* (DSM-III) (3rd ed.). Washington, DC: Author.

Anderson, J.R. (1983). *The architecture of cognition.* Cambridge, MA: Harvard University Press.

Aronson, N. (1984). Science as a claims-making activity: Implications for social problems research. In J.W. Schneider & J.I. Kitsuse (Eds.), *Studies in the sociology of social problems.* Norwood, NJ: Ablex.

Asch, S. (1956). Studies of independence and submission to group pressure. A minority of one against a unanimous majority. *Psychological Monographs, 70.*

Balch, R.W., & Taylor, D. (1977). "Seekers and saucers: The role of the cultic milieu in joining a UFO cult." *American Behavioral Scientist, 20:* 839–860.

Bugliosi, V., & Gentry, C. (1974). *Helter skelter: The true story of the Manson murders.* New York: W.W. Norton.

Cicourel, A.V. (1964). *Method and measurement in sociology.* New York: Free Press.

Cicourel, A.V. 1974. *Cognitive sociology: Language and meaning in social interaction.* New York: Free Press.

Delgado, J. (1969). *Physical control of the mind: Toward a psychocivilized society.* New York: Harper & Row.

Douglas, J.D., & Waksler, F.C. (1982). *The sociology of deviance: An introduction.* Boston: Little, Brown.

Fagan, B.M. (1984). *The Aztecs.* New York: W.H. Freeman.

Festinger, L. 1957. *A theory of cognitive dissonance.* Stanford, CA: Stanford University Press.

Festinger, L., Riecken, H.W., & Schachter, S. (1956). *When prophecy fails.* Minneapolis: University of Minnesota Press.

Freud, S. (1938) *The basic writings of Sigmund Freud* (A.A. Brill, Ed. and Trans.). New York: Modern Library.

Gergen, K.J. (1985). The social constructionist movement in modern psychology. *American Psychologist, 40,* 266–275.

---

*Diagnoses of shared delusion (*folie à deux* phenomena—e.g., see Westermeyer's contribution in this volume) suggest that clinicians view sharing a belief with certain others—those who are under the control of a patient and who have no independent social standing—as not really counting. By extension, delusion might be attributed to a whole group or nation under the control of a tyrant, for example, the Manson family (Bugliosi & Gentry, 1974). Clear definitions of control and of independent social standing are required in order to diagnose *folie à deux* objectively.

Georgoudi, M., & Rosnow, R.L. (1985). Notes toward a contextualist understanding of social psychology. *Personality and Social Psychology Bulletin, 11,* 5–22.

Key, W.B. 1974. *Subliminal seduction.* New York: New American Library.

Leiter, K. (1980). *A primer on ethnomethodology.* New York: Oxford University Press.

McCullagh C.B. (1984). *Justifying historical descriptions.* New York: Cambridge University Press.

Maher, B., & Ross, J.S. (1984). Delusions. In H.E. Adams & P.B. Sutker (Eds.), *Comprehensive handbook of psychopathology.* New York: Plenum Press.

Mannheim, K. (1936). *Ideology and utopia: An introduction to the sociology of knowledge.* New York: Harcourt, Brace & World.

Pasztory, E. (1983). *Aztec art.* New York: Harry N. Abrams.

Scott, G.G. (1980). *Cult and countercult.* Westport, CT: Greenwood Press.

Schneider, J.W., & Kitsuse, J.I. (Eds.). (1984). *Studies in the sociology of social problems.* Norwood, NJ: Ablex.

Simonton, D.K. (1976). Does Sorokin's data support his theory? A study of generational fluctuations in philosophical beliefs. *Journal for the Scientific Study of Religion, 15,* 187–198.

Sorokin, P. (1957). *Social and cultural dynamics.* Boston: Porter Sargent.

Soustelle, J. (1961). *Daily life of the Aztecs* (P. O'Brian, Trans.). Stanford, CA: Stanford University Press.

Sowa, J.F. (1984). *Conceptual structures: Information processing in mind and machine.* Reading, MA: Addison-Wesley.

Stryker, S. (1984). Science as rhetoric: Nothing to lose but our gains. *Contemporary Sociology, 13,* 251–254.

PART THREE

Approaches to Treatment

CHAPTER 13

The Treatment of Delusions in Schizophrenic Patients

DOUGLAS W. HEINRICHS

Maryland Psychiatric Research Center and University of Maryland School of Medicine

Delusional beliefs occur in the context of a wide range of medical and psychiatric illnesses (Manschreck, 1979). In most cases they are conceptualized as secondary to a more fundamental pathogenic process and can be expected to resolve when that underlying process is adequately treated. In the case of schizophrenia the situation is somewhat different. Delusions constitute an important component of most modern criteria for diagnosing the syndrome (Schneider, 1959; Spitzer, Endicott, & Robins, 1975; American Psychiatric Association, 1980). Perhaps because we have so little understanding of the fundamental pathogenic mechanism, resolution of delusions with treatment cannot be assumed. Indeed, in many cases delusions persist in an enduring way, so that the chronic management of delusions and their behavioral consequences is an important issue in the treatment of schizophrenia.

Since their introduction in the mid-1950s, neuroleptic drugs have become the mainstay of the treatment of schizophrenia. A large number of carefully controlled studies have unequivocally demonstrated the efficacy of these drugs in treating acute psychotic episodes in schizophrenics and in delaying—though not preventing—subsequent decompensation (Davis, Schaffer, Grant, Kinard, & Chan, 1980). These studies have generally focused on a broad range of schizophrenic symptomatology, not on delusions in particular. Delusions are among the symptom dimensions benefited by neuroleptics, but these drugs do not seem to be selectively or specifically antidelusional. Furthermore, there has been no evidence to suggest a differential antidelusional effect of one neuroleptic compared to any other, although a given patient may be more responsive to some neuroleptics than to others. When delusions are part of an acute psychotic episode, the resolution of the psychosis by neuroleptic treatment usually leads to a reduction in delusions, although some residual level of delusional belief remains in many cases

(Harrow, Rattenbury, & Stoll, this volume). Furthermore, a significant subset of schizophrenics have chronic fixed delusions that are not episodic and that show little response to neuroleptics.

Traditional psychotherapeutic treatment of schizophrenia derives largely from psychoanalytic theory, following the lead of pioneers such as Federn (1952), Fromm-Reichman (1950), and Sullivan (1962). Since in this framework specific symptoms are viewed as expressions of underlying intrapsychic conflicts or defects, the goal of treatment has usually been conceptualized in global terms rather than as resolution of specific symptoms, such as delusions. Only a small number of controlled outcome studies have sought to assess the efficacy of traditional psychotherapy in schizophrenia, and the results have not been encouraging. Only two studies (Marks, Sonoda, & Schalock, 1968; Karon & Vanderbos, 1972) purport to demonstrate any value for psychotherapy, while four others report negative results (May & Tuma, 1965; Bookhammer, 1966; Rogers, Gendlin, Kiesler, Truax, 1967; Missier et al., 1969). The largest, and methodologically best, study (May & Tuma, 1965) found no value for psychotherapy alone compared to standard hospital management, and only a minimal suggestion of an advantage to psychotherapy plus neuroleptics compared to neuroleptics alone. However, since most of the studies have severe methodological flaws, the verdict remains unsettled.

The growing evidence for a biological basis for at least the vulnerability to chronic schizophrenia combined with the established value of neuroleptic medication has led to an increased reliance on a traditional medical model. While such a model can be sufficiently broad to encompass psychological and social factors (Engel, 1977), it assumes that the patient suffers from a disease that can be named and described and that the patient and his or her family can be educated about the illness and how to manage it. This strategy of psycho-education would be expected to have a beneficial effect on the course of the illness by providing more informed environmental support, eliciting optimal cooperation with treatment, combating hopelessness and demoralization, and reducing the stigma of the illness. The literature has described the incorporation of psycho-educational strategies into numerous treatment programs (Mendell & Allen, 1977; Goldstein et al., 1978; Anderson, Hogarty, & Reiss, 1980; Scher, Wilson, & Mason, 1980; Fink, 1981; Shenoy, Shires, & White, 1981; Falloon et al., 1982; Leff et al., 1982; Heinrichs & Carpenter, 1983). Several controlled studies (Goldstein et al., 1978; Falloon et al., 1982; Leff et al., 1982) have demonstrated a significant benefit of such programs. Most of these studies have focused on global aspects of outcome such as relapse rate, social and occupational functioning, and overall symptom level. The role of psycho-education in treating specific symptoms such as delusions has not been adequately studied.

Maher (1974) has suggested that delusions represent explanatory theories for the abnormal experiences to which the schizophrenic is subject. Hence, by providing a medically grounded alternative explanation for such experiences, direct educational strategies could be expected to dramatically reduce delusional beliefs. While this approach remains to be tested, dramatic resolution of delusions in response to the provision of such alternative explanations has not been described by workers using psycho-educational strategies with chronic schizophrenics. Johnson, Ross, and Mustria (1977) described the resolution of a delusional belief in a young man by a reattribution procedure that had a strong educational component. However, it is questionable whether the patient was schizophrenic. Rudden, Gilmore, and Frances (1982) reported three cases in which delusions were resolved by a confrontation strategy based on a reality testing assessment compatible with a psychoeducational stance. However, in each case the patient did not hold the delusional belief with fixed conviction, and none suffered from chronic delusions. Probably none were schizophrenic by current criteria. Whether such approaches could succeed with schizophrenics who have chronic, fixed delusions is questionable.

Positive and negative reinforcement strategies derived from a behavior modification approach have been employed by a number of workers (Rickard, Digman, & Horner, 1960; Ayllon & Haughton, 1964; Kennedy, 1964; Meichenbaum, 1966; Nydegger, 1972; Wincze, Leitenberg, & Agras, 1972; Liberman, Teigen, & Patterson, 1973; Patterson & Teigen, 1973; Davis; Wallace, Liberman, & Finch, 1976; Bulow, Oei, & Pinkey, 1979) in attempts to reduce delusional speech. Reinforcers have included interpersonal attention, verbal response, tokens, and tangible reinforcers such as food. Positive, negative, and combined positive and negative reinforcement strategies have also been employed. Most reports have focused on one or a small number of cases. Several larger studies employing token economies have been reported (Gripp & Magaro, 1971; Presly, Black, Gray, Hartie, & Seymour, Lentz, 1977), although these have generally focused on broader dimensions of outcome with only incidental attention to delusions per se. The results of these behavioral studies have been quite uniform. It is possible to significantly reduce the amount of delusional speech while the reinforcement strategy is being applied, but when generalization to other settings is examined improvement has been found to be absent or negligible (Wincze et al., 1972; Liberman et al., 1973; Patterson & Teigen, 1973; Davis et al., 1976). Furthermore, those studies that have included a no-treatment follow-up (Liberman et al., 1973; Bulow et al., 1979) have found a loss of benefit after active treatment is discontinued. Nydegger (1972) reported continuing benefit after discharge, but this was apparently due to continued application of a social reinforcement strategy by the patient's family.

These behavioral strategies are unique in constituting treatments specifically directed at delusions. Yet the lack of generalization and endurance make their actual value to the patient doubtful. Furthermore, a more fundamental concern about this approach is that none of these studies assess whether delusional beliefs are actually altered. The patient simply talks about them less. The lack of generalization and rapid extinction combined with descriptions of some of the cases (Davis et al., 1976) suggests that beliefs are not altered; nor is it apparent that patients trained to speak less about their delusions will be less likely to act on them in destructive ways. Davidson (1969) has suggested that prohibiting delusional speech while failing to attend to the antecedent experiences that prompt delusions may actually aggravate the problem. By cutting off access to the delusions, the clinician using such an approach is clearly in a poor position to assess the likelihood of dangerous behavior based on delusional beliefs. Furthermore, since for many patients delusional material constitutes the most subjectively important aspect of their lives, it is difficult to see how a clinician who refuses to discuss them can establish a viable therapeutic alliance with the patient. This may be especially important in outpatient settings where the absence of an alliance often leads to the patient terminating treatment.

Given the limited empirical data available on treatment specific for delusions in schizophrenic patients, the rest of this chapter will focus on six hypotheses that have evolved based upon my treatment of a large number of schizophrenic patients over the past decade. I believe that these hypotheses can be particularly well illustrated by the case histories of two schizophrenics with permanent delusions who have been in long-term treatment with me. Case reports, of course, have little value in proving issues, but when organized around specific questions, they can be useful for developing hypotheses for further study.

Hypothesis 1. Data relevant to delusions in schizophrenic patients emerge gradually over the course of treatment. Such data generally support Maher's (1974) hypothesis, which suggests that delusions seek to explain abnormal or unusual personal experience. Furthermore, data supporting this hypothesis are inclined to emerge after some time has elapsed in the treatment relationship—they may be easily missed during an initial diagnostic or research interview.

Hypothesis 2. The nature of the abnormal experience upon which delusions are based may be of multiple types, including abnormal feeling states and aberrant perceptions of the outer world. Furthermore, the type of abnormal experience has important differential implications for the approach to and success of treatment.

Hypothesis 3. The delusional stance of the patient importantly influences the establishment and maintenance of the therapeutic relationship. The ability of the therapist to alter the underlying abnormal experience is an important prerequisite to an effective therapeutic alliance.

Hypothesis 4. The delusional stance of the patient importantly influences the patient's view of and acceptance of neuroleptic treatment.

Hypothesis 5. Direct education provided to the patient about the nature of the schizophrenic illness usually fails to resolve symptoms, including delusions, due to the impact on the self-image of the patient of accepting the medical explanation.

Hypothesis 6. The experience of passivity plays or comes to play an important role in the delusional expression of schizophrenic patients.

In order to facilitate the following discussion it is useful to begin by providing summaries of two illustrative cases.

Case Summary: Mr. S.

Mr. S., at the time he began treatment with me, was a 25-year-old single, White man. He had had two psychiatric hospitalizations the previous year and had been diagnosed as suffering from chronic paranoid schizophrenia. He was described by his parents as having been a very easygoing child. His developmental milestones were normal. During junior high school he was described by his family as becoming very shy with everyone, especially with girls. He successfully graduated from high school. During his high school years, he episodically abused a range of drugs, including alcohol, LSD, PCP, and amphetamines. He had had one long-standing relationship with a girl who broke off the relationship several years prior to his first hospitalization. The patient stated that he began hearing voices at age 21 following the drowning death of a close friend. This friend had also been somewhat involved in the drug scene and had had a psychiatric hospitalization shortly before his death. Mr. S. described an enduring, irrational guilt concerning his friend's death by drowning; even though he had not been present, he felt somehow responsible. Shortly following his friend's death, he became increasingly convinced that people were picking on him, intent on harming him and "depriving me of something." Due to his progressive suspiciousness and paranoia he was fired from his job at a municipal fire department. Since that time he has not been able to maintain ongoing employment. He became increasingly preoccupied with his friend's death and his own sense of responsibility. He struggled to understand how he might have caused his friend's death and began to believe that somehow he had inadvertently brought it about by using mind control or other telepathic means. He also began to have passivity experiences, thought broadcasting, and a range of other paranoid delusions. He was first seen at the insistence of his family for psychiatric evaluation two years prior to entering treatment with me. After about a year of outpatient treatment with neuroleptics, he was hospitalized for one month following a period in which he experienced an increase in his paranoid thinking, agitation, erratic and disruptive behavior, and threats of violence. Shortly after his discharge from the hospital the same symptoms reemerged, and he was hospitalized for a second time. Throughout this time the patient was extremely angry and complained that people were "depriving me of something." He felt that he had to kill the people who were doing this to him in order to free himself. During his hospitalizations he was treated with neuroleptics and became less angry and agitated. Although be became less obsessed with his delusional concerns, they did not disappear. In addition to his psychotic symptoms, the patient experienced an ongoing sense of passivity and a range of negative or deficit symptoms, including apathy, reduced motivation, anhedonia, social withdrawal, and free-floating anxiety. Almost any kind of environmental stress resulted in a marked exacerbation of his suspiciousness and preoccupation with his delusions. As a result he became progressively agitated, frightened, and withdrawn, but he was also periodically aggressive and confronting. When he was most upset, he would demonstrate some looseness of associations.

The patient has been in treatment with me for approximately four and a half years. During this time a predictable cycle in the treatment has repeated itself four times. In the initial phase, shortly after discharge from a hospital, the patient is cooperative with treatment and is reasonably stable. He is able to question the reality of his delusional beliefs. The therapy focuses on a discussion of these beliefs as well as a discussion of his concerns about his inadequate accomplishment occupationally and interpersonally. In addition, there is considerable discussion of his negative symptoms, including a profound anhedonia that he finds extremely distressing. After a period usually lasting several months, the patient becomes more convinced of the reality of his delusions and more angry at the people he feels are responsible. During this phase he becomes more erratic in taking his neuroleptic medication. Initially the therapeutic relationship is spared, but with time he becomes suspicious and angry towards me as well. At this point he discontinues his drugs and, after a short time, angrily discontinues therapy, claiming that I have nothing to offer him and want to hurt him rather than help him. He becomes more erratic, angry, and threatening toward family and others in his environment, ultimately leading to an involuntary hospitalization, following which the cycle is repeated. At the time of this writing the patient has once again discontinued treatment, is demonstrating a deterioration in his clinical course, and an involuntary hospitalization in the near future is likely.

CASE REPORT: MR. D.

Mr. D. is a divorced White man employed as an accountant who entered treatment with me at the age of 48. His first psychiatric hospitalization occured at age 40 following his divorce. At that time he was described as being anxious and generally suspicious of others but without clear evidence of psychosis. His hospitalization lasted only a few days, but shortly thereafter he was rehospitalized for several weeks with similar complaints. Following his second hospitalization he was in outpatient treatment for over seven years and maintained without hospitalization on a low dose of oral neuroleptics. His psychiatrist moved to another city, which led to his contacting me for treatment.

Mr. D. was the older of two children. He did well in school. Following high school he spent three years in the Army and subsequently completed college, always with excellent academic performance. He married at age 23 and subsequently had five children. He worked as an accountant and was quite successful until the time of his divorce. Surrounding the turmoil of his divorce he was out of work for slightly over a year but after that became permanently employed and continues to have an excellent work record. He has stayed quite involved with his children but otherwise has been very aloof socially, has few acquaintances, and no close friends.

The patient states that at age six he overheard a conversation between his parents and his father's brother. He recalls being confused by the conversation and frightened by the degree of anger expressed by all the participants. His understanding of the conversation was that he had in fact been the product of an affair between his mother and the brother of the man he had thought to be his father. He states that following that conversation the issue was never discussed again, but his father began to treat him very differently. While he treated him appropriately in public, he was extremely neglecting and hostile towards the patient in private. The patient recalls numerous examples of the father treating his sister kindly and neglecting him. By early adolescence he became convinced that his father wished to see him dead and recalls a couple of instances of near accidents that he believes his father intentionally contrived to kill him. The patient states that his divorce resulted from the fact that his youngest child was found to have a medical condition that he was told was always genetically transmitted. Since neither his family nor his wife's family had a history of this disorder he became convinced that his wife had been unfaithful. He found this a painful recapitulation of his own birth and divorced his wife.

The patient also describes a number of instances beginning in early adolescence that were characterized by curious alterations in perception. He describes, for instance, being on a playground with friends when suddenly everything lost its color and became somewhat distorted in shape with harsh, exaggerated outlines. He found this a disorienting experience, but it passed in a manner of five to ten minutes. Similar experiences have occurred from time to time since then.

He describes an airplane trip to California around the time of his marriage at age 23 during which the plane passed through an extremely dense fog. The experience was quite eerie and unsettling and upon landing in California the patient had the conviction that everything was very strange and that he in fact was in some other place that duplicated California. He was unable to describe any objective differences in his environment but simply had the sense that nothing was real or as it seemed. The patient described a similar experience almost 20 years later. This involved a trip to Florida that followed shortly after an extremely brief involvement with a woman that he broke off due to his anxiety. He landed in Florida, again to find that the world seemed altered in some strange way. People seemed to be robots and to be somehow dead inside. He felt that time had changed and that he was in a different year, and that everyone and everything had been substituted in some kind of doubling process. The patient has continued to be preoccupied with these experiences up to the present time. He has developed an elaborate system involving duplicate worlds between which he has been switched unwittingly. From time to time the world seems increasingly unreal, which he takes to mean that he will shortly be transported to yet another world that will seem on the surface to be exactly the same as the real one. The patient understands that these beliefs are seen by others as bizarre, and he himself struggles with how such a thing can be possible, yet he is firmly convinced of their reality.

The patient has throughout the years developed an elaborate system of other beliefs. He feels that the world is filled with hidden messages and meanings that he must try to decipher. He is preoccupied with the meanings of various numbers. He has developed an elaborate number-letter substitution system for decoding the meaning of life from comic strips and popular songs. Employing this system he believes that he can determine which horses will win races and which stocks will do well on the market. The patient from time to time follows these leads in betting and in investing but always with amounts of money that he can afford to lose. Most of the time the patient experiences these hidden messages as being impersonal, there to be read by anyone who knows how; at other times, however, they become intensely personal and directed toward him. At these times he becomes extremely anxious. He becomes concerned about his own fate and that of the world at large, and at times has the overwhelming belief that unless he takes certain actions all the world will be destroyed. At times he has attributed the power for this destruction to his sister and in the past to his mother, who is now deceased. He feels that he has on a number of occasions saved the world from destruction by buying certain stocks or betting on certain horses.

The patient has also described a frequent experience that he must do certain things for reasons that are unclear to him. Usually these involve driving to certain shopping malls or going in and out through certain doorways. He feels that the necessity to do these things is somehow put into his head from outside, and he has over the years developed the belief that an intelligent being lives inside his head that can direct him as if he were a figure on a video game. He finds this process on most occasions more perplexing than frightening, although at times he becomes concerned about what he might be forced to do.

On two occasions, one several years before entering treatment with me and the other shortly after beginning treatment with me, he became profoundly panicked, feeling the world was coming to an end and that he must somehow get help. These experiences were accompanied by sensory alterations in which things changed in color and shape in a kaleidoscopic manner. In both cases the patient was successfully treated with neuroleptic drugs and therapeutic support on an outpatient basis with quick resolution of the episodes.

During his treatment with me the patient has not required rehospitalization. He remains convinced of the reality of his delusional beliefs and discusses them at length in therapy. He does, however, understand how others will respond to them and has learned not to discuss them with family or coworkers.

Hypothesis 1: The Emergence of Mechanisms of Delusion in the Course of Treatment

Mr. D. had delusional beliefs dating at least since adolescence. However, the records of his two hospitalizations make no mention of them, and indeed during the first several months of treatment with me there was no evidence of delusional material in our sessions. Only gradually, as the patient became more trusting, did he begin to reveal his truly bizarre inner world. This revelation occurred in gradual stages. He would speak for a while about his beliefs, carefully monitoring my response. He would then hesitate to go further, as if to allow me to digest the material and only then proceed to tell me more. The full discussion of his intricate belief system emerged only after several years of therapy. When his beliefs were first discussed they were simply presented as his beliefs. Only with very careful discussions, encouraging the patient to describe the circumstances of their emergence, did the underlying theme or sense of his beliefs become apparent. The fundamental theme seemed to be that things are not as they seem, that the world we call real is but a veneer below which is a real world that is quite different. Most people, the patient believes, never move beyond or question this veneer and so live with little anxiety. He, however, has been initiated by a series of strange experiences into the fact that reality is much more complex. He feels driven to understand it. At times this process is intellectually fascinating to him and exhilarating. At other times, however, he is fearful of what he will discover. He is also concerned that he is learning more than he is meant to know and that if he learns too much something disastrous will occur. Three types of direct experiences seem to have determined the patient's need to seek this extraordinary level of explanation: (1) his periodic sensory aberrations, in which the world becomes visually transformed and altered into something other than it appears; (2) his episodes of passivity experience, in which he feels controlled and that his behavior is determined by other forces; and (3) experience of having overheard the conversation between his father and his uncle, during which he discovered that he was not his father's son. From that time on he felt that the family lived a lie in public, acting as if things were as they always had been said to be, but in private their behavior reflected the reality that he in fact had been fathered by another man. Thus, at this very personal level, his world was not what it seemed.

Mr. S. demonstrated delusional beliefs from early in his psychiatric treatment. Initially he talked extensively about delusions relating to the death of his friend. He also talked about how other people tried to hurt him and deprive him of things. However, it was only after a number of months of treatment that we were able to tie these beliefs to an underlying experience. In his case it is the intense experience of anhedonia, in which he feels deprived of a sense of pleasure and satisfaction. The anhedonic experience makes no sense to him. He can find no reason why he should feel so little pleasure in any activity and why he should feel so emotionally dead. He resents this state immensely, and it has become clear that most of his delusional beliefs center around an attempt to explain how he has been deprived of a capacity for pleasure and satisfaction. Somehow it has been taken from him by others. He has been robbed. His satisfactions and pleasures have been stolen from him. His specific delusional experiences reflect this in concretized form. Perhaps if he had a job, a sports car, or a lover, things would be different. Others have these things; why doesn't he? He has come to believe that others have contrived to deprive him of these things and that his anhedonia is the result. At times he feels that his only hope is to kill the people who prevent him from having happiness. It is in this state that he becomes angry and aggressive, and ultimately requires hospitalization.

The full nature of the delusional experiences of both of these patients has emerged gradually in the course of treatment. More importantly, the connection between delusional beliefs and primary aberrations in their inner experience of themselves and their world emerged only after a considerable period of treatment. Beliefs that initially seemed to be inexplicably bizarre came more and more to be seen as creative attempts to understand powerful and idiosyncratic experiences. In the case of Mr. D., the environmental events and perceptual experiences that led to the conviction that the world is not as it seems provide the basic problem for which he has sought understanding. In the case of Mr. S., his profound anhedonia, his inner experience of non-feeling, has led to his struggle to understand why he is deprived of the basic satisfaction to which others seem to have such easy access. These two cases illustrate what for me has seemed to be a common process in the therapy of schizophrenics: An understanding of the mechanism of delusions gradually emerged that conforms to Maher's (1974) theoretical framework. An appreciation of this process raises concerns as to whether Maher's theory could be adequately tested from a single cross-sectional evaluation of patients, however sophisticated the method used.

Hypothesis 2: Multiple Sources of Aberrant Experience

While for both Mr. D. and Mr. S. unusual and profound inner experiences seem to relate importantly to the emergence of delusional beliefs, the nature of those inner experiences varies considerably. In the case of Mr. D., primary sensory alterations of the world play an important role. Dramatic visual distortions in which the world becomes profoundly altered in appearance perplex him and lead him to seek some explanation. This is coupled with primary passivity experiences that seem irrational and nonsensical to the patient. In addition, Mr. D. experienced an important environmental event with respect to the concern over the identity of his father and his family's subsequent reaction, leading to the notion that the world is not what it seems.

With respect to this latter element, of course, there is the concern as to whether this in fact was a real family event or simply part of his delusional transformation. There is no way of achieving absolute certainty in this regard. However, the way in which this issue emerged in therapy argues, I believe, for its basis in reality. All other aspects of Mr. D.'s delusions were introduced tentatively at first; however, once he realized I found it acceptable for him to discuss them and would not reject him or panic at their strangeness, he went on to discuss them with considerable enthusiasm. He seemed to enjoy the intellectual rumination about how all of these strange things could occur and found the opportunity to discuss them in the sessions satisfying and a considerable relief. Whenever the issue surrounding his father emerged, however, he became anxious and depressed. He relived the experience with considerable affect, which was in dramatic contrast to his usually detached discussion of his delusional beliefs. On one occasion when I urged him to discuss this matter in more detail than he was comfortable, he missed the subsequent session and for a time considered terminating treatment. Since that time we have been able to discuss it upon occasion but only in limited doses and always with considerable dysphoria on the part of the patient.

Mr. S. also seemed to elaborate his delusional beliefs as an attempt to understand an abnormal inner experience. In his case, however, it was not directly a transformation of perception or his view of the outer world; rather it was an altered inner state, namely his anhedonia, his inner sense of deadness and emptiness, that was so inexplicable and such a torment to him.

The implication of these different origins of altered inner experience for treatment are important. Mr. D. is clearly focused on understanding perceived peculiarities of the outer world. As such he is able to engage in meaningful discussions about that world and how to assess its reality. He is able to benefit from an appreciation of how his experience of the world differs from others. Although it does not lead him to relinquish his delusional beliefs, it allows him to encapsulate them in an adaptive manner. He is able to separate his delusional interpretations of the world from the apparent public reality that he shares with others. As a result he is able to live effectively in that public reality, to work and to relate effectively with his children, and to maintain some superficial friendships. He is able to accept the importance of living effectively in this publicly acknowledged world and realizes that an important component of that is to indeed keep his private world private. The therapy sessions play an important role in that regard, allowing him a forum for exploring and discussing his inner reality that is safe and removed from the rest of his interpersonal interactions. He has been able to recognize the times at which his preoccupation with his private vision has made him so anxious or so distracted that it has jeopardized his functioning, and he has been able to effectively distance himself from his delusional world at such times. Hence he has continued to function at a reasonably high level and to avoid rehospitalization.

For Mr. S., however, such efforts have proven futile. The direct experience of deprivation of all that is satisfying and pleasurable in life has dominated his experience. Discussions of outer reality and attempts to aid the patient's reality testing have provided little benefit. He is able to partially appreciate the difference between his experience of the world and the publicly shared reality from time to time, but his own inner distress, so directly experienced, inevitably undoes any progress in this area. His increasing despair over ever having happiness becomes transformed into anger and accusation, leading to a profound disruption of reality testing and to aggressive behavior that inevitably results in hospitalization. Perhaps an inner feeling state as basic as anhedonia is so directly experienced—is so unmediated by perceptions of the outer world—as to make any question of its reality nonsensical. Such states are not alternatives to some publicly shared reality and may be as difficult to question as whether a person is having physical pain. The ineffectiveness of existing therapeutic approaches with such inner feeling states may contribute to the poorer prognosis associated with negative or deficit symptoms such as anhedonia in schizophrenia (Anderson & Olsen, 1982; Pogue-Geile & Harrow, in press).

Hypothesis 3: The Mechanism of Delusion and the Therapeutic Relationship

Mr. D. has been able to maintain a stable therapeutic relationship for over seven years. In contrast, Mr. S. has consistently disrupted the therapeutic relationship and has been able to reengage in treatment only after a period of restabilization in a hospital. The nature of the delusional mechanism in each case sheds light on this differential outcome. Mr. D. struggles to make sense of a confusing and perplexing outer reality. He experiences the therapeutic setting as a place where this exploration can be conducted and experiences the therapist as an ally who can help him keep his bearings in this process. He accepts that his unusual experiences are not shared by me and yet knows that I accept them as subjectively real for him. Hence he is able to acknowledge as a legitimate, shared therapeutic task the exploration of reality from our respective vantages and finds that process useful. Mr. S. has been unable to achieve any stable perspective on a mutual therapeutic goal. He knows only that I have been unable to alter his inner emptiness, his anhedonia. That I am unable to give him what he needs becomes transformed in time to me being unwilling to give it; hence I become simply another instance of a depriving world. For a time he seems to draw some consolation from the fact that I understand and acknowledge his inner dilemma, but this is soon lost in his anger at my inability to change it in any way.

The essence of a stable therapeutic alliance resides in the ability of the patient and clinician to have a shared task that can be understood within the framework that each participant brings to the treatment. At first glance this may seem impossible with a delusional patient. After all, his or her beliefs about the world are clearly not accepted by the therapist. However, one of the important therapeutic gains from understanding delusional mechanisms as a function of aberrant experience is that the therapist can accept the reality of the underlying experience as subjectively valid, even when the resulting explanations (delusional beliefs) are disputed. Success in this regard seems more likely when the aberrant experience involves distortions in the perception of the outer world as opposed to aberrent inner feeling states. This conforms with the impression of Rudden, Gilmore, and Frances (1982) that a more favorable response to the treatment of delusions is likely for schizophrenics who have highly charged involvement with the outside world, compared to those who are withdrawn from the world.

Hypothesis 4: Delusions and the Acceptance of Neuroleptic Medication

Mr. D. acknowledges a considerable benefit from antipsychotic medication. It allows him to have more control over the degree to which he thinks about his private world; it strengthens his ability to concentrate effectively on his job and to interact adequately with others. It decreases his subjective experience of the strangeness of the world around him, even though he persists in his belief that what people call real is but a veneer behind which much else lurks. In contrast, Mr. S. is unable to view neuroleptics as providing any benefit in his life. He becomes angry at their failure to alter his anhedonia and instead is inclined to episodically turn to alcohol or stimulants in an attempt to feel some inner life and pleasure. He has come to see the medication as simply another mechanism by which others deprive him of his inner feeling. Hence, he is inclined to reject them. When I have discussed with him the importance of taking his medication, he invariably responds that they fail to make him feel any satisfaction or pleasure and claims instead that they actually deaden him even further. Just as an effective therapeutic relationship depends upon a shared view of how the relationship is valuable for the patient, an effective use of neuroleptics requires the same sort of shared view. The patient, as he develops theories to explain his inner experience, will incorporate into those theories the role of neuroleptic drugs. The way drugs are incorporated is likely to depend upon the capacity of those drugs to in some way alter the aberrant inner experience that forms the basis of the delusional elaboration.

Hypothesis 5: Delusional Mechanisms and the Impact of Direct Education

Maher (1974) has argued that since delusions are based upon attempts to understand idiosyncratic experiences of the world, an effective treatment should involve presenting the patient with an alternative explanation in terms of the way his illness has altered his experience. However, both Mr. D. and Mr. S. are typical of delusional schizophrenics in that a presentation of such explanation does not lead to a relinquishing of the delusional belief. This can be explained by considering the impact that the delusional belief has on the patient's self-image and self-esteem. This is not to say that such factors account for the formation of the delusion in the first place; rather, it is to suggest that once in place the delusion becomes an important component in the patient's image of himself and that giving up his delusional belief can seriously undermine his view of self. In the case of Mr. D., his elaborate belief system provides intellectual stimulation and involvement with what he regards as profound aspects of reality that are intrinsically satisfying. Beyond this he gains considerable satisfaction from his sense that he has a grasp of what is real that others have failed to attain. To replace this with the notion that all can be explained in terms of an aberrant mental or neurological process that alters how he experiences the world is totally unacceptable. At several points during the therapy I have suggested ancillary diagnostic procedures such as EEG and CT scan. The patient has consistently rejected any such workup and seems anxious, defensive, and somewhat offended that I would suggest it.

Mr. S. has also been consistently unwilling to consider the explanation that his aberrant inner experiences reflect a disease state. He has experienced such a suggestion as one more deprivation, namely, deprivation of normalcy. He has refused any participation in group treatment or aftercare day treatment because the association with other obviously psychotic patients offends him. He interprets it as an accusation that it is somehow his flaw or his fault that he is unable to feel and finds much more comforting the notion that he has been actively deprived of happiness by others. It seems to give him a cause around which to rally and some undefined hope that somehow he will be able to steal back what has been taken from him. This is not to suggest that psycho-educational approaches are of no value—quite the contrary. They can be extremely useful in helping patients and families understand the nature of psychiatric symptomatology and in planning effective coping strategies. However, it is not likely that the explanations provided by such direct educational approaches would make the schizophrenic's delusional hypotheses unnecessary.

Hypothesis 6: Passivity Experiences and the Mechanism of Delusion

Although the range of delusional beliefs in schizophrenics is wide, a group of delusional beliefs termed *passivity experiences* has often been assumed to play a particularly important role in schizophrenia. Such delusions have been the backbone of some popular diagnostic criteria for schizophrenia such as those proposed by Schneider (1959). The core feature of the passivity experience is that a psychological or bodily process usually experienced as emanating from the self, or for which the self is responsible, is experienced by schizophrenics as being imposed upon them from without by a mechanism over which they have no control. Examples include the belief that thoughts are put into or taken out of their heads, that feelings or urges that they experience are put there by another or belong to another, or that certain of their bodily sensations or motor acts are actually under the control of another. Not all schizophrenic patients manifest explicit passivity delusions, nor are such delusions pathonomonic of schizophrenia. However, the prominent role they play in schizophrenic illness is understandable if delusional beliefs are viewed as efforts to explain aberrant inner experiences or perceptions of the outside world. Such aberrant experiences are typically experienced by the patient passively; that is, they happen outside the realm of his or her voluntary control and are likely to be experienced as imposed upon him or her in a way that is not easily understood. Mr. D's episodes of perceptual alteration, for instance, occur without warning and are not consciously willed by him. He feels helpless to either start or stop this process when it occurs. Similarly, his sense that he must carry out certain acts feels like a mandate that is imposed upon him, even when he experiences it as nonsensical. He states that he does not know why it is important for him to do these things, and he does not even have a clear notion of what will happen if he doesn't, except that he has an inexplicable sense that to resist the mandates is dangerous.

For Mr. S., the inner deadness and inability to experience normal satisfactions and pleasures does not derive in any logical way from his own experience. It is something that has happened to him. His feelings have been stolen from him against his will. Given that the underlying abnormal experience that is the root of delusional belief is typically experienced passively by schizophrenic patients, it is not surprising that the theories such patients develop to explain their experiences frequently contain the belief that others somehow control the inner workings of their mental life. The experiencing of the self as an object controlled by others can influence patients' behavior profoundly, even when explicit delusional explanations are not employed. Mr. S., for instance, after about two years of treatment with me, was arrested for his role in breaking into a warehouse and stealing some merchandise. The patient stated that he was riding in his car with an acquaintance who said that they would go to the warehouse and steal the merchandise. The patient was told to drive to the back of the building and to sit in the car until the other man returned with the stolen goods. The patient did this and was waiting in the car when the police arrived. In exploring with the patient the basis of his judgment to go along with the crime, it became apparent that the patient in fact exercised no judgment at all. He experienced the comments of the other man not as a suggestion that he could decide to accept or reject but as a command that simply was to be followed. The patient simply failed to consider that he had an option not to go along with the crime. The patient's beliefs concerning the circumstances of the crime were not explicitly delusional; that is, he did not voice the conviction that the other man had the power to make him stay in the car by some mysterious means. The patient simply assumed a passive stance that never reached the level of an explicit delusional formulation. In many patients explicit passivity delusions are but the tip of an iceberg of pervasive passivity that influences their day-to-day behavior more profoundly than is usually appreciated.

CONCLUSIONS

Based on the foregoing clinical discussion and literature review the following guidelines are offered for treating delusional schizophrenics until more specific and efficacious treatments are developed.

1. Consider neuroleptic treatment for delusions that appear *de novo* as part of an acute psychotic episode. Residual and fixed delusional beliefs require ongoing attention in therapy.

2. Acknowledge the subjective importance of the delusional beliefs and encourage discussion about them in the therapeutic sessions—but not to the exclusion of other important reality-based topics.

3. Explore the context in which the delusions arose, seeking to identify the aberrant inner experiences that have prompted them. This task is ongoing over the course of therapy.

4. Seek to identify and apply where possible the interventions—pharmacologic and psychosocial—that can alter those experiences in a desirable direction.

5. Seek to develop a shared view of the rationale for treatment interventions—including some discussion of the schizophrenic illness—that is understandable in terms of the patient's own experience and that considers the patient's need to preserve self-esteem. This usually means that the explicit goal is not to eradicate delusional beliefs but to manage them in a way that allows the patient to function optimally, for example, reducing their emotional intensity, minimizing destructive actions based on the beliefs, and appreciating the consequences of talking about the beliefs in situations such as the workplace.

6. Help the patient to appreciate the contrast between his or her idiosyncratic views and those of other people with whom the patient must interact.

This can form the basis for the patient understanding the reaction of others to his or her delusional speech.

7. Strategies to reduce delusional speech are appropriate when targeted to special settings such as work and when accompanied by a willingness to discuss the problem in the therapeutic session. A reality-based rationale for such strategies, such as keeping a job, should be explicitly shared with the patient.

8. Be alert to the patient's underlying passivity and how it alters his or her behavior, regardless of whether the passivity is part of an explicit delusional belief. Help the patient appreciate his or her capacity to be an active agent in his or her own life.

9. Monitor any plans the patient has to act on his or her delusional beliefs. Help the patient realistically assess the likely consequences of such action and be prepared to take needed initiative to protect the patient or others. When such protective action is required, explicitly state its rationale to the patient in terms of the adverse consequences to be prevented.

10. Educate family or other significant caretakers in the patient's life about the patient's delusional beliefs and help them develop concrete strategies for coping with the beliefs, stressing that it is unlikely that direct confrontation can compel the patient to reject the delusional beliefs.

REFERENCES

American Psychiatric Association. (1980). *Diagnostic and statistical manual of mental disorders* (DSM-111) (3rd ed.). Washington, DC: Author.

Anderson, C.M., Hogarty, G.E., & Reiss, D.J. (1980). Family treatment of adult schizophrenic patients: A psychoeducational approach. *Schizophrenia Bulletin, 6* (3), 490–505.

Andreasen, N., & Olsen, S. (1982). Negative versus positive schizophrenia. *Archives of General Psychiatry, 39,* 789–794.

Ayllon, T., & Haughton, E. (1964). Modification of symptomatic verbal behavior of mental patients. *Behavior Research and Therapy, 2,* 87–97.

Bookhammer, R.S. (1966). A five-year clinical follow-up of schizophrenia treated by Rosen's direct analysis. *American Journal of Psychiatry, 123,* 602–604.

Bulow, H., Oei, T., & Pinkey, B. (1979). Effects of contingent social reinforcement with delusional chronic schizophrenic men. *Psychological Reports, 44,* 659–666.

Davis, J.M., Schaffer, C.B., Grant, A., Kinard, C., & Chan, C. (1980). Important issues in the drug treatment of schizophrenia. *Schizophrenia Bulletin, 6,* 70–87.

Davis, J.R., Wallace, C.J., Liberman, R.P., & Finch, B.E. (1976). The use of brief isolation to suppress delusional and hallucinatory speech. *Journal of Behavior Therapy and Experimental Psychiatry, 7,* 269–275.

Davison, G.C. (1969). Appraisal of behavior modification techniques with adults in institutional settings. In C.N. Frank (Ed.), *Behavior therapy: Appraisal and status.* New York: McGraw-Hill.

Engle, G.L. (1977). The need for a new medical model: A challenge for biomedicine. *Science, 196,* 129–136.

Falloon, I.R.H., Boyd, J.L., McGill, C.W., et al. (1982). Family management in the prevention of exacerbations of schizophrenia: A controlled study. *New England Journal of Medicine, 306* (24) 1437–1440.

Federn, P. (1952). *Ego psychology and psychoses.* New York: Basic Books.

Fink, P. (1981). The relatives group: Treatment for parents of adult chronic schizophrenics. *International Journal of Group Psychotherapy, 31* (4), 453–468.

Fromm-Reichman, F. (1950). *Principles of intensive psychotherapy.* Chicago: University of Chicago Press.

Goldstein, M.J., Rodnick, E.H., Evans, J.R., et al. (1978). Drug and family therapy in the aftercare treatment of acute schizophrenia. *Archives of General Psychiatry, 35* (10), 1169–1177.

Gripp, R.F., & Magaro, P.A. (1971). A token economy program evaluation with untreated controls and comparisons. *Behavior Research and Therapy, 9,* 137–149.

Heinrichs, D.W., & Carpenter, W.T. (1983). The coordination of family therapy with other treatment modalities for schizophrenia. In W.R. McFarlane & C.C. Beels (Eds.), *Family therapy in schizophrenia.* New York: Guilford Press.

Johnson, W.G., Ross, J.M., & Mustria, M.A. (1977). Delusional behavior: An attributional analysis of development and modification. *Journal of Abnormal Psychology, 86,* 421–426.

Karon, B.P., & Vanderbos, G.R. (1972). The consequences of psychotherapy for schizophrenic patients. *Psychotherapy: Theory, Research, and Practice, 9,* 111–119.

Kennedy, T. (1964). Treatment of chronic schizophrenia by behavior therapy, *Behavior Research and Therapy, 2,* 1–6.

Leff, J., Kuipers, L., Berkowitz, R., et al. (1982). A controlled trial of social intervention in the families of schizophrenic patients. *British Journal of Psychiatry, 141,* 121–134.

Liberman, R.P., Teigen, J., Patterson, R., & Baker, V. (1973). Reducing delusional speech in chronic paranoid schizophrenia. *Journal of Applied Behavior Analysis, 6,* 57–64.

Maher, B.A. (1974). Delusional thinking and perceptual disorder. *Journal of Individual Psychology, 30,* 98–113.

Manschreck, T.C. (1979). The assessment of paranoid features. *Comparative Psychiatry, 20,* 370–377.

Marks, J., Sonoda, B., & Schalock, R. (1968). Reinforcement versus relationship therapy for schizophrenics. *Journal of Abnormal Psychology, 73,* 397–402.

May, P.R.A., & Tuma, A.H. (1965). Treatment of schizophrenia: An experimental study of five treatment methods. *British Journal of Psychiatry, 111,* 503–510.

Meichenbaum, D. (1966). The effects of instructions and reinforcement on thinking and language behavior of schizophrenics. *Journal of Abnormal Psychology, 71,* 354–362.

Mendell, W.M., & Allen, R.E. (1977). Treating the chronic patient. *Current Psychiatric Therapy, 17,* 115–126.

Missier, M., et al. (1969). A follow-up study of intensively treated chronic schizophrenic patients. *American Journal of Psychiatry, 125,* 1123–1127.

Nydegger, R.V. (1972). The elimination of hallucinatory and delusional behavior by verbal conditioning and assertive training: A case study. *Journal of Behavior Therapy and Experimental Psychiatry, 3,* 225–227.

Patterson, R.L., & Teigen, J.R. (1973). Conditioning and post-hospital generalization of nondelusional responses in a chronic psychotic patient. *Journal of Applied Behavior Analysis, 6,* 65–70.

Paul, G.L., & Lentz, R.J. (1977). *Psychological treatment of chronic mental patients: Milieu versus social learning programs.* Cambridge, MA: Harvard University Press.

Pogue-Geile, M.F., & Harrow, M. (in press). Negative and positive symptoms in schizophrenia and depression: A follow-up study. *Schizophrenia Bulletin.*

Presley, A.S., Black, D., Gray, A., Hartie, A., & Seymour, E. (1976). The token economy in the National Health Service: possibilities and limitations. *Acta Psychiatrica Scandinavica, 53,* 258–270.

Rickard, H.C., Digman, P.J., & Horner, R.F. (1960). Verbal manipulation in a psychotherapeutic relationship. *Journal of Clinical Psychology, 16,* 364–367.

Rogers, C.R., Gendlin, E.T., Kiesler, D.J., & Traux, C.F. (1967). *The therapeutic relationship and its impact.* Madison: University of Wisconsin Press.

Rudden, M., Gilmore, M., & Frances, A. (1982). Delusions: When to confront the facts of life. *American Journal of Psychiatry, 139,* 929–932.

Scher, M., Wilson, L., & Mason, J. (1980). The management of chronic schizophrenia. *Journal of Family Practice, 11* (3), 407–413.

Schneider, K. (1959). *Clinical psychopathology* (M. Hamilton, Trans.). New York: Grune & Stratton.

Shenoy, R.S., Shires, B.W., & White, M.S. (1981). Using a Schiz-anon group in the treatment of chronic ambulatory schizophrenics. *Hospital and Community Psychiatry, 32,* 421–422.

Spitzer, R.L., Endicott, J., & Robins, E. (1975). Research Diagnostic Criteria (RDC). *Psychopharmacology Bulletin, 11,* 22–24.

Sullivan, H.S. (1962). *Schizophrenia as a human process.* New York: W.W. Norton.

Wincze, J.P., Lietenberg, H., & Agras, W.S. (1972). The effects of token reinforcement and feedback in the delusional verbal behavior of chronic paranoid schizophrenics. *Journal of Applied Behavior Analysis, 5,* 247–262.

CHAPTER 14

The Treatment of Delusions in Patients with Paranoid, Paraphrenic, and Affective Disorders

HUGH C. HENDRIE, STEPHEN R. DUNLOP, and NIZAR EL-KHALILI

Indiana University School of Medicine

"Since time immemorial delusion has been taken as the basic characteristic of madness. To be mad was to be deluded and indeed what constitutes a delusion is one of the basic problems of psychopathology."

KARL JASPERS (1964)

Most psychiatrists would agree with the above quotation, but in fact most psychiatric practitioners and most textbooks of psychiatry tend to spend little time discussing the form, content, and treatment of delusional symptoms per se. Rather, the diagnosis and management of delusions are discussed in the context of the various psychiatric syndromes in which they appear. This emphasis on syndromes makes considerable heuristic sense, parallels the development of knowledge in the rest of medicine, and will be our approach in this chapter. Yet careful consideration of delusions cannot be dismissed so readily because much of our current classification of psychiatric disorders still rests to a considerable extent upon the determination of differing delusional subtypes. In the *Diagnostic and Statistical Manual of Mental Disorders* (DSM-III) (American Psychiatric Association [APA], 1980), for example, delusions represent three of the six cardinal criteria for schizophrenia, one of which has to be present to make the diagnosis. Delusions, however, count only if they are of a certain type, that is, bizarre, or not with persecutory or jealous content except if accompanied by hallucinations. In the recent follow-up study reported by Cloninger, Martin, and Guze (1985), three of the four symptoms that seemed to distinguish schizophrenia from other psychiatric disorders with high specificity and sensitivity were

295

delusions—specifically, control delusions, persecutory delusions, and mood incongruent delusions. These subdivisions of delusions primarily involve analysis of content (not entirely—one involves the coexistence of hallucinations and delusions). It is possible, however, that delusions occurring in the various syndromes also represent quite separate psychopathological processes and thus would respond to different treatment approaches.

Perhaps the best known exponent of this viewpoint was Jaspers (1964, p. 107), who in his major tome *General Psychopathology* separated delusions proper from delusionlike ideas and overvalued ideas. Delusions proper— "the vague crystallizations of blurred delusional experiences which cannot be sufficiently understood in terms of the personality and the situation"—are the characteristic symptoms of schizophrenia. Delusionlike ideas that emerge understandably from preceding affects of shattering guilt-provoking experiences are found more often in affective disorders. Overvalued ideas that constitute "isolated notions that develop comprehensibly out of given personality and situation" (Jaspers, 1964, p. 107) are characteristic of the paranoid group of patients. Maher (this volume) elegantly presents a similar hypothesis from a rather different perspective.

Of course, Jaspers is not without his critics. Kind (1967) objected to the concept of psychological irreducibility. The limits of understanding, he states, are fluid, not static, and depend to a considerable extent on the degree of personal involvement of the therapist. We will argue later that both delusions proper and delusional-like ideas may be present in the same syndrome, that is, affective disorders in the guise of mood incongruent and mood congruent delusions. Nevertheless, Jaspers's concepts and those of his colleagues in the German school of phenomenology remain provocative and influential.

Delusions occur in many psychiatric disorders. Our proposed differential diagnostic schema follows closely the DSM-III (APA, 1980) classification system (see Table 14.1). The major division is between syndromes in which the presence of delusions is not essential for diagnosis and those in which delusions represent the most prominent and necessary feature (although accessory symptoms can and do occur). Although delusions are necessary in the diagnosis of organic delusional states and paraphrenia, these syndromes are put into the first category because equally important additional symptoms must be present. Paraphrenia, the paranoid states of the elderly, is listed in Table 14.1 although it is not a separate diagnostic category in DSM-III (APA, 1980). However, because it presents with sufficiently unique features—a different premorbid history from earlier onset schizophrenic patients, and a relationship with sensory loss—we felt justified in following the European tradition, including it as a separate disorder (Bridge & Wyatt, 1980).

TABLE 14.1.   Differential Diagnosis of Delusional Symptoms

	Delusions Are Part of a Psychiatric Syndrome
Schizophrenia	
Major Affective Disorders	-Mania -Depression
Other Psychotic Disorders	-Schizophreniform -Schizo-affective -Brief Reactive Psychosis
Organic Brain Disorders	-Delirium -Dementia -Organic Delusional States
Paraphrenia	
	Delusions Are the Psychiatric Syndrome
Paranoid Disorders	-Paranoia -Shared Paranoid Disorders (Folie a deux) -Acute Paranoid Disorder
Exotic Disorders	-de Clerambault (Erotomania) -Capgras Syndrome (Illusions of imposters) -Lycanthropy (Delusions of becoming a wild beast) -Cotard's Syndrome (Delusions of nihilism) -Monosymptomatic hypochondriachal psychosis

The various syndromes we have grouped together under Exotic Disorders (*exotic* referring to the names and also to the delusional content of these syndromes) appear from time to time in the literature. Each case report usually elicits criticism from those who believe that such cases only represent unusual subtypes of the more mundane psychiatric disorders such as schizophrenia or organic brain disorder (Pearce, 1972; Rudden, Gilmore, & Frances, 1980; Shrabers, Weitzel, & Shingleton, 1980; Ellis & Mellsop, 1985; Munro, 1985). The few patients with these syndromes seen by the senior author of this chapter would tend to support the latter view; for example, the only lycanthrope encountered was a patient with psychopathic personality who had taken lysergic acid. However, we would agree with Munro that while the bulk of these patients have other disorders, there is a small core with the unique syndromes. These are probably best classified under paranoia. This seems true at least for monosymptomatic hypochondriachal psychosis.

Heinrichs (this volume) addresses the problem of the treatment of delusional symptoms in schizophrenia. We will discuss in this chapter the treatment of the paranoid disorders, the delusional affective disorders, and paraphrenia.

One further issue, however, should be addressed before reviewing the syndromes. The literature on the course, prognosis, and response to treatment of delusional symptoms in any of the psychiatric disorders is not extensive and tends to be confusing and contradictory. One difficulty may lie in the relative dearth of detailed studies on the course of psychiatric disorders over lengthy periods and a lack of interest by researchers in the process of recovery (Ciompi, 1984; Strauss, Hafez, Lieberman, & Harding, 1985). Another reason may lie in the previously mentioned possibility that delusional symptoms represent different psychopathological processes and thus respond to different treatment approaches. A final problem is one that is addressed in this volume by Harrow and his colleagues. Delusions may be a multidimensional clinical phenomenon. Kendler, Glazer, and Morgenstern (1983) suggest two such dimensions: delusional involvement, which is the intensity of the patient's involvement with the delusional beliefs, and delusional construct, which refers to the structure, content, and encapsulation of the delusion. Improvement may occur on one or the other of these dimensions relatively independently. This concept certainly makes a great deal of clinical sense. It is not uncommon to see patients in practice who improve behaviorally by paying less attention to or sealing over (McGlashan, Docherty, & Siris, 1976) their delusions while still insisting on the inherent truth of the beliefs. Studies such as those now being carried out by Harrow should help to clarify this issue.

THE PARANOID DISORDERS
(DELUSIONS ARE THE SYNDROME)

Paranoid disorder as a separate disease category now appears in both DSM-III (APA, 1980) and the *International Classification of Diseases* (9th ed.) (ICD-9) (World Health Organization, 1978), although the authors of DSM-III still express uncertainty about differentiating paranoid disorder from paranoid personality and paranoid schizophrenia.

Paranoia was the subject of a recent review by Kendler (1984), who prefers the term *delusional disorder*. His proposed diagnostic criteria for this disorder include persistent, nonbizarre delusions lasting at least one month; absence of prominent affective symptoms or, if they are present, they have occurred only after the onset of the delusions; absence of characteristic schizophrenic symptoms; and no evidence of organic brain disorder. The characteristic features of the delusions occurring in this disorder are coherence and nonbizarreness. Kendler concludes that delusional disorder does represent a distinct psychotic illness on the basis that demographic characteristics are different from those found for schizophrenia and affective disorders, a low incidence of schizophrenia or affective illness occurring in the relatives of delusional disordered patients, and a relative diagnostic stability over time (although a small percentage of patients so diagnosed do develop schizophrenia).

While delusions are the characteristic primary symptoms of paranoid disorders, accessory symptoms do occur. Paranoid patients are often suspicious, hypervigilant, hostile, and belligerent with some ideas of reference. They are prone to act upon their delusional beliefs. Mood disturbances associated with the delusions with somatic and/or phobic anxiety symptoms that may not meet the DSM-III (APA, 1980) criteria of full affective disorders are not infrequent. The prevalence of paranoid disorders is unknown. Kendler (1984) estimates the incidence to be about one to three new cases per year per 100,000 population.

The exotic paranoid disorders, of which there are many, are defined by the content of the delusions (Nash, 1983). A few examples are included in Table 14.1. De Clerambault's syndrome is characterized by the delusional conviction of being in amorous communication with another person usually of a higher rank. In Capgras's phenomenon, the sufferer becomes convinced that someone close is really an imposter, usually a tormentor. Nihilistic delusions are the prominent feature in Cotard's syndrome; the delusions can be particularly intense and all encompassing, leading to the feeling that nothing exists and sometimes, paradoxically, that the patient is immortal. The lycanthrope is convinced that he or she has been transformed into a wild beast. As mentioned previously, the vast majority of patients with these delusions are usually suffering from schizophrenia, affective disorder, or organic brain disorder. Monosymptomatic hypochondriachal psychosis is characterized, as its name suggests, by a fixed hypochondriachal delusion. In this syndrome, there is evidence that at least a percentage of these patients have a unique disorder that is akin to paranoia in clinical features, course, and prognosis. The hypochondriachal delusion may consist of a belief that the patient possesses an offensive body odor, has some anatomical abnormality, or is suffering from an infestation with parasites, insects, or worms.

Pharmacological Treatment of Paranoid Disorders

Amid the confusing and often contradictory literature on the treatment of paranoid disorders, there seems to be general agreement on only two points. The prognosis, at least for the pure paranoid disorders, is poor (Day &

Semrad, 1978), and there are few, if any, well-controlled treatment outcome studies (Taylor, Sierles, & Abrams, 1985). Rettersol (1971) provides an exception to the generally gloomy view of outcome. In the large group of patients whom he personally followed, he reported a favorable outcome in approximately 80 percent. The characteristics of his good prognosis patients included being married, having a premorbid personality characterized by hypersensitivity rather than schizoidness, an onset after the age of 30, a clear-cut precipitating event, and associated depressed mood and ideas of reference. However, his population seemed to consist of a mixed group of patients who would fit into our present categories of schizo-affective disorders and delusional depression, as well as paranoid disorders.

The reasons for the lack of controlled studies are relatively obvious. The disorders are not common and probably only a small proportion of individuals with the various forms of paranoia present themselves for treatment at mental health facilities. There are no widely accepted diagnostic criteria. Also, by the very nature of the illness, paranoid patients are unlikely to be compliant and would make poor subjects for complex placebo-controlled studies.

Neuroleptics

In the absence of acceptable scientific data, many authorities recommend a pragmatic treatment approach to patients with paranoid disorders, including the judicious use of neuroleptic medication. This view is based upon evidence that neuroleptics are effective in the treatment of delusions seen in other psychiatric syndromes such as schizophrenia, affective disorders, and organic brain disorders, evidence that will be examined elsewhere in this volume. However, this viewpoint is by no means universally held. Rappaport (1978) concluded that at least some paranoid schizophrenics improve more rapidly without medication.

Two follow-up studies involving small numbers of patients who were treated with phenothiazines have been inconclusive. Mooney (1975) reported on 12 patients with pathological jealousy who were so treated. The short-term results seemed promising, with 8 of the 12 improving. However, on follow-up, which lasted from four months to five years, the eventual outcome was not as good; five patients seemed considerably better, two slightly better, one unchanged, and four worse. Some of these patients, however, apparently were diagnosed paranoid schizophrenics. Winokur (1977), in a retrospective analysis of patients admitted to the University of Iowa hospital who fit the criteria for delusional disorder, found five who had been treated with phenothiazines. Three of these were judged to be considerably improved at discharge. In two of these patients who had follow-up data, only one remained at least socially recovered after two to three years.

Pimozide

Pimozide is one of the diphenylbutylpiperidine class of drugs, a nonphenothiazine with neuroleptic properties; its chemical structure is closely related to the butyrophenones, and like them it has a relatively prolonged pharmacological action (Pinder et. al., 1976; Bernstein & Swift, 1979).

In contrast to the other neuroleptics, pimozide may be a specific, effective treatment for monosymptomatic hypochondriachal psychosis (MHP), especially in patients who present with delusions of parasitosis, according to several studies. Riding and Munro (1975) first reported the virtual disappearance of somatic delusions in five cases of MHP when the patients were treated with two to six mg of pimozide daily. The beneficial effect was of rapid onset and contrasted the lack of clinical effect on a patient with dysmorphobia. Hamann and Avnstorp (1982), in a double-blind crossover clinical study, found that whereas 10 of 11 patients with delusions of parasitosis improved during the pimozide period, two patients improved in the placebo period. The improvement was noted for both the delusions and the itching.

In a review of dermatologists' use of pimozide in treating patients suffering from delusions of parasitosis, Lyell (1983) reported that of 66 patients treated, 44 improved and 16 were unimproved. Six patients were lost to follow-up. The improved response, however, varied: Some patients lost their delusional beliefs entirely; for other patients, the delusion persisted but was less compelling emotionally. The dosage used by dermatologists varied from 2 to 12 mg per day. Side effects mentioned included Parkinsonism and drowsiness, which sometimes limited the usefulness of the drug. One dermatologist was so impressed by the drug's action that he referred to the management of parasitosis as being divided into two epochs, BP and AP (before pimozide and after pimozide). As a rule, relapse occurred on stopping the drug, but control could be reestablished by starting medication again.

In addition to being a selective dopamine blocker, pimozide also displays substantial potency as an inhibitor of ^{3}H-naloxone binding with activities comparable to morphine and fentanyl. Creese, Feinberg, and Snyder (1976) have suggested that this activity, which occurs in the presence and absence of sodium, indicates an opium antagonist profile. This is in contrast to other butyrophenones and phenothiazines, which have weak affinity for the opiate receptor. It has been suggested that this pharmacological action produces a centrally mediated antipuritic effect and that this clinical action then fosters extinction of the delusions of parasitosis (Bernstein & Swift, 1979).

Pimozide has also been reported to be effective in the treatment of other paranoid disorders. Amery et al. (1972), in a multicentered nonplacebo controlled study of patients with paranoid symptomatology, concluded that pimozide was an effective drug for symptom control. In their total of 25 patients, there was 1 with a diagnosis of paranoia, 4 with involutional paraphrenia, 10 with a paranoid psychotic reaction, and 2 with paranoid personality disorder. The remainder were diagnosed as paranoid schizophrenics. Other case reports in the literature describe pimozide as being effective in other manifestations of MHP (Munro & Pollock, 1981). In addition, Munro (1984) has reported on a patient with delusional jealousy who made an excellent response to pimozide. Pimozide has recently been approved by the Food and Drug Administration in the United States for treatment of Gilles de la Tourette's disease. While the evidence that pimozide is specifically effective in the treatment of some types of delusional disorders is certainly not overwhelming, it is sufficiently compelling to justify more carefully controlled clinical trials in this country.

Antidepressants

Antidepressant drugs are generally not considered the treatment of choice in delusional patients except in the context of an affective disorder, and even with these patients they are not particularly successful when used alone. However, there are in the literature a few reports of successful use in patients with paranoid disorders.

Akiskal, Arana, Baldessarini, and Barreira (1983) reported on five patients with paranoid disorder with some atypical features who responded to antidepressant medication. The atypical features included evidence of a phasic course with somatic complaints, some alterations in the circadian cycle, previous history of phobic anxiety or panic symptomatology, a family history of affective disorder, and a history of previous successful response to thymoleptic drugs. None of the patients met the DSM-III (APA, 1980) criteria for affective disorder or schizophrenia, although one patient later was diagnosed as suffering from bipolar disorder. The choice of the antidepressant which included doxepine, imipramine, amitriptyline and phenelzine, depended upon the associated features of the disorder.

Using the antidepressant trazodone, Sheehy (1983) successfully treated a patient with paranoia who also had prominent anxiety symptoms and obsessive features. This patient had previously not responded to neuroleptic medication. Brotman and Jenike (1984) reported on two cases with monosymptomatic hypochondriachal psychosis who responded to the antidepressants doxepine and imipramine. One patient was suffering from dysmorphobia (i.e., that she had disfiguring facial wrinkles) and one from the olfactory reference syndrome (i.e., that he had an offensive anal odor).

All the above authors emphasized that their patients were not suffering from a major affective disorder but did have some associated features of anxiety, depression, or obsessive compulsive disorder. These reports suggest that a trial of antidepressants may be justified in paranoid patients with affective symptoms.

Psychosocial Treatment of Paranoid Disorders

Controlled studies on the psychopharmacological treatment of paranoid disorders are few in number. In the psychodynamic literature on paranoid disorders, controlled studies are nonexistent, at least in the search conducted by the present authors. Case studies and theoretical speculations are numerous, although in these papers often little distinction is made between paranoid disorders and paranoid schizophrenia.

There seem to be two schools of thought regarding psychodynamic therapy with delusional patients. One recommends a relatively immediate attempt to correct the delusional reality distortion. The other suggests at least an initial avoidance of confrontation and emphasizes the importance of establishing a relationship between therapist and patient and strengthening the nondelusional aspects of the patient's psyche. These opposing viewpoints are well described by Boverman (1953), who advocated the first approach, and Molden (1964), who advocated the second. In the absence of controlled studies, however, the existence of relative benefits of either approach is purely speculative.

The literature on behavioral approaches to the deluded patient consists primarily of individual case reports in which the response to the specific behavioral intervention is compared to control conditions (e.g., Brink, 1980; Carstensen & Fremouw, 1981). Response is usually defined in terms of observable patient behavior, both verbal and nonverbal. As is the case in the psychodynamic literature, there is often little attempt at distinguishing clinically among the varying psychiatric syndromes. Most case studies, however, are conducted with relatively chronic inpatient populations. Despite the widely different theoretical backgrounds, one cannot help but be impressed by the similarities in the clinical approach of the psychodynamic and behavior therapists to the treatment of delusions. One group of behavior therapists advocates techniques focusing directly on delusional beliefs, while another addresses itself to reinforcing nondelusional behavior. Some programs incorporate both approaches. Most case studies report reductions in delusional behavior during the therapeutic intervention; few, however, demonstrate that this change in behavior is persistent or that it generalizes to the nonexperimental situation.

Two studies seem particularly worthy of mention because they do address the question of confrontation in the treatment of delusional patients, although both of these studies deal with a chronic paranoid schizophrenic patient population. Both are based upon the hypothesis of psychological reactance as exposed by Brehm (1966). This hypothesis predicts that direct confrontation with a paranoid patient by an authority figure (i.e., the therapist) would result in strengthening, not weakening, the delusional belief. Watts, Powell, and Austin (1973) therefore constructed a belief modification procedure, which consists of the following principles:

1. A hierarchy of target beliefs is constructed, rated according to the strength of the belief. In the treatment sessions, the least strongly held belief is discussed first.
2. The subjects are not asked to abandon their beliefs, but rather to consider the facts and arguments and entertain possible alternate explanations.
3. The discussion focuses not on the belief system itself, but rather on the supporting evidence for the belief.
4. The patients are encouraged to voice arguments against their beliefs.

In a pilot study with three chronic schizophrenic patients over a period of four months, the belief modification approach was compared to a control condition and to conditions of relaxation and desensitization techniques. Only the belief modification system produced a significant reduction in the strength of the beliefs compared to the control condition.

Milton, Patwa, and Hafner (1978) extended the Watts et al. (1973) study by contrasting the effects of belief modification with a more confrontational technique in 14 inpatients with chronic systematized delusions divided into two equal groups. Each approach was used for five treatment sessions; the strength of the delusional belief was rated at the end of the treatment period and then again after six weeks. Both approaches produced a slight but not significant drop in the strength of the delusional beliefs at the end of the treatment session. After the six-week follow-up period, however, the patients who had received the belief modification procedure continued to show a reduction in the strength of their delusional beliefs. In contrast, the patients receiving confrontation therapy showed no significant reduction. The author also pointed out that although the confrontation patients showed a slight overall reduction in the strength of their delusional beliefs, in four of the seven patients there was an actual increase in delusional intensity, which is consistent with the Brehm (1966) hypothesis.

These studies also obviously do not address either the problem of generalizability or the problem of long-term persistence of results; nor do they consider the nonschizophrenic paranoid patient. However, they do demonstrate that it is possible to address systematically questions such as whether one should confront directly or indirectly the delusions of a paranoid patient.

PARAPHRENIA

Paraphrenia, as described in ICD-9 (World Health Organization, 1978) is a psychosis characterized by conspicuous hallucinations with accompanying delusions, associated sometimes with affective symptoms and disordered thinking in a well-preserved personality. In ICD-9 it is subsumed under the general category of paranoid states. It was reintroduced into the literature in the 1950s by Roth (1955), who considered it to be a form of late onset schizophrenia, a view shared by others (Grahame, 1984). Post (1980) attempted to subdivide this patient population into three clinical categories according to their predominant characteristic: hallucinations, persecutory delusions, or classical schizophrenic symptoms. The clinical utility of these subtypes, however, is not clear. This syndrome is not rare, accounting for about 10 percent of first admission elderly psychiatric patients to the hospital (Roth, 1976). It also seems to have a strong correlation with sensory loss, particularly deafness, although there is no general agreement as to the strength of this relationship (Cooper, Kay, Curry, & Garside, 1974; Cooper & Porter, 1976).

Pharmacological Treatment of Paraphrenia

There is more agreement among clinicians regarding the effectiveness of neuroleptics in the treatment of paraphrenia than in the treatment of paranoid disorders. Much of this consensus rests on the series of studies conducted by Post (1966, 1973, 1978, 1980). In three similar groups of paraphrenic patients, he compared the results of giving no medication, phenothiazines for initial control of symptoms with no maintenance, and phenothiazines with adequate maintenance dosage. Almost all of his patients who received no medication did poorly, 13 of 19 remaining psychotic, and the remaining 6 having continuing symptoms. In the follow-up period the group maintained on phenothiazines performed best, 89 percent remaining symptom-free, compared to 50 percent symptom-free in the group in which the phenothiazines were discontinued. Post pointed out a number of methodological flaws in this study, including inconsistent and variable follow-up procedures. Nevertheless, his results are impressive.

Whanger (1973), in an uncontrolled study on elderly patients with various diagnoses who exhibited paranoid symptoms, also reported an 80 percent remission rate after treatment with trifluoperazine and haloperidol. This remission rate was the same regardless of diagnosis. His study also emphasized the importance of maintenance therapy—relapse occurred when the medication was stopped.

Raskind, Alvarez, and Herlin (1979), however, reported poor results with oral neuroleptic medication in a group of involuntary, seriously ill outpatients suffering from paraphrenia. They consequently instituted a six-week treatment period with five mg of fluphenazine enanthate administered intramuscularly, and compared their results with a matched group of patients who had received oral haloperidol in the previous year. Eleven of thirteen of the patients receiving parenteral fluphenazine improved compared to only three of thirteen of the oral medication group. The authors concluded by emphasizing the importance of treatment compliance in assessing results in delusional patients, particularly in an outpatient setting.

The choice of neuroleptic and the dosage level in elderly patients has been supported in reviews (e.g., Gulevitch, 1977). There is no evidence that one neuroleptic drug is any more clinically effective than another with this population. Choice depends primarily on the differential side effect profiles of the drugs. Prien, Haber, and Caffey (1975), in a survey of prescription practice in veterans hospitals with elderly patients, found mellaril to be the most popular antipsychotic, presumably because of its lower incidence of extrapyramidal reactions. Other clinicians suggest the use of the high potency neuroleptics such as haloperidol and thiothixene because of their lesser anticholinergic properties (Branchey, Lee, Amin, & Simpson, 1978). Whanger (1973) represents the commonly held view that elderly patients respond well to much lower doses of neuroleptics than younger patients. He recommends dosages in the levels of two mg of stelazine or one mg of haloperidol per diem. This practice also obviously cuts down on the risk of side effects.

DELUSIONS IN AFFECTIVE DISORDERS

Delusional Depression

Depression is characterized by a pervasive and persistent disturbance in mood associated with disturbances in (1) thought content (lowered self-esteem, thoughts of death, suicidal thoughts, feelings of guilt); (2) thought processing (slowing of thought and processes, difficulty in concentration); and (3) appetite, sleep, energy, and involvement with the environment. The presence of delusions is not a necessary or characteristic feature of the syndrome. The point at which disturbances in thought content in the affectively disturbed become delusions is a matter of judgment. Most clinicians would probably agree that delusions are present when the vague preoccupations of depressed patients (e.g., "I am sick and unworthy") take on the quality of concrete, fixed and false beliefs (e.g., "My bowels have turned to stone; I must be executed"). In these circumstances, the delusions that have a recognizable connection to the general disturbances of thought content in depression are considered mood congruent (the delusion-like ideas of Jaspers?). Mood incongruent delusions may also be present in depressed patients. These delusions are often of a kind typically seen in schizophrenia (corresponding to Jaspers's delusions proper?). How to classify such depression has been a continuing problem in nosology. In the Research Diagnostic Criteria (Spitzer, Endicott, & Robins, 1978), patients presenting with mood incongruent delusions could be classified as schizo-affective or depressed, depending on the clinician's decision concerning the exact nature of the delusions or their relationship in time to the affective symptoms. In DSM-III (APA, 1980), no criteria are given for schizo-affective disorder and its use is discouraged. Depressions in the course of schizophrenia are to be classified as separate from the major affective disorders. Nonschizophrenic patients with bizarre delusions can be classified with major affective disorders, with the mood incongruent delusions marked in the last digit of the five-digit diagnostic code. These complications in nosology result in some confusion in the literature concerning the relevance of delusions to the treatment of affective disorder. An additional problem is the tendency of most authors to classify hallucinations with delusions. Most commonly, patients are classified as suffering from psychotic or nonpsychotic depression. Authors then tend to discard from analysis, or consider separately, those patients considered to have an admixture of schizophrenia and affective disorder (schizo-affective disorders or equivalents). However classified, delusions, while not characteristic, are not uncommon in depressed patients, especially inpatients, in whom delusions occur in 10 percent to 20 percent of cases by most estimates. In a review by Leckman et al. (1984) on subtypes of major depression seen in a large collaborative study, 21 of 133 patients (16 percent) met criteria for delusional depression.

Treatment of Delusional Depression

The relevance of the presence of delusions or other psychotic phenomena to the treatment of affective disorder can be resolved into a series of questions. Does the presence of delusions affect the response to treatment of a single episode of affective disorder? Does this effect depend upon the type or content of the delusion (mood congruent or mood incongruent)? Is the effect different in depressed and manic patients? Do delusions have implications for the long-term prognosis of affective disorder? Underlying these specific questions is the more general one: Are delusional (psychotic) and nondelusional (nonpsychotic) affective disorders separate and distinct illnesses or does the presence of delusions simply denote a disorder of greater severity? If delusional affective disorder is a separate illness, then one could expect not only a differential response to treatment and a different prognosis, but also a different spectrum of illness in relatives and eventually a different biology. Apart from the enunciation of general principles regarding the handling of delusional patients, there are no systematic studies of specific psychosocial approaches to the psychotic affectively disturbed patient. Our review of treatment will, therefore, focus only upon the pharmacological and somatic therapies.

The occurrence of delusions in depression has been of interest at least since the 1920s. Kantor and Glassman (1977) have reviewed the literature concerning delusions and the prognosis of depression before the introduction of somatic therapy. They were impressed that a review of the work of Lewis (1936), using modern diagnostic criteria, revealed that at least some delusional patients had a poorer prognosis than the nonpsychotic patients. With the introduction of electroconvulsive therapy (ECT), there was less interest in the presence of delusions in affective disorders because all patients seemed to respond favorably to this treatment method. However, with the advent of antidepressant medication as the treatment of choice, there has been a renewal of interest in the differential response of affectively disturbed patients. In 1975, for example, Glassman, Kantor, and Shostak reported a poorer response to imipramine in delusional unipolar depressive patients than in nondelusional unipolar patients. In their 1981 review, Glassman and Roose concluded that most studies have found that delusional patients respond less well to tricyclic antidepressants alone than nondelusional depressed patients. The delusional patients respond better when neuroleptics are added to the tricyclic treatment regime or electro-convulsive therapy is used. There is one exception to this general finding. Quitkin, Rifkin, and Klein (1978) reanalyzed data classifying patients as psychotic or nonpsychotic based on the "E" factor of Lorr's multidimensional scale for rating psychiatric patients. In two thirds of the patients who were considered delusional using this criterion, no distinction could be seen between their response to tricyclics and to chlorpromazine. Quitkin et al's. paper, however, suffers from an unusually broad definition of psychotic depression. Glassman and Roose (1981) also examined the response of delusional depressed patients to placebo in a study involving 21 delusional and 60 nondelusional unipolar depressed patients. During the one- to two-week placebo period of the study, none of the delusional patients but 18 of the 60 nondelusional patients improved. Curiously, the authors did not report on the further treatment of their patients. They did report, however, that delusional patients had significantly more psychomotor retardation, reported more depressive mood, and were significantly more depressed, using the total Hamilton score, than the nondelusional patients. These findings, the authors pointed out, cannot answer the question as to whether delusions in depressed patients indicate simply greater severity or constitute a separate illness. The presence of delusions does seem to predict, however, the absence of placebo response.

Charney and Nelson (1981) conducted a retrospective review of their clinical experience with 54 delusional and 66 nondelusional depressed patients excluding patients with schizo-affective disorder. They found no significant differences between their patients on demographic or most patient history variables. They did find, however, that 95 percent of the delusional patients with recurrent illness had had a previous episode of delusional depression, compared to only 8 percent of the nondelusional patients with recurring illness. Similarly, 89 percent of all prior depressive episodes were delusional for the delusional patients while only 12 percent of the previous episodes were delusional for the nondelusional patients. When specific symptoms were examined from the Hamilton scale and other sources, agitation, referential thinking, ruminative thinking, and self-reproach were more common in the delusional depressed patients. The nondelusional patients were significantly more commonly retarded, anergic, and anxious. The delusional patients were also more severely depressed on a 7-point scale for severity. In this study the patients were not all treated in the same fashion. Nine delusional patients were treated with tricyclics alone, only two of whom responded. Twenty-six received antipsychotics only; eight of these responded. When tricyclics and antipsychotics were used together on 37 patients, 25 responded. Nine of eleven responded to ECT. For the nondelusional patients the pattern was very different. Thirty-two of forty receiving tricyclics alone responded. Only one received antipsychotics alone and did not respond. Nine of ten receiving tricyclics and antipsychotics responded and only one of four receiving ECT responded. A comparison of the treatment response of the delusional and nondelusional patients revealed that the nondelusional patients responded significantly better to tricyclic antidepressants than the delusional patients. The major contribution of Charney and Nelson's paper is the apparent finding of a repeated pattern of delusional depression in patients who have once had an episode of depression with delusions. Further, the paper supports the concept of a differential treatment response. The pattern of other symptoms associated with delusional and nondelusional depression is not consistent with the findings of Glassman and Roose (1981), however.

A recent study reported by Nelson, Khan, and Orr (1984) contributes an interesting observation on the course of symptomatic improvement in delusional and nondelusional patients treated with tricyclic antidepressants. Their sample was small, 13 delusional and 12 nondelusional hospitalized depressives. In their study, which defined recovery as a four-week Hamilton score of less than 8, they found that only 2 of 13 delusional patients had reached that criterion compared to 7 of 12 of the nondelusional patients. In

11 of the 13 delusional patients, delusional thinking had completely disappeared even though the patients had made a less than complete symptomatic recovery. Again, the delusional patients in this study were more severely ill than the nondelusional patients as measured by the total Hamilton score at the beginning of the study.

In several earlier reports, the differential response to treatment of delusional versus nondelusional patients seems to be accounted for mainly by female patients. Moradi, Muniz, and Belar (1979), consequently undertook a retrospective review of their experience with the treatment of 12 male patients with delusional depression. No patient treated with tricyclics alone improved, whereas all treated initially with neuroleptics improved.

It should be noted that all of the above studies excluded patients with schizo-affective disorder, and thus probably most patients whose delusions would fall into the mood incongruent category.

There are many other clinical reports on the treatment of delusional depressed patients involving small numbers of patients. Nelson, Bowers, and Sweeney (1979) described three patients whose delusional thinking was worsened with tricyclic antidepressive therapy. Two of the three responded to the addition of neuroleptics and one to ECT. Shingu, Kawai, and Yamada (1979), in a report from Japan, described three cases of delusional depression that responded to L-DOPA. This rather surprising finding contrasts both the reported usefulness of neuroleptics, dopamine antagonists, in delusional patients, and the report by Bunney, Brodie, Murphy, and Goodwin (1971) of worsening of psychotic symptoms in depressed patients treated with L-DOPA. To explain this apparent contradiction, the authors proposed a two-stage process in the development of delusional depression. The first stage consists of anxiety, agitation, and insomnia, with delusions of persecution, followed by a second stage characterized by stupor and delusions of poverty and guilt. They speculate that the catecholamine system shifts from overactivity in stage one to exhaustion in stage two. L-DOPA then becomes effective in stage two, whereas presumably neuroleptics would be effective in stage one. Minter, Verdugo, and Mandel (1980) reported a case of delusional depression that responded to the MAO inhibitor tranylcypromine. Lieb and Collins (1978) described four cases that responded to tranylcypromine that had been unsuccessfully treated with tricyclic antidepressants. Price, Conwell, and Nelson (1983) reported on six patients who did not respond well to tricyclics and neuroleptics; three of the six, however, did respond when lithium was added.

Amoxapine, which combines antidepressant and neuroleptic effects, might be considered especially effective in psychotic depression. Anton and Sexauer (1983) reported that four patients responded positively to this medication. The authors noted that these patients seemed to be getting a neuroleptic effect as represented by their elevated prolactin levels.

To summarize, most studies support the concept that delusionally depressed patients tend to respond more poorly to antidepressants alone. The studies reviewed also support the hypothesis that delusional patients tend to be more severely depressed than nondelusional patients. Whether or not psychotic depression represents a unique illness remains open to question. Unfortunately, most studies exclude from their samples patients who show any evidence of schizophrenic-like phenomena, thus eliminating most patients with mood incongruent delusions. Thus, at least for single episodes, scant research addresses the question of whether mood congruent and mood incongruent delusions are differentially related to outcome.

Turning now to the relationship of delusions to the long-term prognosis of depressed patients, the most recent and most comprehensive data are contained in a report by Coryell, Lavori, Endicott, Keller, and Van Eerdewegh (1984) concerning the follow-up of patients admitted to a large collaborative study on the psychobiology of depression. The population consisted of 24 schizo-affective patients, 56 patients with psychotic depression, and 274 nonpsychotic depressed patients who were followed for six months. The schizo-affective patients were distinguished from the psychotic depressed patients by (1) the type of delusion (i.e., mood incongruent), (2) the presence of a marked thought disorder and inappropriate or blunted affect, and/or (3) disorganized behavior. Patients may also have been considered schizo-affective if they had been psychotic when the affective symptoms were not present. On follow-up, the psychotically depressed patients were intermediate between the schizo-affective and nonpsychotic patients in measurements of symptom severity, but not significantly different from either. The schizo-affective patients were significantly more symptomatic than the nonpsychotic patients. On measures of social adjustment at outcome, both the schizo-affective and psychotic groups had significantly poorer adjustment than the nonpsychotic patient population. These differences did not seem to be due to differences in treatment. The authors compared this patient sample with a similar sample of patients who were admitted to hospitals between 1935 and 1945 and who were subsequently followed. The outcomes for these patients showed a similar pattern. Over the short term, schizo-affective patients faired worst, nonpsychotic patients best, and psychotic depressed patients occupied an intermediate position. At follow-up 12, 18, and 24 months later, the psychotic patients increasingly resembled the nonpsychotic patients rather than the schizo-affective patients. These findings are consistent with the results of Coryell and Tsuang (1982) on the follow-up of a proband population of 500 in Iowa. Again, the delusional patient faired less well in the short term than the nondelusional patient, but after 40 years the status of the delusional and nondelusional patients was indistinguishable. This study is marred, however, by the very considerable dropout in long-term follow-up (from the original 225 patients to 41 patients in the 10- to 20-year follow-up).

These studies suggest that schizo-affective patients, and thus probably patients with mood incongruent delusions, have a significantly worse long-term prognosis than either mood congruent delusional or nondelusional depressed patients. Over the long term, the latter two groups show a similar outcome.

Delusions in Mania

Since Kraepelin, psychotic symptoms, delusions, and hallucinations have been frequently reported in manic patients. Young, Schreiber, and Nysewander (1983) noted that some studies have reported delusions in up to 73 percent of manic episodes and hallucinations in 48 percent, but most studies indicate lower frequencies. In a recent prospective study by Louden, Blackburn, and Ashworth (1977), 37 percent of manic patients were rated as having psychotic symptoms. Young and his coauthors found psychotic symptoms in 10 of 40 manic patients using the Mania Rating Scale. As with depressed patients, the psychotic symptoms of manic patients tended to be related to the severity of symptoms overall. In the Young et al. study, the psychotic patients had higher severity scores on all symptoms excluding those involving thought content.

Treatment of Delusional Mania

Perhaps because of the relative frequency of delusional symptoms, less attention has been paid to the relationship between therapeutic response and the presence of delusions in manic patients. Most studies fail to reveal obvious differences in outcome (Rosen, Rosenthal, Dunner, & Fieve, 1983). In some but not other studies in which distinctions between types of delusions have been made, persecutory delusions predict a poor response while grandiose delusions predict a good response (Young et al., 1983).

The long-term prognosis for bipolar patients seems not to be affected by the presence of psychotic symptoms according to most sources. One exception is the study of Rosenthal, Rosenthal, and Dunner (1979), in which psychotic patients stayed well longer than nonpsychotic patients on lithium. The same group of investigators has reported a poorer social outcome in psychotic patients compared to nonpsychotic patients, a rather contradictory finding. It is worth noting that in this latter report, 63 of 89 patients could be considered to have had psychotic symptoms over the whole course of their illness.

In summary, as contrasted with unipolar patients, the presence of psychotic symptoms is a frequent phenomena for bipolar patients throughout the course of their illness. There is little evidence that, apart from an indication of increased severity, delusional symptoms alter the short- or long-term prognosis for these patients. It is possible, however, that if more attention were paid to the type of delusions (specifically, mood congruent versus mood incongruent), a pattern similar to that of unipolar depression would emerge; that is, mood incongruent delusions would confer a poorer prognosis.

In this chapter we have discussed the treatment of the paranoid disorders, paraphrenia, and the psychotic affective disorders, with the major emphasis being on pharmacological approaches. With paranoid disorders, the most interesting observation is the apparent specificity of the drug pimozide in the treatment of at least some subtypes of these disorders, particularly monosymptomatic hypochondriachal psychosis. Paraphrenic patients do seem to respond to neuroleptics. The presence of delusions in affective disorders does seem to affect the response to antidepressant medication and at least to short-term prognosis. The lack of attention in the scientific literature to the natural history of delusions and to the possibility that delusions may consist of different types of psychopathological processes leaves in doubt the answers to many questions regarding treatment.

REFERENCES

Akiskal, H.S., Arana, G.W., Baldessarini, R.J., & Barreira, P.J. (1983). A clinical report of thymoleptic-responsive atypical paranoid psychoses. *American Journal of Psychiatry, 140,* 1187–1190.

American Psychiatric Association. (1980). *Diagnostic and statistical manual of mental disorders* (DSM-III) (3rd ed.). Washington, DC: Author.

Amery, W., Boom, A.J., Huisman, N.G., Kujpers, H., Van der Wiel, H.J., & Reyntjens, A. (1972). A series of multicentric pilot trials with pimozide in psychiatric practice. IV. Pimozide in the treatment of patients with paranoid symptomatology. *Acta Psychiatrica Belgium, 72,* 677–684.

Anton, R.F., & Sexauer, J.D. (1983). Efficacy of amoxapine in psychotic depression. *American Journal of Psychiatry, 140,* 1344–1347.

Bernstein, J.E., & Swift, R. (1979). *Relief of intractable pruritus with naloxone. Archives of Dermatology, 115,* 1366–1367.

Boverman, M. (1953). Some notes on the psychotherapy of delusional patients. *Journal of International Psychiatry, 16* (39), 139–151.

Branchey, M.H., Lee, J.H., Amin. R., & Simpson, G.M. (1978). High and low potency neuroleptics in elderly psychiatric patients. *Journal of the American Medical Association, 239,* 1860.

Brehm, J.W. (1966). *A theory of psychological reactance.* New York: Academic Press.

Bridge, P.T., & Wyatt, R.J. (1980). Paraphrenia: Paranoid states of late life I European research. *Journal of the American Geriatrics Society, 28* (5), 193–200.

Brink, T.L. (1980). Geriatric paranoia: Case report illustrating behavioral management. *Journal of the American Geriatrics Society, 28* (11), 519–522.

Brotman, A.W., & Jenike, M.A. (1984). Monosymptomatic hypochondriasis treated with tricyclic antidepressants. *American Journal of Psychiatry, 141* (12), 1608–1609.

Bunney, W.E., Brodie, H.K.H, Murphy, D.L., & Goodwin, F.K. (1971). Studies of alphamethyl-para-tyrosin, L-DOPA, and L-tryptophan in depression and mania. *American Journal of Psychiatry, 127,* 872–881.

Carstensen, L.L., & Fremouw, W.J. (1981). The demonstration of a behavioral intervention for late life paranoia. *The Gerontologist, 21* (3), 329–333.

Charney, D.S., & Nelson, J.C. (1981). Delusional and non-delusional unipolar depression: Further evidence for distinct subtypes. *American Journal of Psychiatry, 138,* 328–332.

Ciompi, L. (1984). Is there really a schizophrenia. The long-term course of psychotic phenomenon. *British Journal of Psychiatry, 145,* 636–640.

Cloninger, C.R., Martin, R.L., Guze, S.D., & Clayton, P.J. (1985). Diagnosis and prognosis in schizophrenia. *Archives of General Psychiatry, 42* (1), 15–25.

Cooper, A.F., Kay, D.W.K., Curry, A.R., & Garside, R.F. (1974). Hearing loss in paranoid and affective psychoses of the elderly. *The Lancet, 2,* 851–854.

Cooper, A.F., & Porter, R. (1976). Visual acuity and ocular pathology in the paranoid and affective psychoses of the elderly. *Journal of Psychosomatic Research, 20,* 107–114.

Coryell, W., Lavori, P., Endicott, J., Keller, M., & Van Eerdewegh, M. (1984). Outcome in schizoaffective psychotic and non-psychotic depression. *Archives of General Psychiatry, 41,* 787–791.

Coryell, W., & Tsuang, M.T. (1982). Primary unipolar depression and the prognostic importance of delusions. *Archives of General Psychiatry, 39,* 1181–1184.

Creese, I., Feinberg, A.P., & Snyder, S.H. (1976). Butyrophenone influences the opiate receptor. *European Journal of Pharmacology, 36,* 231–235.

Day, M., & Semrad, E.R. (1978). Paranoia and the paranoid states. In A.M. Nicholi (Ed.), *The Harvard guide to modern psychiatry.* Cambridge, MA: Belknap Press.

Ellis, P., & Mellsop. G. (1985). De Clérambault's syndrome—A nosological entity? *British Journal of Psychiatry, 146,* 90–95.

Glassman, A.H., Kantor, S.J., & Shostak, M. (1975). Depression, delusions, and drug response. *American Journal of Psychiatry, 132,* 716–719.

Glassman, A.H., & Roose, S.P. (1981). Delusional depression. *Archives of General Psychiatry, 38* (4), 424–427.

Grahame, P.S. (1984). Schizophrenia in old age (late paraphrenia). *British Journal of Psychiatry, 145,* 493–495.

Gulevitch, G.D. (1977). Psychopharmacological treatment of the aged. In J.D. Barchas, P.A. Berger, R.D. Ciaranello, & G.R. Elliott (Eds.), *Psychopharmacology from theory to practice.* New York: Oxford University Press.

Hamann, K., & Avnstorp, C. (1982). Delusions of infestation treated with pimozide: A double-blind crossover clinical study. *Acta Dermatovenereologica, 62,* 55–58.

Jaspers, K. (1964). *General psychopathology* (J. Hoenig & M.W. Hamilton, Trans.). Chicago: University of Chicago Press.

Kantor, S.J., & Glassman, A.H. (1977). Delusional depressions: Natural history and response to treatment. *British Journal of Psychiatry, 131,* 351–360.

Kendler, K. (1984). Paranoia (delusional disorder). *Trends in Neuroscience, 7,* 14–17.

Kendler, K.S., Glazer, W.M., & Morgenstern, H. (1983). Dimensions of delusional experience. *American Journal of Psychiatry, 140* (4), 466–469.

Kind, H. (1967). The psychogenesis of schizophrenia. *International Journal of Psychiatry, 3* (5), 383–388.

Leckman, J.F., Weissman, M.M., Prusoff, B.A., Caruso, K.A., Merikangas, K.R., Pauls, D.L., & Kidd, K.K. (1984). Subtypes of depression: Family study perspective. *Archives of General Psychiatry, 41* (9), 833–838.

Lewis, A. (1936). Melancholia: Prognostic study and case material. *Journal of Mental Science, 82,* 488–558.

Lieb, J., & Collins, C. (1978). Treatment of delusional depression with tranylcypromine. *Journal of Nervous and Mental Diseases, 166,* 805–808.

Louden, F.B., Blackburn, I.M., & Ashworth, C.M. (1977). A study of the symptomatology and course of manic illness using a new scale. *Psychological Medicine, 7,* 723–729.

Lyell, A. (1983). Delusion of parasitosis. *British Journal of Dermatology, 108,* 485–499.

McGlashan, T.H., Docherty, J.P., & Siris, S. (1976). Integrative and sealing-over recoveries from schizophrenia: Distinguishing case studies. *Psychiatry, 39,* 325–338.

Milton, F., Patwa, V.K., & Hafner, R.J. (1978). Confrontation versus belief modification in persistently deluded patients. *British Journal of Medical Psychology, 51,* 127–130.

Minter, R.E., Verdugo, N., & Mandel, M. (1980). The treatment of delusional depression with tranylcypromine: A case report. *Journal of Clinical Psychiatry, 41* (5), 178.

Molden, H.C. (1964). Therapeutic management of paranoid states. *Current Psychiatric Therapies, 4* (108), 108–112.

Mooney, H. (1975). Pathological jealousy and psychochemotherapy. *British Journal of Psychiatry, 111,* 1023–1042.

Moradi, S.R., Muniz, C.E., & Belar, C.D. (1979). Male delusional depressed patients: Response to treatment. *British Journal of Psychiatry, 135,* 136–138.

Munro, A. (1984). Excellent response of pathological jealousy to pimozide. *Canadian Medical Association Journal, 131* (8), 852–853.

Munro, A. (1985). De Clérambault's syndrome—A nosological entity. *British Journal of Psychiatry, 146,* 561.

Munro, A., & Pollock, B. (1981). Monosymptomatic psychoses which progress to schizophrenia. *Journal of Clinical Psychiatry, 42* (12), 474–476.

Nash, J.L. (1983). Delusions. In J.O. Cavenar & H.K.H. Brodie (Eds.), *Signs and symptoms in psychiatry.* Philadelphia: Lippincott.

Nelson, J.C., Bowers, M.B., & Sweeney, D.R. (1979). Exacerbation of psychosis by tricyclic antidepressants in delusional depression. *American Journal of Psychiatry, 136,* 574–576.

Nelson, W.H. Khan, A., & Orr, W.W. (1984). Delusional depression, phenomenology, neuroendocrine function, and tricyclic antidepressant response. *Journal of Affective Disorders, 6,* 297–306.

Pearce, A. (1972). De Clerambault's syndrome associated with a folie à deux. *British Journal of Psychiatry, 121,* 116–117.

Pinder, R.M., Brogden, R.N., Sawyer, P.R., Speight, T.M., Spencer, R., & Avery, G.S. (1976). Pimozide: A review of its pharmacological properties and therapeutic uses in psychiatry. *Drugs, 12,* 1–40.

Post, F. (1966). *Persistent persecutory states of the elderly.* Oxford, England: Pergamon Press.

Post, F. (1973). Paranoid disorders in the elderly. *Postgraduate Medicine, 53* (4), 52–56.

Post, F. (1978). The functional psychoses. In A.D. Isaacs & F. Post (Eds.), *Studies in geriatric psychiatry.* Chichester, England: Wiley.

Post, F. (1980). Paranoid, schizophrenia-like and schizophrenic states in the aged. In J.E. Binen & R.B. Sloane (Eds.), *Handbook of mental health and aging.* Englewood Cliffs, NJ: Prentice Hall.

Price, L.H., Conwell, Y., & Nelson, J.C. (1983). Lithium augmentation of combined neuroleptic-tricyclic treatment in delusional depression. *American Journal of Psychiatry, 140,* 318–322.

Prien, R.F., Haber, P.A., & Caffey, E.M. (1975). The use of psychoactive drugs in elderly patients with psychiatric disorders: Survey conducted in twelve veterans administration hospitals. *Journal of the American Geriatrics Society, 23,* 104.

Quitkin, F., Rifkin, A., & Klein, D.F. (1978). Imipramine response in deluded depressive patients. *American Journal of Psychiatry, 135,* 806–811.

Rappaport, M. (1978). Are drugs more than palliative in the management of schizophrenia. In J.P. Brady & H.K. Brodie (Eds.), *Controversy in psychiatry.* Philadelphia: W.B. Saunders.

Raskind, M., Alvarez, C., & Herlin, S. (1979). Fluphenazine enanthate in the outpatient treatment of late paraphrenia. *Journal of the American Geriatrics Society, 27,* 459.

Rettersol, N. (1971). *Prognosis in paranoid psychoses.* Springfield, IL: Charles C. Thomas.

Riding, J., & Munro, A. (1975). Pimozide in treatment of monosymptomatic hypochondriachal psychosis. *Acta Psychiatrica Scandinavica, 52,* 23.

Ritzler, B.A. (1981). Paranoia—Prognosis and treatment: A review. *Schizophrenia Bulletin, 7* (4), 710–728.

Rosen, L.N., Rosenthal, N.E., Dunner, D.L., & Fieve, R.R. (1983). Social outcome compared in psychotic and nonpsychotic bipolar I patients. *Journal of Nervous and Mental Diseases, 171,* 272–275.

Rosenthal, N.E., Rosenthal, L.N., Dunner, D.L., et. al. (1979). Psychosis as a predictor of response to lithium maintenance treatment in bipolar affective disorder. *Journal of Affective Disorders, 1,* 237–245.

Roth, M. (1955). The natural history of mental disorder in old age. *Journal of Mental Science, 101,* 281–301.

Roth, M. (1976). The psychiatric disorders of later life. *Psychiatric Annals, 6,* 57–101.

Rudden, M., Gilmore, M., & Frances, A. (1980). Erotomania: A separate entity. *American Journal of Psychiatry, 137* (10), 1262–1263.

Sheehy, M. (1983). Successful treatment of paranoia with trazodone. *American Journal of Psychiatry, 140* (7), 945.

Shingu, K., Kawai, I., & Yamada, K. (1979). Three cases of unipolar delusional depression responsive to L-DOPA. *Folia Psychiatrica et Neurologica Japonica, 33,* 511–515.

Shrabers, D., Weitzel, W.E., & Shingleton, D. (1980). L'illusion de Capgras—Syndrome or phenomenon? *Journal of the Kentucky Medical Association, 78* (3), 125–127.

Spitzer, R.L., Endicott, J., & Robins, E. (1978). Research diagnostic criteria: Rationale and reliability. *Archives of General Psychiatry, 35,* 773–782.

Strauss, J.S., Hafez, H., Lieberman, P., & Harding, C.M. (1985). The course of psychiatric disorder, III. Longitudinal principles. *American Journal of Psychiatry, 142* (3), 289–296.

Taylor, M.A., Sierles, E.S. & Abrams, R. (1985). *General hospital psychiatry.* New York: Free Press.

Watts, F.N., Powell, E.G., & Austin, S.V. (1973). The modification of abnormal beliefs. *British Journal of Medical Psychology, 46,* 359–363.

Whanger, A.D. (1973). Paranoid syndromes of the senium. In C. Eisdorfer & W.E. Fann (Eds.), *Psychopharmacology and aging.* New York: Plenum Press.

Winokur, G. (1977). Delusional disorder (paranoia). *Comprehensive Psychiatry, 18* (6), 511–520.

World Health Organization. (1978). *Mental disorders: Glossary and guide to their classification in accordance with the ninth revision of the International Classification of Diseases.* Washington, DC: Author.

Young, R.C., Schreiber, M.T., & Nysewander, R.W. (1983). Psychotic mania. *Biological Psychiatry, 18* (10), 1167–1173.

CHAPTER 15

Research Hypotheses for Intervention with Delusion-prone Individuals

KENNETH HELLER

Indiana University

The purpose of this short chapter is to discuss some suggestions concerning the modification of delusional beliefs. The stimulus for these remarks comes from the previous chapters, which, for the most part, focus on propositions concerning the functions and hypothesized etiology of delusions. While highlighting intervention possibilities is the primary goal of this chapter, it is important to view the suggestions discussed as research *hypotheses* only. This is because empirical studies of attempts to modify delusional beliefs are rare. Thus, these comments are offered in the hope of stimulating comparative studies of different intervention procedures that might be used with delusional individuals.

DELUSIONS AS A RESPONSE TO THREAT

Neale proposes that some delusions (particularly grandiose delusions in mania) are precipitated by events that activate feelings of low self-esteem in persons with unstable self-regard. Delusions are said to serve a defensive function guiding cognitive activity away from distressing material. If low or unstable self-esteem aroused by stressful events is postulated to be a predisposing factor in the development of delusions, it would follow that appropriate therapies for delusional patients would be those that either reduce the threat to self-esteem produced by impinging events or that help the individual cope better with threatening events.

When the threatening elements in particular settings are identified, research can be conducted to determine whether modification of these elements would reduce their aversive properties. The psychotherapeutic treatment setting can be used as an example of how such an analysis might be conducted. That the psychotherapeutic setting might include threatening, delusion-instigating elements probably would be viewed with skepticism by many practicing clinicians. After all, they approach their work with benevolent intentions and attempt to project a safe and trustworthy image. But consider the treatment environment from the patient's point of view. The physical setting of the doctor's office may be unfamiliar and quite different from what the patient is accustomed to for private self-disclosure. In addition, the stereotype of the psychotherapist as a mind reader, or as an expert in identifying crazy people, might cause the patient to experience awe and trepidation in an initial therapeutic encounter. The patient with tenuous adjustment may have doubts about his or her own sanity, may fear being found out, changed, or manipulated by the therapist, and may fear the therapist's power to hospitalize. The ambiguous therapeutic instructions, "Tell me whatever comes into mind" or "Let's talk about your early childhood" may seem strange and irrelevant. The minimal cues offered by most therapists in their attempts to project an image of benevolent passivity can serve to provoke further anxiety.

Goldstein, Heller, and Sechrest (1966) discuss a number of these threatening elements in the therapeutic setting. Their recommendations to reduce the threatening nature of the therapeutic encounter focus on decreasing the ambiguity of psychotherapy. This could be accomplished by structuring the therapeutic task so that the patient knows what is expected. Stating clear goals for therapy and discussing the procedures by which these goals can be reached would reduce ambiguity, as would periodic discussions of the therapeutic task and the relationship between therapist and patient. On the other hand, an ambiguous stimulus field may magnify the problems for delusional patients who have difficulty in accurately reading interpersonal cues and who misperceive the intentions of and project internal feeling states upon others.

Goldstein, Heller, and Sechrest (1966) offer two other suggestions for minimizing the threat associated with therapeutic messages. The first is delayed compliance, which for delusional individuals means actively suspending or holding in abeyance a final evaluation of potentially threatening alternatives to delusional attributions. A therapist might present alternative attributions in a tentative way, asking the patient simply to think about it or saying, "Look the situation over yourself and then come to a decision." Delayed compliance reduces threat by reducing the urgency of attitude change, giving the appearance that such change is completely under the patient's control.

Phrasing one's message as a two-sided argument is a second approach to reducing threat associated with presenting a point of view discrepant with a delusional belief. In this instance, two-sided communication means acknowledging counterinterpretations. For example, rather than simply saying to a patient, "I know that your wife is not plotting against you" (a one-sided message that merely states the basic proposition), a therapist might say, "I know that your wife's actions could be interpreted as a plot against you, but there are other really good explanations for her behavior." This suggestion comes from early research on persuasive communication, in which it was found that two-sided messages that acknowledge counterarguments are more effective when the listener already knows the counterargument or is likely to be exposed to it later, or when the listener initially disagrees with the communicator's position. The value of a two-sided communication is that it increases the credibility and perceived objectivity of the communicator (the therapist, in our example). At the same time, the delusional individual is encouraged, by example, to adopt a more objective attitude that involves weighing the evidence for and against various counterexplanations. It also reduces threat by not seeming to force compliance. As in the previous suggestion for delayed compliance, the delusional individual is exposed to counterarguments but is not forced to adopt them.

Exposing a patient to *tentative* counterarguments resembles an approach advocated by Sullivan (1956). For example, Sullivan describes a patient who denied his marriage with the statement, "I was never married to this woman, she is not my wife." Sullivan warns against a direct confrontation—even one phrased in a benevolent manner. He recommends answering in a tentative way, such as, "I can understand your having *doubts*, or even a tendency to deny the marriage" (Sullivan, 1956, pp. 369–370). The patient did not express doubts; he was convinced that he was unmarried. Introducing the concept of doubt is a counterinterpretation to the patient's assertion that he is unmarried, but it is stated in a tentative manner. It may receive no attention at the moment, but it sets the stage for the patient to recognize later that perhaps he had been motivated to deny an unpleasant marriage. Introducing the idea that the patient might be doubting his marriage allows the patient to later conclude on his own, "I got so used to saying, 'How in hell *could* I have married this woman,' that finally I decided I hadn't" (Sullivan, 1956, p. 370).

DISCRIMINATION TRAINING TO INCREASE THE ACCURACY OF INFORMATION UPON WHICH DELUSIONAL BELIEFS ARE BASED

Maher views delusions as theories that provide order and meaning to subjective experience. Because these beliefs have explanatory power for the individual they will not be readily abandoned until they can be replaced by a theory that better explains subjective experiences. Several alternatives for corrective action follow from this formulation. Maher advocates the early detection of developing delusions and the "presentation of counterevidence before the 'solution-relief' experience has been reached," because once formed, delusions, like other strongly held beliefs, are resistant to change. Thus Maher emphasizes the need for the presentation of counterevidence fairly early. The practical problem this suggestion poses is in identifying delusion-prone individuals before delusions have developed.

One possibility is to consider difficulty in cue reading as a risk factor for the development of delusions. Maher, Johnson, and Kihlstrom (all in this volume) cite evidence that cue reading deficiencies serve such a role and are linked to delusion formation. One possible intervention then would be to identify those with cue reading difficulty and provide them with cue discrimination training. Clearly, there would be a large number of false positives— persons with cue reading problems who would never become delusional. There also would be a group of deficient cue readers who might never develop delusions but who might be subject to other problems (e.g., learning disabilities, hyperaggressiveness). Still, as a preventive intervention to reduce the frequency of delusions, cue discrimination training might be worth an empirical test, particularly if it could be shown that the costs and negative consequences associated with such training would be relatively low.

While training in cue reading would be the most important ingredient in an intervention program for delusion-prone individuals, it would not be sufficient as the sole program element. According to the model of social competence proposed by McFall (1982; McFall & Dodge, 1982), an observer's judgment of social competence is based upon the successful completion of a series of related social skills. The first steps in skilled behavior involve the accurate perception and interpretation of social stimuli (what we have been calling *cue reading*, and what are referred to as *decoding skills* in the McFall model). However, in addition, the individual must be able to find the appropriate responses that fit the particular social situation (decision skills), and then must be able to successfully implement and monitor the appropriate behaviors (encoding skills). Thus, helping an individual develop alternative appropriate social responses (increasing the repertoire of social behaviors), giving instruction in choosing socially appropriate responses, and encouraging practice in correct responding all may be necessary.

DEVELOPING DELUSION-TOLERANT SETTINGS AS AN ALTERNATIVE TO CHANGING DELUSIONAL BELIEFS

Many therapists approach the task of working with delusional individuals assuming that the therapeutic task is to convince the client that their delusional beliefs are not congruent with fact and are untrue. Viewing delusions from the symbolic interactionist perspective, Heise (in this volume) points out that the diagnosis of delusions is not made on the basis of truth or falsity but according to criteria of social relevance. An implication is that the focus of therapeutic activity should be the *mismatch* between what the delusional individual insists on talking about and what others are willing to tolerate.

If the individual is getting into trouble because he or she insists on saying things that other people do not want to hear, a therapeutic goal could be simply to help the individual stop talking about what is discomforting to others. Delusional individuals have been known to monitor their behavior and discuss their beliefs with only a select few. However, this is clearly not a universal solution because most delusional individuals know that others react negatively to their revelations, and yet they either cannot or will not stop pressing their views despite the negative audience.

A second therapeutic strategy that could be derived from Heise's position is for a therapist to look for a social circle that supports or is tolerant of discrepant thinking, and then to help the individual join that supportive group. This is not to suggest that delusional individuals should band together, because individuals with strongly held but competing beliefs are not likely to tolerate one another very well. This suggestion emphasizes the importance of the support of like-minded individuals. Commonly shared beliefs, according to Heise, are not delusions and are unlikely to be socially disruptive. Some might argue that delusions are so idiosyncratic that a sympathetic listener is not likely to be found, but in fact history is replete with examples of individuals who were able to attract sympathetic and cooperative colleagues for a wide variety of beliefs, even those in which the group's belief led to its demise, as in the Jonestown incident.

The concept of plurality of settings is at the heart of the suggestion that delusional individuals should be linked to groups of like-minded others. Most therapists assume an environmental milieu that is fixed and unitary. Their mission is to help individuals change so as to better fit the dominant culture. However, other options are possible. Price (1979) believes that treatment gains can be maximized by enhancing person-environment congruence. Not only can persons be encouraged to change to fit settings, but settings can be selected, changed, or created to fit the needs of individuals. This, however, requires a therapist who sees environmental settings as modifiable and who recognizes that a plurality of behavior settings (Barker, 1968) already exists. The task then would be to find, create, or help change existing settings to better accommodate client needs.

Applying this principle to delusional individuals means that a therapist might first attempt to find supportive others or community groups that have a history of tolerance for unusual ideas or behaviors (such as the community in Gheel, Belgium; Coleman, Butcher, & Carson, 1984) or that already share the same beliefs (for example, a club interested in extrasensory perception). If such a group did not already exist, perhaps it might be created by an interested group, such as a local mental health association. Such organizations already sponsor social clubs and big brother pairings for patients and volunteers. It would not be difficult for these groups to specifically emphasize tolerance of unusual ideas.

Such a suggestion does fly in the face of the common assumption that delusional ideation is symptomatic of disorder. If delusions demonstrate the presence of illness then an individual is not well until he or she gives them up. A therapist from this perspective would openly encourage the discussion of delusional beliefs only for purposes of refuting them. However, Heise's alternative conceptualization is that the decision as to what constitutes an illness is made on the basis of social relevance. A person whose views fit or were tolerated by an existing social group would not be called to the attention of mental health experts.

At this point, it is an empirical question as to which intervention would reduce the social disruption associated with delusions—to have these views accepted by a significant social group or to continually challenge them. Although there are case studies of therapists who have accepted and reinforced patient delusions as part of treatment (e.g., Lindner, 1954), there seems to be no comparative tests of different therapeutic approaches to delusions. I hope such research can be stimulated.

REFERENCES

Barker, R. (1968). *Ecological psychology*. Stanford, CA: Stanford University Press.

Coleman, J.C., Butcher, J.N., & Carson, R.C. (1984). *Abnormal psychology and modern life*. Seventh edition. Glenview, Ill.: Scott, Foresman.

Goldstein, A.P., Heller, K., & Sechrest, L.B. (1966). *Psychotherapy and the psychology of behavior change*. New York: Wiley.

Lindner, R. (1954). *The fifty-minute hour*. New York: Bantam Books.

McFall, R.M. (1982). A review and reformulation of the concept of social skills. *Behavioral Assessment, 4,* 1–33.

McFall, R.M., & Dodge, K.A. (1982). Self-management and interpersonal skills learning. In P. Karoly & F. Kanfer (Eds.), *Self-management and behavior change: From theory to practice*. New York: Pergamon Press.

Price, R.H. (1979). The social ecology of treatment gain. In A.P. Goldstein & F.H. Kanfer (Eds.), *Maximizing treatment gains: Transfer enhancement in psychotherapy*. New York: Academic Press.

Sullivan H.S. (1956). *Clinical studies in psychiatry*. New York: W.W. Norton.

PART FOUR

Reflections, Observations, and Final Comments

CHAPTER 16

Delusional Processes: An Interactive Developmental Perspective

JOHN S. STRAUSS

Yale University School of Medicine

The understanding of delusions is a key to knowledge about severe mental disorders. But, strangely, little is known about these symptoms, and they have rarely been studied. It is for these reasons that this volume and the reports presented in it are particularly important. These reports reverse an unfortunate trend by exploring the phenomenology, etiology, and possible basic processes that are involved in delusional thinking.

The comments in this chapter will aim at attempting to provide a partial synthesis for many of the important points made in the reports of this volume. To begin this process, it is helpful first to review some of the major ideas suggested about the cross-sectional characteristics of delusions. Perhaps most striking is the diversity of delusional contents and forms that has been described. In addition, several authors have noted that delusions can occur in many diagnostic entities. Together, these observations emphasize that delusions are relatively general processes with many possible contents, origins, and associated symptoms, signs, and levels of social function.

A second major point that several contributions to this volume have made is that although delusions may in some way be different from normal thinking, there are many similarities between delusional ideation and normal processes of judgment (Maher, Johnson).

A third important point made about the nature of delusions is that they are not defined so much by their deviation from some absolute truth as by their relationship to social benefits (Heise). It was even noted (Westermeyer) that delusions, in some social contexts at least, may have a major and extremely useful social role.

This report was supported in part by NIMH Grants MH00340 and MH34365.

How can we understand this complex process, which is so diverse and abnormal but relates to normal thought as well as to social beliefs and functions? Although several suggested answers to this question have been proposed (Maher, Kihlstrom, Oltmanns), we should also consider the precepts of Piaget and others who have said that to understand a phenomenon that is mysterious in cross-section, it is essential to take a longitudinal perspective. Taking such a perspective with delusions suggests some possible explanations, and points to the kinds of research that might be crucial to advance our understanding further.

As a framework for this longitudinal perspective, the interactive developmental model (Strauss & Carpenter, 1981; Strauss, Hafez, Lieberman, & Harding, 1985) provides a way of thinking about many of the findings presented in this volume. This model suggests that the sequences and patterns of interactions that take place between the person and the environment influence the origins and course of mental disorders. It suggests further that only by understanding how the psychological, biological, and social forces involved in these interactions occur is it possible to understand the phenomena of disorder and recovery processes. The developmental part of the model describes the characteristics in the person (and the environment) as accruing over time in definable and generally irreversible ways to generate both changes and continuities in the person and the disorder. Viewing delusions as a resultant of the interactions between the individual and the environment evolving over time—almost as in adding ingredients and carrying out procedures in the baking of a complicated cake—can begin to provide a relatively comprehensive synthesis of the available information.

First, we can start by taking a developmental perspective to consider both the relationship of delusions to normal judgment processes and the existence of a social component in delusional thinking. Early stages of the person/environment interaction may contribute to delusions if children have problematic social relationships, which may in turn lead to their developing social aberrations. A child who has relatively weak or erratic social links may have more difficulty incorporating social norms about reality (Heise) and even cultural beliefs.

Although certain beliefs in children, such as the imaginary playmate, are not usually considered pathological, it may be that the socialization of the developing person through experiential processes narrows the range of acceptable beliefs and increasingly defines deviant ones as problematic, which in fact they may be. In essence, certain social and material experiences may tend to sharpen and maintain the judgmental processes that Maher and Johnson suggest are compromised in the formation of delusions. Problematic family experiences may be particularly powerful influences on the development of these judgmental processes (Wynne & Singer, 1963; Lidz, Cornelison, Fleck, & Terry, 1957).

In extending this speculation, we might recall the report of Heinrichs, as well as the work of others, which suggests that premorbid social functioning is not only a risk indicator for functional psychoses, but is also a predictor of their outcome. Strangely, although the etiologic and prognostic associations of poor premorbid adjustment are among the most widely replicated findings in the study of mental disorders, there are relatively few speculations about the mechanisms involved. The reports in this volume suggest one such mechanism: the prevention of and recovery from delusional thinking may be promoted by social experiences. The person with poor social skills and experience is less likely to be able to use corrective experiences and may be vulnerable to disorder and have a poorer prognosis for this reason. It has been noted, for example, that delusional patients who, through their own control or through trusting ward staff, participate in research projects may use these experiences to begin to question their delusional thinking (Sacks, Carpenter, & Strauss, 1974).

Other contributions to the development of delusions are also suggested by the reports in this volume. Heinrichs posits that underlying personality characteristics influence the nature or the occurrence of delusions. Such characteristics may be another ingredient contributing to vulnerability to or at least to shaping the direction of problematic judgments.

The meaning of a situation for the person—meanings that develop over time—might also help to forge this vulnerability and spark the manifestation of delusions (Neale). Delusions of mania may be particularly likely to have some of their origins in family situations, where there is pressure on the child to rescue the family in some psychological or even material way (Cohen et al., 1959; Lieberman & Strauss, 1984). Furthermore, specific life events that produce conflicts around this issue may be especially likely to set off a manic episode. Neale's efforts to define psychoanalytic concepts in an operational way without losing their essence suggests a particularly important research path for exploring the role of situational meaning in delusions.

Finally, in this process of contributing to vulnerability and then to onset, as Gaines reports, cultural factors may be involved as well. Mary's situation, as reported by Gaines, reflected her intense experience in attempting to understand the unfamiliar meaning system of the subculture in which she was involved. This lack of cultural familiarity may have first increased her disorganization and then perhaps increasingly fixed her delusional system.

But the contributions of these factors—childhood social experiences, personality, social functioning, meaning, and culture—seem unlikely to involve a random mix, as though they were thrown into a pot regardless of quantity or timing. Rather, certain sequences of occurrence and amounts of these ingredients might be essential in determining the interactive developmental evolution that generates delusions and determines their course.

Strauss et al. (1985) have described longitudinal processes in psychiatric disorder that are reported by and observed in patients. These processes include (1) *simple phases*, with plateaus of functioning ("woodshedding") and sudden changes ("change points"); (2) *complex phases*, involving the evolution of different interacting domains of function (e.g., symptoms and social relationships); (3) specific person/environment interactions involving *sequences* (e.g., positive feedback loops), and (4) longer term *patterns* (e.g., gradual deterioration followed by sudden improvement). A major point in describing such longitudinal processes is to counter the erroneous but often implicit assumption that the precursors and course of disorder involve a homogeneous linear process.

It seems likely that in the origins and course of delusions there are such nonlinear but definable temporal sequences, perhaps with critical periods of vulnerability or resistance to change, generated by the various factors described above. Thus, a man with a suspicious personality, poor premorbid social adjustment, and rare social experiences from which to develop consensual judgment processes, may be effective occupationally at a fragile but consistent plateau until he encounters a meaning situation to which he is particularly vulnerable—such as a disorienting stay in a foreign culture. Beginning distortion of judgment might be rapidly escalated through a positive feedback sequence involving alienation of his few colleagues, isolation, increased anxiety, judgment breakdown, and further alienation of colleagues. Delusions developed during this experience might persist until influenced later by a corrective social contact.

The part of the interactive developmental perspective just discussed views the evolution of delusions over a long time period. It is also important to amplify the microscopic longitudinal perspectives involved in such a model. The work of Chapman (1966), Conrad (1958), Melges and Freeman (1975), Docherty, Van Kammen, Siris, and Marder (1978), and others provides such a microscopic perspective on the possible sequences of delusion formation. Other studies, such as that by Sacks et al. (1974), provide information on the process of delusion resolution. One point made extremely clear by these studies is that in many instances, delusions are formed and resolved through a series of microprocesses. These processes are probably of major importance for understanding and treatment. A more detailed investigation of these microlongitudinal processes could help test the hypotheses generated in several reports in this volume: that delusions have a perceptual base (Maher); that delusions are similar, at least in early stages, to normal processes and aberrations of judgment (Chapman and Chapman); and that vulnerability to strong stimuli might also be part of the delusion formation process (Chapman, 1966; Strauss, 1967).

Few detailed microlongitudinal studies of delusions have been conducted. Yet they are obviously possible and seem likely to produce important findings. As a side effort of one of the present author's longitudinal investigations, for example, subjects were given a five-card Rorschach test. On initial evaluation, one of the subjects had felt persecuted by the devil who she thought was commanding her to remain standing. At follow-up this subject reported no such delusional ideation. On the Rorschach, however, she said that one card looked like the devil telling somebody to do something. The evolution of delusional thinking in such patients in relation to shifts in ability to form judgments more generally is only one possible focus for microstudies of these processes.

The work of Chapman and Chapman and other such studies have already provided much useful information, and these efforts could be focused even more specifically on a microlongitudinal perspective to clarify the various sequences that occur in the onset of and recovery from delusions. Such investigations could also explore events that might be associated with these sequences and their various stages. Microstudies of this kind might even help to resolve the question of whether delusions do serve a useful function, either for the individual (providing organization and explanation) or for the social context more broadly. This fundamental question, particularly difficult because it is teleological, was raised by Bleuler (1911/1950), Jackson (1887), and Freud (1911/1958), and is reflected in this volume by the report of Westermeyer.

The present volume presents a considerable amount of what is known about the nature of delusions and the progress that has been made. This information, viewed through a synthesizing conceptual framework, could provide the next step in understanding these central phenomena of severe mental disorder.

REFERENCES

Bleuler, E. (1950). *Dementia praecox or the group of schizophrenias.* New York: International Universities Press. (Original work published 1911).

Chapman, J. (1966). The early symptoms of schizophrenia. *British Journal of Psychiatry, 112,* 225–251.

Cohen, M.B., Baker, G., Cohen, R.S., et al. (1959). An intensive study of twelve cases of manic-depressive psychosis. In D.M. Bullard (Ed.), *Psychoanalysis and psychotherapy: Selected papers of Frieda Fromm-Reichmann.* Chicago: University of Chicago Press.

Conrad, K. (1958). *Die Beginnende Schizophrenie.* Stuggart, Germany: Thieme.

Docherty, J.P., Van Kammen, D.P., Siris, S.G., & Marder, S.R. (1978). Stages of onset of schizophrenic psychosis. *American Journal of Psychiatry, 135,* 420–426.

Freud, S. (1958). Psychoanalytic notes on an autobiographical account of a case of paranoia (dementia paranoides). In *Standard edition of the complete works of Sigmund Freud* (Vol. 12). London: Hogarth. (Original work published 1911).

Jackson, H. (1887). Remarks on evolution and dissolution of the nervous system. *Journal of Mental Science, 33,* 25–32.

Lidz, T., Cornelison, A., Fleck, S., & Terry, D. (1957). The intrafamilial environment of the schizophrenic patient. *American Journal of Psychiatry, 114,* 241–248.

Lieberman, P., & Strauss, J.S. (1984). The recurrence of mania: Environmental factors and medical treatment. *American Journal of Psychiatry, 141,* 77–80.

Melges, F.T., & Freeman, A.M. (1975). Persecutory delusions: A cybernetic model. *American Journal of Psychiatry, 132,* 1038–1044.

Sacks, M.H., Carpenter, W.T., & Strauss, J.S. (1974). Recovery from delusions: Three phases documented by patient's interpretation of research procedures. *Archives of General Psychiatry, 30,* 117–120.

Strauss, J.S. (1967). The clarification of schizophrenic concreteness by Piaget's tests. *Psychiatry, 30,* 294–301.

Strauss, J.S., & Carpenter, W.T. (1981). *Schizophrenia.* New York: Plenum Press.

Strauss, J.S., Hafez, H., Lieberman, P., & Harding, C.M. (1985). The course of psychiatric disorder: III. Longitudinal principles. *American Journal of Psychiatry, 142,* 289–296.

Wynne, L., & Singer, M. (1963). Thought disorder and family relations of schizophrenics. *Archives of General Psychiatry, 9,* 199–206.

CHAPTER 17

Delusions as the Product of
Normal Cognitions

BRENDAN A. MAHER

Harvard University

Several contributors to this volume suggested that it would be appropriate for me to offer a commentary on the chapters insofar as they are related to my model of delusions as normal cognitions. I am grateful for this opportunity: In order to avoid abusing this privilege, I will make these comments brief.

Some of the questions that have been raised about the model were anticipated in the original chapter (this volume). Others are new. The most important question may be stated as, Why do most people fail to develop delusions when faced with anomalous experiences? The thrust of this question is directed at the basic thesis of the model that delusions are produced by normal cognitive processes. By implication, the counterthesis is that only some kinds of people develop delusions when faced with anomalous experiences: hence there must be traits or other individual dispositions toward delusion formation. It is not entirely clear where the burden of proof in the matter lies. There is a case to be made that psychological processes should be assumed to be normal until their pathological nature has been demonstrated independently, and nobody seems to have yet established that the processes of logical inference are basically impaired in delusional subjects. One possible answer to the fundamental question, however, includes several components.

By definition, beliefs that are classified as delusional are not held by the majority of people in the culture concerned. If a belief is held by most people, no matter how illogical it is and no matter how much it flies in the face of evidence, then it tends to be regarded as nondelusional. There is no need to belabor this point, as it has already been made in several chapters. Importantly, the observation that most people do not exhibit delusions does not of itself constitute an empirical finding—it is a fundamental part of the definition of delusion! The mere infrequency of certain kinds of beliefs tells us nothing about the probable pathology of the cognitive processes that went into developing the beliefs unless we have already decided that low frequency of a behavior is *prima facie* proof that it reflects pathology. There are many problems with this criterion, including the fact that it necessarily defines all new scientific hypotheses as pathological.

The second component of the answer is that the assertion that normal people fail to develop delusional types of theory to account for their anomalous experiences is totally lacking in evidence. It has been shown that individuals with no prior psychiatric history explain strange experiences in ways that duplicate substantially the kinds of explanation that are usually classified as delusional (see Maher, this volume). The central fact that delusions occur in so many different conditions demands either that delusional thinking is actuarially normal under specified circumstances, or that there are many more people with deviant information processing than has been generally recognized. In brief, the premise of the question is open to challenge at the outset. For the premise to be accepted as a basis of criticism it must be shown that a majority of people who have anomalous experiences do not develop strange or delusional explanations of them. It is not sufficient to point to the fact that most people do not have beliefs that are labeled as delusional; it is necessary to show that most people *with anomalous experiences* do not develop beliefs that will be labeled delusional. By the same token, the argument that many people do not have delusions even though they experience the kind of medical pathologies that produce delusions in some people is unconvincing unless there is a clear operational technique for determining that the patients' experiences in such illnesses are uniformly anomalous. This does not seem to have been established empirically; it does not even seem to have been investigated. The proper stance on this issue is that the matter has not been proven one way or the other, as is so true of much that is written about delusions.

A second objection that the model provokes may be stated this way: Surely most people really do respond to counterevidence much more reasonably than delusional patients. Is there not a trait of selective perception in delusion-prone people that far exceeds in narrowness that of non-deluded persons, in a way that accounts for their imperviousness to such evidence? The Chapmans (this volume) express agreement with the model at the point at which it likens the cognitive activities of the deluded patient with those of the normal scientist. They do so on the grounds that professional scientists are notoriously inhospitable to data that controvert their own theories. In conceding this, the Chapmans are really suggesting that scientists, in their own way, are more pathological in their narrowness of focus, and hence more like deluded patients, than are the vast bulk of what is assumed to be the normal, nonscientist sector of the population. These latter, unlike either scientists or deluded patients, do consider counterevidence carefully and abandon their theories more readily when the data do not fit.

The response is that this is simply not so. The work of Ross and his associates provides evidence of the readiness of normal subjects to retain improbable beliefs on the basis of slim positive evidence and much negative evidence. If there is better evidence to the contrary, then it will be necessary to amend the model to conform to the data. But the data are not forthcoming as yet. In fact, the main corpus of contemporary data from the large literature on social cognition suggests that—to the distress of some social psychologists—most people seem to place their trust in personal experience rather than in general theories of probability and knowledge of the principles of sampling biases.

Some delusions seem to arise not through a process of selectively ignoring relevant data, but through attending to real aspects of the environment that many other people have failed to notice at all, or have not thought worthy of comment. The human body, for example, is marginally asymmetrical in most people, especially in the face. Typical representations of the body and face ignore this asymmetry, so much so that when a patient notices the asymmetry and becomes concerned about it, the patient's perception is deemed to be mistaken. We ask why the patient does not recognize that his or her body is symmetrical, why the patient is impervious to counterevidence instead of first ascertaining exactly what the evidence was that led the patient to the perception of asymmetry.

Johnson has demonstrated eloquently in her contribution to this volume that simple anomalous sensory experiences may be described in metaphorical terms which, if taken literally, would lead us to view the experience as quite pathological. The common experience of formication reported by some substance abuse patients derives its name from the tendency to liken the itching feeling to that of ants crawling under the skin. In the same manner, certain experiences arising from temporary interruption of peripheral circulation are described as pins and needles. While this use of language may not be a major component of the delusion formation sequence, it is not trivial, and deserves perhaps more note than it has been given—the more so as it occurs in the general population with some frequency.

A third question has to do with the distress that is so often experienced by deluded patients, and that seems to arise directly from the content of the delusion. If the explanation is serving a purpose for the patient, why does it not serve a happy purpose? The answer to this is that the anomalous experiences are often distressing. They are often painful, confusing, and alarming, and all of these effects are increasingly anxiety-provoking as long as they remain unexplained. The stress effects of uncertainty are by now well established. Behavioral medicine has generated a literature that makes it clear that a definite diagnosis that one is seriously ill is accompanied by some relief from the anxieties that surround the presence of the major symptoms of an illness that has not yet been diagnosed. "Better the devil that you do know than the devil that you don't," is a proverb that may contain an important psychological truth. Delusions, like other explanations, are not intended to create happiness; they are intended to explain distressing puzzles.

In conclusion, it simply is not good enough for us to rely on an implied rational common sense control as evidence that abnormal cognitive processes are at the root of delusions. When we do this we are confusing prescriptive assertions about thinking, which are rules about how people *ought* to form beliefs, with descriptive assertions, which are observed regularities in the way that people actually do form beliefs.

We need well-controlled comparisons of the cognitions of deluded patients with those of both nondeluded psychiatric populations and nonpsychiatric populations before we can confidently claim that delusions are due to a pathology of cognition. These comparisons require a serious attempt to ascertain the evidential basis of the patients' beliefs, a careful assessment of the role of language usage in creating quasidelusional descriptions of normal but infrequent experiences, a fine-grained analysis of the line-by-line longitudinal development of delusional systems—as suggested by Strauss, for example—and perhaps most important of all, demonstration of cognitive malfunctioning independent of the delusion itself, but of a kind that could plausibly account for the delusion.

Finally, an adequate model should either be (1) comprehensive enough to explain the phenomena of delusions in the wide range of disorders in which they appear, or (2) provided with a systematic method for the analysis and classification of delusional structures and processes (not content) that would permit us to distinguish differences between the delusions that are found in specific conditions.

Author Index

Subject Index

(*continued from front*)

Women in the Middle Years: Current Knowledge and Directions for Research and Policy *edited by Janet Zollinger Giele*

Loneliness: A Sourcebook of Current Theory, Research and Therapy *edited by Letitia Anne Peplau and Daniel Perlman*

Hyperactivity: Current Issues, Research, and Theory (Second Edition) *by Dorothea M. Ross and Sheila A. Ross*

Review of Human Development *edited by Tiffany M. Field, Aletha Huston, Herbert C. Quay, Lillian Troll, and Gordon E. Finley*

Agoraphobia: Multiple Perspectives on Theory and Treatment *edited by Dianne L. Chambless and Alan J. Goldstein*

The Rorschach: A Comprehensive System. Volume III: Assessment of Children and Adolescents *by John E. Exner, Jr. and Irving B. Weiner*

Handbook of Play Therapy *edited by Charles E. Schaefer and Kevin J. O'Connor*

Adolescent Sexuality in a Changing American Society: Social and Psychological Perspectives for the Human Service Professions (Second Edition) *by Catherine S. Chilman*

Failures in Behavior Therapy *edited by Edna B. Foa and Paul M.G. Emmelkamp*

The Psychological Assessment of Children (Second Edition) *by James O. Palmer*

Imagery: Current Theory, Research, and Application *edited by Aneés A. Sheikh*

Handbook of Clinical Child Psychology *edited by C. Eugene Walker and Michael C. Roberts*

The Measurement of Psychotherapy Outcome *edited by Michael J. Lambert, Edwin R. Christensen, and Steven S. DeJulio*

Clinical Methods in Psychology (Second Edition) *edited by Irving B. Weiner*

Excuses: Masquerades in Search of Grace *by C.R. Snyder, Raymond L. Higgins and Rita J. Stucky*

Diagnostic Understanding and Treatment Planning: The Elusive Connection *edited by Fred Shectman and William B. Smith*

Bender Gestalt Screening for Brain Dysfunction *by Patricia Lacks*

Adult Psychopathology and Diagnosis *edited by Samuel M. Turner and Michel Hersen*

Personality and the Behavioral Disorders (Second Edition) *edited by Norman S. Endler and J. McVicker Hunt*

Ecological Approaches to Clinical and Community Psychology *edited by William A. O'Connor and Bernard Lubin*

Rational-Emotive Therapy with Children and Adolescents: Theory, Treatment Strategies, Preventative Methods *by Michael E. Bernard and Marie R. Joyce*

The Unconscious Reconsidered *edited by Kenneth S. Bowers and Donald Meichenbaum*

Prevention of Problems in Childhood: Psychological Research and Application *edited by Michael C. Roberts and Lizette Peterson*

Resolving Resistances in Psychotherapy *by Herbert S. Strean*

Handbook of Social Skills Training and Research *edited by Luciano L'Abate and Michael A. Milan*

Institutional Settings in Children's Lives *by Leanne G. Rivlin and Maxine Wolfe*

Treating the Alcoholic: A Developmental Model of Recovery *by Stephanie Brown*

Resolving Marital Conflicts: A Psychodynamic Perspective *by Herbert S. Strean*

Paradoxical Strategies in Psychotherapy: A Comprehensive Overview and Guidebook *by Leon F. Seltzer*

Pharmacological and Behavioral Treatment: An Integrative Approach *edited by Michel Hersen*

The Rorschach: A Comprehensive System, Volume I: Basic Foundations (Second Edition) *by John E. Exner, Jr.*

The Induction of Hypnosis *by William E. Edmonston, Jr.*